MARTIN LUTHER

Bernhard Lohse

MARTIN LUTHER

An Introduction to His Life and Work

T. & T. CLARK

EDINBURGH

Translated by Robert C. Schultz.

English Translation Copyright © 1986, by Fortress Press.

Originally published under the title
Martin Luther — Eine Einfuhrung in sein Leben und sein Werk,
copyright © Verlag C. H. Beck, Munich, West Germany, 1980.

T. & T. CLARK LTD,
59 GEORGE STREET, EDINBURGH EH2 2LQ.

First printed in the U.K. 1987.

British Library Cataloguing in Publication Data

Lohse, Bernard
Martin Luther: an introduction to his life and work.
1. Luther, Martin, *1483–1546*
2. Reformation—Germany—Biography
I Title
284.1′092′4   BR325

ISBN 0–567–09357–3

CONTENTS

PREFACE

In this volume, I shall attempt to give a basic overview of the important problems and dimensions of Luther research. I shall also try to encourage those of you who read this book to begin to study Luther for yourselves. I will therefore suggest some possible areas for the reader's own further research.

Such an introductory overview has not yet appeared—at least I am not aware of one—in spite of the constantly growing list of publications dealing with Luther and the Reformation. Heinrich Böhmer had a somewhat similar purpose in his book *Luther in the Light of Modern Research*,[1] but he actually developed his material in quite a different way. Böhmer gave much more attention to Luther's life and personality than I intend to. In contrast, I shall begin this book with a brief description of the world in which Luther lived and the significant phases of his life. I shall, however, give the most attention to Luther's writings and to his theology. In doing this, I have always tried to direct the reader's attention to developments in Luther research and, simultaneously, to suggest possible tasks in our study of Luther that still require attention. I thereby intend to encourage you who read this book to undertake your own personal studies of Luther.

Obviously a summary presentation of this kind cannot make any claim to completeness. Its size is limited by the realities of contemporary publication practices as well as by my consideration for the patience of its intended readers. In order to achieve the purpose of this book, it was necessary to make difficult choices about what should be included or omitted at various points. Frequently, I have drawn attention to significant events and problems only by referring to them as examples. Another author would undoubtedly have chosen differently at many points. This book, however, must itself demonstrate whether it has achieved the goals for which it was written.

References to Luther's works are given in terms of the Clemen Edition when possible, but in every case there is a reference to the Weimar Edition. An English translation is cited whenever possible, usually the fifty-five volume American Edition of *Luther's Works (LW)*[2].

Since I have finished this manuscript, Herbert Wolf's excellent introduction to Luther's Works from the perspective of Germanic studies has
appeared.[3] I could not take this important work into consideration in
writing this book. Wolf's book, however, does not deal with the material
covered in this book. Rather, these two books complement each other.

Hamburg   BERNHARD LOHSE
June 1980

1 | LUTHER'S WORLD

1.1 Frederick III and Maximilian

Luther lived during the reigns of three German emperors. When Luther was born in 1483, Frederick III was emperor. He ruled for fifty-three years, from 1440 to 1493. This was the longest reign of any German emperor. Frederick III was politically as well as militarily incompetent, unable to meet the demands of his time. He lost control of the empire. Frederick III did, however, succeed in arranging the marriage of his son, Maximilian I (1493–1519), to Mary of Burgundy, heiress to Franche-Comté (on the border between France and Switzerland) and the Seventeen Provinces of the Netherlands. This marriage laid the basis for the meteoric rise of the Hapsburgs. Through this marriage, Maximilian not only established an alliance with Burgundy but also gained the enmity of France. The resulting conflicts between the Hapsburgs and France dominated political and ecclesiastical history during the first decades of the sixteenth century.

Maximilian I was politically more effective than his father had been. He began to reform the empire in 1495. Even though his reforms enjoyed wide popular support, however, he was able to complete only part of what he intended. One of Maximilian's reforms was the introduction of a general tax that was regularly collected throughout the empire. He was, however, still sometimes forced to continue the custom of levying special taxes on the different territories. As a result, he never developed the financial base for gaining firmer control of the whole empire. For example, he could not maintain a central army.

Another reform was introduced in 1495, when Maximilian was able to establish a supreme court for the empire. This court set limits to the unrestrained power of the nobility, who operated on the principle that "might makes right." He thereby strengthened the central administration of the empire.

Maximilian, who has been called "the last of the knights," was more successful in his support of humanistic studies and the literary arts than in political reform. As a result of his support, Humanism—the then-new

1

cultural movement that was already influential in many other countries—
was gradually able to gain a foothold in the German Empire as well.

1.2 Charles V

As far as Luther and the Reformation are concerned, Charles V (1519–
56) was the most important emperor of all. In 1497 Maximilian's son,
Philip the Handsome, was married to Joanna the Mad, daughter of Ferdinand of Aragon and Isabella of Castile. At the time that this marriage was
planned, there were no plans for combining Spain with the German
Empire. The others who preceded Joanna in the line of succession died,
however, and she inherited the throne of Spain. After her husband, Philip,
died in 1506, Joanna herself sank ever more deeply into mental illness. As
a result, her son Charles, while still a minor, became heir apparent to the
greatest kingdom ever established in the West. Charles inherited not only
the Austrian territories of the Hapsburgs, but also Naples and the Netherlands, which Maximilian had acquired, and, most important, Spain as well
as the American territories owned by Spain. There was, of course, no
natural way of unifying all these different territories and any long-lasting
unification of Spain and the German Empire was simply unthinkable.

Nevertheless, this enormous concentration of power in the hands of
Charles V was of decisive significance not only for the German Empire
but for all of Europe as well. The other European powers, particularly
France under Francis I (1515–47), viewed the increasing dominance of
the German emperor with great concern. Even the papacy was afraid that
its ecclesiastical state would be encircled by Charles V. Francis I and
Charles V waged war almost continuously, especially for control of Milan.
The extended dominion of Charles also had serious consequences for the
German Empire. On the one hand, Germany was indeed very important
to Charles—it not only contained the lands of the Hapsburgs that he
inherited from his father but had also elected Charles as emperor. Germany was, however, still only a part of his kingdom, and as a result he
sometimes gave little attention to it and left it to take care of itself.

Because of his father's early death and his mother's illness, Charles V
spent his childhood in the Netherlands. As a result, he was much more
fluent in Spanish and French than in German, a language he never
adequately mastered. Nevertheless, the fact of his German ancestry
helped Charles win election to the German throne, an office that even the
king of France tried to win. In the final analysis, however, Charles won his
campaign for emperor because the wealthy banking house of the Fuggers
supplied him with massive amounts of money. Money was an important
factor in his election because the princes who elected the emperor
demanded that he pay a high price for their votes.

Charles's basic intention for the German Empire was to strengthen the central administration and reduce the autonomy of the churchly and princely estates. Because he was involved in so many wars and could not wage them without the support of the estates, however, he constantly made compromises with them.

The religious conflict, which had already begun before his election, quickly intensified afterward and for years actually shaped the political controversies throughout the empire. Thus Charles's reign was characterized by two conflicts, the one between the emperor and the estates, and the other between the "Catholics" and the "Protestants." In both basic conflicts, the lines of opposition were constantly shifting. For example, the Roman Catholic estates did not support Charles's policies against the Protestants when these policies seemed to threaten the independence of all the estates. Similarly, Charles deliberately sought the support of the Protestants whenever such support seemed helpful in achieving his own goals.

1.3 Francis I and Henry VIII

As for the other European powers at that time, France, being more centralized, was stronger than the German Empire. Its ruler, Francis I, and Charles V were involved in decades of conflict over the control of northern Italy as well as over Charles's hereditary rights in Burgundy. These issues were not resolved until Charles won the war and peace was established by the treaty of Crépy in 1544. Even after peace was established, France succeeded in extending its eastern border to include some territory that had formerly been German.

England at the time was ruled by Henry VIII (1509–47), a typically unscrupulous Renaissance ruler. He at first supported Charles but later sided with France. Henry had married Catherine of Aragon, the widow of his older brother and an aunt of Charles V. The pope, who had given a special dispensation permitting the marriage, later refused Henry's request for a divorce. Henry responded by repudiating the authority of the Roman pope and establishing the Anglican Church as the state church of England (1531–34). Henry, however, did not introduce any Protestant policies or practices. England first became one of the leading European powers only during the reign of Elizabeth I (1558–1603), after standing up to Spain and defeating the Spanish Armada in 1588.

1.4 The Netherlands

In many respects, the Netherlands, which at that time also included approximately the present territory of Belgium and Luxembourg, can be described as the focal point of European politics in the sixteenth century.

Maximilian I had incorporated the Netherlands into the German Empire. It became very important to Charles V because its geographical location provided the link by which he held his many countries together.

When Charles abdicated the throne in 1556 and his inheritance was divided, the Netherlands was assigned to the Spanish branch of the Hapsburgs. The Netherlands, however, revolted against these alien rulers from Spain and their persecution of Protestants. After ten years of rebellion against Philip II (1556–98), the most powerful ruler of that time, they were able to establish their independence. As a result, the Netherlands became the center of a growing movement for greater spiritual and intellectual freedom that gradually spread to other European countries.

1.5 The Turkish Threat

The Turks were also very important during Luther's time. Charles V not only waged almost constant war against Francis I, but also the danger of Turkish attacks in southeastern Europe gave him little chance to catch his breath. In 1526, Suleiman the Magnificent (1520–66), an extraordinarily capable ruler, conquered Budapest. In the fall of 1529, a Turkish army for the first time camped outside the gates of Vienna. Although promptly compelled to retreat, the Turks were again expected to attack both Hungary and Austria. The emperor continually had the utmost difficulty convincing the estates that they should provide the financial and military aid he needed to withstand the Turks. Frequently he was able to obtain the needed support only by making concessions. The Turkish threat to the empire was to last well over a century. This fact was particularly significant for the people of the sixteenth century because the Turks threatening Europe were also heathens threatening Christianity. This symbolism provided rich nourishment for the apocalyptic expectations of the time.

The reigns of the emperors under whom Luther lived were thus in many ways entwined with European politics as a whole. The history of Luther and of the Reformation must always be seen in this larger context.

1.6 Luther's Home: The County of Mansfeld

To be sure, Luther and the Reformation were far more directly influenced by the actions of the German princes and estates than by the politics of the other great European powers. Luther, of course, thought of himself as a German. First of all, he came from the small county of Mansfeld, which may be considered his home. Later on, while Luther was living and working in Wittenberg, his development was determined by events in Electoral Saxony. The tension between the territories and the central government, present since the beginning of the history of the German

Empire, was especially strong in the sixteenth century. Even as strong a ruler as Charles V could not prevent the scales of power from tipping in favor of the territories. The larger territories especially, but also some of the larger cities, were constantly expanding their spheres of influence.

1.7 Territories and Cities of the German Empire

Even a casual inspection of the map of fifteenth-century Germany provides an impression of the multiplicity of territories. The imperial register of 1495 lists a total of more than 350 territorial states, counties, free imperial cities, abbeys, imperial orders of knights, and many more. Among these, the secular and ecclesiastical electors, who ruled over territories of very different sizes, all exercised considerable influence simply because they cast the votes that elected the emperor. The duchies of Württemburg, Bavaria, Saxony, and Braunschweig-Lüneburg were all very important simply because they were so large. The Landgrave of Hesse ruled over one of the most important territories. The bishops of Bamberg, Würzburg, Münster, and Bremen controlled extensive areas. The imperial cities are not to be omitted from this list. For example, the cities of Nürnberg and Ulm owned as much land as some of the more significant territories. Naturally, the accumulation of money and economic power in the cities made them even more influential. In addition to all these territories, there were numerous smaller states, many of which frequently were totally enclosed within the boundaries of a larger state. Only a few princes ruled over larger unified territories. It would be hard to find a more colorful map than a map of the German Empire at the time of the Reformation.

The Reformation did not produce any substantial changes in this situation. In comparison to Germany, countries such as England and France were already quite centralized. One goal of Henry VIII's decision to break with Rome and establish the independence of the English church from the pope was to increase the influence and power of the king. This same motive was also one that determined the church politics of Scandinavian rulers. In the German Empire, however, an emperor could not hope to gain power by supporting the Reformation. Since the majority of the estates, unlike the majority of the people, remained loyal to the old church, it was unthinkable that there could ever be a Protestant emperor in the sixteenth century. A Protestant emperor simply could never have survived the struggles for power. On the other hand, the territorial princes as well as the free cities and all the other estates would all, under certain conditions, have greatly benefited from a decision in favor of the Reformation.

None of this should be interpreted as implying that decisions for or against the Reformation were made simply on the basis of political calculations. On the contrary, despite the corruption of the church as well as the people's many grievances against the church, deep personal religious piety was most often the decisive reason for supporting or opposing the Reformation. This assertion is verified by the fact that many people, even the princes themselves, often suffered greatly for the sake of their faith. Nevertheless, it is still important for us to view the struggle surrounding the Reformation within the social context of the times and thus take the reciprocal influences of political developments and theological controversies into account.

1.8 The Growth of the Power of the Princes

Developments in the later fifteenth century brought stricter order to the territories and, as a result, increased the power of the princes. Some competent princes succeeded in simultaneously strengthening their sovereign rights over against the empire and, in spite of much opposition, establishing their control of the estates. Since the territorial rulers were dependent on the taxes paid by the estates, however, they could not govern without the cooperation of the estates. As a result, territorial constitutions were developed in order to regularize the relationship between the princes and the estates. In this process, the estates conceded that the princes had the right to collect taxes and therefore had the right to administer the financial affairs of the territories. In order to exercise this right, the princes developed a group of civil servants.

Likewise, many territories at the end of the Middle Ages had established territorial or privy councils presided over by the prince. At first the knights were members of these privy councils. Gradually, however, the knights were replaced by lawyers. Thus, a special, central institution developed that both advised the prince and at the same time administered policies. The formation of such a central institution compelled the princes to set up permanent residences in order to keep in touch with these administrative offices. This is how a primitive form of the modern state first developed in the territorial states rather than at the level of the empire.

The princes also had considerable influence in decisions about affairs of the church. The Roman curia, the administrative organ of the church of Rome, had already begun to disintegrate during the popes' exile in Avignon and the consequent papal schisms. The obvious inability of the curia to initiate and maintain the sorely needed reform of the church made it possible for the European countries that were generally becoming more powerful to assume many more rights in the church. As far as fifteenth-century England and France are concerned, we may already speak of territorial churches. Such a development was not possible in the German Empire because the central government was so weak. Some princes in the fifteenth century were, however, given the right to initiate reforms and to make supervisory visitations. Reforms carried out in many fifteenth-century cloisters would have been impossible without strong backing from the princes. The later establishment of many Protestant churches as territorial churches in the sixteenth century was thus only a later stage in a continual development which began in the late Middle Ages. During the time of the Reformation, this development also appeared in Roman Catholic territories.

1.9 Economic Development

Developments in the economy also played an important role in increasing the significance of the territories. In this regard, the latter part of the fifteenth and the sixteenth centuries were a time of radical change. During this time, the economic practices of early capitalism developed. The significance of such accumulations of capital is clearly demonstrated by the prestigious position of the Fuggers' bank. Without their financial support, Albert of Mainz could not have gained control of three dioceses, an action clearly contrary to ecclesiastical law.

The early sixteenth century also brought new methods of production, particularly methods of manufacturing that were much more progressive than the earlier methods. The mining industry was particularly important, especially in Saxony. The mines near the border of Saxony and Bohemia produced copper, silver, and tin.

Silver had been mined in Saxony since the twelfth century. Mining became an important industry only during the second half of the fifteenth century, however. Karlheinz Blaschke[1] has compared this development to the nineteenth-century California Gold Rush and, in fact, there are many points of comparison: both movements resulted in population shifts, increased flow of money, the accumulation of wealth for those involved in mining but also poverty for others. No other industry was as significant for the economy of sixteenth-century Saxony as the mines were. Without the economic power based on its mining industry, Saxony would not have achieved the high level of culture it enjoyed in the sixteenth century. The rulers of Saxony also owed their political influence to profits of the mining industry.

1.10 Saxony

Saxony was Luther's homeland. Its rulers from the House of Wettin had subdivided the territory in 1485. Ernest received the area around Wittenberg and Torgau, the greater part of Thuringia, as well as the western Harz

Mountains and the Vogtland. Most important of all, he was given the right to be an elector of the emperor. On the other hand, Albrecht received the largest territory, the territory of Meissen and the city of Leipzig, as well as the northern part of Thuringia extending as far as the Werra River. Both parts of Saxony were thus intertwined. Therefore it is not surprising that their relationships were very tense and that they were involved in many disputes in the early decades of the sixteenth century. This rivalry reached its peak when Duke Moritz of Saxony, despite his personal Lutheran faith, fought on the side of the emperor against the Protestant estates during the Smalcald War (1546–47). The emperor rewarded him by giving him large sections of Electoral Saxony as well as the office of elector.

When Saxony was divided, the only university was located in Leipzig in Ducal Saxony. As a result, Frederick the Wise, who ruled Electoral Saxony from 1486 to 1525, founded a new university in Wittenberg in 1502. Even though it was the only university of Electoral Saxony, it did not really get started for fifteen years. It first became significant as a result of the Reformation. During part of the sixteenth century, it was the most prestigious German university.

In both parts of Saxony, there were no large cities even by sixteenth-century standards. No city had a population of more than 10,000 inhabitants. Görlitz, the largest city of Saxony, had 9,000 inhabitants. Leipzig had about 6,500 inhabitants. Zwickau, where Thomas Müntzer was active for a time, had about 3,200 in 1561. Wittenberg in the early part of the sixteenth century had only a little more than 2,000 inhabitants. Other German cities, such as Nürnberg, Cologne, Strassburg, or Lübeck, were at that time much larger and much more important than the Saxon cities.

1.11 The Situation of the Church

At the beginning of the sixteenth century, the Western church was basically unchallenged. All the grievances that had been complained about for decades, all the abuses in piety and in indulgences, as well as the inadequacies of its theology, did not cause people to leave the church. On the contrary, even the most passionate criticisms of the church showed that its critics knew what the real work of the church was. It has been correctly observed that the period around 1500 was the most pious period in the history of Germany. Of course, it is also true that there were such strong and even contradictory tensions in the image of the church and piety during the latter part of the Middle Ages that it is hardly possible to identify common characteristics in the manifold forms of religious life. An accurate picture of religious life at the time can be formed only by focusing on the different types and tendencies individually.

1.12 The Reform Councils of the Fifteenth Century

Viewed from the outside, the Western church around 1500 was flourishing. The papal schism that developed after the end of the exile of the popes in Avignon (1378–1415) was finally resolved by the Council of Constance (1414–18). As a result, the greatest and most damaging scandal of Western Christianity was finally settled. The papacy, however, could not have healed this schism on its own; rather, it needed the help that only a council could provide. Whereas the popes of the High Middle Ages had made increasingly unreasonable demands of the emperors and other rulers, their power was now limited from within the church by the conciliar movement. Both the Council of Constance and the Council of Basel (1431–49) declared that a general council was superior to the pope. The popes, however, did not accept these decrees. On the contrary, they did everything possible to subordinate the councils to the popes. The popes' experiences with the councils of the fifteenth century partially explain why they were reluctant to call a council in the sixteenth century. The popes' drive for power and their unwillingness to reform the church were major reasons that led them to reject the councils. As far as the conciliar movement was concerned, it had obviously passed its peak by the middle of the fifteenth century.

1.13 The Need for a Reform of the Church

A thorough reform of the church was needed, but the energy needed to carry it out was lacking. There were many problems and abuses, particularly in the area of papal finances. The popes always needed more and more money to finance the wars that the ecclesiastical state became involved in. They also needed ever-increasing amounts to maintain their wastefully expensive life style as princes of the church. Thus the increasing number of indulgences in the late Middle Ages had, above all, financial causes. And the church used ecclesiastical penalties to enforce the payment of the assessments and taxes that it levied. Ecclesiastical offices were also sold to generate income.

Even worse than these exploitative financial practices, the clergy did not take their ecclesiastical duties very seriously. Many bishops thought of themselves primarily as worldly rulers rather than as priests. Celibacy—more accurately, chastity—was frequently not practiced. More and more masses were celebrated as a way of meeting the clergy's financial needs. This fact combined with their theological confusion about the real meaning of the sacrifice of the Mass were the cause as well as the result of additional abuses.

At every diet of the German Empire the *Gravamina nationis Germanicae*—the list of abuses that the diet was asked to correct in the church in the German Empire—was always presented. Although the term was first used in an official statement issued in Frankfurt in 1456, such a list had already been presented at the Council of Constance in 1417. Such demands that abuses be corrected were still presented to the imperial diets in the early years of the Reformation. Demands for secular and ecclesiastical reforms were merged in these lists. Basically, however, the papacy was seen as the real enemy—robbing the German nation of its wealth, its freedom, and its dignity.

The church clearly demonstrated that it was incompetent to respond adequately to such demands for reform. This was never more clear than at the Fifth Lateran Council (1512–17), which was convened just before the Reformation began. Although the council passed many resolutions intended to reform various abuses in ecclesiastical taxes and fees, it was completely unable to stop the selling of ecclesiastical offices or to prevent one individual from holding several offices. The censorship of printed religious material was planned but not put into effect.

The total inconsistency of the church's attempts to reform itself is revealed by the fact that when the text of the papal bull on the reform of the church, read at the ninth session of the Fifth Lateran Council, was sent to Albert of Mainz, it was accompanied by a special offer forbidden by this very papal bull. The offer was: the pope would permit Albert to carry out his illegal plan to hold a number of ecclesiastical offices simultaneously in exchange for a fee of ten thousand ducats. To assist him in raising this money, he was authorized to sell indulgences. These very indulgences were the reason for the drafting of Luther's Ninety-five Theses.

1.14 The Reform Movements

Nevertheless, some isolated reform movements developed during the late Middle Ages. The most important by far was the *devotio moderna*, the "modern style of devotion." Beginning in the Netherlands toward the end of the fourteenth century, this movement resulted in a reform of the monasteries. Through the work of the Brethren of the Common Life, a lay group that practiced this form of spirituality, it also nurtured a personal spirituality among lay people that was one of the most noble fruits of the medieval church. Men and women who were members of the Brethren of the Common Life lived in convents and practiced the imitation of Christ. Through their schools, they exercised widespread influence. The

Brethren of the Common Life did much that prepared the way for the Reformation. Later, most of them became supporters of the Reformation.

1.15 Huss and the Hussites

The movement started by John Huss (c. 1369–1415) was of particular importance for the church of the late Middle Ages. The Hussites were the first large group in the West to gain and maintain independence from Rome, that is, to have a confession of faith other than that of the Roman Church. Huss was greatly influenced by the writings of the English theologian, John Wyclif (c. 1328–84), who advocated the reform of the church. This influence was so extensive that Huss copied whole sections of Wyclif's work. This does not mean that Huss was spiritually and intellectually dependent on Wyclif. Rather, Huss adopted only those parts of Wyclif's writings in which he himself firmly believed.

A study of Huss's use of Wyclif's material shows that Huss generally was more cautious in his work than Wyclif was. Huss never was as sharp in his criticism of certain practices and teachings of the church at that time, nor as radical in his own suggestions for reform as was Wyclif. Both of these "pre-Reformers," however, shared a similar regard for the Holy Scripture as the law of God which the church was to follow and as the standard by which the actions and teachings of the church were to be judged. They compared the medieval church—worldly, rich, and mighty—to the early church which lived in apostolic poverty. Wyclif and Huss were sharpest in their criticism of indulgences. Huss defined the church as the number of the predestined. He asserted that Christ is the only head of the church.

Huss had many followers in Bohemia. The hierarchy reacted as sharply as possible, even excommunicating him. The king of Bohemia and a large part of the nobility as well as of the people supported Huss, however. As a result he was able to continue his work for some time after his excommunication. When Huss refused to renounce his teachings at the Council of Constance, however, he was burned at the stake as a heretic. This happened in spite of the emperor's official guarantee that he could return safely to Bohemia. His death became a scandal in Bohemia. Both emperor and pope were considered to be his murderers.

The Hussites formed two groups, the moderate Utraquists, who basically demanded only the distribution of the wine to the laity during communion, and the radical Taborites. Then in 1420 the pope declared a crusade against the heretics in Bohemia, and the wars against the Hussites began. The Hussites defended themselves fanatically. Beginning in 1427 they invaded the German Empire, reaching as far as Brandenburg and Austria. They saw themselves as spreading the kingdom of God by violence. The Taborites considered the Old Testament the norm of all of life, rejected any kind of hierarchy, and held all goods as common property.

After the Utraquists gained control of the Hussite movement, the Council of Basel came to terms with them in the *Compactata* (the Treaty of Prague, 1433). Even though the papacy never recognized these agreements and actually annulled them in 1452, the Hussites were still able to assert themselves. In 1467 the Unity of the Brethren *(Brüderunität)* split off from the Hussites. This group understood itself as an internal, Hussite reform movement in conformity with the principle of the gospel. They tried to live according to the Sermon on the Mount. In the sixteenth century the German Empire still remembered the horrors of the Hussite wars. In some areas, there were groups that secretly held the teachings of the Bohemians. All the other, older heresies had almost totally disappeared by 1500, but the influence of the Hussites cannot be minimized. People in the early sixteenth century were still impressed by the Hussite criticism of the many abuses in the church as well as by their example of life based on a divine "law." Most important, the question as to whether Huss had been unjustly condemned and executed in Constance was frequently discussed. The Hussites provided the West with an example of successful resistance.

1.16 The Intellectual Situation

The situation at the end of the Middle Ages, not only with regard to the church and piety, but also in intellectual life, was very complex. Optimistic expectations of the future and apocalyptic visions of disaster existed side by side. The late Middle Ages was as much the era of the Renaissance as it was the era of the dance of death. New beginnings, such as those made by Albrecht Dürer in the fine arts, were deeply rooted in specific medieval ways of thinking. Once again we need to be careful not to try to oversimplify the great variety we encounter. Rather, we should try to take the diversity of the various intellectual and cultural movements into consideration.

1.17 The Universities

As far as intellectual life was concerned, significant differences had developed between England and France on the one hand, and Germany on the other, by the High Middle Ages. In France and England as well as in Italy, universities had been established since the year 1200. In the German Empire, however, universities were not established until the middle of the fourteenth century; the oldest were in Prague (1348), Vienna (1365), Heidelberg (1386), Cologne (1388), Erfurt (1392), and Leipzig (1409). The most important university in the early sixteenth century was still the

Sorbonne in Paris. Among the Reform theologians who taught there were Peter of Ailli (1350–1420), who played a decisive role in overcoming the papal schism, and John Gerson (1363–1429), who participated in the Council of Constance. Even after 1500, theologians at the Sorbonne taught that the councils were superior to the pope. German universities exercised no similar influence. They began to be influential only as a result of the Reformation.

There were also differences in the teaching of theology and philosophy. The most significant scholars had taught in England and France. Most of the great medieval systems of philosophy and theology were developed in Paris. Naturally these great works of the Dominicans and the Franciscans were also studied in Germany. Germany, however, did not generate any substantial contribution to scholastic thought. The major original German contribution took the form of German mysticism. Johannes Eckhart (d. 1327), John Tauler (d. 1361), and Henry Suso (d. 1366) undoubtedly were deeply indebted to previous generations of mystics. It is also true that it is difficult to draw a clear line of demarcation between scholasticism and mysticism. Nevertheless there can be no doubt that late medieval mysticism developed a unique form in Germany. The influence of this mysticism continued into the sixteenth century. Mysticism also played a significant role in the development of the German language.

1.18 Scholasticism and Late Scholasticism

By 1500 the era of great scholastic systems had come to an end. Thomas Aquinas and John Duns Scotus no longer dominated the field, even though their systems were still frequently held and taught. In their place, William of Ockham (1285–1349) was now the most influential scholar. He was born and raised in England. In the feud between Ludwig of Bavaria and the popes, he took the side of the emperor and supported this position in his carefully thought-out writings. Through his consistent application of Aristotle's principles of science and scholarship, Ockham successfully challenged the synthesis of philosophy and theology that had been asserted by earlier scholasticism. Ockham did not teach the theory that philosophy and theology are two completely separate truths, but he did consider them to be two different kinds of knowledge.

As a theologian, Ockham no longer followed a speculative method but rather examined critically the theological usefulness of philosophical concepts. For example, in the doctrine of God, the concept of God's freedom was central. On this basis, the Creator was radically differentiated from all created beings. In the doctrine of human being (anthropology), as well as in the doctrines of sin and grace, the radical distinction between the absolute and contingent powers of God resulted in two different approaches. On the one hand, Adam's sin was described as having devastating effects on all later generations only because God imputed this sin to all later generations. On the other hand, Ockham's respect for the authority of the church fathers caused him also to describe original sin as the lack of original righteousness—that is, of the special righteousness that Adam had before he fell into sin. Similarly, Ockham both described grace as the nonimputation of sin and asserted that people are able to fulfill the law through their own power.

The idea of God's freedom as well as the contingent nature of creation and all that happens was so dominant that the representatives of other scholastic systems could not help being influenced by Ockham or, at the very least, by his formulation of the question. Even theologians like Gregory of Rimini (c. 1300–1358), who tried to develop a deeper insight into sin and grace based on Augustine's teaching, were influenced by Ockham, at least in their doctrine of God. Gabriel Biel (c. 1410–95), who taught at the University of Tübingen, spread Ockham's teaching through his lectures and writing. He did not, however, affirm Ockham's critical thinking about the papacy and the church.

1.19 Humanism

Scholasticism had passed its peak shortly before the Reformation began, but Humanism, which had come to Germany from Italy, achieved its highest development in the early sixteenth century. Of course, there were differences between the varieties of Humanism taught on either side of the Alps. The revival of interest in classical Greek and Roman cultures and in the rhetorician as the ideal person was common to all Humanists. The secularism that so often resulted from this in fifteenth-century Italy, however, appeared comparatively less frequently in Germany. Quite to the contrary, German Humanism was very religious. This is already apparent in Rudolf Agricola (1443/44–85), and is particularly manifest in Johannes Reuchlin (1455–1522) or Erasmus (1469–1536).

Classical and Christian reform motifs can, as a result, hardly be distinguished in the work of the German Humanists. Whereas Italian Humanists established their own "academies," German Humanists gathered in small groups that kept in touch either through personal contact or through correspondence. Conrad Celtis (1459–1508) founded more such learned sodalities than almost anyone else. He himself was more active as a poet than as a teacher. In 1487 Emperor Frederick III crowned him as poet laureate, the first German to receive this honor. Celtis, like many other Humanists, wanted to reassert the old German values. To achieve this, they published collections of German proverbs and of

German historical sources. Needless to say, this work was often quite amateurish.

Some princes, especially Maximilian I, encouraged these humanistic tendencies. Since the emperor gave his personal support to the efforts of the Humanists, Germany became more of a center of Humanism than almost anywhere else in Europe. At the same time, the nationalist element was becoming stronger in German Humanism. People hoped to develop German law, German grammar, and even, perhaps, a German form of the church. If Humanism thus produced a national romantic movement, it also simultaneously produced a humanistic enlightenment, best exemplified by Erasmus. This enlightenment left no room for the glorification of one's own national tradition. There were thus many diverse forces at work within Humanism. All these diverse tendencies within Humanism, however, shared the common characteristic of affecting only small circles of educated people. The common uneducated person could not participate in the various Humanist movements.

Humanism also penetrated the universities. In the beginning, we cannot make a general distinction between scholasticism and Humanism. Tensions and contradictions gradually developed, however, because the Humanists' return to the ancients presupposed a devaluation of the Middle Ages. The scholastic methods of scholarship were also increasingly rejected. The poor education of most of the priests was a welcome target of ridicule. Satires were written on the morality of the higher clergy. The Humanists' renewal of a cultural ideal influenced more and more universities and schools. Many of the Reformers, although Luther was not one of them, were decisively influenced by Humanism.

As far as the feeling about life in general is concerned, there were many sharp contrasts at the beginning of the Reformation. The Humanists thought they were at the beginning of a new era that would replace the dark Middle Ages. In other circles there were apocalyptic expectations that the world would soon come to an end. Belief in witches and the antichrist often not only existed alongside humanistic cultural ideals, but simultaneously appeared in the same circles, and even in one and the same person. The controversy between Reuchlin and the Dominicans of Cologne as to whether the rabbinical literature should be destroyed or preserved (1510–20), did not simply pit Humanism and scholarship against the Inquisition or even enlightenment against obscurantism; rather, Reuchlin's own attitude toward Judaism was owed to the spirit of the times. Those who wanted to destroy the rabbinical texts were ridiculed by the satirical *Letters of Obscure Men* (1515/17).[2] Most of these letters were written by Erfurt Humanists.

The old and the new, the conservative and the revolutionary spirits were often interchangeable. The Reuchlin who was highly praised by fellow Humanists decisively rejected Luther's Reformation. When his great-nephew Melanchthon sided with Luther, Reuchlin broke off contact with him. The reverse also occurred, however. People who were very much at home in the Middle Ages became supporters of the Reformation after 1517. It would be a mistake to try to predict who would support Luther on the basis of their position at the beginning of the Reformation. Even though the world seemed to most people to be ready for reform, the Reformation was not the kind of reform that many were looking for.

1.20 Is the Idea of Historical Periods Valid?

Given these differing attitudes toward the Reformation, there is no reason to be surprised that scholars respond in such different ways to questions about the boundary between the Middle Ages and the modern age. In dealing with this question, we encounter many other problems that can only be partially dealt with here.

First of all, we must ask whether we wish to continue to distinguish between ancient, medieval, and modern periods, or consider this distinction—first proposed in the late seventeenth century by Christopher Cellarius (1638–1707)—inappropriate.

If we wish to continue to make this common distinction, we must then identify the unique characteristics of the medieval period in contrast to the ancient and modern periods. Obviously, we will be able to make such a distinction only if we are especially clear about the boundaries separating the medieval from the ancient as well as from the modern world. Cellarius thought that the Middle Ages began with Constantine the Great and ended with the fall of Constantinople, approximately at the end of the fifteenth century. Since then many other, often quite different, boundaries have been proposed for the Middle Ages. Ultimately the reasons for such distinctive definitions of these periods are found in the variety of viewpoints from which individual scholars view history. Frequently, different boundaries are set on the basis of whether one is studying political, cultural, religious, or economic history.

Similar questions arise if we describe the modern world as sharing a common boundary with the Middle Ages. If so, what is the basic nature of the modern world in contrast to the medieval world? Similarly, if we reserve a special period for the Protestant and Roman Catholic Reformations between the medieval and modern periods, we must again ask what specifically distinguishes this age of Reformation from the medieval and modern periods. Here, too, different decisions result, depending on whether we are most interested in economic, social, political, cultural, or ecclesiastical and theological questions. The mere fact, however, that we may be particularly interested in social history, for example, does not make it necessary for us to deny the great significance of theological factors in the sixteenth century.

Finally, any attempt to distinguish between the historical periods will to a great extent be determined by our own world view. A Marxist will think differently than a Christian, a Protestant than a Roman Catholic who possibly might conclude that Luther's Reformation was significant primarily because it destroyed the unity of Christianity. Others may judge that the development of the modern ideas of freedom and tolerance are most important. This position would be taken, for example, by many agnostics.

The question of distinguishing different historical periods, at least with reference to the distinction between the medieval and the modern periods, cannot be answered in a way that excludes all objections. Whether and however we distinguish between periods, it is even more important for us to remain open to all viewpoints and different ways of making such a distinction. At the same time, we need to continue to search for an answer that takes as many factors as possible into consideration. Whatever position we take, we should assume from the very beginning that there is no abrupt transition from one age to another. Rather, the transitions are gradual. Thus we will find some elements of the late Middle Ages that are really typical of the modern world. This would be true, for example, in terms of intellectual history of the Nominalists' work in epistemology. In terms of political history, it would be true of the new political theory of Marsilius of Padua (d. 1342/43). Finally, in terms of political practice, it would be true of Machiavelli's (d. 1527) theories of political practice that anticipate the development of the European national states and their absolute forms of government. In terms of the history of art, we might describe the process by which portraits of individuals were becoming fashionable. In terms of the church and theology, we can refer to Luther's refusal to go against the testimony of his own conscience and of the Bible by recanting and thereby subjecting himself to the authority of the Roman Catholic Church. Similarly, Luther's liberation of human reason and secular government from authoritarian domination by ecclesiastical authority is part of the beginning of a new epoch in contrast to the Middle Ages.

On the other hand, elements we would consider distinctive of the Middle Ages can be found in all areas of sixteenth-century life. Reference could be made, for example, to the numerous forms of superstition and to the various forms of intolerance that were almost omnipresent, even though with varying levels of intensity. Similarly, we could refer to the way in which uniformity of faith in a given territory was taken for granted, to the massive and very substantial concepts of the devil and the antichrist, as well as to the very limited areas of cultural and spiritual freedom that had just begun to be won.

Luther occupies the most permanent place in this manifold process of transition between the Middle Ages and the modern age. Depending on how we look at Luther, we can see him either as a conservative or as a progressive force in this process. Whatever one's opinion, we should not overlook the fact that we can never do full justice to the particularity and uniqueness of any historical personage by merely defining this person's place in the flow of history. As far as Luther is concerned, his whole person was involved in the entire substance of his proclamation. Anyone who wants to understand Luther must therefore come to terms with the substance of his preaching and teaching.

2 | QUESTIONS RELATED TO LUTHER'S LIFE

2.1 The Abundance of Sources

It is a generally acknowledged principle of historical study that we can understand and value someone's work only in the context of that person's whole life. This is especially true of Luther. His theological insights were always of existential significance for his own personal life. His vast literary production was not based on a preconceived plan, but rather developed primarily as Luther's response to the manifold controversies in which he was involved. Of course, this does not contradict the fact that Luther always worked out of a basic and comprehensive theological perspective. This basic perspective was, however, constantly reworked in response to each new situation.

We know more about Luther's personality and about the details of his daily life than we do about anyone else in the sixteenth or any earlier century. On the basis of the large number of his published works and his lecture manuscripts, as well as the manuscripts or transcripts of his sermons, and particularly his letters, we are able to trace his biography in terms of daily and hourly events. The enormous number of contemporary reports and the manifold connections between Luther's life on the one hand and major political developments on the other hand, as well as the comments about Luther made by his contemporaries, make it unusually difficult to write a biography of Luther. Useful biographies of the young Luther (up to the time of the controversy over indulgences in 1517–18 and even through the Peasants' War and the late 1520s) are available. It has been a long time, however, since anyone has attempted to write a comprehensive biography of the older Luther. The work of Heinrich Bornkamm (1979) remains an unfinished fragment.[1] For a long time, Luther scholars have recognized the need for an extensive biography of Luther that reliably describes the details of his life and presents a balanced evaluation of his work in the context of the first half of the sixteenth century. The production of such a biography, however, still remains one of the great unfulfilled tasks of Luther research.

19

2.2 The Task of a Biography of Luther

Anyone attempting to write a biography of Luther must do more than
carefully describe the details of his life in the context of the political and
cultural history of the time. Rather, the author must take a personal
position in regard to Luther from the very beginning and expose his or
her own value judgments. This is particularly true of writings about
Luther.

The author of such a biography of Luther must begin by determining
the significance of various historical factors such as the decay of the
church at the end of the Middle Ages, the then-new movements of the
Renaissance and Humanism, the uneasy coexistence of the territories and
the empire, the economic reorganization of the empire, and the ferment-
ing process of social change which was already strongly influential in the
later fifteenth century and which reached its peak during the Peasants'
War.

In determining his or her own position on these matters, the biographer must also come to terms with the question of whether the
religious problems with which Luther struggled can be regarded as a
contemporary expression of a totally different basic problem, or whether
they are to be seen as questions which, in constantly varying forms, are
asked by people of all periods and which Luther may have especially
recognized and experienced in his own life. And when the biographer has
decided whether the basic problems discussed by the Reformers are
"real" problems, he or she must also decide whether Luther's answers are
genuinely Christian, that is, biblical, or whether Luther was a radically
one-sided theologian. These basic perspectives are quite separate from
the critical task of every scholarly study—which must be taken with
equal seriousness whether one basically affirms the Reformation or basically rejects it as traditional Roman Catholic scholarship has.

2.3 Luther's Childhood

The biographer's own response to these questions will already be reflected in the way in which Luther's childhood is described. The basic
facts about his family, his birth in Eisleben on November 10, 1483, his
early years in Mansfeld, where his father worked in the copper mines and
by hard work achieved modest prosperity, are, of course, well known. It is
also clearly established that Luther's ancestors were farmers on the west
side of the Thuringian Forest. But what is the significance of the fact that
Luther, a man of peasant, not noble ancestry, could play a role that was
previously reserved for the aristocracy?

Furthermore, we must also decide whether Luther's early years in the
remote county of Mansfeld should be viewed in the context of the

tensions of his times, or whether Luther first came into contact with these tensions at a later time. Granted that Luther's parents admittedly gave him a strict upbringing, how did this affect his personal development? Is there a relationship between the strictness of his father and his conception of God as judge—an idea which was a very significant factor in his personal spiritual temptations? Can such a relationship be proved or is it even probable? Are there other factors that affected Luther's personal development and thus shaped his work as a reformer? Or should one say that Luther's personality was quite special and in some ways perhaps even abnormal—perhaps due to some genetic predisposition?

2.4 Luther's Upbringing

The question of Luther's personal development has been raised repeatedly by scholars representing various disciplines. As far as his parental training at home was concerned, Luther later remembered receiving several hard beatings. Methods of child-rearing at that time were, however, generally quite strict when compared with modern methods. Luther's experiences were, therefore, not unusual. Quite apart from this fact, Luther and his parents always felt deep affection for one another. Luther felt deep devotion to his parents until they died. Many attempts have been made to interpret Luther's later life in terms of a deep conflict with his father, but these can hardly be substantiated from the sources.

Luther's religious experience at home was also not unusual for that time. His parents were pious people who certainly not only shared the widespread superstitions of their time, but who could also think realistically and rationally. Finally, the most conspicuous fact is that nothing in Luther's childhood and adolescence indicates the nature of his later life and work.

2.5 Luther's Schooling in Magdeburg and in Eisenach

Luther's experiences in Magdeburg and Eisenach were more important for his development. In 1497/98 Luther attended the cathedral school in Magdeburg. Here his teachers were Brethren of the Common Life. Thus, during his adolescence, Luther was closely acquainted with what was probably the deepest kind of lay spirituality of the entire Middle Ages. As a result, Luther was acquainted with the strength as well as the decay of the church of the late Middle Ages.

Luther completed his basic schooling in Eisenach from 1498 to 1501. There, Luther was a frequent visitor in the pious, cultured, and distinguished patrician homes of the Schalbe and Cotta families. The atmosphere of these homes reflected their Franciscan spirituality. Music was also cultivated in these families. Luther made many friends in Eisenach, some of whom remained his friends for the rest of his life. Luther had many positive experiences in Magdeburg as well as in Eisenach. This fact alone should warn us against painting Luther's childhood and youth in too-dark colors.

2.6 Luther's Studies in Erfurt (1501–5)

Luther's studies in Erfurt were of special significance for his later development. Between 1501 and 1505, Luther finished his basic studies in the liberal arts. As part of this schooling, Luther mastered grammar, rhetoric, and Aristotelian logic, and also became thoroughly familiar with the ethics and metaphysics of Aristotle.

Ockham's Nominalism dominated the scene in Erfurt, although Ockham's later writings produced in support of Ludwig of Bavaria, and therefore those that were critical of the papacy and the church, were ignored. Luther learned a form of Ockhamism that had been revised by Gabriel Biel (d. 1495), a moderate disciple of Ockham who had taught in Tübingen. Even as a student, Luther was exposed to the Ockhamist critiques of Aristotelianism and Thomism. Although certain humanistic tendencies were present in Erfurt at the time, Luther probably did not come in contact with them.

Luther's later studies in theology, beginning in 1507, also primarily exposed him to Biel's modified version of Ockhamist theology. At first, Luther learned to see other traditions only as these were presented by the Ockhamists. For this reason, scholars have repeatedly asked whether late medieval Ockhamism and the critical, even destructive, questions that it raised against Thomism did not constitute the negative presupposition for the gradual development of Luther's Reformation theology.

There can be no question that other traditions besides Ockhamism were also important for Luther. And although Luther read very little of Aquinas, he began to read Augustine and many works of the mystics early in his studies. Thus both in his later studies of theology and in preparing his own first lectures on theology, Luther came to terms with large masses of the traditions of the early and medieval church. Since there is no clarity about the individual authors and works that Luther read, however, we cannot always say with certainty that a particular tradition was known to Luther and is therefore a part of the background against which his own statements must be understood.

2.7 Luther's Entry Into the Cloister (1505)

Luther intended to fulfill his father's wishes and study law after receiving the degree of master of arts in 1505. This plan for his career changed radically on July 2, 1505, when Luther was caught in a fierce thunderstorm near Stotternheim, close to Erfurt. In his fear he called on St. Anna, the patron saint of the miners, and swore, "I will become a monk." On the one hand, this oath was not the result of careful consideration but rather slipped out of his mouth in a time of great distress. On the other hand, it was more than merely accidental that Luther made such a promise. He had probably thought of becoming a monk before, even though he had not considered it intensively. The great number of monasteries, the high percentage of the population who were members of monastic orders, as well as the always-present question about the salvation of one's soul were reason enough for anyone to think about his or her own worthiness in the eyes of the eternal judge.

Undoubtedly, the fact that Luther had not made his oath freely and on his own initiative resulted in his being uneasy about his decision. After returning to Erfurt, he tried to decide whether such an oath was binding. His teachers gave him different answers. Luther took the most difficult answer as correct and burned his bridges behind him. On July 17, 1505, Luther entered the Black Cloister of the Augustinian Hermits in Erfurt. It is important to note that Luther did not choose this particular monastery, as is sometimes claimed, because it was so strict in its asceticism. Rather, he chose it because it represented the same method of philosophical and theological scholarship as the university's faculty of liberal arts did. Luther hoped that he would be able to continue his studies along the same lines as before.

2.8 Luther's Spiritual Temptations

Luther's spiritual temptations (*Anfechtung*) were the most important of his real reasons for entering the monastery. Luther's concept of such temptation is typical of his thinking and combines many perspectives and problems, some of which are theological, others personal. Finally, Luther's spiritual temptations focus on the question of the worthiness of people before God, that is, on the question, How can I find a merciful God?

The theological presupposition for Luther's pointed way of asking this question lies in the works-righteousness of late medieval theology which Luther eventually rejected. This works-righteousness ascribed to people the ability to love and trust God above everything else, and thereby to fulfill the First Commandment. The question as to whether one had this ability became particularly acute when examining oneself before confession as well as while fulfilling the works of satisfaction prescribed by the priest as part of the absolution. Luther's understanding of spiritual temptation also included a variety of different experiences derived from the

medieval practice of prayer, from anxiety about not being good enough
to meet God's demands, from fear about impending death, as well as from
the frightening uncertainty as to whether one had been predestined to
salvation or was not one of the chosen. At the end of the Middle Ages
such spiritual temptations were experienced by innumerable people.

Unless people had such spiritual temptations, they would not have
been willing to purchase an indulgence for themselves or for their family
members who were languishing in purgatory. Pastoral care as well as
widely distributed literature, the so-called art of dying *(ars moriendi)*,
helped people deal with such spiritual temptations in the face of approaching death. Their intention was to give comfort and help to people
so that they would not be trapped in despair but would rather be able to
gain the necessary courage and confidence to trust themselves to God's
will. At least in the years before Luther succeeded in making his reforming breakthrough, the unique character of his spiritual temptations consisted in the fact that Luther suffered and thought through the theological
questions raised by his spiritual temptations from the perspective of the
concept of God, and did so with radical seriousness. What is unique for
Luther is not the kind of spiritual temptations but rather the intensity
with which he experienced these temptations and his theological reflection on the questions which they raised.

Later in his life Luther once said of these temptations:

> I myself "knew a man" [2 Cor. 12:2] who claimed that he had often suffered
> these punishments, in fact over a very brief period of time. Yet they were so
> great and so much like hell that no tongue could adequately express them,
> no pen could describe them, and one who had not himself experienced
> them could not believe them. And so great were they that, if they had been
> sustained or had lasted for half an hour, even for one tenth of an hour, he
> would have perished completely and all of his bones would have been
> reduced to ashes. At such a time God seems terribly angry, and with him the
> whole creation. At such a time there is no flight, no comfort, within or
> without, but all things accuse. At such a time as that the Psalmist mourns, "I
> am cut off from thy sight" [Cf. Ps. 31:22], or at least he does not dare to say,
> "O Lord, ... do not chasten me in thy wrath" [Ps. 6:1]. In this moment
> (strange to say) the soul cannot believe that it can ever be redeemed other
> than that the punishment is not yet completely felt. Yet the soul is eternal
> and is not able to think of itself as being temporal. All that remains is the
> stark-naked desire for help and a terrible groaning, but it does not know
> where to turn for help. In this instance the person is stretched out with
> Christ so that all his bones may be counted, and every corner of the soul is
> filled with the greatest bitterness, dread, trembling, and sorrow in such a
> manner that all these last forever.
>
> To use an example: If a ball crosses a straight line, any point of the line
> which is touched bears the whole weight of the ball, yet it does not embrace

the whole ball. Just so the soul, at the point where it is touched by a passing eternal flood, feels and imbibes nothing except eternal punishment. Yet the punishment does not remain, for it passes over again. Therefore if that punishment of hell, that is, that unbearable and inconsolable trembling, takes hold of the living, punishment of the souls in purgatory seems to be so much greater. Moreover, that punishment for them is constant. And in this instance the inner fire is much more terrible than the outer fire. If there is anyone who does not believe that, we do not beg him to do so.[2]

In his spiritual temptations, Luther thus experienced the wrath of God. He already inwardly experienced the pain of purgatory in this life. And although this is the core of his spiritual temptations, there are special dimensions that appear in various ways. For Luther's spiritual temptations did not end when he came to the understanding of the gospel that characterized the Reformation. Rather they reappeared from time to time—even though in somewhat different form. Luther went through a particularly difficult period in 1527. He was repeatedly tortured by questions as to whether or not he really was in the right and the world of enemies that confronted him in the wrong and why he had ever begun to teach in a way that led to the Reformation. Was he the only one who was wise and all the others in error? Was it really true that all of his predecessors for so many centuries had not known what was true?

How are we to evaluate such spiritual temptations? Are they nothing more than an expression of the constantly recurring question about the meaning of history and of one's own life? Must we describe Luther's experience of the divine wrath as pathological? Might we not rather say that the common way of living life one day at a time is ultimately a terrible illusion that most people have always used to deceive themselves about the emptiness of life and the abyss of nothingness?

2.9 Attempts to Explain the Spiritual Temptations

Luther's sudden decision to enter the monastery and the spiritual temptations under which he repeatedly suffered, as well as many other events in Luther's life, have repeatedly evoked medical interpretations. Luther's various illnesses long ago attracted closer attention and have repeatedly been analyzed from a medical perspective.[3]

The American scholar Preserved Smith was the first to publish a psychoanalytic interpretation of Luther.[4]

The most comprehensive investigation of Luther's illnesses as well as of his personality and of the psychosis attributed to him is that of the Danish psychiatrist Paul J. Reiter.[5] Apart from his various illnesses, Luther for a long time suffered from gallstones and finally died of angina pectoris. In addition to this, Reiter asserted that early in his life Luther already suffered from an anxiety neurosis that was related to his father fixation. This psychological crisis of his youth reinforced his basic tendency toward depression. Luther basically always saw his father as an oppressive and threatening shadow. Reiter asserted that these gloomy influences of his family life were far more influential for Luther than anything else in the world around him. Neither Luther's entry into the monastery, nor his ordination as a priest, nor his Reformation breakthrough changed his psychological makeup. Reiter asserted that Luther's psychosis runs through his whole life like a red thread.

Reiter did not in any way deny the greatness of Luther's achievement: "His psychosis in no way takes away the halo of his genius. On the contrary, it is an essential component of the external and inner constellation of forces which made it possible for him to be the real founder and the greatest leader of the Reformation. Without this psychosis, Luther would hardly have become a genius."[6] In spite of this positive evaluation, Reiter was totally unable to understand the unique character of Luther's religion and theology. The doctrines of justification and of predestination in their entirety appeared to him to be nothing more than an "unassimilable remnant of his neurosis."[7] Reiter concluded that Luther's theology is basically an "ideological systematization of the emotional disturbances" of a hypochondriac.[8]

Reiter's work remains useful insofar as he describes Luther's numerous acute illnesses. Regardless of whether Luther's personality may in one way or another have been normal or not, Reiter is to be charged with having no understanding of theological questions. Thus Reiter asserted that we ought "not assume the presence of divine or demonic powers or mystical elements as long as it is possible to explain events in Luther's life on a totally natural basis."[9] Such an assertion does not do justice to the nature of religious and theological phenomena. Finally, Reiter's methods frequently do not meet the criteria of historical-critical scholarship so that his far-reaching conclusions have no adequate basis in the sources.

Luther was interpreted in a somewhat different way by the American psychoanalyst Erik H. Erikson. Erikson tried to provide a psychoanalytic and historical study of Luther. His work is, however, no more adequate in terms of historical-critical method than that of Reiter. Erikson asserted that the young Luther was involved in an oedipal struggle with his father and that this resulted in an identity crisis. Since there was no adequate, solid basis for such an interpretation in the sources, however, Erikson was only able to reconstruct it on the basis of questionable reports and by sometimes misinterpreting statements. This is particularly the case in his treatment of "the fit in the choir" during which Luther is supposed to have called out "I am not" (that is, not the person possessed of a demon described in Mark 9:17). Erikson interpreted this statement falsely, simply on the basis of his misunderstanding of the grammar. But quite apart from this, there are very strong doubts as to whether this event ever occurred in history—yet Erikson gave it a key position in the development of his thinking. Erikson also attributed to Luther a supposedly long and extended identity crisis and a moratorium in finding his identity. Neither of these can be adequately established on the basis of the sources. On the other side, however, Erikson showed more understanding of Luther's theological questions than Reiter does.[10] Reiter, however, has defended his position and expressed his criticisms of Erikson in a manuscript, published after his death,[11] in which he criticized Erikson as having found too easy a solution to the problems at many important points.

Any psychiatric or psychoanalytic study of a person who lived several hundred years ago confronts extraordinary difficulties. It is extremely difficult for us to determine the significance that ideas then universally accepted could have had for the personal development of the individual. Certainly it is not particularly helpful in understanding a person like Luther to deny the uniqueness of the religious factors. We thus continue to need a description of Luther from a medical viewpoint that does justice to Luther in both historical and theological terms. If such a description should ever be written, it would be necessary for theologians to be very open to the psychoanalytic and psychiatric dimensions. It would, however, be equally necessary for the psychoanalysts and psychiatrists to be ready basically to admit the unique character of religious ideas and experiences.

2.10 Luther's Ordination to the Priesthood and His Study of Theology

On February 27, 1507, Luther was ordained to the priesthood in Erfurt. After his ordination, he was assigned to study theology. Luther thus had the possibility of studying, in a scholarly way, the questions that caused him existential concern. In October 1508 Staupitz, the vicar-general of the order, transferred Luther to the cloister of the order in Wittenberg. Luther was assigned to continue his theological studies and also to give lectures on moral philosophy in the faculty of the arts in Wittenberg. Luther's lectures on Aristotle's *Nichomachean Ethics,* which he held in 1508–9, have not been preserved. In March 1509 Luther received the degree of bachelor of biblical studies *(baccalaureus biblicus)* from the theological faculty of Wittenberg. In the same year, he became a "sententiarius," that is, he began to give lectures on the *Sentences* of Peter Lombard, the basic dogmatic treatise of the High and late Middle Ages. Luther's working copies of Lombard and of some of the writings of St.

Augustine have been preserved. Consequently, we have marginal notes
that Luther made in these books in 1509–10.

Probably, Luther and Staupitz got to know one another much better in
the winter of 1508–9 in Wittenberg. Staupitz was a very wise pastor who
was personally formed by the *devotio moderna* and on this basis he was
able to be of some help to Luther in his spiritual temptations. Neither
through his interpretation of biblical passages nor through his theological
reflections, however, was he able to overcome Luther's terrors in the face
of God the divine judge. Scholars still have not yet entirely clarified
Staupitz's theological position. In particular, we still are not clear about
the extent to which Staupitz's theology was genuinely oriented to
Augustine.

2.11 Luther's Journey to Rome and His Acceptance of the Lectureship on Bible in Wittenberg (1512)

In November 1510 Luther, together with another monk from his cloister,
was sent to Rome to protest against the reunification of the cloisters of
the order that were more strict in their observance of the monastic rules
with those cloisters that were somewhat more relaxed. This reunification
had been ordered by Staupitz. Luther's own cloister belonged to the
group that observed the rule more strictly. Such a protest on the part of
his monastery, of course, had no hope of being successful and their plea
was eventually rejected in Rome. This journey to Rome does not appear
to have been very significant for Luther at the time. It was only when
Luther looked back on it from the perspective of later life that he used his
memories as a basis for criticizing the secularization of the Roman
Church. In that context, he remembered and reported specific examples
of such secularization from his experience in Rome.

After his return to Erfurt, Luther supported a compromise proposed by
Staupitz, although the majority of the Erfurt cloister was opposed to it.
Thereupon, Staupitz in 1511 once again sent Luther to Wittenberg. From
then on, Luther took up permanent residence in Wittenberg. In October
1512 Luther received the degree of doctor of theology. At the same time
he accepted the appointment as professor of Bible with the responsibility
of giving exegetical lectures in the biblical books.

2.12 Luther's Early Lectures

Up until the time of Luther's final move to Wittenberg there are many
factors in his life that are not clear or are even disputed, particularly with
regard to his trip to Rome. In contrast, Luther's life since the autumn of
1512 can be traced exactly. In 1513 Luther began his academic work as a
professor of theology. He continued this work for more than thirty years.

In his lectures Luther interpreted the books of the Bible chapter by chapter.

During his early years in Wittenberg, Luther exercised a variety of offices in his order on the side. In the autumn of 1511, he was the house preacher of the cloister. In May 1512 he became the subprior of the cloister as well as director of the program of general studies that was associated with the cloister. In May 1515 he became the district vicar of the order. In this office, he was responsible for the supervision, at first of ten and, later, of eleven cloisters of the Saxon congregation of his order. Luther was very conscientious in carrying out the duties of the offices that he held. He also carefully kept the monastic rule of the order. In addition, beginning in 1514 Luther was also the pastoral administrator of the parish church in Wittenberg.

Most important of all for Luther, however, were his lectures. In 1513–15 he lectured on the Psalms,[12] in 1515–16 on Romans,[13] in 1516–17 on Galatians,[14] and in 1517–18 on Hebrews.[15]

Even the choice of the biblical books that Luther interpreted is significant. The Psalms were at that time understood primarily as the prayers of Christ. On this basis Luther took the opportunity to concentrate totally on the message of Christ in his interpretation. Words such as humility, pride, judgment, trust, and the gospel received new meaning in the light of the cross of Christ. In terms of a theological understanding of people, Luther now also began to concentrate heavily on people's personal relationship to God. Just as Christ humbled himself on the cross, people must humble themselves under God's judgment. Only on this basis is it possible to share in divine grace (cf. below, 5.2.2–4).

Luther developed these basic themes with careful reference to previous commentaries on the Psalms. Following these lectures on the Psalms, Luther lectured on the Pauline epistles—Hebrews was traditionally ascribed to Paul. Even the choice of books to be interpreted indicates that Luther was particularly concerned with questions about the righteousness of God and the justification of people.

This did not mean that Luther ignored the numerous other themes that are present in these books. Even these early lectures, however, clearly demonstrate the characteristic perspective of Luther's theology: he considered every question from the viewpoint of damnation and salvation, from sin and grace, or from the attempt to realize oneself in contrast to receiving the "alien" righteousness of Christ.

2.13 The Development of a New Theology

Apparently Luther made his Reformation discovery about the righteousness of God and the justification of people in these years (see below, 5.3).

Many scholars feel that this discovery already occurred in 1514 but others date it as late as 1518, that is, after the beginning of the controversy. No matter what one's opinion of this matter, Luther's great Reformation breakthrough must be understood in the context of his total theological development after 1513. These developments did not result in Luther leaving the organized church. Indeed, Luther was not even aware of such a contrast between himself and Rome before the controversy on indulgences.

Luther was, however, aware of his increasing opposition to scholastic theology. On the basis of Augustine, he attacked the Pelagians of his own time and asserted the bondage of the human will in all matters related to salvation. He also asserted that we are saved alone through divine grace which we receive in faith. This new theology found its clearest expression in Luther's theses prepared for the *Disputation Against Scholastic Theology* of September 4, 1517.[16] In these theses, Luther declared his opposition to the theology that was most common at the time. And it was basically accidental that the conflict between Luther and Rome developed not on the basis of these theses but rather in response to his far-less-radical Ninety-five Theses on indulgences of October 31, 1517.[17]

2.14 Conflict with Rome

Since his acceptance of the professorship in Wittenberg, Luther had been able to concentrate his attention on his duties as an academic teacher and was not involved in external conflicts. The controversy that began with the publication of the Ninety-five Theses, however, suddenly and permanently forced Luther out of the quietness of his study and demanded that he engage in many struggles. These controversies at first were concerned with the Roman Church which felt itself to be attacked by Luther's theses and suspected that he represented heresies similar to those of John Huss in the early fifteenth century.

It would be quite mistaken to assume that Luther either before or after 1517 was carrying out any preconceived program of Reformation and that the break with Rome came about as a result of such a program. There is no question that Luther in 1517 (sometimes even earlier) and far more emphatically in the years after 1517 made a variety of demands for reform. Luther, however, never pursued or presented a definite program for a Reformation. He was primarily concerned that the Word of God as it is known to us in the Scripture would once again become the sole norm of the preaching and life of the church and that human teachings and rules would not be given any binding authority in contrast to the Word of God.

The Roman Church at this time also clearly accepted the authority of

the Scriptures without reservation. It differed from Luther in the fact that
it uncritically assumed agreement between the Scripture and the tradition. The Reformation scriptural principle and its criticism of the num-
berless traditions on the basis of the Scriptures, however, took on such a
tremendously influential role particularly because of the many and longstanding abuses in the life of the church. It was also reinforced by the
Humanists' demand for a return to the "sources" as the primary authority.
As a result, theologians loyal to Rome were for almost the entire first half
of the sixteenth century forced to hold positions that were very difficult
to defend because they lacked both the humanistic skills of interpretation
and knowledge of the original biblical languages.

Although the controversy between Luther and Rome was never finally
ended, it took place primarily from 1517 to 1521. It reached its high
point with Luther's excommunication by the church and with the emperor's declaration that Luther was an outlaw. This was also the temporary conclusion of the controversy. In the following period, neither side
produced any substantially new arguments of any significance. Luther,
however, continued to make many significant modifications and clarifica-
tions of his position. These are found in writings such as *The Bondage of
the Will* (1525)[18] and in the Smalcald Articles (1537).[19]

2.15 Luther on the Wartburg (1521–22)

The year 1521 marks a turning point in Luther's life. It was during this
year that he was, for reasons of personal safety, taken to the castle on the
Wartburg and was thus prevented for a considerable period of time from
actively participating in events in Wittenberg. As a result, events there
developed differently than Luther had hoped they would. It was also in
1521 that it first became clear that there were many different movements
represented among Luther's large number of followers.

Almost all of these movements shared one thing in common. They
demanded that certain reforms be carried through more quickly and
more emphatically than Luther thought they should. This difference
reflects varying understandings of the divine law in the Old Testament as
well as of the significance of the Holy Spirit. Almost without exception,
these were the questions that resulted in the divisions within the Reformation itself. Although these differences within the Reformation first
became evident at this time, their roots lay in the fact that quite different
late medieval traditions were at work among various groups of supporters
of the Reformation. Scholars have long attempted to determine more
definitely the nature and extent of the influence of these traditions and
their implications for the gradual differentiation of various forms of the
Reformation but they have not yet achieved conclusive results. Andreas

Karlstadt (c. 1480–1541) was the leader of the Wittenberg Reformation during Luther's absence. Melanchthon somewhat reluctantly followed his leadership. And after his return from the Wartburg in March 1522, Luther critically differentiated his own position from the actions of these Wittenberg Reformers.

During the following years Luther's activity extended over a much larger geographical area. The Reformation spread quickly and many territories sought Luther's advice as they began to introduce reforms into the life of the church. Luther also extended his influence through the publication of a large number of books and pamphlets as well as through his extensive correspondence. In addition, Luther continued to hold his lectures and to preach regularly.

After 1523 the Reformation was threatened by the shadow of the approaching Peasants' War. In a variety of writings, Luther dealt with the theological justification of the conflict asserted by the rebels on the one hand and, in quite a different style, by Thomas Müntzer's publications on the other. It was also during this time that Erasmus attacked Luther's understanding of the human will (1524).[20] Luther's answer to that attack (1525)[21] resulted in the division between Luther and the major elements of the Humanist movement.

2.16 Luther's Marriage

Shortly after the Peasants' War came to its terrible end, Luther married the former nun Katharina von Bora on June 13, 1525. At the time, this action by Luther aroused a great negative reaction. This reaction did not mean that Luther was the first former monk who no longer considered himself to be bound by his oath of celibacy—he had many predecessors in this action. Rather, the negative reaction centered on Luther's timing of his marriage.

At this time, the Peasants' War still had not come to an end in many areas. And the terrible vengeance of the princes and nobles had already begun to fall on the rebels. How could Luther get married at such a time? The peasants had allied themselves with the Reformation and had attempted to realize the freedom that it promised in terms of their own understanding of that freedom. As a result, an apocalyptic time had come on the Reformation. How was it possible for Luther to think of his own personal happiness at such a time?

Even Luther's closest supporters were critical. Melanchthon—in his letter of June 16, 1525, to Joachim Camerarius—complained that Luther had not said anything to anyone about what he was going to do. In addition, he had picked the entirely wrong time in which to do such a thing.[22]

Luther personally, however, saw his action as primarily an act of faith in opposition to the devil and all apocalyptic expectation. In addition, Luther had decided to marry after very carefully thinking through the situation and he carried out his intention in a very deliberate way. This was not a marriage of love in the modern sense of the term. Ever since the monks had gradually deserted the cloister in which he lived, and the monastic community had been gradually dissolved, Luther basically had taken care of himself. By 1525, he badly needed someone who would take charge of the household and see that Luther himself was taken care of. In addition Luther had unsuccessfully attempted to find an acceptable husband for Katharina. He finally solved the problem by marrying her himself. On June 21, 1525, he wrote to Amsdorf, "I feel neither passionate love nor burning for my spouse, but I cherish her."[23]

Both partners in this marriage felt great love for each other. Kate managed Luther's always-expanding household with skill and prudence. The large building of the Black Cloister, which the elector gave to Luther as his personal property, became a center of hospitality. Friends and guests came in large numbers. Students lived as paying guests with Luther as they did with many other professors. The growing family frequently gathered together to make music. Kate often found it difficult to make ends meet financially. Luther was very generous and did not think too seriously about financial matters. His salary was indeed adequate and he received a number of raises. He declined to collect the tuition fees to which he was entitled from the students, however. He also received no honorarium for his writings. The printers are said to have offered him four hundred gulden a year—more than his salary as a professor—for the exclusive rights of publication. Luther, however, declined every honorarium. He never made a penny of profit from his huge literary production. He felt that whatever he was able to do in this area was something that he ought to do without pay.

Admittedly, the tasks that Luther had to manage did not become smaller through his establishing a family and the controversies also did not cease. In addition to his lectures, Luther worked intensively on his translation of the Old Testament. His translation of the New Testament, the so-called September Testament, had already appeared in 1522. The translation of the Old Testament appeared gradually until the whole Bible had been translated by 1534. Another very significant task was the organization of the Lutheran territorial churches. The Reformation movement had reached far and wide but until the middle 1520s had hardly resulted in any actual reformations of the organizational life of the church. In addition there was considerable uncertainty as to how the life and preaching of the church were to be defined as a result of the

Reformation. The organizational system of the old church was now partially nonexistent but the new had not yet taken shape. The declaration of the Diet of Speyer in 1526 appeared to provide a legal basis for the full introduction of the Reformation in the church.[24] As a result, in 1527 the visitation of the churches and the schools began in Electoral Saxony. Luther participated in this visitation. Questions of church order were as a result always a matter of concern for Luther, not only in Electoral Saxony but far beyond its borders.

2.17 The Controversy About the Lord's Supper

In addition, the controversy about the Lord's Supper between Luther and Zwingli began in 1525 (see below, 3.29–35). Zwingli began the controversy with his polemical attack against Luther's very cautious emphasis on the real presence of the body and blood of Christ in the Sacrament. Before this happened, Luther and Zwingli had both undergone considerable development in their doctrine of the Lord's Supper. As a result, Luther emphasized the real presence while Zwingli interpreted the words of institution in a figurative sense. There were a variety of other theological problems underlying this difference in the doctrine of the Lord's Supper. As a result, the controversy did not simply focus on a single problem but rather raised the most basic questions about the theology and the organization of the church of the Reformation. Ultimately, the interpretation of the incarnation, sin, the relationship between body and spirit in the biblical in contrast to the classical tradition, and also the basis of the certainty of salvation were at stake.

As the controversy proceeded, almost all the significant theologians of the Reformation became involved in it. Once again it became clear that there were very significant differences among various branches of the Reformation. Not all of them adopted either Luther's or Zwingli's position; rather, there were many attempts at compromise.

As far as Luther himself was concerned, he increased his emphasis on the real presence during the controversy with Zwingli and began to assert the doctrine of ubiquity. According to this doctrine, the ascended human nature of Christ is omnipresent as a result of its union with the divine nature of Christ, even though it is only available to us "for our salvation" in the elements of the Lord's Supper. Under pressure from his opponents, Luther now made use of a variety of scholastic ways of thinking. In addition, after the appearance of the divisions within the Reformation, Luther intensified his emphasis on teaching as a way of giving leadership to the Reformation.

The Marburg Colloquy in 1529 brought the two opposing viewpoints somewhat closer together. Finally, however, the basic controversy between Luther and Zwingli could not be resolved. And, as a result, it was not possible to reunite the Reformation movement. On the contrary, the Reformation could now be introduced only at the level of the individual territories, one territory at a time. A more comprehensive unity was not possible. This also marked the end of Landgrave Philip of Hesse's bold plans for an alliance of the Reformation territories which would set limits to the great power of the House of Hapsburg. Although a limited theological agreement resulted from the colloquy, this agreement had no long-lasting significance.

2.18 The Diet of Augsburg (1530)

The year 1530 presented the Reformation with a severe test. The edict of the Diet of Worms of 1521 had basically been carried out only in the territories governed by the Hapsburgs. The other territories had been content to make more or less noncommittal statements. This inaction had been possible only because Charles V had become involved in armed conflict with Frances I of France immediately after the conclusion of the Diet of Worms. As a result, the emperor himself had, for many years, not been able to give attention to the implementation of the edict.

Now in 1530 Charles was finally able to return to the territory of the German Empire. He did so with the firm intention to resolve the religious controversy at the Diet of Augsburg in 1530. Because he wanted to create a good climate for negotiations, he intentionally formulated the summons to the diet in very mild terms. No one, however, had any reason to expect that the emperor would not, in case of a final breakdown in negotiations, bring all the force that he could bring to bear on the "Protestants."[25]

Being excommunicated by the church and outlawed by the emperor, Luther himself could not appear at the diet. During the diet, however, he took up residence at the castle of Coburg, the southernmost point of Electoral Saxon territory. Here he was as close as he could possibly be to Augsburg and he was able to exercise some influence on events there, at least through his correspondence. The primary burden of responsibility rested on Melanchthon, however—both in the composition of the Augsburg Confession as well as in the confidential negotiations, which were basically far more important than the confession itself. Melanchthon was not only a great scholar but was also deeply concerned about the future of the Reformation. For this reason, he was more inclined to make concessions than Luther was.

It was very painful to Luther that he was not able personally to be present with his friends in Augsburg. The exchange of views through correspondence involved many delays. Insofar as he was able, Luther encouraged the Lutherans in Augsburg. He also exercised his influence

with a publication *Exhortation to All Clergy Assembled at Augsburg.*[26]
This was a courageous defense of the work of the Reformation. In spite of
the nervous tension he was under at this time, Luther now found, as he
also had when he was on the Wartburg, inspiration for writing about
questions that were not high on the day's agenda. For example, he
published *The Beautiful Confitemini,* an interpretation of Psalm 118,[27]
The Keys,[28] an important discussion of questions related to confession,
absolution, and church discipline, as well as *A Sermon on Keeping
Children in School.*[29] In addition, he wrote *On Translating: An Open
Letter,*[30] in which he made significant contributions to the discussion of
hermeneutics, the art of interpretation, as well as publishing his own
German translation of Aesop's Fables.[31] Thus, even in this stressful year,
Luther continued his own work without interruption.

When Luther thought about the situation in Augsburg he was pleased
that the Lutherans were so courageous in their confession even though
he was also critical of the Augsburg Confession at some points.

The decrees of the Diet of Augsburg renewed the Edict of Worms. As a
result, the situation of the Protestant states was seriously threatened.
They responded by joining together in the Smalcald League (1531), a
political and military alliance in which they committed themselves to
mutual defense in case the emperor used military force to resolve the
religious question.

In earlier years, Luther had rejected the idea that anyone had a right to
active resistance and in its place had recommended the use of passive
resistance. Since the Reformation had already been introduced into many
territories, however, this viewpoint was no longer viable. Luther now
accepted the opinion of the lawyers that the authority of the emperor
was not superior to the authority of the estates. Reluctantly, Luther gave
up his opposition to a defensive alliance but continued to warn against
trusting in weapons instead of in God. Luther's discussions of the right of
resistance, written in the 1520s and early 1530s, contain a variety of
different approaches to the question. It was only as a result of these
discussions that Luther's position on resistance as well as his doctrine of
the two governments of God were more thoroughly and sharply defined.

2.19 The Truce of Nürnberg (1532)

The Truce of Nürnberg was agreed to in 1532 and resulted in the first
armistice. Luther interpreted this as a confirmation of his own view that
the goals of the Reformation would not be achieved through the use of
force. The protection provided by the military alliance, however, continued to make possible a comparatively undisturbed development of the
Reformation. During these years, both the theological faculty (in 1533)

and the whole university of Wittenberg (in 1536) were reorganized. In this process, the practice of holding scholastic disputations, which Luther considered to be quite valuable, was reintroduced. Luther himself frequently presented theses and took part in such disputations. These disputations explored many kinds of doctrinal questions, although it was only natural that the themes were most often determined by the then-current controversies. Luther had long been known as an exegete, a preacher, a popular author, and a translator of the Bible. Through his participation in these disputations, he also established himself as a teacher of the church.

2.20 The Wittenberg Concord (1536)

In the 1530s the theologians of central Germany, who usually followed Luther's leadership, and those theologians from southern Germany who supported the Reformation gradually reached agreement on the doctrine of the Lord's Supper. Luther's influence had become stronger in southern Germany after the death of Zwingli in 1531. And as a result of Martin Bucer's mediation, Luther in 1536 agreed to the text of the Wittenberg Concord, an explanation of the Lord's Supper drafted by the southern German Reformers.[32] Full union was still not achieved, however, because too many other differences remained unresolved.

At the same time, controversies continued to arise among the Reformers, particularly as a result of the so-called antinomian teaching of Johann Agricola. This controversy was particularly important because it dealt with the heart and center of the Reformation, the understanding of justification and of the distinction between the law and the gospel. Luther expressed his opposition to Agricola in several disputations and series of theses and in the process continued to define his own position more precisely.[33]

2.21 The Colloquies on Religion (1540–41)

The council that had originally been summoned to meet in Mantua in May 1537 did not convene as scheduled, but rather first began its work in Trent in 1545. The emperor responded to the delay by once again taking the initiative and attempting to resolve the controversies over religion. In 1540–41 a series of religious colloquies was held in which many leading theologians participated. Among the Protestants were Melanchthon, Bucer, and also Calvin, who at this time was living in Strassburg. Luther did not take part in these negotiations.

The Roman Catholic theologian John Gropper and Bucer arrived at agreement in the doctrine of justification itself. This agreement was expressed in the so-called Regensburg Book (1541) but was rejected by

Luther.[34] He thought that the viewpoint of the Reformation was not adequately represented in this agreement. More significantly, however, as Luther grew older he was increasingly filled with an unlimited and very deep mistrust of the papacy. Since these discussions were not able to achieve agreement in the question of transubstantiation and since the newly proposed compromise was also not accepted by Rome, none of these efforts was successful. Thereupon, Charles V began to carry out the plan that he had earlier often considered: to first conquer the Protestants with military force and then to force them to return to the Roman Catholic Church.

In pursuing this goal, the emperor found an ideal weapon in the unfortunate double marriage that Landgrave Philip of Hesse, the political leader of the Protestants, had entered into in 1540 (cf. below, 3.37). The political decline of German Protestantism actually can be dated from the date of this double marriage. Under the law, bigamy itself was punishable by death. And as the whole affair became a public scandal, the emperor used it to force Philip to remain politically neutral although he did not insist that he stand trial.

As a result, the Smalcald League was decisively weakened and the emperor was able to pursue his goals with hope of success. Luther in any case did not live to experience the catastrophe of the Smalcald War (1546–47). He was not even really aware of the emperor's long series of preparations for military conflict. Had he been aware of these, it is quite possible that he might have further revised his understanding of the right to resist.

2.22 Luther's Last Years

Luther's last years were once again overshadowed by numerous quarrels and controversies within Protestantism. Alongside the many current questions of varying importance that were constantly on the agenda, Luther was particularly concerned that the princes were exercising too much influence over the Protestant Church. And his efforts to establish Lutheran bishops (particularly Nikolaus Amsdorf as bishop of Naumburg in 1541–42) served not only to preserve episcopal dioceses in the Reformation but also corresponded to Luther's personal understanding of the way in which the Protestant Church should be structured. He was not able, however, to prevent the developments that resulted in the princes' gaining control of the church's organizational structure.

Luther was very concerned about the possible future of both the Protestant Church and the German people. Already in his treatise *Dr. Martin Luther's Warning to His Dear German People* (1531)[35] elements of apocalyptic expectation are clearly evident. As Luther grew older, his concerns and fears intensified. For example, he thought that the end of the world was very near. Precisely for that reason, Luther felt that the government should do everything it could to delay the divine judgment as long as possible. When this strong apocalyptic expectation is taken into account, we can understand why Luther, in his last years, asserted that Jewish worship services should be forbidden. Luther, like many of his contemporaries, felt that what happened in the synagogues was public blasphemy. They felt that such blasphemy had to be prevented, otherwise they would call down God's immediate judgment upon themselves (cf. below, 3.41).

For this same reason, Luther's polemic against the papacy became as sharp as we can possibly imagine during the last years of his life. His attacks were simply unrestrained. At the same time, however, the polemics of some of his Roman Catholic opponents were no less excessive. It would obviously not be appropriate to explain the character of Luther's polemics as an expression of his personal pathology. Rather Luther's polemical style must be primarily evaluated in the total context of his Reformation theology (cf. below, 3.39).

2.23 Luther's Death

Luther was in very poor health for a long time before he died. The physical and emotional strain under which he lived, particularly in the period around 1521, resulted in insomnia that Luther was never able to overcome. Since approximately 1525 he suffered from gallstones, an illness that periodically reoccurred and almost proved fatal in Smalcald in February 1537. This illness created frequent and long periods of pain for Luther. In addition, he suffered from a chronic ear infection. As he grew older, he gradually began to develop angina, a heart problem that caused him quite a bit of trouble and finally led to his death. In spite of this variety of often severe illnesses, however, Luther's creative power remained unbroken throughout his life. For that reason alone, it is not possible to explain his spiritual temptations on the basis of his illnesses. On the contrary, Luther remained active up until just before his death.

Shortly before his death, he undertook a trip to Eisleben in order to resolve a legal controversy between the counts of Mansfeld. While in Eisleben, on February 18, 1546, Luther died. His body was buried in the Castle Church in Wittenberg.

3 | LUTHER'S ROLE IN THE COMPLICATED CONTROVERSIES OF HIS TIME

3.1 Theological, Ecclesiastical, and Political Conflicts

Luther first became known to a wider public in 1517. In the following decades, a large number of controversies about diverse issues developed. Luther was not only involved in most of these controversies but also evoked many of them through his Reformation theology.

It would certainly be an error to assert that the ecclesiastical and theological controversies of those decades were the cause of all the other conflicts of the age; however, it would be equally one-sided to describe the arguments in these controversies as only the expression of various political and economic conflicts. The fact is, rather, that the theological and ecclesiastical controversies of the time were inseparably involved with the conflicts of interest among politicians, the estates, and economic groups. Frequently it is not even possible to distinguish clearly the various themes and viewpoints from one another.

It may even be the case that the attempt to make such a clean distinction between theological and other motives is clear evidence of a misunderstanding of the nature of religion. For religion does not exist in a vacuum, but is constantly involved with questions of real life. As far as the sixteenth century was concerned, questions related to theology and the life of the church were in the foreground. In no other period of German history were religious questions as significant for the decisions of individuals as well as for political decisions. As a result, Luther played a central role in all of the controversies after 1517.

3.2 The Controversy Escalates and Focuses on Scripture

The controversies of the sixteenth century dealt with a wide variety of questions. For example, a controversy might begin by dealing with certain abuses in the church. This would soon lead to an attack on the authority of the pope and the church. It was inevitable that more and more problems became involved in the controversy. Basically, of course, only a few questions were finally at issue. These central questions were the authority and understanding of the Holy Scriptures. It was the understanding of Scripture that was at stake in the controversies between Luther and Rome as well as among the various groups in the Reformation in Saxony, and also between Luther and Zwingli.

This was also the case in the controversy between Luther and Müntzer. Although political questions also played an important role in the latter controversy, it was ultimately a controversy between two parties who understood the Scripture in completely different ways. The two sides in the controversy represented two basically different viewpoints, each of which—in a way completely different from the other—claimed that it had the authority of the Scripture on its side.

The basic elements of this new understanding of Scripture are already apparent in Luther's early lectures. Luther shared with Humanism the concern to base his interpretation on the original text, as much as this was possible. But there is absolutely no contemporary parallel for Luther's intensive efforts to return to the original meaning of the Scripture. For Luther, the Bible was not only the most important source of teaching and preaching but also the means through which God still makes the word of judgment and of grace heard in our world. In this understanding of the Scripture as the medium as well as the message, Luther differs from all those who merely emphasize the literal content of the Scripture.

Luther's conviction that God still speaks to us today through the medium of the Scripture became the basis for the almost prophetic authority with which Luther, confident that he was supported by the Scripture, set himself in opposition to the papal hierarchy. In his early lectures Luther did not yet interpret the Bible in such a way that he came into critical conflict with the hierarchy. Even in these early lectures, however, there is a comprehensive criticism of various movements in the church and particularly in monasticism. Luther was particularly disturbed by the unbelief and self-security that he encountered precisely among those who considered themselves to be "pious."

In his early lectures, Luther did not refer to the radical critique of the church by Wyclif in the fourteenth century. Wyclif had criticized the secularization of the church as well as the alliance between the state and the church. John Huss had repeated this critique in a somewhat more cautious form in the fifteenth century. Over against these previous criticisms of specific abuses and corruption in the church, Luther's critique of the church is quite unique in focusing on spiritual elements in the life of the church.

3.3 The Dispute Over Indulgences

The first great controversy that was focused on Luther and that indeed was also induced by him was the controversy about indulgences. In his early lectures, Luther had already expressed specific but scattered objections to the practice of indulgences. And in two sermons, one of which was probably delivered on October 31, 1516, Luther had warned of the dangers of indulgences. Luther did not reject the possibility of an indulgence in principle, but rather identified a contradiction between true contrition and the desire to receive an indulgence.

What was an indulgence? The practice of indulgences must be understood in the context of the sacrament of penance. Penance first begins with the sinner experiencing contrition. Then the sinner confesses her or his sin to the priest and receives absolution from the priest. Finally the priest requires the penitent to perform some kind of satisfaction. This satisfaction was laid upon penitents as a way by which they could experience the punishment of their sins that had not been removed by the absolution. This understanding of satisfaction was based upon the presupposition that a sinful act not only results in guilt but also incurs a temporal punishment that must be endured either here upon earth or in purgatory.

During the High and late Middle Ages, a number of the church's teachings had been further developed and given specific formulation on the basis of this understanding of the sacrament of penance and the associated development of the teachings about indulgences. These included doctrines such as God's judicatory activity, the church, purgatory, and the "treasury of the church"—which was constituted by the excess merits of Christ and the saints, and became the resource out of which the church provided indulgences to other people.

The practice of indulgences first began to develop in the eleventh century and was originally understood as affecting only the temporal punishments imposed by the church itself. Later, indulgences were issued releasing penitents from the temporal punishments of purgatory. Then, an indulgence was issued releasing the recipient from punishment and all guilt. Finally, indulgences were issued on behalf of members of the recipient's family who had already died, releasing them from the punishments of purgatory. The theologians disagreed among themselves on many aspects of the practice and effectiveness of indulgences. At the time of Luther, there was still no official teaching of the church about indulgences. As a result, there was—even by the time of Luther—no adequate clarity about this complex set of practices, which were so very important in the pastoral work of the church.

The practice of selling indulgences was of immense significance for the financial structure of the church. Indulgences were one of the major sources of the income that the papal state required to meet its strong need for money and to finance the many wars in which the papacy was involved. The curia also needed the income from the sale of indulgences to finance its luxurious life style. Over and above this, indulgences were sometimes issued to finance major economic projects that would otherwise not have been achievable. To this extent, the indulgence served some of the same functions that were later served by borrowing. For innumerable faithful, the purchase of an indulgence was an opportunity to make use, in some way, of the church's help in protecting themselves from the dangers of purgatory and eternal judgment. Thus the sale of indulgences both met the financial needs of the curia and simultaneously responded to the popular desire for salvation. This led to a rapid development of the business of dealing in "holy goods." No less a person than Luther's own prince, Elector Frederick the Wise, was a pious merchandiser of indulgences. As late as 1522 he sent his personal agent to Venice to purchase religious relics. Once a year, he put these on display so that people might gain release from the punishments of purgatory by visiting the exposition and piously viewing the relics. In 1518 the total value of the indulgence gained by viewing all the relics in this collection corresponded to the remission of 127,800 years of suffering in purgatory.

Luther's Ninety-five Theses of October 31, 1517,[1] criticized the then-current practice of indulgences. Luther made his criticisms public because it was his duty, both as a pastor and a doctor of theology, to be concerned about preserving pure teaching and preaching in the church. Since the doctrine of indulgences had not been defined as a dogma of the church, Luther felt quite free to raise the most critical kinds of questions. It was his intention to clarify and resolve the many kinds of problems connected with the sale of indulgences. Of course, considering the widespread use of indulgences and the curia's financial interest in them, it was very dangerous for Luther to attack the practice of indulgences in this way.

3.4 Were the Ninety-five Theses Really Posted on the Church Door?

Scholars disagree as to whether or not Luther actually nailed the Ninety-five Theses to the door of the Castle Church in Wittenberg on October 31, 1517. Although this nailing of the theses has been celebrated as a symbol of Protestantism for centuries since, the Roman Catholic Church historian Erwin Iserloh in 1961 raised questions about the historicity of the posting of the Ninety-five Theses. He pointed to the fact that the posting of the theses is first mentioned in Melanchthon's introduction to volume 2 of Luther's Latin works. Melanchthon, however, did not write this until some months after Luther's death. Melanchthon did not move to Wittenberg until August 1518 and is demonstrably not very well informed on many details of the early period of the Reformation. Thus it is quite understandable that Melanchthon might have been in error about the posting of the theses. According to Iserloh, his viewpoint is supported by the additional fact that Luther wrote both of the letters that he sent to his ecclesiastical superiors on October 31, 1517, as private letters. This would also indicate that he had not yet published the theses.

As a result there has been considerable debate about the historicity of the posting of the theses—but no generally accepted conclusion has been reached. Iserloh's arguments are not really convincing, but no one has succeeded in proving the historicity of the accounts of the posting of the theses. The decision in this matter is really of some importance. If Iserloh is right, then the responsibility of the hierarchy is all the greater because they did not react to Luther's correspondence. This lack of response made it necessary for Luther to raise his questions in the public forum. On the other hand, if the theses really were posted, Luther's own role in generating the controversy that developed as a result is of greater significance.

3.5 The Ninety-five Theses

How did it happen that Luther's Ninety-five Theses received such an overwhelming response? One would not necessarily have expected that on the basis of their content. The theses Luther prepared for his *Disputation Against Scholastic Theology*[2] held on September 4, 1517, were much more radical. In these theses Luther attacked the influence of Aristotelian philosophy on the development of the whole of theology. In contrast to this, the Ninety-five Theses dealt primarily with indulgences and penance. As he had done previously, Luther did not reject every use of indulgences, but rather limited their efficacy to the remission of temporal punishments imposed by the church. In addition, he protested against the false sense of security that indulgences created.

Luther's criticism of indulgences was indeed quite moderate. In the background, however, could be heard the first sounds of an earthquake that was to shake the entire church. Others became aware of this larger implication sooner than Luther did. Luther did not understand repentance primarily in terms of the sacrament of penance but rather in terms of the comprehensive process that is presupposed by the New Testament's usage of the term "repentance." In this perspective, Luther began to develop a new understanding of the office of the ministry. The priest could only remit guilt insofar as he declared that it was remitted by God. The doctrine of the treasury of the church was also attacked by thesis 62 which asserts: "The true treasure of the church is the most holy gospel of the glory and grace of God."[3] Since Luther had prepared the Ninety-five Theses for use in a disputation, he did not have to agree unconditionally with the opinions that they presented. In spite of this, however, the Ninety-five Theses are of far-greater significance. For, when Luther introduced theses 42–51 with the phrase "Christians are to be taught that . . . ," he went far outside the basic frame of theses prepared for use in disputations.[4]

It is therefore not surprising that the rapidly growing controversy which centered around Luther's Ninety-five Theses did not give intensive attention to the question of indulgences but rather focused on questions related to ecclesiastical authority, the papacy, obedience, the doctrine of the sacraments, or even suggested that there might possibly be an opposition between Scripture and human teachings.

In this controversy the defenders of the Roman Church were simply unable to understand what Luther was really concerned about in his criticism of the practice of indulgences as well as in his basic understanding of Scripture. Quite the opposite was true. Not only Johannes Tetzel, but John Eck as well, staked their reputations on their attempts to reveal Luther as a heretic. Suspicions spread very quickly that Luther was renewing the false teaching of Huss. Since Huss had been condemned by the Council of Constance, Luther was also threatened with being burned at the stake. The suspicions of his opponents, however, only had the effect of forcing Luther to move forward step by step and to expand both his critique and its theological basis.

The amazingly rapid spread of the Ninety-five Theses as well as the discussion about them was only possible because the art of printing had already been developed for a few decades. This art of printing, combined with the special political and cultural conditions which at that time existed only in Germany, provided the decisive presupposition for the very large response to Luther's criticism. The resulting powerful effect on public opinion of Luther's work made it impossible for Luther to be done away with as simply and quickly as Huss had been. Thus the art of printing is of considerable significance for the end of the unified world of the Middle Ages and the development of the pluralistic modern age.

3.6 "The Heidelberg Disputation" (1518)

In April 1518 Luther was given the opportunity to conduct the public disputation at the meeting of his order in Heidelberg and to prepare the theses that were to be discussed.[5] Luther used the theological and philosophical theses that he prepared for the disputation in Heidelberg to present his basic Reformation theology about the sinfulness of people, the bondage of the will in relationship to God, the working of God's grace without human cooperation, and faith without reference to the daily controversies of the time, and also to give very sharp and clear formulation to his teaching. In opposition to a "theology of glory," Luther asserted his "theology of the cross."[6] The theologians who at that time represented the scholastic position quite understandably did not feel that Luther's sharp condemnation of them was based on a proper understanding of their position. Luther's use of the concept of the theology of glory as a description of scholasticism can indeed not be accepted as historically valid. At the same time, however, this characterization focuses our attention on certain very definite limitations and one-sided formulations that the theology of that time had not avoided.

3.7 Luther's Examination by Cajetan (1518)

The Diet of Augsburg was held in the autumn of 1518. One of the things which took place on the margin of the diet was that the Saxon elector took the initiative in arranging for Luther to be examined by Cardinal Cajetan in Augsburg. The curia was forced against its will into agreeing with the elector's plan because it needed the support of the Saxon elector in the vote for the successor to Emperor Maximilian I. The elector had interceded on behalf of his Wittenberg professor for a variety of reasons. The elector was of course concerned that Luther would not receive a fair trial in Rome, but he also wished to protect his recently founded Wittenberg University. Thus at the very latest after the autumn of 1518, Luther's case was involved with a variety of interests in the larger world of politics. As far as the curia was concerned, it lost valuable time as well as the opportunity of possibly suppressing the Reformation movement in its very beginnings by giving priority to its political concerns rather than to Luther's trial for heresy.

When he examined Luther in October 1518 Cajetan began by simply demanding of Luther that he repudiate his false teachings. When Luther asked to be told what his false teachings were, the cardinal could not avoid becoming involved in a discussion of the content of Luther's teaching. As a result, they discussed the doctrines of the treasury of the church, the authority of the papacy, the relationship between Scripture and ministry, as well as the necessity of faith for the saving reception of the sacraments. Cajetan could understand Luther's critique of indulgences; however, he sharply rejected Luther's view of the papacy. Luther had admittedly only occasionally expressed his view of the papacy as a marginal note to other discussions. Cajetan, however, had written a treatise in preparation for his conversation with Luther. This treatise expressed his suspicion that Luther's attitude really revealed the intention of "establishing a new church." For Cajetan, the church as an objective reality always took priority over the subjective certainty of the individual. For Luther, however, Christian faith is not possible without the certainty of salvation.

3.8 Luther's Appeal to a Council

On November 28, 1518, shortly after his examination in Augsburg, Luther appealed to the pope for a trial before a general council of the church. Luther based his appeal on the decisions of the councils of Constance and Basel that a council which had legitimately assembled in the Holy Spirit represented the holy catholic church and was superior to the pope in questions of faith. For this reason, Luther was certain that the pope could do nothing to interfere with an appeal to a council.[7] In spite of many assertions to the contrary, it can be considered quite certain that Luther's appeal to a council did not simply represent his joining the conciliar movement that remained active in the early sixteenth century. Rather, Luther already at this time thought of the council as being under the authority of the divine word. An example of the way in which Luther's critical attitude rapidly became sharper is provided by the fact that Luther, at the end of 1518, began to express the suspicion that the antichrist was in charge in the Roman curia.[8]

3.9 The Leipzig Debate (1519)

The conflict between Luther and Rome reached another high point during the Leipzig debate in July 1519. Originally, the debate was planned as a disputation between Eck and Luther's colleague Karlstadt, but Eck's preparatory theses were primarily addressed to Luther. As a result, the leading champions on each side debated one another in Leipzig. They also took the leadership in the controversies of the following decades. It was Eck's intention to reveal Luther as a heretic and he succeeded in doing so. Luther revealed his heresy by denying that the decisions of a council were infallible. This became particularly clear when he asserted that many of the teachings of Huss condemned by the Council of Constance were good Christian teaching.[9]

Luther thus established a clear opposition between the authority of Scripture and the authority of the church. Luther did not understand the authority of the Scripture in a legalistic way but rather felt that only those teachings that were based on Scripture could be considered binding in the church. Luther cited John Gerson and Augustine in support of this way of thinking although he admittedly did not do full justice to their positions.[10]

3.10 The Bull Threatening Excommunication (1520)

Luther's controversy with Rome came to a preliminary conclusion when the papal bull threatening his excommunication was issued. Although the political interest of the curia repeatedly resulted in a delay in Luther's trial, the process moved more rapidly after the spring of 1520. Both Cajetan and Eck took an active role in the process. Since the condemnation of Luther was based on the opinions that the universities of Cologne and Louvain had issued in 1519 condemning certain Lutheran teachings, the process proceeded quite rapidly. The bull *Exsurge Domine* of June 15, 1520,[11] threatened Luther with excommunication and condemned forty-one statements of his as "heretical, scandalous, erroneous, offensive to pious ears, misleading to simple minds, and contradictory to catholic teaching." The condemned statements are partially not understandable because they were taken out of context. No basis was given for the condemnation. Thus item 33 in the bull condemned Luther's statement that "the burning of heretics is contrary to the will of the Holy Spirit," which would mean that the bull considers the burning of false teachers as being according to the will of the Holy Spirit. Luther was summoned to recant within sixty days after the bull had been published and was threatened with excommunication if he did not do so. Luther did not do what he was asked to do. Rather he burned the bull together with the books of papal decrees and volumes of scholastic theology on December 10, 1520, outside the Elster Gate of Wittenberg.[12] Luther's final excommunication was proclaimed in Rome on January 3, 1521, in the bull *Decet Romanum Pontificem*.[13]

3.11 Luther's Three So-called Main Reformation Writings

In the year 1520 Luther wrote his three so-called main writings of the Reformation: *To the German Nobility Concerning the Reformation of the Christian Estate*,[14] *The Babylonian Captivity of the Church*,[15] and *The Freedom of a Christian*.[16]

The intensification of the controversy in the years after 1518, as well as Luther's constant rethinking of the condition of the church in the light of the Scriptures, led Luther to condemn very sharply a variety of manifestations of decay in the church and in the world. Luther in his open letter addressed to the nobility turned to the secular authorities and asked them to help in setting aside abuses. This became the first step in a process that later resulted in the state church system as well as in further strengthening the position of the territorial princes. Given the situation which then existed, however, the secular princes were the only ones who could intervene in a helping way after the ecclesiastical authorities had failed to carry out their functions. Any alternative solution involved the danger of a revolutionary upheaval.

In *The Babylonian Captivity,* Luther attacked the medieval doctrine of the sacraments and concluded that only Baptism and the Lord's Supper, possibly also penance, could be considered as sacraments. In his treatise, *The Freedom of a Christian,* Luther developed the dialectical formula of the simultaneous freedom and bondage of the Christian and on this basis developed the elements of a Reformation ethic. Luther dedicated his treatise on freedom to Pope Leo X and wrote him quite a long letter when he sent it to him. This was the result of the remarkable attempt to arrive at a reconciliation which Karl von Miltitz undertook on his own initiative. In spite of this, however, it is not possible to assume a contradiction between Luther's usual criticism of the papacy and the many seemingly reverential expressions of Luther's dedicatory letter. The accusation that Luther here was simply acting for political effect is also hardly right. It is clear, however, that the question of the papacy was still not a closed question as far as Luther was concerned. And it was his intention not to do something that would frustrate the possible success of Miltitz's efforts before they had even begun. Luther's attempts to resolve the dispute between himself and the papacy became meaningless only after he was finally excommunicated. As a matter of fact, Luther never again showed the same kind of readiness to compromise, even on a limited basis, which he showed in the autumn of 1520.

3.12 Luther's Critique of Monastic Vows

Luther's controversy with Rome reached its conclusion with his critique of monastic vows. He expresses his basic criticisms in his book *The Judgment of Martin Luther on Monastic Vows,* written in the autumn of 1521.[17] Luther did not absolutely reject the possibility of making or keeping monastic vows in every case but he did reject the idea that such vows were eternally binding. In the context of the situation at that time, no one paid much attention to Luther's admittedly limited affirmation of monastic vows. On the contrary, innumerable monks and nuns found that Luther's treatise gave them permission to leave their convents with a good conscience. Actually most of the monastic communities in Germany at that time were to a large extent dissolved. Luther's criticism of monastic vows must also be understood in the context of a new evaluation of secular work. He no longer saw the special work of the monk but rather the "normal," everyday work of secular vocations as fulfilling God's command (cf. below, 4.16).

3.13 The First Differentiations in the Reformation Movement (1521–22)

The first differences within the Reformation itself began to appear during the final phase of the controversy with Rome. These differences had already begun to become apparent after the Diet of Worms, however, when Luther, for reasons of personal safety, lived on the Wartburg. During this time, from May 1521 to March 1522, two basic factors became clear. The first was that the Reformation movement that Luther had evoked was in no way dependent for its success or failure on his person; rather, it became clear that the movement would continue without him as its leader or spokesman. The second was that, particularly in Wittenberg where others assumed leadership roles as spokespersons of the Reformation, there were significant differences of opinion among the reformers themselves.

Looking back on the whole situation, it is now clear—although this was completely ignored at the time—that these differences were the result of two different factors. On the one hand, various reformers represented a variety of traditions of the early and medieval church that continued to determine their thinking. On the other hand, various reformers had differing understandings of the nature of Reformation theology. For some time, there has been intensive research into the strength and the specific characteristics of these traditions as well as about the unique ways in which reformers tried to find new formulations of central theological themes. Some of Luther's supporters and co-workers became his theological opponents. Yet all without exception were decisively influenced by their contact with him. Luther's significance for the development of many of them was basically as a catalyst. We cannot deny that his friends and co-workers were independent thinkers and workers in their own right. Consequently, if we are to understand the Reformation movement, we must recognize that it was from its very beginning a pluralistic movement.

The topics in which the differences appear most clearly are those related to the binding character of the laws of the Old Testament for Christians, the significance of the Holy Spirit for the interpretation of the law, and the nature and extent of the reforms that were needed. An examination of almost all the later controversies in the Reformation would confirm that the dividing principles are almost always formulated in terms of the law and the Spirit.

3.14 The Wittenberg Reformers

During the summer of 1521, when the question of the validity of monastic vows was most seriously discussed, Karlstadt maintained that such
vows were binding. At the same time he also declared that breaking such
a vow was a sin, although not a very serious sin because the making of
such a vow had already been an act of personal disobedience against God.
Beginning in the autumn of 1521, there were also arguments as to
whether or not the Mass should still be celebrated if only the bread were
distributed to the people, and whether or not the Decalogue's injunction
against images meant that the pictures and statues of the saints should be
removed from the churches.

Melanchthon, who had been in Wittenberg only since 1518 and who
was only twenty-four years old in 1521, was not able to arrive at any clear
decision on these matters. In this, he was in a marked contrast to the
much-older Karlstadt who had been born about 1480. And then, at the
end of December 1521, the so-called Zwickau prophets appeared with
their enthusiastic and apocalyptic sermons claiming special authority for
themselves. They added greatly to the general confusion.

After several sometimes tumultuous, even riotous, events, the city
council of Wittenberg under the leadership of Karlstadt introduced new
laws on public order on January 24, 1522. The new laws forbade all
begging, required that all pictures and images in the churches be removed, and permitted each church to have only three altars. A new order
of the liturgy of the Mass was also introduced. The government of
Electoral Saxony at first remained neutral because it did not consider
itself to be competent in religious matters. At the same time, however, the
government was quite concerned about the disturbances that preceded
and followed the introduction of these new laws.

3.15 Luther's View of Freedom and Order

In many respects, Luther and Karlstadt did not differ all that much in their
thinking about the necessary reforms. Luther made a secret visit to
Wittenberg in early December 1521. At that time he reported that he was
impressed by some of the reforms. He was, however, unhappy about the
disturbances that accompanied the introduction of these reforms. In
particular, he did not want the reforms to be introduced without the
cooperation of the authorities: "But what becomes of order? For it was
done in wantonness, with no regard for proper order and with offense to
your neighbor. If, beforehand, you had called upon God in earnest prayer,
and had obtained the aid of the authorities, one could be certain that it
had come from God."[18]

This attitude had been developing within Luther for some years. After 1522 it became one of the most important points under dispute in the controversies between Luther and the other reformers. Luther saw the relationship between freedom and order differently than the radicals among the Wittenberg Reformers did. Luther was particularly concerned that the consciences of the people first be properly instructed. Luther also wanted to preserve Christian freedom. He felt there was no need to make changes too quickly. Luther was well aware that the compulsion to make changes quickly could easily conceal a new form of legalism. Luther thus felt that changes should be made very gradually, particularly out of his concern for weak consciences. Karlstadt, however, felt that being concerned for the weak meant preventing the weak from being misled in their piety through pictures and images. Furthermore, he asserted that the freedom of the gospel could not long exist if it did "not produce its own result." Karlstadt felt that the new understanding of the gospel must also produce the necessary fruits.

3.16 A Clearer Understanding of Government

The controversies of the winter of 1521/22 gave Luther occasion to develop further his theology at many points. His theology was particularly affected in terms of his understanding of the government and of the law—particularly in terms of the relationship of the law to the gospel. The traditional theological categories for expressing this problem were the relationship between the letter and the Spirit.

In his early period, Luther had primarily interpreted the law in a Pauline sense. He now emphasized that the law is also effective in the secular realm and distinguished between the theological and the political functions of the law. The theological function of the law is to convict people of sin. The political function of the law is to maintain external order. The theological function of the law is defined in contrast to the righteousness of faith. The law's political function can lead people only to a point of civil righteousness but no further. At the same time, Luther now had occasion to rethink the dialectical relationship of the law and the gospel, a distinction that in terms of its substance is closely related to the Reformation view of justification.

As far as the doctrine of the Holy Spirit is concerned, Luther emphasized that the letter and the Spirit belong together—the Spirit makes use of the letter of the Scripture just as the real meaning of the Scripture is first opened for us through the enlightenment of the Holy Spirit.

Luther, during this controversy with the Wittenberg Reformers, more clearly developed his earlier viewpoints and protected them against misinterpretation. In so doing, he did not really introduce anything new but rather only stated his earlier teachings in a more precise form. And as far as his understanding of the gospel is concerned, he had already stated it in substance in his *First Lectures on the Psalms,* where he sometimes even explicitly used the concepts of judgment and gospel.

Questions about the people's right to revolt and the authority of the secular government had already become burning issues by the end of 1521. In the following years, they continually gained in importance until the Peasants' War and even into the following years. Luther had already demonstrated that he rejected civil disturbance and rebellion by his negative reaction to a number of fights between students and citizens of Wittenberg in July 1520. Luther was present at a mass gathering and noted, as he wrote Spalatin on July 14, 1520, that "Satan chaired the meeting."[19] Luther left the gathering and on the following Sunday preached against insurrection and revolt.

In early December 1521 Luther left the Wartburg and returned to Wittenberg for a few days. During his visit, he heard considerable talk about plans for a revolution. He responded by writing *A Sincere Admonition by Martin Luther to All Christians to Guard Against Insurrection and Rebellion.*[20] In this treatise Luther, on the one hand, supported the most radical criticism of the papacy as the antichrist and expressed his firm expectation that the divine wrath will itself punish the evil practices of the papacy. On the other hand, Luther asserted that God has forbidden us to rebel. His only recommendation was that the secular authority and the nobility should "take action" in their own territories.[21]

3.17 Luther's Treatise on "Temporal Authority"

Very soon, that is, late in 1522 a completely new situation developed. In Ducal Saxony, in Bavaria, and elsewhere the "tyrants" ordered that all copies of Luther's translation of the New Testament be turned in so that they could be confiscated. Now Luther felt that he was faced not with the question of revolt but rather of the limitations of secular or temporal authority. Luther dealt with this question in his treatise *Temporal Authority: To What Extent It Should Be Obeyed* (1523).[22]

In the process of writing this treatise, Luther also developed the set of concepts that is usually referred to as his teaching on the "two kingdoms." This summary designation is both too oversimplified and also too systematically integrated to do justice to the complexity of Luther's thinking.

It was not only the particular occasion for writing this treatise itself but also Luther's observation that the secular princes frequently misused their power and exploited the poor people that led Luther to say that God wanted to do away with the princes.[23] Luther felt that the princes' exploitation and abuse of the people had gone beyond all limits. He described the princes as workers in a rendering plant who are skinning the peasants and scraping their bones. Neither justice, nor honor, nor faithfulness can be found among the princes. In discussing the temporal authority of the secular princes, Luther distinguished between the power that was given them in earthly matters and power over people's souls. The latter power belongs to God alone.

Luther, in this treatise on temporal authority, spoke about the doctrine of the two kingdoms without explicitly using this concept. He asserted that all people are to be divided into two groups. On the one hand, there are those who belong to the kingdom of God, that is, all true believers in Christ who are under Christ. These have no need of the secular sword and secular justice. If the world were made up only of Christians, temporal authority would be superfluous. For such people would do what is right of their own accord and would not need any instruction. "Just so, by the Spirit and by faith all Christians are so thoroughly disposed and conditioned in their very nature that they do right and keep the law better than one can teach them with all manner of statutes; so far as they themselves are concerned, no statutes or laws are needed."[24]

On the one hand, Luther of course recognized that no one belongs naturally under this kingdom of God. On the other hand, all those who are under the law, that is, all those who are not Christians, live under the kingdom of this world.

> There are few true believers, and still fewer who live a Christian life, who do not resist evil and indeed themselves do no evil. For this reason God has provided for them a different government beyond the Christian estate and kingdom of God. He has subjected them to the sword so that, even though they would like to, they are unable to practice their wickedness, and if they do practice it they cannot do so without fear or with success and impunity. In the same way a savage wild beast is bound with chains and ropes so that it cannot bite and tear as it would normally do, even though it would like to.[25]

Just as Luther spoke of two kingdoms, so he also spoke of two governments of God. "For this reason God has ordained two governments: the spiritual, by which the Holy Spirit produces Christians and righteous people under Christ; and the temporal, which restrains the un-Christian and wicked so that—no thanks to them—they are obliged to keep still and to maintain an outward peace."[26] The terminology of the "two governments" gives stronger expression than that of the "two kingdoms" to the fact that we are, in both cases, dealing with God's order and institution. In addition, the terms "kingdoms" and "governments" must be seen both in terms of their differences from each other and in terms of their mutual relationship.

This world cannot be ruled with the gospel. And the gospel has not abrogated secular justice and the sword but rather has given us a new perspective on them by defining their limitations. The gospel thus shows us both what constitutes the mission of the secular government and what its limitations are. Secular government, for its part, provides for peace and order and thereby provides the necessary conditions for the proclamation of the gospel.

Using these basic ideas, Luther independently reworked the old theme of the two powers and reformulated it in a way that very much corresponded to his Reformation theology. At the same time, he summarized and clarified his own viewpoints, which he had expressed more casually. Luther, however, did not thereby intend to develop a comprehensive doctrine that he could schematically apply to every situation. On the contrary, even though Luther continued to use the distinction between the two kingdoms or governments which he developed at this time, he always made that distinction in any given situation in terms of the actual facts of that situation. It is particularly to be noted that Luther never simply abandoned the secular realm to the temporal authority, but rather always involved himself in political developments and in the process of decision making, both by consultation with the decision makers and by advocacy of a particular course of action. (Cf. below, 5.8.)

3.18 Luther's Writings on the Peasants' War

The basic ideas of Luther's treatise on temporal authority were reinforced in his writings on the Peasants' War. Whatever ethical judgment one may reach about Luther's response to the demands of the peasants and to their revolt, one should never forget that Luther himself was at that time primarily concerned with avoiding a confusion of the two kingdoms. He saw this danger as inherently present in the position taken by the peasants. It was in reference to *The Twelve Articles* of the peasants,[27] which were issued at the end of February 1525 in Swabia, that Luther, in the latter half of April 1525, wrote his *Admonition to Peace, A Reply to the Twelve Articles of the Peasants in Swabia.*[28]

In this publication Luther tried to address the consciences of both parties. He rebuked the lords and the princes because their political policy of oppression made them ultimately guilty for the revolt. He disagreed with the peasants—for whose demands he showed partial understanding—because they were trying to seek justice for themselves and thereby attempting to sit as judges in their own case. They also claimed to be a Christian confederation and thereby misused the name of Christian for secular purposes. Finally Luther criticized them because in demanding their divine rights, they were taking God's name and sinning against the Second Commandment. Luther emphasized that our redemption through Christ is entirely compatible with our lack of freedom on this earth.

Luther's very severe treatise *Against the Robbing and Murdering Hordes of Peasants,*[29] which challenges the princes to suppress the revolt with all possible means, must also be understood in the context of Luther's treatise on temporal authority of 1523. Particularly in interpreting this writing of Luther against the peasants, our evaluation must give great importance to the complicated history of its development and the process of its being printed. It is entirely possible that Luther's final public statement made during the course of the Peasants' War itself was an exhortation to peace and to reconciliation.[30]

Obviously, it is not possible to arrive at an adequate evaluation of Luther's role in the Peasants' War simply on the basis of his motives. His opponents, that is, the peasants and Thomas Müntzer, as well as the princes, also deserve to be understood in terms of their motives. Such an investigation of the various starting points of the parties involved, their definitions of their own goals, and their various assessments of the situation, as well as of the constantly changing alliances of friends and foes, will provide the student with good training in understanding the complexities of political reflection and decision making that also seeks to be Christian and ethical. In addition, the student will want to give attention to an analysis of the economic situation that provides the context for the peasants' revolt. The attitude of the territorial princes and the varying attitudes to the Peasants' War prevalent in different classes of the population should also be taken into account. Finally, the student will also want to give attention to the religious, sometimes chiliastic and utopian elements of the peasants' revolt and to evaluate them in terms of their interaction with other causes of the revolt. Some scholars have suggested that the religious and Reformation-related factors of the Peasants' War are of greater significance than any other motivating factors. From this viewpoint, Heiko A. Oberman has described the Peasants' War as a "revolution of faith."[31]

In any case, we should today be able to take it for granted that our understanding of the various participants in the Peasants' War is determined neither by apologetic nor by polemical viewpoints. Were we to be influenced by such considerations, the arguments of the parties then in conflict are all too likely to be distorted in a way that converts them into our current controversies. At the same time, it is of course true that we cannot, in evaluating Luther's attitude during the Peasants' War, ignore the far-reaching effects of this war on later developments. Here too, however, we should not ascribe too much significance to the attitudes of individuals in terms of their significance for developments on the larger scale.

3.19 Thomas Müntzer

Among Luther's opponents at this time, Thomas Müntzer is particularly significant. This is true in many ways: in terms of the development of Müntzer's theology and Reformation activities as a possible alternative to Luther; in terms of the development of the relationship between Luther and Müntzer; and finally in terms of the long-range effects that the activities of each had on later developments. The study of the latter factor has led to surprising conclusions in recent decades.

The intensive research of the past decades has given us a much more accurate knowledge of the development of Müntzer's theology and his activity as a reformer as well as of his active participation in the Peasants' War. As a result of these studies, it has been necessary to make many corrections of earlier studies of Müntzer both in specific details and in overall conclusions.

In spite of such advances in our knowledge many important problems remain to be solved. We do not yet have really reliable knowledge of the traditions that formed and shaped Müntzer. There is still much that we do not know even about the decisive influences on Luther and this is even more true of our knowledge of Müntzer. We are quite certain that Müntzer received very significant stimulation from German mysticism. It is also possible that he was influenced by the thinking of the Taborites. It is at present still very difficult to prove this in any detailed way, however. We are also completely uncertain about the extent of any scholastic influence on the young Müntzer. The view—formerly widely held—that Müntzer was decisively shaped by Luther is no longer tenable. On the contrary, Müntzer, much more clearly than many others, demonstrates the fact that the Reformation was made up of a variety of layers and was not simply a homogeneous movement. He indeed placed great hopes in Luther for a while but he was quickly disappointed. As early as the end of 1521, Müntzer had formulated the basic thoughts which were essential to his thinking and which he held to the time of his early death.

This makes it quite clear that Müntzer could not have been formed and shaped by the Wittenberg Reformers during the period 1521–22. It now seems that his contacts with groups advocating social reform in Zwickau in 1520–21 were much more significant.

The relationship between Luther and Müntzer began with a period of mutual admiration ending in 1519. It was then gradually transformed, first into a careful process of distancing themselves from each other, and then into an increasingly sharper polemic which finally resulted in a mutual hatred that could hardly be surpassed in its intensity. For Müntzer the process of establishing critical distance between himself and Luther became one of the essential dynamics in the further development of his own theology. Given the fact that Müntzer was not at any decisive point shaped by Luther, it is still true that his criticism of Luther was more significant than any other factor in defining the form and shape of his own theology.

The opposite is also true—that is, Luther felt that Müntzer was the best example of the final effects of enthusiasm. Luther saw Müntzer as personally incorporating enthusiasm's distortion of the gospel, its blurring of the Reformation's distinction between law and gospel, its proclamation of a new spiritualized legalism, its revolt against and rejection of the authority of government, and thus also its endangering of all secular order and the public peace. In his controversy with Müntzer, Luther thus further developed and more clearly defined important points and aspects of his own theology. This is particularly true of his doctrine of law and gospel as well as of government. On the other hand, however, Luther no longer expressed certain spiritualistic thoughts that still appeared, for example, in his interpretation of *The Magnificat* published in 1521.[32]

In saying this, it is necessary to emphasize that Luther did not understand these ideas as they would have been understood by the radical spiritualists. To this extent, the conflict with Müntzer led Luther to strengthen his own opposition, as well as to define it more narrowly.

We must not overlook Müntzer's significance for the early developments in Protestant worship. In 1523, that is, earlier than Luther, Müntzer translated the Latin liturgy of the Mass into German and in the process omitted those parts that were not acceptable to the Reformation. He also reformulated the prayers of the canonical hours that had been prayed by the clergy and used them as the basis of his orders of daily service. He also arranged to have new agendas printed. In addition to this, he translated some well-known Latin hymns and thus laid the foundation for congregational singing in Protestant worship. "Thus it is really Müntzer who is the father of evangelical [Protestant] worship and evangelical hymnody."[33] In this connection we need to raise a question that will not be easy to answer: Was there any connection between Müntzer's liturgical reforms and his advocacy of social revolution, an area in which his views were also very clearly formulated by this time? As far as Luther was concerned, Müntzer's example definitely stimulated him to carry out his own reform of worship and to compose Protestant hymns.

The final long-term result of the controversy between Luther and Müntzer remains more historically significant than any of the other conflicts in which Luther was involved. This is also true of its significance for our present situation. For centuries Müntzer has stood in the shadow of Luther. The negative picture of Müntzer that was so common for so long was to a large extent painted by Luther as well as by Melanchthon and other supporters of Luther. In this picture, Müntzer appeared as the destroyer of all secular order and as the counterfeiter of the gospel. The nineteenth-century Communists were the first who saw themselves as building on Müntzer's work and claimed him as the ancestor of their own political movement. As a result, Communist thinking was for a long time dominated by a glorified picture of Müntzer. It has only recently become possible for Marxists as well as many non-Marxists to develop increasingly neutral and unprejudiced studies of Müntzer. As a result, we now need to be more concerned that Luther is fairly presented in these studies than about a distorted presentation of Müntzer's position. At the same time, the study of the conflict between Luther and Müntzer provides us with very good examples of both the validity and the limitations of Luther's political ethics. In our study of this controversy, however, it is important to remember that, from beginning to end, both participants saw their disagreements as basically concerned with theological issues.

3.20 Can Soldiers Be Saved?

Luther's treatise, *Whether Soldiers, Too, Can Be Saved*,[34] was written in 1526—in the context of events related to the Peasants' War. Although Luther in this book deals directly with the problem of insurrection, it was written as an answer to a different question. A certain Colonel Assa von Kram had asked Luther whether it was possible to both have Christian faith and do the work of a soldier in wartime. In writing this response, Luther was not primarily concerned with expressing his political views or even writing an ethic of war. Rather he responded as a pastor to the question placed to him with the intention that, as Luther puts it, "I agreed to your request and promised to provide this book in order—to the best of my ability—to give the best advice to these weak, timid, and doubting consciences, and so that those who do not care may be better instructed."[35]

Here as in the controversy with Rome and in harmony with his general reluctance to support any particular program of reform, Luther was primarily concerned with instructing the conscience of his readers. Luther no longer saw the conscience as subject to the decision of the church, with the result that we may no longer act contrary to our own conscience. On the other hand, however, Luther saw the conscience as basically being under the authority of the Holy Scripture. We therefore have no basis for interpreting Luther as teaching that the conscience is autonomous. The question as to what we may or may not do with a good conscience before God was really the central problem for Luther.

Luther was admittedly convinced that a good conscience enables us to act energetically in pursuit of our goals. "For whoever fights with a good and well-instructed conscience can also fight well. This is especially true since a good conscience fills a man's heart with courage and boldness. And if the heart is bold and courageous, the fist is more powerful. . . ."[36] At least as far as Luther was concerned, however, this assertion of a relationship between our good conscience and our freedom of action does not provide any basis for deriving a good conscience from success and a bad conscience from failure.

In order to answer the colonel's question, Luther distinguished between the office and the person or between the work and the doer of the work. The office as such is given by God. This is also true of the offices of judge and executioner. Likewise the married estate as such is good. This is, however, a different question than whether the actions of particular individuals in any office and estate are good or bad. Luther further defined the question, "I am dealing here with such questions as these: whether the Christian faith, by which we are accounted righteous before God, is compatible with being a soldier, going to war, stabbing and killing, robbing and burning, as military law requires us to do to our enemies in wartime. Is this work sinful or unjust? Should it give us a bad conscience before God? Must a Christian only do good and love, and kill no one, nor do anyone any harm?"[37]

As far as the office of the soldier is concerned, Luther took the then-traditional position that, according to Romans 13 and 1 Peter 2, the office of the sword had been instituted by God in order to punish those who do evil and to protect the godly. "For the very fact that the sword has been instituted by God to punish the evil, protect the good, and preserve peace [Rom. 13:1–4; I Pet. 2:13–14] is powerful and sufficient proof that war and killing along with all the things that accompany wartime and martial law have been instituted by God."[38] Since God has instituted this office, it is ultimately God who uses the horrors of war to bring such terrible punishments on people. The soldiers are only the means or the tools that God uses. And if one were to assert that the use of the sword in war is unjust, one would also have to hold that the punishment of the evildoer in peacetime is unjust. If, however, one work of the office of the sword is right and just, then the other must also be.

Accordingly, the question that Luther identified as requiring particular consideration was the question of personal ethics. In Luther's own terms this question read: how can we use this office properly? Luther began to answer this question by pointing out that the Christian is not commanded to fight. Beyond this, however, it is necessary to distinguish between different possible kinds of war. First of all, there can be a war between equals, in which none of the participants has sworn to be true to any of the others or in which none of them is subject to the others. Second, a sovereign can wage war against the subject. Third, the subject can wage war against the sovereign.[39]

In terms of the third possibility, Luther held that no subject ought to wage war against any superior to whom obedience is required according to Romans 13. Revenge belongs to God and no one can sit as judge in one's own case. Luther warned against any attempt to overthrow the government. "The mad mob, however, is not so much interested in how things can be improved, but only that things be changed."[40] The sovereign, however, specifically the emperor in this case, may in case of insurrection wage war even against the princes. As far as war among equals is concerned, only defensive war is allowed. Luther never approved aggressive war. "Whoever starts a war is in the wrong. And it is only right and proper that he who first draws his sword is defeated, or even punished, in the end."[41]

As far as the subjects are concerned, they have the duty of using their lives and their property in support of those in authority and of answering a call to report for military service. In particular, the nobility and the feudal lords owe such obedience to the government—in this case, Luther thought of the government as the princes who rule over larger territories. In no case may anyone wage war in order to enrich himself; rather a soldier should carry out his difficult task solely out of a sense of responsibility and duty. But what about the case in which the lord whom a soldier serves is acting unjustly? Luther answered that if we are certain of that, we should fear God more than man and not participate in a war against the advice of one's own conscience. If we are not certain of that, however, we should go ahead and fight without worrying. In such a case, we need not have a bad conscience before God.

3.21 Luther's Writings on the Turks

In his later writings on going to war against the Turks as well as on resisting the emperor, Luther also explored problems of conscience from a pastoral perspective. In response to questions about war against the Turks, Luther gave unlimited affirmation of the justice and necessity of efforts to defend the West against attack but rejected the idea of a crusade which was so common at that time. A crusade against the Turks could no longer be considered a defense of Christendom but would rather be a purely secular matter. In the event of such a crusade, Luther felt that the emperor would no longer have the right to designate himself as "The Patron of the Church and The Defender of the Faith." Christendom itself can fight on its own behalf only with the sword of the Spirit, namely with God's Word and prayer.

3.22 Luther's Understanding of the
Right of Resistance

The Diet of Augsburg of 1530, which decided to implement the Edict of
the Diet of Worms authorizing the use of force against the Protestants if
they did not repent, gave a very high priority to the question of resistance. Even then, however, Luther basically continued to examine the
problem from the perspective of the care of souls and of troubled
consciences. On the basis of the presuppositions that he had already
developed in his earlier treatise *Whether Soldiers, Too, Can Be Saved* (cf.
above, 3.20) Luther now concluded that, even under these circumstances, the Protestant princes had no right to resist the emperor. Only
after being instructed by the lawyers that the emperor acts in roles other
than that of sovereign power over the princes, did Luther abandon his
opposition to a defensive alliance such as the Smalcald League which was
formed in February 1531. All the same, however, although Luther wrote
many opinions on the great variety of political problems of his time, there
is not a single one in which he clearly affirmed this alliance.

In terms of his view of government and of the two kingdoms, there is
therefore no further development of Luther's basic position. We are,
however, able to identify specific applications of the viewpoint that he
had already expressed in 1523. Any historical formulation and evaluation
of his position must also take into account the alternative positions that
were available at the time. In addition, a comparison with later, especially
with present-day, viewpoints on these matters can help us clarify the
validity and the limitation of Luther's teaching about authority.

3.23 Luther's Controversy with Erasmus (1524–25)

The years 1517–20 were the years of Luther's break with Rome. The
years immediately following, 1521–25, marked his break with the more
radical Reformation movements centered around Karlstadt, Müntzer, and
the peasants. In 1524–25, Luther and Erasmus, the spiritual leader of the
Humanists, came to a parting of the ways. The break was particularly
painful for both sides, even though it was not a complete break since
Melanchthon and many other reformers continued to maintain the ideas
of Humanism.

At the time, the break primarily involved Erasmus and Luther. They
were the most significant representatives of the two movements. Their
confrontation, however, had far-reaching effects on their followers on
both sides. In this process, it is important to remember that Humanism,
perhaps even more than the Reformation, was a multisided movement of
various groups that cannot be described with a few simple slogans. There
were geographical differences, for example, between Italian, French,

English, Dutch, and German Humanists. The differences between the periods of humanism were no less important. Early Humanism appeared in the universities and generally did not stand in opposition to scholasticism. The mature period of Humanism, beginning with the sixteenth century, increasingly criticized the scholastic form of instruction as well as a great many abuses in the church. In addition, there were many differences between the smaller groups of Humanists, the "sodalities," each of which had its own character.

As in so many other cases, the scholars are also not entirely in agreement about Erasmus. More recent research has strongly emphasized the theological character of his work. This theological side of his work is particularly manifest in his editions of the Greek New Testament and of the church fathers as well as in his commentaries on biblical writings. At the same time, Erasmus's ironic, often bitterly sharp critique of much of the foolishness and corruption of his time cannot be overlooked.

Where did Erasmus's heart really lie? Was it wherever he had reason to hope that a return to the pure sources of Greek and Roman antiquity would fulfill the promise of providing internal and external renewal for a disintegrating Christendom? Or did it lie where Erasmus, through satire, came to terms with the pope and the curia? Or where Erasmus represented a simple piety oriented to the Sermon on the Mount? Was Erasmus a skeptic? Or was he, when measured by the standards of his time, a true Christian? All too often we have no clear answers to these and similar questions.

3.24 Humanism and the Reformation

Humanism and the Reformation: Neither of these terms was a self-designation; both are names first assigned to the movements that they describe by people of later ages. These two movements had much in common. In addition to their common criticism of scholasticism, both shared a scriptural principle, even though each understood it differently. Without the editorial labors of the Humanists, Luther would not even have had a usable edition of the Greek New Testament available. The renaissance in the study of Augustine at the University of Wittenberg was of great significance for the Reformation. It is impossible to imagine these new insights into Augustine's thought without the new edition of Augustine's works produced by the Humanists. And, last but not least, the humanistic movement produced new knowledge of the ancient languages—Hebrew and Greek as well as classical Latin—on which the Reformation was able to build.

Because of these many factors which they shared, the Humanist movement and the Reformation movement were able to cooperate for a while.

Even Erasmus himself was at first not unsympathetic to Luther, although he very early expressed his disapproval of the sharpness and loud tone of the conflict. As the conflict became more and more intense, the situation became increasingly difficult for Erasmus. Many of his students and admirers had already joined forces with the Reformation. Erasmus was in danger of no longer being accepted by either the papacy or the reformers. Finally, he gave in to the pressure of many of the princes and the Roman curia and decided to oppose Luther. This decision was made easier for Erasmus because there were so many points at which he knew he radically disagreed with Luther.

In fact Luther, in a letter to Spalatin written on October 19, 1516, had already criticized Erasmus. Erasmus had interpreted the works-righteousness rejected by Paul as being merely the observance of ceremonial rules. Luther also asserted that Erasmus's understanding of sin did not match that of Augustine during his anti-Pelagian period.[42] Although Luther also made many complimentary references to Erasmus and expressed appreciation for his work in the following years, the real differences between them could not always be hidden. Luther would hardly have taken the initiative in attacking Erasmus. Luther thought too highly of Erasmus's work for that to be possible. Erasmus, for his part, would also not have taken the initiative in beginning the conflict, unless he had been put under pressure to declare his position.

When Erasmus opened the controversy with Luther, he did not choose to discuss any of the commonly argued topics such as the papacy, the authority of the councils, faith and justification, or the doctrine of the sacraments. Rather, Erasmus focused on the question of the freedom of the will. This clearly demonstrated that Erasmus had identified the center of the controversy more clearly than had Luther's other opponents. It was also true that Erasmus could sincerely defend the medieval doctrine of the freedom of the will against Luther. It seemed to Erasmus that Luther's denial of the freedom of the will in matters related to eternal salvation made it difficult to think of any kind of human responsibility. If people have no personal responsibility, Erasmus thought that there was also little reason to try to educate them.

3.25 Erasmus's Treatise "On the Freedom of the Will"

In his *On the Freedom of the Will: A Diatribe or Discourse,*[43] Erasmus described his understanding of free will as "a power of the human will by which a man can apply himself to the things which lead to eternal salvation, or turn away from them."[44] Erasmus was aware that the authors of the Bible expressed a variety of opinions concerning the freedom of the will—as did the ancient and modern church fathers. Yet Erasmus asserted that Luther's denial of the freedom of the will removed all the barriers against godlessness. Erasmus considered it an open question whether God is the primary cause of all activity, achieving certain effects only through secondary causes, or whether God does everything alone. Erasmus's own position was that God is the first cause of all that happens and that the action of the human will is the second cause of achieving salvation.

Beyond this, Erasmus rejected Luther's enthusiasm for making definite theological assertions. "And, in fact, so far am I from delighting in 'assertions' that I would readily take refuge in the opinion of the Skeptics, wherever this is allowed by the inviolable authority of the Holy Scriptures and by the decrees of the Church, to which I everywhere willingly submit my personal feelings, whether I grasp what it prescribes or not."[45] Obviously, Erasmus was not, after all, concerned about understanding the Reformation theology at which Luther had arrived from his study of Paul. And his statements in the discourse on the freedom of the will were even inferior to the statements that he customarily made in discussing questions such as the freedom of the will, the hiddenness of God, or the authority of the church. In *Hyperaspistes* (Erasmus's response to Luther's attack on his teaching), Erasmus expressed his skepticism in a way that was less open to criticism: "I will not permit any skepticism about the clear meaning of the Holy Scriptures or the clear decisions of the church."[46]

3.26 Luther's Treatise on "The Bondage of the Will" (1525)

In his response to Erasmus, Luther mercilessly came to terms with the leader of the Humanists. In terms of the substance of his reply, Luther deals with all three of the topics discussed by Erasmus, that is, the necessity of making theological assertions, the question of the freedom or bondage of the will in terms of salvation, and finally, the doctrine of God with particular reference to the distinction between the hidden and the revealed God.

As far as the first topic is concerned, Luther held that the inner necessity of faith requires definite assertions. Over against Erasmus, Luther emphasized that the Holy Scriptures give clear and unambiguous answers to the basic questions. Since the seal on the grave of Jesus had been broken and the stone rolled away from the entrance to the grave— that is, after the deepest mystery of the incarnation of Christ and the Trinitarian nature of God have been revealed—the Scriptures are never unclear about the central issues: "Take Christ out of the Scriptures, and what will you find left in them?"[47]

In dealing with the second topic, the bondage of the will, Luther attacked Erasmus with equal vigor and asserted that people are free only in relationship to those things that are under them but not in relationship to those that are above them. Anyone who judges differently denies that God is God.

Previously Augustine and many others had asserted that the human will is unable to take any initiative in reaching out for God's grace. At one point, however, Luther transcended the entire tradition: he derived the bondage of the will not from the fall into sin but rather from the created nature of humankind. The finite human will cannot be free in relationship to the infinite will of God.

Sometimes Luther came very close to the view that people have no freedom to choose even in matters that are subject to them and seemed to say that human actions even at this level are directed by God. Luther also made use of the scholastic distinction between two kinds of necessity: absolute necessity or the necessity of the consequent *(necessitas consequentis)* and conditional necessity or the necessity of the consequence *(necessitas consequentiae)*. This distinction was designed to preserve both the understanding that God is the cause of all things and the understanding that one of the things that God has caused is the human freedom to make decisions. Luther really did not do justice to this scholastic distinction, however. At the same time, Luther also tried to avoid the danger of determinism. One problem that Luther discussed is the famous example of Judas, which has often been made the basis for a discussion of the question of the freedom and bondage of the will. Luther asserted that Judas became the betrayer of Jesus out of necessity; not, however, because he was compelled to act in this way but rather because it was his will to do so.[48]

In discussing the third topic, the doctrine of God as revealed and hidden, Luther further developed ideas that he had previously expressed in a variety of ways. He made a sharp distinction between the hidden God *(Deus absconditus)* and the revealed God *(Deus revelatus)*.

It must be noted here, however, that Luther did not make this distinction for systematic theological reasons but rather as part of his interpretation of the disputed passage, Ezek. 18:23–32, which asserts that God does not have "any pleasure in the death of the wicked." Erasmus had cited this passage to support his assertion of a limited freedom of the human will. Luther's distinction between the hidden God and the revealed God must therefore be understood, first of all, as an interpretation of Scripture. Taken in its context, Erasmus pointed out, this passage from Ezekiel is not referring to the hidden and terrible will of God who orders everything according to his plan but rather is discussing the mercy of God that is offered to us in the preaching of the gospel.

Admittedly Luther carried this distinction very far and many of his statements come quite close to a division in the concept of God: "For it is this that God as he is preached is concerned with, namely, that sin and death should be taken away and we should be saved. . . . But God hidden in his majesty neither deplores nor takes away death, but works life, death, and all in all. For there he has not bound himself by his word, but has kept himself free over all things."[49]

At the same time, Luther himself seemed to be trying to avoid being misunderstood as teaching that there are two Gods by interpreting the distinction between the God proclaimed in the gospel and the hidden God as the distinction between God's Word and God's self. He thus went on to say, "God does many things that he does not disclose to us in his word; he also wills many things which he does not disclose himself as willing in his word."[50]

In conclusion, Luther emphasized that we ought not concern ourselves with God's hidden will but, rather, should hold to the incarnation of God in the crucified Christ *(Deus incarnatus)*.

3.27 The Interpretation of "The Bondage of the Will"

Luther's writing against Erasmus has been subjected to a wide variety of interpretations.

Among these interpretations, the following elements are the most important: The traditional idea that God is hidden and cannot be known, particularly strong in the Neoplatonic and mystical traditions, has been compared with Luther's similar statements. Luther's distinction between the hidden God and the revealed God has been compared to the distinction between the scholastic—and particularly late scholastic—distinction between the absolute power of God and the mediated power of God (see below, 5.6.6). The different understandings of necessity in scholasticism have been compared with both Luther's criticism of determinism and his use of this position. Last but not least, however, Luther's treatise on the bondage of the will must be seen against the background of the understanding of human nature in the Renaissance. It is particularly important to remember that the question of the freedom of the will was discussed intensively in Italy at the end of the fifteenth and beginning of the sixteenth centuries. And the understanding of the doctrine of humanity presented by Erasmus in his diatribe or discourse against Luther is at many points far less developed than the discussions of the Italian Renaissance.

Finally, it is necessary to distinguish between the philosophical problems of determinism and indeterminism on the one hand and the theological issues of human freedom and bondage in relationship to God on the other. These two sets of problems are basically distinguished from one another because the question is asked from two quite different viewpoints. Theology is, in any case, primarily concerned with the exegetical problems and with the conclusions that are to be drawn from certain biblical passages, such as Rom. 5:7 and 9—11.

Luther's treatise on the bondage of the will is a very controversial document, however, not only in terms of its relationship to tradition and to other contemporary statements of the doctrine but also in terms of Luther's expressed intention in writing it. In contrast to many attempted interpretations, we must maintain that the basis of Luther's argument is the certainty of faith. Luther's argument is therefore not based on a specific picture of God nor is it to be explained on the basis of Luther's rejection of Erasmus's basic presupposition that human beings must have a certain kind of freedom. The central point of departure for any interpretation of this whole writing of Luther's must obviously be the climax of its concluding section.

> For if we believe it to be true that God foreknows and predestines all things, that he can neither be mistaken in his foreknowledge nor hindered in his predestination, and that nothing takes place but as he wills it (as reason itself is forced to admit), then on the testimony of reason itself there cannot be any free choice in man or angel or any creature.
>
> Similarly, if we believe that Satan is the ruler of this world, who is forever plotting and fighting against the Kingdom of Christ with all his powers, and that he will not let men go who are his captives unless he is forced to do so by the divine power of the Spirit, then again it is evident that there can be no such thing as free choice. . . .
>
> To sum up: If we believe that Christ has redeemed men by his blood, we are bound to confess that the whole man was lost; otherwise, we should make Christ either superfluous or the redeemer of only the lowest part of man, which would be blasphemy and sacrilege.[51]

3.28 Humanism and the Reformation After 1525

The break in personal relationship that developed between Erasmus and Luther as a result of their writings against each other could not be repaired. The same is not true, however, for the relationship between Humanism and the Reformation in general. The many factors that these two movements had in common not only permitted them to form alliances with one another but also basically to preserve those alliances.

This is true even though many Humanists who had at first allied them-selves with Luther now turned their backs on the Reformation. The educational system under the Reformation, however, continued to culti-vate the study of the ancient languages and biblical interpretation. When we think about this and about other ways in which the great contribu-tions of Humanism found their greatest area of practical effectiveness through their use by the Reformation, we must be particularly grateful to Melanchthon.

Even Luther's sharp opposition to Erasmus was not fully accepted throughout Lutheranism. In the Lutheran Confessions, particularly in the Augsburg Confession and its Apology, the question of the freedom of the will is discussed in a much more careful and moderate way. And Luther himself never insisted that his position become the normative position of the Reformation. Occasional statements of the older Luther even make it clear that he really preferred to develop the doctrine of predestination in closer relationship to the doctrine of the person and work of Christ than many sections of *The Bondage of the Will* seem to do. And the very sharp distinctions that Luther made between the hidden God and the revealed God in this work are only occasionally repeated in later writings. Luther, however, never substantially changed the position that he took in the controversy with Erasmus.

3.29 The Controversy About the Lord's Supper (1524–29)

The controversy about the Lord's Supper began at the time of the Peas-ants' War and while Luther was still involved in the controversy with Erasmus. Basically it lasted from 1524 to 1529, but flared up from time to time after that. There can be no question that this became the most significant controversy among Protestants in the sixteenth century. Luther and Zwingli came to a parting of the ways because of their differences on the doctrine of the Lord's Supper. And, after Luther's death, this doctrine became the subject of a controversy between Calvinist and Lutheran theologians that ended with the Lutherans and the Reformed declaring each other to be heretics. This effectively eliminated the pos-sibility of uniting the two main movements of the Reformation in a common church.

In order to understand why the controversy about the Lord's Supper had such far-reaching significance for the Reformation, we must be aware of two factors. First, we must understand that the medieval doctrine of transubstantiation was always presupposed as the background of the controversy. Second, we must be aware that from the earliest days of the church the Lord's Supper or Eucharist has always been at the heart and center of Christian worship. Luther, in 1520, rejected this doctrine of transubstantiation and taught that the bread in the Lord's Supper remains bread even after it has been consecrated. Throughout his life, however, Luther taught—as energetically as any medieval theologian ever had—that Christ's body and blood are present in the consecrated elements.

The liturgical practices followed by the Lutheran Reformers in celebrating the Lord's Supper, particularly their understanding of the consecration as well as the way in which they handled the consecrated bread and wine, clearly illustrate how closely Lutheran sacramental piety was related to medieval piety. That is especially clear in Luther's discussion of the adoration of the consecrated elements. Luther did not reject such adoration but rather, within certain limits, explicitly affirmed it.[52]

3.30 The Development of Luther's Doctrine of the Lord's Supper

Luther's doctrine of the Lord's Supper underwent a number of transformations. The first form of his doctrine of this sacrament appeared in his literary "sermons" written in 1518 and 1519.[53] Luther referred to many documents from this period as "sermons." In reality these "sermons" are usually more like theological tracts and treatises than sermons which were actually preached to congregations. Luther used these "sermons" to discuss topics such as baptism, the Lord's Supper, and penance.

In his discussion of each sacrament, Luther distinguished between the sign, the meaning, and faith. In his discussion of the sacramental sign, Luther agreed with Augustine that the sign is an external sign. It is important to note that he understood this differently than the later Zwingli understood the same statements of Augustine. Luther's new contribution to the discussion—and the point at which his position clearly differed from the medieval doctrine of the sacraments—consisted in the way in which he made faith an element of his definition of the sacrament. As far as the Lord's Supper is concerned, Luther at this time still supported the view that the elements are changed. It is the idea of the fellowship of the communicants, however, that really stood at the center of his thinking. The Lord's Supper brings us into the fellowship of Christ and of all the saints and thereby communicates salvation to us.

We encounter the next stage of Luther's doctrine of the Lord's Supper in 1520. In *A Treatise on the New Testament, That Is, the Holy Mass*,[54] as well as in *The Babylonian Captivity of the Church*,[55] Luther no longer interpreted the Lord's Supper on the basis of a general definition of a sacrament, but rather on the basis of the words of institution. The central place of the words of institution in the doctrine of the Lord's Supper remained a characteristic of Luther's thinking. And the fact that his later opponents also placed the words of institution in the center of their discussion of the Lord's Supper is certainly due to the precedent set by Luther. Luther's interpretation of the words of institution in 1520 was determined by the basic concepts of promise, faith, and testament.

Luther never denied the real presence of the body and the blood of Christ in the elements. In 1523, he made this real presence a central focus of his doctrine, beginning with his treatise, *The Adoration of the Sacrament*. In this treatise, Luther endorsed the adoration of the sacrament within limits. He did reject a mere external adoration and also rejected the custom of establishing sacramental shrines in which the elements were kept solely for the purpose of being adored. He also rejected the custom of processing through the streets with the sacrament so that those in the street could adore it. Luther explicitly defended the spiritual adoration of the sacrament, however, as long as such adoration was not bound to external factors and primarily focused on the words of institution. In formulating his position on these matters, Luther also defined his doctrine of the Lord's Supper in relationship to the doctrine of the Hussites in Bohemia and to the doctrine of the Humanist scholar Honius.

The Hussites had taken the view that Christ is only spiritually present in the sacrament, but they understood this in terms of "another existence" or "another form of being." In spite of some reservations, Luther felt that the Hussites' doctrine of the Lord's Supper was an acceptable teaching in the church. Luther, however, rejected the viewpoint of Honius who interpreted the "this is" of the words of institution as meaning "this signifies." Luther also felt that the doctrine of the Lord's Supper taught by Karlstadt, his colleague on the theological faculty of the University of Wittenberg, was also subject to suspicion. As a result of these developments in Luther's doctrine of the Lord's Supper, the controversy on the Lord's Supper began among the Protestant Reformers themselves.

Luther always felt that his later controversy with Zwingli was only a variation of his original conflict with Karlstadt. Luther's identification of Zwingli's doctrine of the Lord's Supper with that of Karlstadt, however, really does not do justice to the teaching of Zwingli, who was the leader of the Reformation in Zurich.

3.31 Karlstadt's Doctrine of the Lord's Supper

As far as Karlstadt was concerned, his basically charismatic and spiritualized understanding of Christianity had already become apparent in the role in which he played during the Wittenberg riots of 1521–22. This charismatic emphasis was also significant for his doctrine of the Lord's

Supper. In 1524 Karlstadt, in a number of writings, expressed the view
that the external celebration of the Lord's Supper does not have power to
create faith. The celebration of the Lord's Supper is nothing more than a
confession and witness of the congregation as well as a proclamation of
the death of Christ. As Karlstadt understood the words of institution, it is
totally impossible that the body and blood of Christ can really be present
in the elements. Karlstadt felt that there was no way of asserting such a
presence on the basis of the simple meaning of the words of institution.
On the contrary, the bread and wine are to be used only "in memory of
Christ." The decisive element in the celebration of the Lord's Supper,
therefore, is that which comes from the heart of the recipient. For this
reason, we must be certain of salvation before receiving the Lord's
Supper. This spiritual eating of the body of Christ is necessary but the
fleshly eating is useless (cf. John 6:63).

3.32 Luther's Criticism of Karlstadt

Luther rejected Karlstadt's doctrine of the Lord's Supper not only because
Karlstadt disputed the real presence, but even more because Karlstadt
denied that the Lord's Supper is a means of grace. Luther described this as
a new form of works-righteousness. In *Against the Heavenly Prophets*
(1525), Luther not only defended the doctrine of the real presence but
also the doctrine that the life of the Christian is always and under all
circumstances based on the grace of God.[56] He asserted the distinction
between the fact that we have already received forgiveness for all our sins
and the fact that we receive forgiveness each time we receive the sacrament. Forgiveness has been given to us once and for all, but the distribution of this forgiveness is repeated over and over again. In this context,
the real presence of Christ's body and blood became even more significant for Luther. The discussion of the real presence was now a discussion
about the presence of the crucified and ascended Lord.

3.33 Zwingli's Doctrine of the Lord's Supper

Whereas Luther, in the course of his controversy with Karlstadt, came to
place an increasing emphasis on the real presence, Zwingli's personal
development led him in exactly the opposite direction. As a young
theologian, he had not yet—as his *Schlussreden,* published in the spring
of 1523, makes clear—criticized the doctrine of the real presence. He
had, however, already emphasized the spiritual character of the Lord's
Supper. Admittedly, he even adopted Luther's view that the testament of
Christ stands at the center of the Lord's Supper. In addition to this,
however, he also emphasized the idea that the Lord's Supper is a sign of
the covenant of God and the people.

As a result of the influence of the Dutch Humanist Honius on his doctrine of the Lord's Supper, Zwingli interpreted the phrase "this is" in the words of institution as meaning "this signifies." In addition, although careful to distinguish his position from that of Karlstadt, Zwingli basically adopted Karlstadt's emphasis on the spiritual character of the Lord's Supper. Both Zwingli and Karlstadt regarded John 6—rather than the words of institution in the Synoptic Gospels in 1 Corinthians 11—as the most important text in the development of the doctrine of the Lord's Supper. As a result, Zwingli understood the Lord's Supper as the church's act of remembering Jesus and confessing its faith in him. Zwingli, however, also understood this remembering not merely as a memory of the past, but as an act of commemoration, "through which those who firmly believe that they are reconciled to the Father through Christ's death and blood proclaim his life giving death."[57]

Zwingli touched off the controversy over the Lord's Supper, in the spring of 1525, by publishing a statement that challenged the viewpoint of Luther.[58] The fact that Zwingli himself described his doctrine as related to that of Karlstadt made the conflict particularly difficult. Luther saw this as evidence that Zwingli was probably a spiritualist and therefore also an enthusiast.

The writings related to this controversy appeared primarily from 1525 to 1529.[59] In addition to Luther and Zwingli, numerous other theologians participated on both sides of the issue and represented a wide variety of viewpoints. The most prominent among them were Martin Bucer in Strassburg and Johannes Oecolampadius in Basel. During the five years during which this controversy on the Lord's Supper was at its height, it seemed to overshadow any other controversy, even that between the Reformation movement as a whole and the supporters of the papacy.

3.34 Additional Points at Issue in the Controversy About the Lord's Supper

This controversy concerned itself not only with the understanding of the Lord's Supper itself, but also with a variety of other related theological questions, particularly with questions related to the person and work of Christ. General questions related to the understanding of Scripture and to faith were also at issue in this controversy, however. The intensity and extent of this conflict were greater than in almost any later controversies among theologians of the Reformation.

The study of this controversy is particularly important for our understanding of many questions related to Luther's theology. It is, however, possible to define clearly the uniqueness of Luther's position and arguments only in the context of the controversy itself, that is, with reference to the viewpoints of his opponents. As far as Luther's theology is concerned, we can draw conclusions from his contributions to the controversy on the Lord's Supper.

The So-called Scriptural Principle. In his early lectures, Luther interpreted the Scripture from the viewpoint of judgment and gospel and then later from the viewpoint of law and gospel. In the controversy with Rome, he asserted the authority of Christ against the authority of the church. On the basis of the Scripture, he gave new expression to central elements of faith and teaching. In the controversy on the Lord's Supper, however, Luther emphasized the literal meaning of the words of institution. It should be clear, however, that this does not mean that Luther practiced some kind of biblicism. He did, however, begin to think about the relationship between the letter and the spirit in a different way than he had previously, just as Zwingli developed an approach to the interpretation of Scripture distinctively different from that of Luther.

Christology: The Person and Work of Christ. Luther had certainly always emphasized that God is to be found only in the earthly Christ and that the earthly Christ is to be identified with the ascended Lord. The paradox of the covering and the revealing of the deity of Christ is, however, much more sharply defined by Luther in opposition to Zwingli.

The Ubiquity of Christ. In the course of the controversy with Zwingli, Luther developed this special element in his Christology. In order to describe the possibility of the real presence of the body and the blood of Christ in the elements, Luther made use of certain ideas of late medieval theology and developed them further. One of these is the teaching that, since the time of Christ's ascension into heaven, the human nature of Christ is omnipresent. Luther asserts this as a necessary consequence of the unity of the divine nature with the human nature in the person of Christ. Luther thereby rejected the traditional idea that Christ's sitting at the right hand of the Father means that he is limited to a particular place in heaven. Contrary to this idea, Luther thought that Christ, like God, cannot be found in any place and yet is active everywhere. He is present for our salvation, however, only as the earthly, crucified Christ.

At this point, a number of questions need to be asked: How are we to reconcile Luther's use of the scholastic doctrine of ubiquity and his further development of this doctrine with Luther's critical attitude toward nonbiblical elements in the tradition of the church? What is the significance of Luther's new thinking about the ascended Christ? However we respond to such questions, we must always remember that Luther's teaching on the ubiquity of Christ was not developed on the basis of physics or chemistry but rather on theological presuppositions.

The Physical Implications of Receiving the Lord's Supper. Karlstadt and Zwingli both understood the effects of receiving the Lord's Supper in purely spiritual terms. Luther, in the course of the controversy with Zwingli, occasionally also referred to physical effects in the recipient. Sometimes he went so far in his assertions that he made use of ancient concepts from pre-Christian idol worship. What is the significance of these thoughts? Do they contradict Luther's Reformation emphasis on faith?

Objectivity of the Gift of Salvation. Luther's early lectures often leave the impression that he is interpreting the Scripture in an almost existential manner. Medieval methods of interpretation, particularly the use of the tropological method of interpretation (which encouraged figurative and moral interpretation as a way of relating the message of Scripture to contemporary life), provided a point of contact for this approach to Scripture. In the controversy about the Lord's Supper, however, Luther very clearly maintained the objectivity of the gift of salvation.

This emphasis on the objectivity of the gift of salvation raises some very important questions about Luther's own theology. It also raises a number of very significant methodological issues about our interpretation of Luther's theology. We usually assume that it is possible to define Luther's theology at any point on the basis of his controversial writings. Luther's emphasis on the objectivity of the gift of salvation during this controversy demonstrates, however, that Luther held certain presuppositions that he had not expressed in his earlier writings. Since they were not the subject of controversy, it was not necessary for him to state them explicitly. This raises the question as to whether there were other significant presuppositions of his theology that he never expressed in writing because they were never the subject of controversy. What were they? How important were they for his thinking? These questions must be considered by anyone who attempts to describe Luther's theology.

3.35 The Marburg Colloquy (1529)

As far as the controversy on the Lord's Supper was concerned, it was in many respects concluded by the colloquy held at Marburg from October 1 to 4, 1529.[60] This colloquy once again demonstrates the close interrelationship between theology and politics in the sixteenth century. The colloquy was held at the initiative of Landgrave Philip of Hesse. Philip had been thinking about and planning such a colloquy for some years but Luther had previously rejected his proposals. After the Diet of Speyer in 1529, however, the political situation of the Protestants became increasingly difficult. It was no longer possible to deny the necessity of a defensive alliance. As a result, efforts to achieve unity among the Protestants were pursued with more energy.

The Wittenberg theologians and politicians were convinced that theological agreement was the necessary presupposition for entering an alliance with the Swiss as well as with the Protestants in southern Germany. Earlier attempts to overcome the theological controversy about the Lord's Supper had been undertaken here and there soon after it began, but had not achieved their goal. And the attempts at reconciliation made by Strassburg in 1526 also were not successful.

One can therefore say that the Marburg Colloquy would never have taken place if the participants had not been under pressure to work together politically. It would, however, also be false to conclude that the positions taken by various participants in the theological controversy were merely determined by, or manifestations of, political forces and alliances. The end result of the Marburg Colloquy demonstrated that this was not the case. In spite of all the political reasons for reaching unity, the Marburg Colloquy only succeeded in bringing the parties considerably closer together, without achieving the necessary basis for unity.

As a result, Philip's comprehensive plans for an alliance were not realized. The Smalcald League, which was formed in 1531, only included those estates that subscribed to the Augsburg Confession. This close relationship between theological confession and political alliance was relaxed only later. After the Smalcald War, Moritz of Saxony allied himself with the king of France in order to save German Protestantism and the liberty of the princes. The resulting alliance defeated Charles V decisively. A hundred years later, during the Thirty Years' War, the principle that an alliance could be formed only on the basis of a common confession was completely abandoned. But even at this later time, it would still be one-sided to ignore the fact that questions of theological confession continued to play a role in the forming of political alliances.

3.36 Luther's Later Controversies

Alongside Luther's particularly important controversies with the enthusiasts, with Erasmus, or with Zwingli were a number of other controversies that were as important for their long-range effect on the history of the Reformation as they were for Luther and his opponents.

Basically, Luther's whole life was marked by controversies of various kinds. After 1517 Luther no longer experienced a time that could really be characterized as a time of rest. Among these controversies, those among the Reformers themselves became increasingly important—even after the temporary conclusion of the controversy about the Lord's Supper. This is true even though Luther himself felt that his conflict with Rome was by far the most significant controversy in which he was engaged. Although they cannot be discussed in detail, brief reference needs to be made to some of these later controversies.

The antinomian controversies began to develop as early as 1527 and then reappeared in a much sharper form in 1537. These controversies came about as a result of the way in which Luther's student, and later co-worker, Johann Agricola, taught about the preaching of the law. Since this controversy dealt with the doctrine of the distinction between law and gospel, it dealt with the heart and center of Reformation theology. This is one of the reasons why it was such a vehement controversy. And once again, a fuller study of this controversy would demonstrate that a variety of previously existing movements came together in the Reformation.

When the Anabaptists established their revolutionary government in Münster in 1534–35, the Reformation was once again held responsible for all their excesses. These accusations were not even silenced by the fact that Protestant as well as Roman Catholic estates participated in the overthrow of the Anabaptist regime. As a result of the events in Münster, Luther and the other Reformers increasingly solidified their opposition to the Anabaptists.

During 1540 and 1541, Roman Catholics and Protestants engaged in a series of colloquies on religion. These meetings were held in Worms and Regensburg. They were accompanied by a large number of opinions, memoranda, position papers, and critiques. At times it seemed that agreement had been achieved. Luther, however, was absolutely skeptical about these attempts to arrive at a common position. His attitude, combined with the uncompromising position of the Roman curia, contributed to the failure of these attempts which in and of themselves were very close to achieving success. Neither side had the basic minimum of trust in the honorable intentions of the other party that is absolutely necessary for such conversations to succeed. It was the lack of this kind of trust—rather than the impossibility of arriving at statements that could be accepted by both parties—that finally caused the failure of these colloquies on religion. Even when the participants succeeded in arriving at joint formulations—as they were able to do in very important points of controversy—each side mistrusted the other and assumed that the other side would interpret such formulations to its own advantage and to the disadvantage of the other.

3.37 The Bigamy of Philip of Hesse

Among the various controversies, a particular problem was presented by the bigamy of Landgrave Philip of Hesse in March 1540. This bigamy marked the beginning of the collapse of the Smalcald League.

In spite of personal reservations, several Reformers, including Luther, had agreed to the plan for such a bigamy. Philip of Hesse (1504–67) had early in life entered into a marriage with Christine of Saxony. As was common in such marriages among the nobility, there was no satisfying personal relationship. Under the pressure of his strong need for sexual satisfaction, Philip concluded that he could no longer remain faithful to his marriage vows. With the consent of his wife he entered into a second marriage with a lady of the court, Margarete von der Saale, in March 1540. Before taking this second wife he had consulted, in December 1539, with Luther and Melanchthon and received their consent to this action.

In spite of all attempts to keep the matter secret, this bigamy became known. When this happened, Luther advised Philip to deny everything. Nothing was of any use, however. The scandal grew and grew. And since bigamy was punishable by death, Philip was personally in danger. The emperor, however, used the opportunity to achieve his political goals. He put pressure on Philip to enter into a separate agreement with him in which Philip abandoned his policy of opposition to the emperor. In exchange the emperor promised that he would not bring charges against Philip because of his bigamy—unless the emperor were engaged in war against all Protestants. Philip agreed to this on June 13, 1541.

Philip was the political leader of the Protestants. As a result of his bigamy and the resulting agreement with the emperor, he was politically paralyzed and unable to act. The Smalcald League became increasingly less powerful and the advance of the Reformation into new territories was halted. Because he had succeeded in neutralizing Philip, Charles V was also able to defeat the Protestant estates a few years later in the Smalcald War. After winning this victory, the emperor was able to impose the Augsburg Interim (1548) on the Protestants and thereby severely damage the position of the Reformation territories and churches.[61]

Even though Philip of Hesse must bear the major share of guilt for the far-reaching consequences of his bigamy, Luther himself carried a considerable share of responsibility because of the advice that he, as his confessor, gave to Philip. This confessional advice deserves to be investigated and evaluated objectively. For example, it should be understood in the context of contemporary attitudes about bigamy. In addition, we must also take into account the fact that Philip of Hesse did not give Luther correct information on some important matters. As a result, Luther gave his confessional counsel on the basis of presuppositions that were partially false. It is also interesting to note that Luther, years earlier (1520), had expressed the opinion that in cases of doubt bigamy is preferable to divorce.[62] In a similar situation—during the long and difficult discussions as to whether the marriage of Henry VIII to his first wife, Catherine of Aragon, could be dissolved—papal officials in Rome itself for a time considered the possibility of bigamy. This makes it clear that in spite of the fact that bigamy was forbidden, bigamy at that time seemed to be a possible resolution of a difficult situation. Finally it must be noted that Luther did not consider this matter as a lawyer or as a politician but rather from the viewpoint of a pastor. In spite of all this, however, this particular confessional counsel had disastrous results.

While discussing Luther's participation in these developments that were of such extraordinary significance for the Reformation, brief reference should be made to Luther's widespread activity as an advisor and as a source of expert opinion in various controversies. For example, Luther was intensely involved in controversies such as the recapture of Württemberg for Duke Ulrich in 1534, the controversy [between Elector John Frederick and his cousin Moritz] over the property of the monastery in Wurzen in 1542, and the military campaigns against Braunschweig from 1542 to 1545. And it is not accidental that Luther at the very end of his life was intensely involved in efforts to resolve the disagreements between the counts of Mansfeld.

Throughout his whole life, Luther carried the burden of being involved in a great variety of such problems. It is important to note that Luther, in his attempts to resolve such problems, always functioned as a theologian. Neither his theology nor his practical application of theology to life recognized certain areas as being subject to their own laws. At the same time, however, he did not try to resolve questions in a biblicistic way, that is, he did not use an individual biblical passage as a pattern for his suggested resolution of a problem.

3.38 Luther's Role in the Development of the State Church

Luther's involvement in the development of the new structure of the Protestant church, particularly in terms of the new role assumed by the secular government, is particularly important. We will, therefore, pay special attention to this area of Luther's activity. It will once again be necessary to take a wide variety of factors into consideration in order to arrive at an accurate understanding of Luther's part in this whole development. It is certain that Luther played a decisive role in the development of the state church. Scholars are still not agreed, however, as to what Luther was really trying to accomplish.

The Protestant territorial churches were established with the help and assistance of the territorial governments. In order to understand how this resulted in the establishment of state churches, we need to remember that the basic elements of this process were already present at the end of the Middle Ages. During the sixteenth century, not only Protestant but also Roman Catholic princes assumed almost equal significance in the life of the churches in their territories. The development of Protestant state churches therefore must be seen as part of the much broader processes that led to the development of independent territorial states. For a time, this development reached its high point in the ascription of total and absolute power to the state. Our awareness of this larger historical trend, however, obviously ought not reduce the significance of the roles played by individual persons and forces in the process.

Another factor that must be taken into consideration in our analysis of this matter deals with the question about the basic relationship between the church defined in spiritual terms as the body of Christ and the church defined as an external institution, or in other words, the relationship between spirit and law.

In Roman Catholic areas, the existing relationship was usually accepted uncritically. Protestants, however, always tended to contrast the spirit with the law, or the visible church with the invisible church, and to play them off against each other. Thus Rudolf Sohm (1841–1917) represented the view that the existence of church or canon law is always a contradiction of the nature of the church.[63] Sohm defined the church only as the invisible church or as the body of Christ. More recent students of Protestant church law have abandoned this assertion of a radical opposition between the spirit and law in favor of a concept that, with the aid of a spiritual church law, attempts to combine the visible and the invisible. Whatever position one takes on this matter will affect one's evaluation of the increasingly powerful role played by the princes in the government of the sixteenth-century churches.

A third factor, closely related to the second, is that varying doctrines of the church will also evaluate these developments in the sixteenth century in quite different ways. Recent research has clearly demonstrated that earlier students of this problem have distinguished the visible church from the invisible church in ways that did not do justice to the thinking of Luther and the Reformation. Today, we usually say not that the church is invisible, but that the real nature of the church is hidden. As a result, it can still be known through certain "signs" such as the sacraments or the proclamation of the gospel. Although Luther constantly emphasized the spiritual character of the church, he always described the church as existing as a tangible and identifiable entity within the created world. In this respect, Luther's doctrine of the church is analogous to his understanding of the incarnation.

A fourth factor that is of basic significance for our understanding of the princes' involvement in the government of the church is the then commonly accepted understanding of the role of government and the extent of its authority. It was taken for granted in theory as well as in practice during the Middle Ages that the spiritual and secular powers represented one another in an emergency and, when necessary, helped one another out by either one assuming the duties of the other. The bishops and the hierarchy remained loyal to the papacy, however, and resisted the introduction of the Reformation. As a result, no one was left who could assume the responsibility of introducing changes in the life of the church except the secular government. It was, at the time, absolutely unthinkable that the congregations themselves might have taken the initiative. Not only were they not prepared to do so but the common view of the close relationship between the secular and the spiritual authorities provided absolutely no basis for such an initiative. Even Müntzer at first attempted to gain the support of the government for his utopian reform plans. Only after the government refused to assist him did he begin to ascribe power to the people. Obviously, however, even though no one was able to do anything without involving the government, the nature and function of the government were still understood in different ways. To this extent, the role to be played in the Reformation by the government and the princes was described in different ways. It is in this connection that Luther's specific understanding of the nature of government is significant for our discussion.

Even in his early years before the Reformation began, for example in his lectures on Romans in 1516, Luther expressed his opinion that the secular authorities apparently administered their affairs in a better and more successful way than the ecclesiastical authorities did. For this reason, Luther suggested that "perhaps it would be safer if the temporal affairs also of the clergy were placed under the secular power."[64] In his treatise *To the Christian Nobility of the German Nation Concerning the Reform of the Christian Estate*, written in 1520, he appealed to the secular authorities to carry out a series of very necessary reforms in the life of the church as well as in the life of society.[65] The church itself had failed to carry out even the most absolutely necessary reforms. On the basis of the universal priesthood of the baptized, however, the government officials could fill the gap. Admittedly, Luther at the same time warns them against false self-confidence. And he himself considered the specific proposals that he made in his treatise addressed to the nobility only as examples of corrective measures that might be undertaken rather than as a prescriptive program for reform.

In the years following the Diet of Worms, the role of the government became even more important for Luther. As described above (see above,

3.15–17), this was obviously true during the Wittenberg riots. Luther became even more appreciative of the function of government as he came to terms with the events of the Peasants' War. This revolt of the peasants, however, also showed Luther what kind of ideas could be asserted in the name of the gospel and therefore also of the Reformation. In the light of all this, it seemed to Luther more and more important to undertake the task of providing a structure for the Protestant church. The Reformers began to undertake this task with a careful visitation of the congregations in Saxony. They were particularly concerned with providing for the strengthening of the life of the congregations, examining the teaching and life of the pastors, and providing remedies for abuses. Since the bishops remained loyal to the papacy, only the secular government had the authority to order such a visitation.

In 1526 the Diet of Speyer concluded that every estate of the empire should respond to the Edict of Worms in such a way that each could answer for their actions to both God and the emperor. In and of itself, this decree merely placed the implementation of the Edict of Worms in the discretion of the individual estates of the empire. In the Protestant territories, however, this decree was very quickly interpreted to mean that each estate was free to decide whether to make specific reforms or even to introduce the whole Reformation (see above, 3.16). Practically, this interpretation anticipated the regulation of these matters that would be agreed to in the religious Peace of Augsburg (1555).

In 1525 Luther had already requested the elector to authorize a visitation of the congregations. Others had made the same request even earlier. Now, after the Diet of Speyer, the Saxon elector John the Constant implemented these proposals. Such a visitation of the churches and schools was carried out in Electoral Saxony from 1527 to 1530. As a result of this visitation, the Reformation movement took on the form of a Protestant state church.

This process had unusually far-reaching results. For example, in spite of many variations it remained the basic external form of the German Protestant churches until 1918.

Until 1918, German Protestantism was characterized by very close cooperation between government and the church. This arrangement assigned responsibility for the outward welfare of the church to the state.

In actual practice, however, the state also exercised far-reaching influence on the church's teaching. The Augsburg Confession, the basic confessional writing of Lutheranism, was signed not by Protestant theologians but by the political estates of the empire. This fact is a symbolic expression of the reality that the Reformation in Germany resulted in

Protestant state churches under the supervision of the secular authorities.

The Diet of Augsburg itself was organized in such a way that the theologians had neither voice nor vote in the discussions. They functioned only as advisors to their princes. As a result, the entire process of forming the confessional statements of the Reformation in Germany was finally determined by representatives of the various governments, who of course represented specific theological viewpoints. Scholars have long disagreed about the role that Luther intended the government to play in the visitation of the churches and schools in Electoral Saxony. Obviously we cannot expect Luther—or anyone else then involved—to be aware of the far-reaching consequences of the decisions that they made in 1525 and 1526. In that historical situation, it seemed absolutely necessary to reform the life of the church without further delay. We ought not burden those who made these decisions with responsibility for all of the effects that these decisions had in later history. To understand these decisions properly, we must ask what they meant in the context of the situation in which they were actually made and how those making these decisions understood that situation. At the same time, however, these decisions were also made on the basis of definite presuppositions about the nature and function of the church and of government. Any evaluation of such decisions must also consider the validity of these presuppositions.

Two very important documents were produced in 1527 that give us insight into the thinking of Elector John of Saxony as well as of Luther. The elector's instruction to the visitors (*Instruction und befelch dorauf die visitatores abgefertiget sein*), which defined their authority and provided guidelines for their activity, was issued on June 16, 1527. After the visitation had already begun, Melanchthon, in the summer of 1527, composed another set of guidelines for the visitors. Luther revised this text at several points and it was then published in 1528 with a preface by Luther as *Instructions for the Visitors of Parish Pastors in Electoral Saxony.*[66]

There are clear and obvious differences between the two texts. Whereas Luther had turned to the government for help because no one else was in a position to carry out the Reformation, the elector acted solely on the basis of his authority as the head of the government. He understood that the visitors received their "power and authority" from him. The elector expected them to act in the same way that he expected any of his official representatives to act. There was no clear distinction between spiritual and secular authority in the elector's instructions. On

the contrary, we find here the roots that would later result in the development of the government of the church by territorial princes.[67]

Luther wrote his preface to the instructions after the elector's instructions had been issued. In obvious disagreement with the elector's position, Luther described the visitation of the churches as the responsibility
of the bishops.

It is very clear that Luther wished to preserve an episcopal form of
church government. The gospel having been once again restored to its
place of honor, he wrote,

> we would like to have seen the true episcopal office and practice of visita-
> tion re-established because of the pressing need. However, since none of us
> felt a call or definite command to do this, and St. Peter has not countenanced
> the creation of anything in the church unless we have the conviction that it
> is willed of God, no one has dared to undertake it. Preferring to follow what
> is certain and to be guided by love's office (which is a common obligation of
> Christians), we have respectfully appealed to the illustrious and noble
> prince and lord, John, Duke of Saxony, First Marshall and Elector of the
> Roman Empire, Landgrave of Thuringia, Margrave of Meissen, our most
> gracious lord and prince, constituted of God as our certain temporal sov-
> ereign, that out of Christian love (since he is not obligated to do so as a
> temporal sovereign) and by God's will for the benefit of the gospel and the
> welfare of the wretched Christians in his territory, His Electoral grace might
> call and ordain to this office several competent persons.[68]

This passage can be read to mean only that the elector should act solely
in his role as a Christian brother and not because he is the elector. Luther
clearly says that although the elector "is not obligated to teach and to
rule in spiritual affairs, he is obligated as temporal sovereign to so order
things that strife, rioting, and rebellion do not arise among his subjects;
even as the Emperor Constantine summoned the bishops to Nicaea since
he did not want to tolerate the dissension which Arius had stirred up
among the Christians in the empire, and constrained them to preserve
unity in teaching and faith."[69]

How are these differences in emphasis between the elector's instruction and Luther's preface to be evaluated? Was Luther really protesting
against the basic tone of the instructions? Or was he possibly silently
correcting them without being fully aware of their implication? Or is
there really no difference worth talking about between the two, especially since Luther, in the following years, cooperated with the government in fulfilling the many tasks that came about as a result of the
Reformation? Even if we were to conclude that the difference between
the instruction and the preface is very small, there is simply no doubt
about the fact that Luther wished to preserve an episcopal form of church

government. Such a form of government, however, was not possible at that time. To this extent, the development leading to the government of the church by the princes could not have been avoided. The provisional arrangement, which Luther helped to establish, however, has obviously proved to have an extraordinarily long life.

In addition to the factors already considered, it is possible that Luther's position as a university professor was also an important factor in the development of the state church in Lutheran territories. H. W. Krum-wiede[70] has drawn attention to the independence of the university from the elector, an independence that, of course, was more and more lost as time went on. His position at the university, however, gave Luther a certain amount of independence even in his relationship to the elector. Luther exercised this independence as a member of the faculty, even though he, as a citizen, was completely dependent on the protection of the elector since the Diet of Worms had declared him an outlaw and the Roman Church had excommunicated him. In spite of this, however, the most important motivating factors in Luther's position are to be found in his theology.

3.39 The Sharp Polemical Tone of the Controversies

As many controversies as Luther was involved in and as long as they lasted we should not overlook the fact that these were very strenuous battles. Crude polemics were taken for granted on all sides of the issue in the sixteenth century and were never unique to Luther. Even the controversies in the late Middle Ages were crude in ways that are hard to match. Having said this, it must also be said that Luther surpassed most of his contemporaries in the coarseness and roughness of his language. This same coarseness and roughness also characterized Luther's language as he sat around his dining-room table, as his published table talk indicates. This characteristic is, however, particularly prominent in his writings. The longer Luther was engaged in controversy, the stronger his polemical attitude and his ridiculing of his current opponent seemed to be. Accordingly we only occasionally find crude comments in Luther's early lectures. This is the case even though Luther had already expressed sharp and substantial disagreement with those who falsified the faith. For example, in his lectures on Romans, Luther interjected a comment, in the middle of the Latin text, about those theologians who depict humans as capable by nature of loving God fully. He called them "Sautheologen," literally, "pig-theologians."[71]

The polemical tone became much sharper, however, after the controversy on indulgences began. This was true of all participants, but especially of Luther. The occasional attempts at reconciliation, such as that by

Karl von Miltitz, may be described as pauses in which the opponents took time out to catch their breath. Then, however, the fact that Luther was excommunicated and declared an outlaw had the effect of a breaking of the dam insofar as sharpness of the controversy was concerned. After 1520 Luther exercised no restraint and no moderation in his attacks on the papacy. Soon, however, new controversies arose among the Reformers themselves. These controversies were conducted with the same hardness as the controversy with Rome. Whether he was dealing with Karlstadt, Müntzer, or Zwingli, Luther's polemics were always sharp although he was quite capable of choosing his nuances carefully. His opponents answered in kind—as one can see from the title of Müntzer's last writing against Luther, *Hochverursachte Schutzrede und Antwort wider das geistlose, sanftlebende Fleisch zu Wittenberg, welches mit verkehrter Weise durch den Diebstahl der Hl. Schrift die erbärmliche Christenheit also ganz jämmerlich besudelt hat*—freely translated as "Well-Provoked Defense Against and Answer to the Mindless, Soft-Living Piece of Meat from Wittenberg, Who Has So Terribly Befouled and Soiled Christendom, Although It Is So Deserving of Pity, by Stealing the Holy Scriptures."

Of course this polemical language was often raw and sometimes obscene. It was the custom on both sides to address opponents with the least-flattering names of animals. In this process, participants in the controversy often betrayed remarkable zoological knowledge. Such customs, however, were comparatively harmless. It was far worse that both sides took it for granted that they each would describe the other as being possessed by the devil. We would miss the point of this were we to understand such expressions as only a matter of literary form. On the contrary, just as Luther saw the antichrist as being at work in the papacy because that which had been added to the gospel had adulterated its purity, so too, people actually thought that they were fighting not only against human opponents but also against the devil. They thought the devil was using their opponents only in order to bring confusion into the pure doctrine and divine order of the church and society. Many New Testament passages could be cited in support of this concept of the devil. As a result, these views were only strengthened by the Reformation's scriptural principle. The widespread apocalyptic expectation of those times also reinforced these views. That seemed to justify fully the indiscriminate transference of traditional language and imagery from the apocalyptic world view onto whomever happened to be the opponent at the time.

Basically none of the various movements involved in these controversies was better or worse than the others at this point. The only differences that can be observed are gradual differences in the level of their attacks on one another. Luther's coarseness, however, was the object of heavy criticism, particularly by Roman Catholics, in the first decades of the twentieth century. In response to such complaints, Protestant scholars tried to defend Luther and to justify it. In recent years, however, discussions of this matter have become much calmer. It is possible, although it is not very likely, that this is the result of a growing understanding of the primitive and rough style of expression that was common in the sixteenth century. It is much more likely that the change is the result of the marked decline in Luther research and in the knowledge of Luther in broader circles. It may also be, however, that the increasing vehemence of expression in our own contemporary public controversies has changed our feeling about the particularly sharp tone of the sixteenth century. However that may be, the sharp tone of polemical argument in the sixteenth century was simply a part of the reality of those controversies. And there is a broad field of investigation open to students who wish to investigate the individual styles of the various participants.

3.40 Luther's Polemic in His Book "Against Hanswurst" (1541)

Some references from Luther's book *Against Hanswurst*[72] will provide a firsthand impression of Luther's polemical style. This treatise is addressed to, or more accurately, directed against Duke Henry of Braunschweig-Wolfenbüttel. In the spring of 1538, open enmity broke out between the duke and the two leading Protestant princes, that is, Elector John Frederick of Saxony and Duke Philip of Hesse. A very energetic literary controversy followed. Luther at first remained silent. At the end of 1540, however, a new writing commissioned by Henry described the Protestants as obstinate, apostate, and blasphemous heretics. Over and above this, the false assertion was made that Luther had referred to his prince as "Hanswurst"—that is, as a buffoon. "We [that is, Duke Henry] have not given any reason to that Saxon [that is, Elector John Frederick], (whom Martin Luther calls his dear pious Hanswurst) to write against us."[73]

In response, Luther wrote his book *Against Hanswurst*. The first sentences read:

> Von Braunschweig of Wolfenbüttel has now published another libel in which he has set out to rub his scabby, scurvy head against the honor of my gracious lord, the elector of Saxony. He has also twice attacked and baited me: first, when he writes that I have called my gracious lord Hanswurst, and then when he attacks the whole essence of the faith, of which I must confess I am one of the foremost exponents at the present time. He curses, blasphemes, shrieks, struggles, bellows, and spits, so that, if people really heard him utter these words, they would gather with chains and bars, just as if (like the man in the gospels [Mark 5:1–10]) he were possessed by a legion

of devils and had to be seized and bound. And though I do not think that this vile fellow is worth a syllable's reply, I will nevertheless—since he is not alone—give our people something to talk about.[74]

In addition, Luther asserted that it did not only his heart but also his kneecaps and ankles good when books like the book written against the elector were written against him. "For it makes me tingle with pleasure from head to toe when I see that through me, poor wretched man that I am, God the Lord maddens and exasperates both the hellish and worldly princes, so that in their spite they would burst and tear themselves to pieces—while I sit under the shade of faith and the Lord's Prayer, laughing at the devils and their crew as they blubber and struggle in their great fury."[75]

Luther experienced such controversies as refreshing him and making him strong and happy. He had earlier said much the same thing in a considerably milder form. For example, in Worms in 1521 he said that he was happy to be the occasion of so great a controversy, because Christ himself had said that he had not come to bring peace but rather a sword.[76]

Luther's ascription of the title of "Hanswurst" to Duke Henry was still a comparatively mild form of polemic. The duke in addition had also to endure being accused of having told lies. Indeed Luther asserted he was a "shameless liar."[77] Luther also repeatedly referred to "the devil and his Hanswurst" in the same breath.[78] To put it in particularly drastic terms: "And that vulgar boor, blockhead, and lout from Wolfenbüttel, that ass to cap all asses, screams his heehaws, judges, and calls men heretical."[79] And since Henry supported the church of Rome, Luther used the occasion for passionate attacks against Rome. The curia, the papacy, and even the whole Roman Church are called "whores" or the "devil's whore." Luther found these and similar phrases ready to use in the prophetic and apocalyptic literature.[80] Luther regretted that the Protestants "were formerly stuck in the behind of this hellish whore, this new church of the pope."[81] Similarly, Luther described the papal church as "a great dragon's head,"[82] or as "the true whore-church of the devil."[83] Not only the duke, but also the pope was called an "ass."[84] The Roman churches were sometimes also described as "brothels and devil's churches."[85] And the polemic against the duke and against Rome can be so merged together that Luther simply spoke of "Pope Harry [Henry] of Rome."[86] Luther had earlier used untranslatable puns to describe the decretals, that is, the decisions of the papal courts, as corrupt.[87] When such statements are combined with his characterization of his old enemy Eck as "Doctor Sow" and of all the papists as "silly asses," the result is a rather picturesque style of writing. Luther could also change the metaphors, particularly by comparing himself with the sheep who is eaten by the wolf.[88]

It was obvious that this kind of sharp polemic suggested, and even demanded, its own illustrations. In fact, Luther some years later did not hesitate to seek the help of Lukas Cranach as the illustrator of his totally and extravagantly polemical writing, *Against the Roman Papacy, an Institution of the Devil* (1545).[89] Apart from Luther's comments on some specific events, this book is Luther's sharpest attack against the assertion that the pope is the head of Christendom. Luther also once again attacked the theory of the *translatio imperii*, that is, that the pope had conferred the authority of the Roman Empire on the German Empire. Luther had already opposed this theory in 1520 in his book, *To the Christian Nobility of the German Nation Concerning the Reform of the Christian Estate*.[90] Luther rejected all the claims of the papacy and asserted that the renunciation of the devil in baptism is also a renunciation of the papacy. Of course, Luther's attacks of many decades against the papacy were now raised to their highest extreme through the pictorial illustrations. Luther himself had given instructions concerning the content of the pictures. The content of some of these pictures is scatological and all of them express a deep hatred of the papacy.[91] This hatred was undoubtedly common among the people. Still, these pictures must also have stimulated the lowest instincts of those who saw them. Luther composed Latin inscriptions and German verses to accompany these pictures. Their basic content is that the pope and his cardinals should be hanged.

3.41 Luther's Writings About the Jews

Luther's attitude toward the Jews was a dark chapter in his dealing with the questions of the time. Undoubtedly, the sharp polemic that was so widespread in the sixteenth century played a great role in this. And yet the problems associated with Luther's attitude toward the Jews lay much deeper than this. Here we are dealing with questions of theology and of "conversion"; with prejudices that, at that time, were taken for granted; and with intolerance. In all of this, it is particularly noteworthy that Luther originally encountered the Jews in a much more open way. Later in life, however, he spoke out against them with such vehemence that leading National Socialists at the time of Hitler felt they were entitled to claim Luther as a patron of their persecution of the Jews.[92] In 1523 Luther published *That Jesus Christ Was Born a Jew*.[93] This treatise demonstrated such an open attitude toward the Jews that it gave reason to think that a new epoch in Christendom's relation to the Jews was about to begin. In contrast, Luther's later writings on this subject made very severe suggestions aimed at isolating Jews from the rest of society.

In evaluating Luther's writings about the Jews, we must take into account the general background of relationships between Jews and Christians at that time as well as the particular events that caused Luther to write these books. In addition, however, we must remember the fact that attitudes toward the Jews in the sixteenth century were not focused on questions of race but rather on the differences in belief. In spite of this, there can be no doubt that Luther in his old age made extravagantly immoderate statements about the Jews, just as he had earlier made such statements about the peasants. By so doing, Luther left the way wide open for those who appealed to his statements as giving his personal approval and authorization for what they were doing even though Luther never intended anyone to do anything of the kind (cf. also above, 2.22).

3.42 Tenderness and Coarseness in Luther's Personality

Just as we are not able to remain silent about Luther's coarse polemic, so we must also emphasize that Luther could also express tender feelings and empathy. The ordinary reader would not suspect such sensitivity from the coarse writer of pamphlets described in the preceding sections. As a husband and as a father to his children, and also as a friend and a colleague in relationship to his prince, Luther could demonstrate empathy and consideration that would be hard to equal.

This quality of his character corresponds to the value that Luther placed on music and the role that the performance of music played in his own home as well as in the Protestant congregations. In this, Luther experienced music as a source of help in his spiritual temptations— music drives away the evil spirits and strengthens faith.

Similarly, we must observe Luther's pastoral work. He acted with goodness and wisdom, but without conveying a false note of permissiveness in his relationships to individual people and their needs. In so doing, he could occasionally also set aside norms which in and of themselves were considered valid, as he did in considering Philip's bigamy, although that particular decision was definitely problematical.

Of course it would be just as one-sided to describe Luther primarily in terms of the positive elements of his personality as it would be to focus primarily on his rudeness. We have already seen that Luther's spiritual temptations break out of the boundaries of the normal—although that alone is not sufficient reason to see them as pathological—so Luther's personality expressed itself in a tremendous variety of ways that often broke through the limits of what is otherwise usual. When we try to understand Luther, we must try to remain open for the enormous variety of his personality and not exclude any particular area. A blind attempt to proclaim him as a hero would be equally as problematical as a similar effort simply to reject him with a negative judgment.

3.43 Luther's Self-Understanding

Luther's own self-consciousness of his historical task is of considerable significance not only in the context of our analysis of Luther's style of controversy but also particularly as a problem all its own. An awareness of Luther's self-understanding of his task can help us to understand his behavior better. (See below, 5.1.4.)

Luther frequently spoke about his life and work. His remarks were characterized by surprising freedom and courage that is as far removed from self-glorification as it is from coyness. In these reminiscences, Luther repeatedly emphasized that he did not embark on his public career voluntarily and certainly not with some sort of prepared plan. On the contrary, God had really forced him to undertake these tasks. As many of the prophets described in the Old Testament did, Luther described himself as having been compelled by God. This means that he did not consider himself to have been called because he had particular talents or because he had achieved certain things. For that reason, Luther also did not consider the issues of the Reformation to revolve around his person. As Luther wrote to Staupitz on October 3, 1519, God could raise up "many Martins."[94] Luther maintained this attitude during the time he spent on the Wartburg in 1521 and 1522. He repeatedly objected to the custom of referring to his followers as Lutherans:

> In the first place, I ask that men make no reference to my name; let them call themselves Christians, not Lutherans. What is Luther? After all, the teaching is not mine [John 7:16]. Neither was I crucified for anyone [I Cor. 1:13]. St. Paul, in I Corinthians 3, would not allow the Christians to call themselves Pauline or Petrine, but Christian. How then should I—poor stinking maggot-fodder that I am—come to have men call the children of Christ by my wretched name? Not so, my dear friends; let us abolish all party names and call ourselves Christians, after him whose teaching we hold. The papists deservedly have a party name, because they are not content with the teaching and name of Christ, but want to be papist as well. Let them be papist then, since the pope is their master. I neither am nor want to be anyone's master. I hold, together with the universal church, the one universal teaching of Christ, who is our only master [Matt. 23:8].[95]

In 1522 Luther expressed himself in a somewhat milder manner on this question: "But if you are convinced that Luther's teaching is in accord with the gospel and that the pope's is not, then you should not discard Luther so completely, lest with him you discard also his teaching, which you nevertheless recognize as Christ's teaching. You should rather say: Whether Luther is a rascal or a saint I do not care; his teaching is not his, but Christ's."[96]

3.44 Luther as Reformer

Never once in any records that we have available did Luther claim to be a reformer of the church. His understanding of the Reformation itself would have prevented him from making this claim. On the eve of the Reformation, before Luther appeared as a public figure, there was a wide variety of thinking about a possible reformation. Many felt that such a reformation was necessary and that it would soon begin. Political and ecclesiastical parties of very different heritages and with very different goals were united to the extent that they all used the key slogan of "reformation." As far as Luther was concerned, he did not claim that he had caused a reformation of the church. The basis for this is not to be found in some kind of modesty but rather in the fact that Luther had a different understanding of reformation than we ordinarily encounter.

Even in the earliest writings in which Luther used the term "reformation," it is clear he was concerned with the proclamation of the pure gospel and the true faith and with the abandoning of human teachings. For this reason, the Reformation is finally not a matter that is achieved by people but rather by God. It should be clearly understood that the so-called scriptural principle of the Reformation is closely related to this understanding of the ongoing reformation of the church. The scriptural principle, however, was basically intended only to create the condition under which reformation could occur. The introduction of this principle as such is not yet identical with reformation.

Luther felt that there were two reasons that prevented the curia from opening itself to the reformation of the church in this sense. First of all, human traditions were so firmly established in Rome that they covered over the divine word and prevented it from making itself heard in its purity. In addition, the unwillingness of the princes of the church to repent prevented their conversion. Luther felt that the leaders of the church were concerned only with the position of the church as a power in this world.

3.45 The Doctor of Theology

The only office to which Luther appealed throughout his life in order to justify his activity was his doctorate in theology. Even at the beginning of the controversy about indulgences, Luther wrote to the pope reminding him that he had been declared a teacher of theology through the pope's own apostolic authority. Luther went on to say that this fact gave him the right to conduct public disputations not only about indulgences but also about the authority to set aside penances and to forgive sins. The latter are far more important questions than indulgences are. Luther asserted that the right that he claimed was confirmed by the customary practice of all the universities and of the whole church.[97]

Later Luther could put it much more pointedly:

> However, I, Dr. Martinus, have been called to this work and was compelled to become a doctor, without any initiative of my own, but out of pure obedience. Then I had to accept the office of doctor and swear a vow to my most beloved Holy Scriptures that I would preach and teach them faithfully and purely. While engaged in this kind of teaching, the papacy crossed my path and wanted to hinder me in it. How it has fared is obvious to all, and will fare still worse. It shall not hinder me. In God's name and call I shall walk on the lion and the adder, and tread on the young lion and dragon with my feet.[98]

Luther himself was firmly convinced that as a doctor of Holy Scripture he shared responsibility for the teaching and preaching of the church. No person, not even an authority of the church, could absolve him from his share of this responsibility.

Luther therefore thought that his primary task was to interpret the Scripture. This was his duty, first of all, as a professor. We should never forget that Luther was a university professor and that the German Reformation is closely related to the reformation of the universities that was occurring at the same time. The reformation of the universities was, by and large, more successful than the Reformation of the church insofar as its basic principles ultimately prevailed even in Roman Catholic universities. In contrast, the Reformation of the church resulted in a schism in the church.

This self-understanding led Luther to make certain specific proposals for reform, for example, particularly in 1520. But this self-understanding also prevented Luther from identifying the desired Reformation with the introduction of a series of individual reforms. Still, however, Luther saw any particular change as a specific example of the fact that the church was giving up its claim to power and placing its trust in the divine Word alone.

We must, of course, admit that this basic view is also one of Luther's limitations. As long as Rome basically rejected Luther and the Reformation, the appeal to the "gospel" was a powerful lesson. In the few cases in which there were relatively serious conversations between Roman Catholics and Protestants in the course of which the supporters of the Reformation needed to explain more exactly what they felt should be changed, the mere appeal to the gospel was no longer adequate. Melanchthon was confronted with this very difficult situation both at Augsburg in 1530 and in the colloquies on religion at Worms and Regensburg in 1540 and 1541. The appeal to the gospel could not, and in any case may not, excuse us from the task of discussing the many real questions about the life and theology of the church and also to join in seeking specific answers to those questions. As long as Protestantism was able to define itself in terms of its almost-permanent opposition to Rome, this very serious weakness of Protestantism could be concealed. Only now, in the age of ecumenism, have Protestants become aware of the tasks that await them.

Luther in any case was of the opinion that he had basically never done anything else. "I simply taught, preached, and wrote God's Word; otherwise I did nothing. And while I slept [cf. Mark 4:26–29], or drank Wittenberg beer with my friends Philip and Amsdorf, the Word so greatly weakened the papacy that no prince or emperor ever inflicted such losses upon it. I did nothing; the Word did everything. . . . I did nothing; I let the Word do its work."[99]

Luther maintained this viewpoint even after he basically had to admit he needed to do something more than merely assert that the divine Word is sufficient to accomplish whatever needs to be done. The unique characteristic of Luther's self-awareness lies in the fact that he never felt that his own person was the issue in the Reformation but that he always focused on the substance of the issue under discussion.

In this sense, however, Luther had a very well developed sense of his own historical mission. No matter how worthy or unworthy he might be, he had been commissioned to act on behalf of the truth of the gospel as it is contained in the Scripture. Luther was unalterably convinced that this truth of the gospel had been newly illuminated for him through his spiritual temptations. It was this gospel that he represented over against a church that had fallen into decay. In this Luther saw himself as one of a long series of witnesses to the truth that stretches from the apostles to the martyrs such as John Huss. For a long time, Luther was firmly convinced that he too would suffer martyrdom and he was personally prepared for that. This readiness to suffer martyrdom gave Luther his amazing courage over against the authorities of the church as well as over against the secular authorities. Luther often demonstrated tremendous security in controversy with a variety of opponents such as Rome, the enthusiasts, the peasants, Müntzer, Erasmus, or Zwingli. This unusual courage is not, therefore, to be explained primarily on the basis of his personal character but must rather be understood finally in the context of the Reformation's self-understanding that it was based on clear statements of Scripture.

Although Luther thereby placed himself far in the background over against the position that he represented, he had the capacity—shared by few of his contemporaries—to recognize the nature and significance of the many historical transitions and problems of the time and address them clearly. He was able to do this not merely because of his personal shrewdness—although this often gave him a surprising clarity in these matters. Rather, Luther had an unusual ability to explore issues thoroughly at a deep level of insight. For that reason, Luther was also able to clarify the spiritual significance of the issues of the day. Luther repeatedly demonstrated this capacity without falling into oversimplication.

One example of Luther's in-depth analysis of an issue is provided by his discussion of the reformation of Wittenberg. Other examples could be found in his analysis of the decisive theological questions involved in the controversies with Rome or with the enthusiasts. During the Peasants' War, Luther recognized that basic questions were the definition of the task of government, and the relationship between obedience and revolt, as well as the possible misuse of the gospel in support of secular goals. Luther saw these problems far more clearly than anyone else did. The same might be said of Luther's appraisal of the wars against the Turks or of his predictions about the future of Germany. His analysis is not only clear but sometimes almost prophetic in character.

A particularly clear example of Luther's ability to get at the root of a problem occurred during the Diet of Augsburg in 1530. The negotiators in Augsburg were making very intensive efforts to achieve a compromise. Luther, who was in Coburg, wrote a letter to Justus Jonas, who was in Augsburg, expressing his opinion that it might be relatively easy to arrive at a mutually acceptable compromise in questions such as the marriage of priests or giving the wine to the laity in the Lord's Supper. Luther, however, was unable to imagine a solution to the problems related to the teachings of the church. Having said this, Luther recommended that a solution be found that would preserve political unity and let the dogmatic disagreements recede into the background.[100] Luther thus made a proposal that was put into effect twenty-five years later in the Religious Peace of Augsburg after the attempts to arrive at a common doctrinal understanding had in the meantime proved to be fruitless.

In all of this, Luther was very deeply aware of the contingent nature of all that happens. Luther knew that events and developments cannot be predicted in advance but rather that history always confronts us with surprises which prove all our rational predictions false. Luther understood that history is full of discontinuities, and that there are sharp breaks between events. Luther's position was that history does not reveal God but rather conceals God from us. (See below, 5.1.) Precisely for this reason, the proclamation of the gospel is all the more important. In this proclamation, God reveals his heart to people and at the same time gives us power to believe that the divine hand is effectively at work under the mask of secular events in this world. Thus Luther's idea that events can never be totally understood or explained strengthened his own sense of mission. For Luther this sense of mission is the confidence that the preaching of the gospel, and only the preaching of the gospel, can give people something to hold on to in this hopeless world.

Luther's understanding of his special mission as well as his capacity to understand clearly the real nature of a variety of situations made what he said effective to a degree that has probably not been equaled by any other German-speaking person. Luther's creative talent in the development of the German language, which has often been commented on, must be seen in this context. Luther did not merely have an unusual command of the German language and its possibilities—although in this respect Luther achieved very much. Rather the effectiveness of Luther's language derived much more from the unique way in which he looked into the depths of events as well as of people.

As a result of this talent, Luther always spoke with an incomparable directness that was right on target. Whether Luther was comforting the dying, giving an opinion on a question of daily politics, expressing himself in a theological controversy, or composing hymns for the Protestant Church, he was able to express what others could only sense. It would be very inadequate to describe Luther as merely the mouthpiece of the people, no matter how much that seemed to be the case in the tumultuous early years of the Reformation. Luther proclaimed the message of the Bible to the people with the full authority of the Bible itself (see below, 5.1.4).

4 | LUTHER'S WRITINGS

4.1 The Absence of Any Pride of Authorship in Luther

It is surprising that, although Luther wrote a very great deal, he had no pride of authorship. On the contrary, he repeatedly subjected his own writings to sharp criticism. In his introduction to the first volume of the Wittenberg edition of his German writings, he wrote in 1539, "I would have been quite content to see my books, one and all, remain in obscurity and go by the board."[1] Occasionally he exempted one or the other of his writings from this severe judgment but that did not basically change Luther's low evaluation of his own literary work.

Luther's evaluations of his work were not an expression of false modesty for he was quite able to value his own writings in comparison to those of his opponents. He was also able to see the way in which other translations of the Bible were dependent on his own. Rather, Luther intended that his writings should always take a place far lower than that given the Bible as the Word of God. And it is in this sense that the ironic and humorous statements about authors taken from the same preface are to be understood.

> If, however, you feel and are inclined to think you have made it, flattering yourself with your own little books, teaching, or writing, because you have done it beautifully and preached excellently; if you are highly pleased when someone praises you in the presence of others; if you perhaps look for praise, and would sulk or quit what you are doing if you did not get it—if you are of that stripe, dear friend, then take yourself by the ears, and if you do this in the right way you will find a beautiful pair of big, long, shaggy donkey ears. Then do not spare any expense! Decorate them with golden bells, so that people will be able to hear you wherever you go, point their fingers at you, and say, "See, See! There goes that clever beast, who can write such exquisite books and preach so remarkably well."[2]

It is remarkable that so many significant aspects of Luther's literary work have still not been adequately investigated. There are many studies of Luther's theology, dealing both with his theological thinking in groups of writings and with his translation of the Bible and its significance for the history of the German language. There is, however, still no adequate

97

study of the types of books that he wrote and of the styles that he used.
There is also no adequate investigation of Luther's writings in the context
of the history of literature. In making these suggestions for further
research, I understand that such research will require the cooperation of
specialists in the history of German literature as well as in theology.

4.2 The Uniqueness of Luther's Style

Up until now, the best—although obviously brief—sketch of Luther as an
author has been provided by Heinrich Bornkamm.[3] In this study,
Bornkamm has evaluated Luther's stylistic characteristics, particularly his
very great humor, his capacity for imagination, his ridicule of his opponents, his ironic view of himself, and his lack of pride of authorship.
Bornkamm also has indicated that Luther in these ways was quite different from Humanists of that time. And, in fact, Luther in his writings did
not use the stylistic literary devices and the forms of literature that were
common among sixteenth-century Humanists. This is true not only of his
German but also of his Latin writings. At the same time, Luther—for a
brief period beginning in late 1518—saw himself as quite closely identified with humanistic concerns.

Bornkamm has also drawn attention to the unique characteristics of
Luther's style, particularly to the rhythm and timbre of his language, the
melody of his vowels, his use of dissonance and alliteration, his capacity
for meaningful and relevant associations, and the richness of his imagery.
Moreover, Bornkamm has specifically demonstrated that Luther's whole
literary production must be viewed in terms of his work as an interpreter
of the Bible. "Luther brought things out of the Bible that had not been
heard before—just as the Bible brought things out of him which had
been previously unheard of."[4] In addition, while Luther in his many
controversies spoke directly to his opponents, he also always made the
Bible "the third partner" in the conversation.[5] Luther came to his clearest
insights about the meaning of the Bible when he was using it in controversy. For example, Luther developed his distinction between the hidden
and the revealed God in responding to Erasmus's attack.

Although the comparison of Luther with the Humanists is in many
respects very stimulating, however, Luther's literary work must also be
compared with the German-language literature of that time. Specific
forms of humanistic literary prose such as encomia, declamations, or
dialogues were frequently used by the Humanists but are conspicuously
absent from Luther's writings. Their absence is not noticed, however,
when Luther's writings are compared with those of Karlstadt, Müntzer,
Zwingli, and with many of the pamphlets of the time. The whole broad
Reformation movement that was developing in the early sixteenth cen-

tury is as a whole quite different from Humanism. Luther's special place in the history of German literature is to be defined in terms of his unique place within this Reformation movement.

4.3 Luther Was Bilingual

It is important to note that Luther was bilingual, that is, he spoke and wrote both Latin and German. This capacity to work in two languages is not unusual in and of itself. Most of the Reformers, for example, Bugenhagen, Zwingli, Bucer, Brenz, and many others, were also able to do this. And it is self-understood that such people frequently used Latin— the language commonly used in the universities for lectures and disputations—as the primary language of their scholarly writings. They used German primarily in writings addressed to a more popular audience.

Luther's linguistic ability undoubtedly found fuller expression in his German than in his Latin writings. This is not only due to the fact that the Latin language was considerably older than the German and was therefore no longer as capable of development but primarily to the fact that Luther, like the great mass of the people, lived, felt, and thought in German. In spite of this, Luther's literary work in both languages must be evaluated as a totality. His German and Latin writings are related to one another in a variety of ways. His early lectures were, of course, delivered in Latin. And it is only from these lectures that we can gain some insight into Luther's intellectual activity at that time. The controversy with Rome was at first carried on almost entirely in Latin. At the same time, however, Luther began to present his thinking in German. When one compares Luther's Latin and German writings, the Latin works, which are intended for scholars, are ordinarily much clearer and sharper, whereas the same ideas appear in his German writings somewhat later and are formulated more cautiously.

4.4 Luther's Writings as Responses to Specific Situations

Luther's Latin and German writings must also be grouped together when we attempt to study the intention and structure of individual works. Certainly, most of Luther's writings were responses to actual situations. Luther was hardly ever able to project and execute an outline for a book. His academic lectures are a very important exception to this. For example, although Luther wanted to write a book "about justification," he never did so. Nevertheless, some of his Latin writings are more carefully constructed and executed than the German writings are. This is true, for example, of *The Babylonian Captivity of the Church* (1520),[6] in which Luther presented a well-organized discussion of the doctrine of the sacraments. He provided a very carefully organized outline for his book on the controversy over monastic vows, *The Judgment of Martin Luther on Monastic Vows,* written in the autumn of 1521.[7] No other writing of Luther's is as clearly structured.

Most of his Latin as well as his German writings, however, do not follow a strict outline. At the same time, Luther did not simply adapt himself to the line of argumentation followed by his opponents and seek to refute them point by point. Rather, he usually began his controversial writings by defining the point at issue as fully as seemed necessary and then discussing the arguments of his opponents in the context of his own position. That is the case, for example, in *The Bondage of the Will.* The question as to whether or not Luther in this process did justice to the views of his opponent is usually hard to answer. We cannot answer this question either by referring to Luther's sharp polemics or by referring to the fact that he usually approached the matter from another viewpoint than his opponents had. Rather, we must answer this question on the basis of the subject matter itself, as Luther was trying to define and express it.

Luther almost always wrote in response to very specific situations that needed his attention and had a very definite purpose. This fact is of considerable significance for the understanding of his whole way of thinking. This means first that Luther's thoughts can only be recovered by carefully tracing his line of argument in the context of a particular controversy. Second, however, Luther based his work on a total viewpoint that must be understood in depth. Luther is sometimes accused of not having been a systematician, but this is not true. Although Luther never wrote a handbook of dogmatics, he was, nonetheless, a very capable systematic thinker.

Seen in these perspectives, there is a significant difference between Luther's Latin and German writings. Luther's Latin writings more clearly reveal the tradition in which Luther stood and the way in which he came to terms with this tradition. It is especially difficult to understand the young Luther, because he often did not come to terms with the traditions explicitly. The question as to which traditions Luther was familiar with and which determined his own thinking has been answered at many points; however, it is still an open question at others. The overwhelming influence of Augustine on the young Luther has been established. But did he only read Augustine through Ockhamistic glasses? Or did he do this at first and then more and more discover the "real" Augustine? Or did Luther from the very beginning interpret Augustine from the viewpoint of the Reformation? We are still often uncertain about the nature of late medieval Ockhamism. We also do not yet know how far the influence of the mystics extended. As a result, much important research remains to be done on the question of Luther's relationship to the Middle Ages.

In addition it is important to note that Luther's writings usually are clearly outlined—although Luther used a variety of structures. In his early period, for example, in the *Explanations of the Ninety-five Theses* (1518),[8] Luther occasionally still used the ponderous methods of scholastic argumentation. This is particularly true of his respect for various traditional authorities—although even at this early time his decisive arguments came from the Scripture. To this extent, his content already breaks through the formal structure of his method.

In many of the German writings of the following years, Luther emphasized the various questions with which he dealt by numbering his sections. It can be argued that this reflects a style of writing disputation theses. The question, then, is whether Luther simply followed the usual practice of numbering the theses to be discussed or whether he only used this as a simple way of arranging his thoughts in a series. In his later writings, Luther occasionally began with a rough outline of the contents. This is the case in the Smalcald Articles (1537)[9]—a Lutheran position paper he prepared for the council that was soon expected to convene—in which he lists the various matters to be discussed in sequence. He also provides such a general table of contents in *On the Councils and the Churches* (1539).[10]

These outlines are usually quite general and Luther did not always follow them strictly when he wrote. Primarily because of the overwhelming load of work that Luther carried, his writings after *The Judgment of Martin Luther on Monastic Vows*[11] are no longer so carefully organized. Once the controversy with Rome developed fully, Luther never again had the necessary leisure to think through an outline before he began to write. The only possible exception would have been during the time he spent on the Wartburg (1521–22), but for other reasons he had no leisure during that period either. Rather, Luther managed a variety of tasks simultaneously: he was a university teacher, a preacher, a reformer, a pastor, and a counselor—both in personal consultations and through his very extensive correspondence. Luther's own natural tendency to be too wordy was reinforced by this lack of time to plan his writing in advance.

4.5 The Change in Luther's Exegetical Method

The form of Luther's lectures shows a very important change in comparison to the traditional form. In his early period, Luther interpreted the biblical text as earlier interpreters had done, using brief notes (glosses) written between the lines and in the margins, as well as inserting more extensive sections of commentary. After the beginning of his second lectures on the Psalms in 1518,[12] Luther abandoned this ponderous method of commenting in favor of an integrated philological and theological interpretation. In doing this, Luther made a significant break with the traditional form of commenting on a text. The cause of this change lay in Luther's new understanding of the Scripture, particularly in his view of the interrelationship between the letter and the spirit. This new form of commentary eventually was universally adopted—simply because it is more appropriate to the subject matter.

4.6 Luther's Relationship to Rhetoric

Luther's relationship to the art of rhetoric is a special topic that has not yet been adequately investigated. Since Humanists at the time of Luther studied and practiced classical rhetoric, it is certain that Luther was acquainted with the various forms and parts of an address as these were taught by the great rhetoricians. Ulrich Nembach has attempted to prove that Luther's sermons follow the form advocated by Quintilian.[13] At the same time, however, Luther also criticized Quintilian's method. The question of Luther's relationship to various methods of rhetoric must of course be explored further in a larger context. It is certainly true, as is demonstrated by Nembach's work, that the numerous parallels between Luther and Quintilian prove that Luther was familiar with Quintilian. We still, however, need to know more about Luther's relationship to Cicero and Aristotle. In addition, a study of Luther's relationship to rhetoric presents us with special problems in terms of the historical sources of Luther's thinking.

As important as these questions about Luther's more formal adoption and transformation of classical forms of rhetoric and expression are, questions about the relationship of the substance of Luther's theology to his rhetorical method(s) are even more important. And even though Luther's hermeneutics, that is, his method of interpretation, as well as his understanding of language have been intensively researched in the past decades, we still do not have very useful studies of these special questions. Klaus Dockhorn[14] has begun such research, but much more needs to be done. Simple generalizations about the opposition between theology and rhetoric in Luther are of as little help as are premature conclusions about their interdependence. Both Luther's use and criticism of rhetoric are far too complex issues to be dealt with in such a simplistic manner.

4.7 Survey of the Types of Literature
Used by Luther

A number of quite different types of literature can be identified in Luther's Latin and German writings, although these types are not always encountered in a pure form. The following classification attempts to group his writings according to their situation in life or the primary intention of each writing. The list makes no claim to completeness but is intended only as a preliminary definition of the types of literature.

Lectures and Commentaries on Biblical Books. In the course of his academic activity, Luther interpreted many of the biblical books, primarily those of the Old Testament. Some of these books were interpreted more than once. Many of these lectures have been preserved either in Luther's own manuscripts or in notes taken by his students. Some of them were edited by Luther himself before being published.

Biblical Interpretations. The boundary between this and the preceding category is not an exact one. Many of Luther's interpretations of biblical books as well as many of his sermons, a writing such as *The Beautiful Confitemini* (an interpretation of Psalm 118),[15] were originally intended for publication and are addressed to a different reading public than the students who heard his lectures.

Academic Disputations. The practice of disputations played a very large role in the life of universities in the late Middle Ages. After 1516 Luther himself conducted many disputations.[16] Many important decisions resulted from these disputations, both in the course of his controversy with Rome[17] and in the later controversies within the Reformation itself. Disputations were often of special significance when the Reformation was introduced into new cities. And Luther felt that disputations were a very valuable method of teaching.

Meditations. These also are mostly interpretations of biblical material, but are generally characterized by being more strongly meditative in nature. Examples are: *The Seven Penitential Psalms* (1517)[18] or Luther's interpretation of *The Magnificat* (1521).[19]

Sermons. Even though many sermons were the result of actual preaching, this particular category describes a kind of treatise that is usually short, although sometimes it can be quite long, dealing with questions related to the church and theology that were particularly important at the time. Examples are: *A Sermon on Indulgences and Grace* (1517),[20] *The Blessed Sacrament of the Holy and True Body of Christ and the Brotherhoods* (1519),[21] *A Treatise on the New Testament, That Is, the Holy Mass* (1520).[22] In later years, Luther used the title of "sermon" much less often as a designation for a particular writing. In this later period, the term was used mostly to designate sermons that were actually preached to congregations.

Treatises. Treatises are closely related to other writings, particularly to the disputations as well as to the controversies. In fact, the treatises themselves most often have polemical character. Examples are: *Explanations of the Ninety-five Theses* (1518),[23] *Resolutio Lutheriana super propositione sua decima tertia de potestate papae* (1519)[24]—a discussion of the power of the papacy that Luther wrote in preparation for the Leipzig Debate—and *The Judgment of Martin Luther on Monastic Vows* (1521).[25] Those treatises on the Lord's Supper that are not entirely polemical in nature can also be included here, such as: *The Adoration of the Sacrament of the Holy Body of Christ* (1523),[26] and *On Translating: An Open Letter* (1530).[27]

Controversial Writings. In this category, we could name a great many of Luther's works, such as *Asterisci Lutheri adversus obeliscos Eckii* (1518),[28] *Ad dialogum Silvestri Prieratis de potestate papae responsio* (1518),[29] *A Prelude of Martin Luther on the Babylonian Captivity of the Church* (1520),[30] *Von den neuen Eckischen Bullen und Lügen* (1520),[31] *Assertio omnium articulorum M. Lutheri per bullam Leonis X. novissimam damnatorum* (1520),[32] *Ad librum eximii magistri nostri Mag. Ambrosii Catharini, defensoris Silv. Prieratis acerrimi, responsio M. Lutheri* (1521),[33] *Against Latomus: Luther's Refutation of Latomus' Argument on Behalf of the Incendiary Sophists of the University of Louvain* (1521),[34] *Against the Heavenly Prophets in the Matter of Images and Sacraments* (1525),[35] most of Luther's writings during the controversy on the Lord's Supper,[36] *Against the Roman Papacy, an Institution of the Devil* (1545).[37]

Writings on the Liturgy. The most important are *An Order of Mass and Communion for the Church at Wittenberg* (1523),[38] *German Mass and Order of Service* (1526),[39] *Exempel, einen rechten christlichen Bischof zu weihen* (1542).[40] In an extended sense, Luther's numerous writings on baptism, the Lord's Supper, repentance, confession and absolution, engagement and marriage, as well as Luther's prayers and hymns[41] could all be listed here.

Pamphlets and Programatic Writings. Here once again it is difficult to draw a definite boundary in relationship to some of Luther's other writings. The most important examples are: *To the Christian Nobility of the German Nation* (1520),[42] *Freedom of a Christian* (1520),[43] *That a Christian Assembly or Congregation Has the Right and Power to Judge All Teaching and to Call, Appoint, and Dismiss Teachers, Established and Proven by Scripture* (1523),[44] *Ein Sendbrief an die ehrsamen und weisen Herren Bürgermeister, Rat und ganze Gemeinde der Stadt Mühlhausen* (1524),[45] *Letter to the Christians at Strassburg in Opposition to the Fanatic Spirit* (1524),[46] *To the Councilmen of All Cities in Germany That They Establish and Maintain Christian Schools* (1524).[47] Luther's writings on the Peasants' War may also be listed under this category: *Admonition to Peace, a Reply to the Twelve Articles of the Peasants in Swabia* (1525),[48] *Against the Robbing and Murdering*

Hordes of Peasants (1525),[49] *Open Letter on the Harsh Book Against the Peasants* (1525),[50] as well as *Whether Soldiers, Too, Can Be Saved* (1526).[51]

Pedagogical Writings. Here again the boundaries are not easily drawn. Examples are: The Large Catechism (1529),[52] *Enchiridion: The Small Catechism for the Ordinary Pastors and Preachers* (1530),[53] and The Smalcald Articles (1537).[54]

Comforting Writings. In the broad sense, these are pastoral writings; but in a narrower sense, they are messages of comfort that were often directed to individual persons. Examples are: *Comfort When Facing Grave Temptations* (1521),[55] *A Sermon on Preparing to Die* (1519 and many editions),[56] *Letter of Consolation to the Christians at Halle* (1527),[57] *Comfort for Women Who Have Had a Miscarriage* (1542),[58] *Ein schöner christlicher Trostbrief des gottseligen Mannes M. Lutheri, an eine hohe und namhafte Person in Niedersachsen geschrieben, die ... mit überflüssigen Gedanken von der Vorsehung Gottes beladen gewesen, sehr tröstlich zu lesen und zu hören* (published about 1550).[59]

Writings on the Jews. Luther repeatedly expressed his opinion on the church's relationship to the Jews, particularly in *That Jesus Christ Was Born a Jew* (1523),[60] *Ein Sermon von des jüdischen Reichs und der Welt Ende* (1525),[61] *On the Jews and Their Lies* (1543),[62] *Vom Schem Hamphoras und vom Geschlecht Christi* (1543).[63]

Writings on the Turks. Luther repeatedly expressed his opinion on the increasing danger to Europe presented by the armies of the Ottoman Empire: *On War Against the Turk* (1529),[64] *Eine Heerpredigt wider den Türken* (1529),[65] *Appeal for Prayer Against the Turks* (1541).[66]

Memoranda, Opinions, Advice. In many opinions, which were very often written jointly with other Wittenberg theologians, Luther took a stand on important questions of the Reformation, of law and order and society, and also on specific problems. Examples are: *Bedenken Luthers (Phil. Melanchthons und Johannes Bugenhagens) Ob ein Fürst seine Untertanen wider des Kaisers oder anderer Fürsten Verfolgung um des Glaubens willen mit Krieg schützen möge* (1523),[67] *Bedenken Luthers auf Bucers Vergleichsvorschläge in betreff des heiligen Abendmahls* (January 16, 1531).[68]

Marginal Notes. Luther made marginal notes (glosses) in many works, some for his own use and some for publication. In his first years as a teacher, in 1509 and 1510, he made some especially important marginal notes in some of the writings of Augustine and Peter Lombard. These marginal notes help us see clearly the beginnings of the thinking that a little later would characterize Luther as Reformer. Occasionally, Luther also added marginal comments to the writings of his opponents and republished them. Examples are: *Duae episcopales bullae, prior pii posterior papistici pontificis, super doctrina Lutherana et Romana* (1524),[69] and *Hermann Rab: Exemplum theologiae et doctrinae papisticae* (1531).[70]

Sermons. Luther preached regularly except when he was prevented by illness or some other problem. Often, however, these sermons are not available to us in manuscript or in an edition supervised by Luther but only in notes made by those who heard them.[71]

Spiritual Hymns and Prayers. Luther wrote numerous hymns and prayers. All of them express his Reformation theology and are also closely related to the organizational development of the Protestant church. It should be noted that Luther did not write any Lenten hymns but did write Easter hymns. Some of the prayers were written for particular kinds of persons or situations, such as his prayer for soldiers (1526),[72] in an epidemic of the plague (1534),[73] against the Turks (1541),[74] and as part of an order for use in exorcism (1545).[75]

Poems. Luther composed a number of German and Latin poems. Many of these are theological in nature and have some relationship to the controversies he was involved in. Examples are: *Nun treiben wir den Papst hinaus,*[76] *Eine andere Auslegung des 128. Psalms in Versweise gestellet: Willst du vor Gott, mein lieber Christ,*[77] *Erasmus hostis omnium religionum et inimicus singularis Christi* (1533).[78] There are other poems with quite different content, for example, the verses Luther wrote to accompany the picture of the late elector, John the Steadfast, *Nach meines lieben Bruders End* (1532),[79] or Luther's description of life at the courts of the princes, *Wer sich nimmt an, unds redlein kann.*[80]

Letters. Luther's unusually extensive correspondence was addressed to all sorts and conditions of people and dealt with the most varied kind of questions. Alongside the personal letters that he wrote to his wife and children and that are full of inner participation in their worries both large and small, there are letters to popes, bishops, princes (particularly Protestant rulers). Luther also maintained an unusually widespread correspondence with other Reformers, pastors, secular councils, and so forth.[81]

The Translation of the Bible. Alongside Luther's regular activity as university professor and the tasks that came to him through the Reformation, his work of translating the Bible is undoubtedly the third most extensive area of his lifework. Luther translated the New Testament in 1521 while he was on the Wartburg. The translation of the Old Testament books appeared one after the other until 1534, when the whole Bible was available in Luther's translation. In this work of translation, Luther was supported by others, particularly by Melanchthon, who also translated the Books of the Maccabees.

Luther was always concerned with improving his translation. For example, his first translation of the New Testament appeared in September 1522 and for that reason is called the September Testament; the second edition, published in December 1522 (the December Testament), already contained hundreds of corrections.

Beginning in 1531, Luther formed a commission of scholars to revise the translation of the Bible. This commission published the Psalter in its basically final form. Similar commissions were active in preparing the whole Bible for its first publication in 1534 as well as in the comprehensive revisions of the Bible from 1539 to 1541. Work on a revision of the translation of the New Testament began in the autumn of 1544, although this project was soon interrupted. The minutes of the meetings of these commissions for the revision of the translation of the Bible give evidence of the very careful way in which they worked.

Table Talk. These are expanded notes or comments that Luther made around the dinner table and which dealt with the most varied kind of questions, primarily related to theology and the church.[82] Luther himself never read this material and did not authorize its publication. As a result, its value as a source is quite limited. We must also ask whether such "table talk" should even be considered part of Luther's writings, since we are dealing here with extemporaneous material. At the same time, we can also be fairly certain about the fact that at this point the boundaries between the oral and written versions are somewhat fluid. And on account of their close relationship with other of Luther's works, the "table talk" can be included among the various types of his work. The important example would be Luther's comments on transubstantiation made on June 10 or 11, 1541. This was later put into writing for Prince George of Anhalt on June 12, 1541.[83] This piece of table talk is of particular significance for our understanding of Luther's criticism of the doctrine of transubstantiation.

Editions of Other Works and Prefaces. Luther republished many works of other authors because he considered their content to be valuable. His purposes were not polemical; rather, Luther felt that the opinion of others would support his viewpoint. Thus in 1516 Luther published the *German Theology* with a short preface and described it as "A spiritually noble little book that truly understands and distinguishes between the old and the new person."[84] In 1518 he published a more complete edition of the book with a longer preface.[85] Luther often wrote prefaces for the works of other authors.

Miscellaneous. There is a whole series of writings that are difficult to classify as being of one type or another and some that are obviously totally unique. The *Supputatio annorum mundi,* commonly referred to as Luther's "chronicles," was published in 1541 and in a much revised edition in 1545.[86] This book contains chronological tables that Luther originally had laid out for himself. He wanted to have a manageable view of biblical history. In preparing this, he used the *World Chronicle* prepared by the mathematician Carion. This work had (with Melanchthon's assistance) been published in 1532 in Wittenberg.[87] The *Supputatio* demonstrates Luther's sense of history, even though he did not do any of his own research in writing it. At the same time it also betrays his apocalyptic expectations. Luther attempted to determine the date of the end of the world. In doing so, he adopted the traditional idea that the world would last six thousand years. In this respect, this kind of literature is related to an apocalyptic writing.

Another example: Luther wrote only one ballad and did so in the form of a historical popular song, *A New Song Here Shall Be Begun* (1523).[88] The occasion was the execution of the first two Protestant martyrs in the marketplace in Brussels. This ballad also is closely related to the substance of the Reformation. It emphasizes our responsibility to witness to our Christian faith and praises the faithful courageous confession of the martyrs. After this, Luther did not write any more ballads. Some of his spiritual songs have some balladlike characteristics, however, particularly *Dear Christians, Let Us Now Rejoice* (1523)[89] and *Isaiah 'Twas the Prophet* (1526).[90]

Alongside the types of literature that have been referred to up until now, there are still others such as the "pamphlet." We have examples of these from quite different situations in Luther's life. An example from the early period is *Scheda adversus Iacobum Hochstraten* (July 13, 1519).[91] This pamphlet was written following the Leipzig Debate. It contains Luther's defense against the attack of the famous heresy-hunter Hoogstraten who had denounced the last thesis Luther had prepared for the Leipzig disputation to the pope as corrupting the church. Luther attacked this new enemy "whom God had raised up against him." In terms of its content, this pamphlet is concerned with questions of the authority of Scripture and of heresy. Luther accused Hoogstraten himself of being a heretic.

An example of a completely different kind of pamphlet is provided by Luther's admonition of May 13, 1543, against the gluttonous and whoring students.[92] This brief admonition warns of the dangerous results of immoral behavior and of sexual unchastity and emphasizes the necessity of keeping the Sixth Commandment. Luther asserted that Wittenberg has

a Christian church and school; they are there so that people can learn
God's word, morality, and discipline. For that reason, whoremongers have
no business in Wittenberg but ought to move elsewhere. This clear
admonition also illustrates Luther's understanding of the tasks of government and of the relationship between spiritual and secular authorities.

It would certainly be possible to define additional types of Luther's
writings. It would also be helpful if scholars would devote more attention
to analyzing the types of Luther's writings. On the other hand, it is also
clear that no particular type of literature appears in a pure form in
Luther's writings. His treatises frequently contain polemical elements;
and his controversial writings contain sections that are typical of other
types of literature. Very often the content has shattered the form. Ricarda
Huch has said it well: "The difference between Luther and a poet is that
Luther never intentionally shaped his material. He was concerned only
with truth and never with beauty."[93]

4.8 The Central Focus on the Question of Truth, the 'Apostolic' Character of Many of Luther's Writings

Luther always focused on Christian truth. This focus—together with his
self-consciousness of once again restoring the original meaning of the
gospel, which had in so many ways been corrupted by the papacy—gave
many of Luther's writings the character of apostolic epistles. This characteristic was not entirely unusual in the literature of that time; it frequently appears in various pamphlets. Luther expressed it both in the
form and in the content of many of his writings and letters. Thus Luther
began many of his writings with the name of "Jesus."[94] The introductory
as well as the concluding sentences of many of his writings sometimes
remind us of Paul's letters.

Thus Luther began *A Sincere Admonition by Martin Luther to All
Christians to Guard Against Insurrection and Rebellion* (1522) in this
way: "Jesus. May God grant grace and peace to all Christians who read
this pamphlet or hear it read. By the grace of God the blessed light of
Christian truth, hitherto suppressed by the pope and his adherents, has
risen again in our day. Their manifold harmful and scandalous deceits and
all manner of misdeeds and tyranny have thereby been publicly exposed
and brought to shame."[95] He concluded the book, "God grant us all that
we may practice what we preach, putting our words into deeds. There are
many among us who say, 'Lord, Lord' [Matt. 7:21] and praise the teaching,
but the doing and the following are simply not there. Let this suffice for
the present as a renewed admonition to guard against insurrection and
giving offense, so that we ourselves may not be the agents for the
desecration of God's holy word. Amen."[96]

Luther's dedicatory letter for *Temporal Authority: To What Extent It Should Be Obeyed* (1523) was addressed to John the Steadfast, elector of Saxony. This letter begins "Grace and peace in Christ."[97] This attitude is expressed even more clearly and more definitively in Luther's introduction to the *Ordinance of a Common Chest: Fraternal Agreement on the Common Chest of the Entire Assembly at Leisnig* (1523).

> Martin Luther, Ecclesiastic. To all Christians in the congregation of Leisnig, my dear sirs and brethren in Christ: Grace and peace from God the Father and our Savior Jesus Christ.
>
> Dear sirs and brethren. Since the Father of all mercies has called you as well as others to the fellowship of the gospel, and has caused his Son Jesus Christ to shine into your hearts; and since this richness of the knowledge of Christ is so active and powerful among you that you have set up a new order of service, and a common fund after the example of the apostles [Acts 2:44–45; 4:32–35], I have seen fit to have this ordinance of yours printed, in the hope that God will so add his gracious blessing that it may become a public example to be followed by many other congregations, so that we, too, may boast of you, as St. Paul boasted of the Corinthians that their effort stirred up many others [II Cor. 9:2]. Nevertheless, you will have to expect and take comfort from the fact that if what you are undertaking is of God it will necessarily meet with vigorous opposition, for Satan never rests or takes a holiday.[98]

It would hardly have been possible to express more strongly the Reformers' self-awareness of having restored the early and therefore authentic Christian church. The parallels to statements of the Pauline epistles are obvious.

4.9 The "Sermon on Preparing to Die" (1519)

Luther, however, could also speak with a simply amazing kind of authority even without using the forms of the New Testament epistles. This is true of his early work such as his lectures on Romans and especially for the beginning of these lectures.[99] This sense of authority shows itself much more strongly in the controversy on indulgences. It is, however, not only expressed in Luther's controversy with Rome, but also in his pastoral ministry. This is the case, for example, in *A Sermon on Preparing to Die* (1519).[100] In terms of its form as well as its content, this sermon belongs to a very broad category of literature on the art of dying *(ars moriendi)*. Comparisons with writings of this type are therefore also particularly instructive for an understanding of Luther.[101]

Luther clearly spoke as a pastor who wanted to help the dying prepare themselves spiritually for their departure from this world by placing their trust entirely in God. Luther also wrote with an authority that has no parallel elsewhere in the literature, however. This authority is derived not only from his Reformation understanding of faith but rather also from his almost apostolic sense of mission.

> You must not view or ponder death as such, not in yourself or in your nature, nor in those who were killed by God's wrath and were overcome by death. If you do that you will be lost and defeated with them. But you must resolutely turn your gaze, the thoughts of your heart, and all your senses away from this picture and look at death closely and untiringly only as seen in those who died in God's grace and who have overcome death, particularly in Christ and then also in all his saints.
>
> In such pictures death will not appear terrible and gruesome. No, it will seem contemptible and dead, slain and overcome in life.[102]

At the end of this sermon, Luther wrote, "What more should God do to persuade you to accept death willingly and not to dread but to overcome it? In Christ he offers you the image of life, of grace, and of salvation so that you may not be horrified by the images of sin, death, and hell. Furthermore, he lays your sin, your death, and your hell on his dearest Son, vanquishes them, and renders them harmless for you. In addition, he lets the trials of sin, death, and hell that come to you also assail his Son and teaches you how to preserve yourself in the midst of these and how to make them harmless and bearable."[103] "After all, you will have to let God be God and grant that he knows more about you than you do yourself."[104]

4.10 Luther's Sense of 'Authority'

In his spoken as well as in his written communications, Luther exercised an almost unheard-of authority. Probably the outstanding example of this is his letter to Frederick the Wise, the elector of Saxony, on March 5, 1522. At that time, Luther was on his way from the Wartburg to Wittenberg. In making this trip, he was acting contrary to the explicit instructions of the elector. In his letter he wrote:

> As for myself, Most Gracious Lord, I answer this: Your Electoral Grace knows (or, if you do not, I now inform you of the fact) that I have received the gospel not from men but from heaven only, through our Lord Jesus Christ, so that I might well be able to boast and call myself a minister and evangelist, as I shall do in the future. . . . I have written this so Your Electoral Grace might know that I am going to Wittenberg under a far higher protection than the Elector's. I have no intention of asking Your Electoral Grace for protection. Indeed I think I shall protect Your Electoral Grace more than you are able to protect me. And if I thought that Your Electoral Grace could and would protect me, I should not go. The sword ought not and cannot help a matter of this kind. God alone must do it—and without the solicitude and co-operation of men. Consequently he who believes the most can protect the most. And since I have the impression that Your Electoral Grace is still quite

weak in faith, I can by no means regard Your Electoral Grace as the man to protect and save me.[105]

And the sharpness of Luther's polemic over against the pope and many other ecclesiastical dignitaries must finally also be viewed in terms of his combined consciousness of an almost apostolic authority and a sense of his pastoral responsibility.

4.11 Research on Luther's Translation of the Bible

Luther integrated literary productivity, theological interpretation, and an "apostolic sense of mission." This appears most clearly in his translation of the Bible. In terms of the amount of work and the length of time that he devoted to this project, but especially in terms of its effect, it is by far his greatest literary work. Through his translation of the Bible Luther significantly influenced the use of the German language both by the common people and in literature for many centuries. This influence has continued far into the twentieth century. It is possibly coming to an end at present, however, because the knowledge of the Bible among large groups of the population has decreased remarkably. Where the Bible is still read, even in worship services, Luther's translation is frequently no longer used. We can, however, still study the history of Luther's effectiveness better than anywhere else by studying the influence of his translation of the Bible.

Of course, the great significance of Luther's translation of the Bible has been recognized for a long time and investigated by many scholars in many ways. In spite of this, we cannot say that this research has already been completed. Quite to the contrary, there are still many specific tasks and even whole areas in which research is only just beginning or in which in any case previous conclusions no longer can be simply accepted without revision.

Wilhelm Walther's work is basic to all recent research.[106] Walther compared Luther's translation of the Bible with older translations. He concluded that Luther's particular intention was to express the gracious will of God to which the Bible bears witness. In this process, however, Luther worked very carefully and did not give a one-sided interpretation of individual Bible passages in order to support his conclusions. Walther's studies of pre-Reformation translations of the Bible have been very stimulating to later scholars and have provided the basic impulse for many studies. Admittedly, Walther did not go far enough in his own work on this point. Rather, Walther, like many later scholars, has only chosen individual examples in order to illuminate Luther's translation; he did not undertake any systematic investigation of larger sections of the Bible.

In the decades following, the studies of Gustav Roethe are particularly noteworthy.[107] Roethe attempted to demonstrate that Luther always translated with the older German translations of the Bible, particularly the Zainer Bible (Augsburg, 1475), before him. Roethe concluded that Luther, however, systematically modernized both the vocabulary and the grammar of these translations. Roethe still concluded, however, that Luther worked independently and creatively—especially when he was translating the Bible. Luther's translation is particularly characterized by being shorter, by being both deeper and simpler, and by using terms directly related to the experience of the senses. As a result, it has rightly become a classical work of the German language. The Bible was renewed in Luther and was born again from his soul.

As far as the relationship between Luther's translation and the older German translations of the Bible is concerned, Hans Vollmer[108] properly warned against devaluing the earlier translations. In a variety of studies, Vollmer cast new light on the interaction between the Bible and German culture. Basically, there was before Luther something very like a German Vulgate. Vollmer, however, had not explored this very remarkable thesis comprehensively and therefore had not tested its validity.

In a brief study, Heinrich Bornkamm attempted to determine the relationship of Luther's translation to the original text, to the Vulgate, and particularly also to Erasmus's edition of the New Testament. He concluded that Luther did not prefer any one source over the others. Bornkamm concluded that Luther particularly did not make use of the Zainer Bible. The similarity between Luther's translation and many older German translations of the Bible is probably due to the fact that they were available to Luther in his memory, but there is no reason to speak of literary dependence. Bornkamm described two major tasks of research in this area: a comprehensive comparison of the style of Luther's translation with that of other versions and an unbiased evaluation of earlier German translations.[109]

In recent decades, Heinz Bluhm has presented his research on Luther's translation of the Bible in numerous essays. His book, *Martin Luther: Creative Translator*,[110] demonstrates that Luther functioned as a coauthor of the biblical texts. Through his Reformation theology, through the power of his language, and through his ability to internalize the statements of the biblical texts and thus to experience their truth in his own life, Luther was, in a certain sense, able to create the text for a second time in German. Sometimes, Luther's translation is even better than the biblical original because it is based on his deep religious experience. Thus Luther created a Bible for the Germans out of the spirit of the original Bible. Bluhm attempted to substantiate this position primarily through an investigation of Luther's translation of Pauline texts.[111]

Siegfried Raeder has attempted to evaluate Luther's method of translation in the context of his biblical hermeneutics.[112] Working primarily with Luther's *On Translating: An Open Letter* (1530),[113] Raeder attempted to demonstrate that Luther's work is based on three presuppositions: being free from the letter of the text, being bound to the letter of the text, and finding the clearest expression of the meaning and substance of the text. In addition, Raeder, on the basis of certain typical examples, demonstrated how Luther himself applied these three basic principles. As a result of this remarkable study, we now see Luther's philological and theological understanding of the text as a unity. Luther's "interpretive translation" of the Bible into his own language rose beyond a merely literal reproduction of the words and—with an amazing freedom in relation to the literal meaning—attempted to arrive at the meaning of the substance of the text.

In fact, an evaluation of Luther's translation of the Bible can only succeed when his hermeneutic is also taken into account. Our study of Luther's translation of the Bible is not simpler but rather more difficult as a result, but it rests on a firmer foundation.

Beyond this, an exact exploration of Luther's translation of the Bible can only be undertaken by comparing, as thoroughly as possible, his translation with the sources available to him. We must also give attention not only to Luther's own translation of the Bible but also to his other translations of particular biblical passages, as well as to his commentaries. As far as Luther's other translations are concerned, it is important to note that he did not always refer back to his own translation of the Bible when he quoted the Bible. Rather, he frequently either quoted from memory or gave a fresh translation. His unusual acquaintance with the basic text of the Bible as well as with the Vulgate and the other German translations very often made it possible for him to quote from memory. And a study of Luther's biblical quotations that appear outside his translation of the Bible often helps us see his translation of the Bible more clearly.

As far as Luther's use of sources is concerned, no extensive explanation of the importance of comparing his translation as fully as possible with earlier translations is necessary. Luther was personally acquainted with some of the older translations of the Bible. In this connection, it should be noted that the traditional pericopes of the ancient church were naturally better known to many people than the larger and more expensive complete texts of the Bible. It is hardly possible to prove that Luther was really dependent on any of these older translations. At the same time, the close relationship between the language and content of Luther's translation and the older translations can help us to improve our understanding of Luther's translations. At the very least, the level of linguistic competence available at the time of Luther can be more exactly determined only through such a comparison.

In addition, however, knowledge of the theological interpretation of specific individual passages or pericopes in all of Luther's writings is of great importance for our evaluation of his translation of the Bible. Only by taking all that we know about Luther's theological interpretation of a passage into account can we determine the theological basis for Luther's translation with adequate certainty. We must also take into account the contemporary situation in which Luther was writing. Naturally, it is only possible to determine that Luther's translation was influenced by contemporary events in those situations in which we can demonstrate an almost direct "application" of the biblical text to a specific situation. These few passages, however, are unusually significant for they show us that Luther's translation of the Bible was intended to make the divine word relevant to his own historical situation. To put it very pointedly, God, who once spoke through the biblical authors in Greek and Hebrew, now communicated the same message in German through Luther's translation.

If we wish to take these various aspects into consideration in understanding the unique character of Luther's translation, we must not merely study individual passages that have been taken out of their context, but rather must very carefully examine longer sections of the text. In this respect, only a few beginnings have been made up until now and these efforts need to be continued.

4.12 Luther and the Development of Modern High German

Further investigation is also needed in order to determine the extent of Luther's participation in the decisive formation and the further development of Modern High German as a literary language. The detailed comparison of Luther's translation with the older translation of the Bible in particular will open up many new viewpoints. Particularly, the index of Luther's German words that is currently being prepared[114] will for the first time permit us to have a complete overview of Luther's use of the German language and will probably bring us many surprises with regard to both the antiquity and the meaning of many words. Obviously, the total picture of Luther's place in the history of the German language will probably not be significantly changed at any basic point through such studies.

The older literature, as well as many popular contemporary presentations, asserts that Luther created Modern High German as a literary language. The primary claim is that Luther's translation of the Bible established a unified and uniform German literary language. As a result of the studies of the last decades, however, it is no longer possible to support this view. The process of development of Modern High German is very complicated and extended over a long period of time. There can be no doubt, even on the basis of our present knowledge of the situation, that Luther played an extraordinarily important role in the history of the German language. Obviously, however, it is necessary to distinguish between Luther's significance for the spoken word and for the written word—although both aspects are naturally related to each other.

Modern High German actually began to develop in the fourteenth century. The East-Central German territories played a particularly significant role at this time. In many ways, the vocabulary that Luther used was already developed in the fourteenth century. Luther also used many grammatical constructions that were already used in the fourteenth century. German mysticism was particularly influential in these developments. It internalized the German language so that the mystics could use it to express their deep personal experiences. In so doing, mysticism not only changed the meaning of some words but also created new words. Without the benefit of this transformation of the German language that had already taken place in the late Middle Ages, Luther would hardly have been able to express his own insights and experiences in the way in which he did. Luther, however, also significantly reinforced and extended these developments that preceded him.

Latin, however, was still the language of choice of educated people in the sixteenth century. In 1520 about 90 percent of the published books were written in Latin. The percentage of German-language books rose slowly but did not exceed the number of Latin publications until late in the seventeenth century. This process of the constant increase in German-language publications took place independently of Luther. As a result of Luther's work, however, and particularly of his translation of the Bible, it was notably strengthened and took place much more quickly.

Several factors reinforced Luther's influence. Indeed, apart from these factors, it is hard to imagine him as having had very much influence at all. Obviously, the most important of these factors was the discovery of printing. Apart from this discovery, Luther would not have experienced the tremendous popular response to himself as a theologian and a reformer. His contribution to the history of the German language would also have been much more limited in scope if the art of printing had not yet been discovered. In addition, developments in the world of politics as well as the world of business made it desirable to use the German language alongside the Latin language. In response to this need, the so-called official language *(Kanzleisprache)* developed at various courts. This process began before Luther was born. Its continuation in the sixteenth century was not dependent on Luther's contributions. Luther himself made use of the official language of the Saxon chancellory. Already during his lifetime, his German was described as coming from Meissen. It was only natural for Luther, as his spelling adequately reveals, to use the Saxon language with which he was familiar. The official language of the Saxon chancellory, however, was particularly well suited to provide the vehicle through which northern and southern Germans could understand one another. To this extent, Luther was working under very favorable circumstances.

Obviously, however, these facts do not in any way lessen Luther's very important contributions to the development of Modern High German. Luther not only contributed to a movement that would have taken place without him but also decisively determined the nature of this movement especially through his translation of the Bible. Many of the words that he coined became part of the language, and other words basically took on the meaning that Luther gave to them. Luther listened to what the common people said in order to write German that they would be able to understand. His own German was not the usual German of that time, however. Rather, Luther was able to address both educated and uneducated people. This became clear already in the first edition of his translation of the New Testament (the September Testament), but was reconfirmed over and over again as his translation of the various Old Testament books appeared. The Luther translation of the Bible immediately became the most commonly used of all the Bible translations. In spite of the substantial price of one-and-one-half Gulden, the approximately three thousand copies of the first edition of the September Testament were quickly sold out. Between 1522 and 1533, eighty-five editions of Luther's New Testament were printed. And the Wittenberg publisher Hans Lufft, in the fifty years following the publication of the complete Bible in 1534, sold about one hundred thousand copies.

4.13 God's Word as Translated and Interpreted by Luther

Luther's translation of the Bible could enjoy this tremendous success only because it was of both the highest literary quality and the deepest religious character. And it was the use of the translation of the Bible that first really spread Luther's thinking among the people. At the beginning of the sixteenth century, possibly 3 to 4 percent of the German people were able to read. Naturally more of these people who were able to read lived in the cities than in the rural areas, and a considerable percentage of these people who were able to participate in the intellectual life of the time owned Luther's translation of the Bible. Since the Bible was consid-

ered to be by far the most important book of all, people read and heard
God's Word in the language and interpretation of Martin Luther. Although
Luther appears to be the prophet for only some of the German people,
we can say without a doubt that he was the proclaimer of God's Word for
all Germans. With regard to the development of Modern High German,
Luther undoubtedly made the Bible become the most significant popular
book, a role that it maintained for centuries. Apart from the work of
Luther, this kind of religious formation of Modern High German as a
literary language would certainly not have taken place.

4.14 Other Bible Translations in
the Early Sixteenth Century

Low German was still so widespread in northern Germany in the sixteenth century that as soon as parts of the Bible appeared in Luther's
translation, they were immediately rewritten in Low German. Obviously,
these translations into Low German, as well as the translations of the
Bible into various other vernacular languages, were decisively influenced
by the spirit of Luther's Bible and the Reformation. As a result, Luther also
spoke indirectly through them. In addition, Luther's translation of the
Bible set limits to the development of Low German as a literary language.
Even in the German-speaking section of Switzerland, Luther's translation
of the Bible was influential, together with the Zurich Bible. It is true that
many idioms and expressions characteristic of the Alemannic dialect
found their way into Swiss editions of Luther's Bible. But Luther also
advanced the influence of Modern High German in Switzerland through
his translation of the Bible.

The powerful influence of Luther's Bible and its significance for Modern High German is also apparent from the fact that even Bible translators
in areas that remained faithful to Rome frequently made use of Luther's
translation. For example, Hieronymus Emser (1478–1527) was one of
Luther's most enthusiastic opponents. When he responded to many re-
quests by publishing his own translation of the New Testament, however,
he made broad use of Luther's translation. Emser's translation was even
published with a foreword written by Duke George of Saxony. And
Revelation or the apocalypse was illustrated with the pictures that Lukas
Cranach had prepared for Luther's translation. The ironical result of this
was that Emser's Roman Catholic translation thereby presented Rome as
the "Babylon" of the apocalypse. In addition, Emser added a postscript
that warned lay people against reading the Bible. And later reworkings of
this translation by Johann Dietenberger and John Eck still clearly reveal
the influence of Luther's translation of the New Testament. Thus Luther

extended his influence even through Roman Catholic translations of the Bible.

4.15 The Ongoing Revision of the Translation of the Bible

As long as he lived, Luther himself constantly revised his translation. Beginning in 1531 a commission for the revision of the Bible was formed.[115] Luther presented proofs of his translations to this commission after he had made his own handwritten corrections on them. During the meetings of the commission, Luther's translation was compared with the original text and with the Latin Vulgate, as well as with a variety of interpretations. The commission also concerned itself with finding the best German expression. In more than a few cases, very substantial changes were made in Luther's original text. Beyond this, Luther throughout his life always rethought the real meaning of various passages and in this process sometimes reached conclusions that were substantially different from his own translation.

A particularly interesting example of this process of revision is found in the lectures on Ps. 90:1 that Luther gave in 1534–35. In the translation of the Psalms, first published in 1524, and in later editions, Luther had translated the Hebrew word *Maon* as "refuge." The sense of the translation of 1524 is: "Lord you have become our refuge from generation to generation." In the editions of the Psalms published in 1531 and 1545 Luther eliminated the word for "become" so that the later translation reads: "Lord God you are our refuge from generation to generation."[116] In his lectures on Psalm 90, Luther suggested a possible change that never actually became part of his revision. He said, "The Hebrew word *Maon* really means 'dwelling place.' ... Since, however, a house serves the purpose of protecting its inmates, this term as employed by Moses means 'refuge' or 'place of refuge.'" In his commentary, Luther then translates "dwelling place" *(habitaculum)* rather than "refuge" *(refugium)*.[117] In this process, Luther was influenced by the wording of the Latin Vulgate, which in its translation of this passage is actually closer to the Hebrew text than Luther's German translation of the Psalms was. The translation "dwelling place" used in the lecture instead of "refuge" is of considerable theological significance. As Luther himself emphasized, the Scriptures usually understand people as God's temples in whom God dwells. In this passage, we are told that people are the inhabitants and that God is, in a certain sense, the house. Thus, according to this verse of Psalm 90, God is our place of residence and the godly people of the Old Covenant also rest in him.[118]

4.16 The Linguistic Gap Between Protestant and Roman Catholic Germany

Even though Luther's translation had indirect effect even in Roman Catholic territories and was influential for the development of the German language as used throughout Germany, it is on the other hand also true that it deepened the gap between the language used in the Protestant and Roman Catholic territories. In territories that remained Roman Catholic, Latin continued to be the language of educated people much longer than in Protestant territories. The superior educational work of the Jesuits, beginning in the latter half of the sixteenth century, enabled them to overcome the advantage that the schools and universities of the Reformation had originally gained. The Jesuits' educational work, with its emphasis on the use of Latin, however, actually delayed the development of a German national language. Such a national language developed later in Germany than in France or England. Apart from this strong emphasis on the use of Latin, it is to some extent also possible to observe differences in the meaning of German words in Protestant and Roman Catholic territories. In many significant cases, the Reformers' understanding of the meaning of words did not prevail. This is particularly clear from the example of a word such as "calling" *(Beruf)*. Luther, of course, did not create the word itself. Rather, the new understanding of this word had already been spread by the German mystics. To be sure, Luther was the first who provided a theological basis for understanding "calling" in the sense of secular work. He was also the first who overcame the assumption that monasticism or ministry are higher than other secular callings. Through the Reformation, this understanding of calling was very widespread and also prevailed linguistically. In Roman Catholic territories, however, "calling" continued to describe the vocation to enter a religious order, as it had in the Middle Ages. As a result, ethics continued to be described in two stages, one for the laity and a higher ethic for the clergy.

4.17 Suggestions and Advice for Reading Luther

How should one begin to read Luther? If someone knows very little about Luther, what book will it be most useful to begin with? How can we work our way more deeply into Luther's thinking? Naturally, the various interests that we bring with us to Luther are different so that there is no one piece of advice that will apply to all. In spite of this, however, there are certain basic rules that we should all take into consideration.

4.18 The Use of Editions

If we wish to engage in serious Luther research, we should use only the scholarly editions of Luther's works, that is, apart from special editions of individual works, the Weimar Edition *(WA)*,[119] the Clemen Edition *(Cl)*,[120] and the new study edition.[121] Editions that modernize Luther's German are useful.[122] Such editions make it easier for beginners to find their way into Luther's German writings. In spite of this, however, these editions cannot take the place of the scholarly editions—not only because of their different orthography and the sound of the words, but also because of the comments in the scholarly apparatus (quotations, sources, references, extensive introductions, etc.). As far as the Latin writings of Luther are concerned, translations will obviously be a help for most students. For scholarly work, however, only the original text should be used.

[For those who read English, the American Edition of Luther's Works *(LW)* is an exceptionally good resource.[123] The nineteenth-century emigrants brought surprisingly large numbers of the Erlangen Edition with them.[124] And the St. Louis Edition is frequently available.[125] Thus, although there are only a limited number of copies of the Weimar Edition available in the United States, much can be achieved through the use of the translation and the older editions of Luther's Works in conjunction with the Clemen Edition. Correlations of the various editions—and also chronological listings of Luther's writings—have been made available by Kurt Aland and others.[126] Heinrich J. Vogel[127] has correlated the American, St. Louis, Weimar, and Erlangen editions of Luther's Works. This is a useful tool in tracing a reference when a specific edition is not immediately available.—Trans.]

4.19 The Importance of Knowledge About the Contemporary Situation

An indispensable presupposition for working with Luther is a basic knowledge of the historical situation in which he worked as well as of his life. This means that we must be acquainted with the basic elements of the political, social, ecclesiastical, and intellectual and cultural situation of the sixteenth century—more specifically, the conditions in the papal curia, the role of the papal church state in politics, the financial exploitation of the empire for the purposes of the curia, sacramental piety, the nature of questions about salvation, the often very explicit superstitions of the time, as well as the nature of class and rank in society and social relationships. Particularly in thinking about the early period of the Reformation and Luther's early writings, we need to be aware of the role and function of a university during the late Middle Ages and its special right to raise critical questions about the most sacred dogmas in the course of academic disputations.

4.20 The Central Themes of Luther's Theology

Anyone who is interested only in one particular question related to
Luther must still give a certain amount of attention to the central aspects
of Reformation theology. Obviously, we are free to focus primarily, for
example, on Luther's relationship to government, on his actions during
the Peasants' War, on his view of law and justice, or on some other
specific question. And naturally, no one can be expected to be acquainted
fully with the whole theological discussion. It is, however, obvious that,
no matter what Luther did, he was primarily concerned with expressing
the primary content of Scripture in its real sense. Any investigation of an
individual problem must therefore take place in relationship to the
central focus of all of Luther's thinking.

For example, no matter how we may evaluate Luther's statements at the
time of the Peasants' Revolt, he finally did not see this as a matter of
political judgment but rather as a question of what, in obedience to the
Bible and with a good conscience, can be done and what must be
forbidden and forcibly prevented. Similarly, Luther's view of law and
justice can only be viewed in relationship to his understanding of law and
gospel as well as of his doctrine of human nature. This principle has
sometimes been expressed by saying that we should not think that we
have understood any particular idea of Luther's unless we have brought it
into relationship to his doctrine of justification. Taking Luther seriously as
a theologian in this way does not mean that we must follow him uncritically, but rather the standards by which we evaluate Luther must
include the standards by which he wanted his own work to be measured.
The critical examination of Luther's thinking is not in any way excluded
in such a procedure.

This means that we can never work our way into Luther's thought on
the basis of only one type of his writings but should always take at least
two types into consideration. For example, if we are studying Luther's
controversy with Rome, we should also study some of his meditative
interpretations of Scripture, such as *The Magnificat*.[128] Similarly, if we are
studying Luther's focus on the authority of government, we should also
take his actual attitude over against ecclesiastical and secular officials into
account. If we are studying Luther's criticism of the medieval doctrine
and practice of the sacraments, we should also take Luther's own doctrine
of the sacraments and his sacramental piety into consideration. Each of
Luther's writings, almost each of his sentences, have their own unique
character. Each instance where we think we have identified a particular
pattern of thought in Luther's writings, however, must be tested to prove
that it does not mean something else. We must, however, not only

positively prove each conclusion that we have identified such a pattern of thought that was unique to Luther, but rather we must also prove that no one else in the church had already expressed the same idea.

A serious word of advice: Because of the variety of contexts that we have already described in Luther's writings, it is especially necessary to warn against quoting his statements out of their context. Precisely because almost all of Luther's writings were written in response to a specific situation and because they each concern themselves with a specific topic, the exact analysis of each individual text is of decisive importance. In many monographs on Luther's thought, this absolutely necessary principle has been violated. As a result, the authors have imposed an alien systematic framework on Luther.

A theologian can be expected to have studied closely a series of Luther's writings. It is highly recommended that a student begin by reading the documents contained in the first four volumes of the Clemen Edition of Luther's selected work for this basic orientation to Luther's work.[129]

[Theodore G. Tappert[130] has edited a similar selection of English translations for the use of the student who can read English, but not Latin or German. Tappert's volumes should be supplemented with the other documents in *LW* 31 and 32; *The Magnificat* (1520/21); *The Bondage of the Will; Confession Concerning Christ's Supper* (1528); The Large Catechism (1528); The Smalcald Articles; and *Against Hanswurst.* —Trans.]

It is never enough for a theologian to be acquainted only with Luther's three Reformation writings of 1520: *To the German Nobility; The Babylonian Captivity of the Church;* and *The Freedom of a Christian.* This is true even though these writings—because of their development of the doctrine of the priesthood of all believers, of the Reformation understanding of the sacraments, as well as of the understanding of freedom—are particularly significant. Together with these writings, *The Bondage of the Will* should be the focal point of a study of Luther. In addition, a theologian must also be familiar with Luther's Ninety-five Theses on Indulgences, some of the sermons of 1519, *The Magnificat,* and The Smalcald Articles. A thorough knowledge of these writings is the necessary basis for gaining a definite overview of the theology of the Reformation.

In addition, a theologian should have some knowledge of Luther's early lectures. Selections from these have been edited in the fifth volume of Clemen and a translation of the lectures on Romans is available in the second supplementary volume of the Munich edition. In addition, a theologian should have read Luther's early exegetical lectures on the Psalms, Romans, Hebrews, and Galatians.[131]

Anyone who is majoring in religion should at least read the three main Reformation writings, The Smalcald Articles, and one or the other of Luther's books dealing with political ethics.

What follows is a detailed discussion of most of Luther's writings referred to above. The sequence is generally organized on a chronological basis.

4.21 The Marginal Notes 1509–10

No one should begin to study Luther's early writings until gaining an overview of his Reformation theology in the period from 1517 to 1520. Luther's marginal notes on Augustine and Peter Lombard from 1509 to 1510[132] present special problems. These first extensive theological comments or glosses were made by Luther for his own use in his desk copies of these books. They can therefore only be understood in the context of the texts of the writings of Augustine and Lombard to which they refer. In addition, the reader must also have an understanding of Luther's corresponding viewpoint after 1517. The briefness of these marginal notes frequently makes it very difficult to interpret their meaning.

4.22 The Early Lectures

The selections of the lectures from the period 1513 to 1518 provided in *Cl* 5 represent a very excellent choice.[133] It is, however, not so easy to work one's way into these lectures. Particular difficulties will be encountered in studying the *First Lectures on the Psalms* (1513–15)—at least as long as the new edition in volume 55 of the Weimar Edition is not yet available. In studying these lectures, it is especially necessary to have some knowledge of the tradition of exegesis before Luther. Much of this required background information will, to a great extent, be provided by the new edition of these lectures. Particularly in studying the *First Lectures on the Psalms*, it is very important not to take Luther's statements out of context. In any case, we must read larger sections of these lectures in order to avoid the danger of a one-sided view of what Luther is saying. The lectures on Romans (1515–16), Galatians (1516–17), and Hebrews (1517–18) are much easier to work with than Luther's *First Lectures on the Psalms*. Each year Luther more clearly thought through and sharply defined his theology, as can easily be demonstrated on the basis of central topics such as sin, grace, righteousness, faith, and good works.

The Heidelberg Disputation[134] clearly defines Luther's understanding of the theology of the cross in contrast to the theology of glory. This contrast together with Luther's rather rough description of his doctrine of grace and election defined the focus of his theological work in his early lectures. Although this disputation took place after the controversy on indulgences had already begun, that is, in April 1518, Luther's statement of his central theological thinking was the basic content of this disputation and the day-to-day events of the controversy receded into the background.

4.23 Luther's Writings Related to the Controversy on Indulgences

Luther's statements on the controversy on indulgences can be fully understood only on the basis of a thorough knowledge of his early lectures. Anyone beginning their study of Luther will, however, still find it easiest to start with the controversy on indulgences. A thorough knowledge of the history of indulgences and particularly of the decree proclaiming the indulgence issued by Albert of Mainz is important for an understanding of Luther's theses.[135] Luther's *Ein Sermon von Ablass und Gnade*[136] provides a good comparison to the *Disputation on the Power and Efficacy of Indulgences,* commonly called the Ninety-five Theses.[137] By comparing and contrasting these two documents, we can see how Luther's Latin and German writings are related to each other. It is useful to ask whether all of the critical questions about indulgences raised in the Latin text of the Ninety-five Theses reappear in the German text of the *Sermon.* If some of these critical comments are not repeated, we need to identify those that are omitted and to explore the reasons for their omission.

In the winter of 1517–18, Luther prepared his *Explanations of the Disputation Concerning the Value of Indulgences,* also called *Explanations of the Ninety-five Theses.*[138] This has properly been referred to as Luther's first true Reformation writing. The significance of the *Explanations* does not lie in their external form, which simply follows the Ninety-five Theses point-for-point, but rather in their content: Luther's new understanding of grace, the sacraments, faith, justification, and ecclesiastical authority is much more clearly and sharply presented here than in the Ninety-five Theses. In reading the *Explanations,* it is important to take into account the fact that Luther by this time had already been accused of heresy. The section titled "Conclusio XV"[139] is particularly significant in terms of Luther's own spiritual temptations. In addition, the *Explanations* indicate that while Luther still recognized the authority of the pope, which he saw as being established by Romans 13, he now obviously understood it only as human authority, that is, as granted to the pope not by God but by the church. Thus, Luther had, by this time, made a very significant change in his understanding of the church.[140] In studying Luther's writings on indulgences, we need to observe which themes are of significance in connection with the question of indulgences and which themes are not directly related to indulgences but increasingly become the focus of the discussion.

4.24 The Sermons of 1519–20

The sermons of 1519–20 stand alone as a specific group of Luther's writings.[141] In these treatises, Luther dealt very specifically with topics such as the sacraments of penance, baptism, and the Lord's Supper. In addition, Luther instructed people how to "prepare to die." He also discussed excommunication, good works, and the liturgy.[142]

These treatises are definitely not polemical but, rather, are intended for the edification of their readers. They presuppose some theological knowledge and at the same time are intended to be read by educated lay people. In these treatises, we can observe the masterful way in which Luther further developed the doctrine of the Lord's Supper and presented it in a very understandable way. The fact that Luther treated penance, baptism, and the Lord's Supper demonstrates that the other four sacraments—ordination, marriage, confirmation, and the last rites—had already receded into the background of his thinking. This is true even though he did not assert that these four are not really sacraments until he wrote *The Babylonian Captivity of the Church*. (See below, 4.27.)

It is important to note that Luther's understanding of the nature of the sacrament at this time had its own character when compared to both the scholastic doctrine and Luther's own later view. Thus his understanding of the gift of the sacraments, particularly the Lord's Supper, very soon changed. For example, Luther began *A Treatise on the New Testament, That Is, the Holy Mass* (1520) by discussing the words of institution rather than with a general definition of the sacraments.[143] In general, these sermons show us Luther's attempt to discuss basic theological questions from the viewpoint of the Reformation in a way that would be useful for a wider public and that was not merely related to the controversies of the day—although Luther was very much engaged in these.

4.25 "On the Papacy in Rome"

Luther's *On the Papacy in Rome, Against the Celebrated Romanist in Leipzig*[144] was published in 1520. This book is of considerable significance—both in terms of our understanding of Luther's controversy with Rome and of its own content. This was the first book that Luther wrote in German dealing with the questions at issue in his controversy with the theologians who represented the papacy. Luther, however, did not take the initiative in carrying on the argument in a writing accessible to persons able to read German. On the contrary, he was responding to an

attack on him published in German by the Leipzig Franciscan Augustine
Alveld. This book had originally been published in Latin under the title
Super apostolica sede (Concerning the Apostolic See). Luther responded
in German only after Alveld had published a revised edition of his book in
German.[145] This illustrates how Luther—particularly in the years immediately following 1517—was often forced by his opponents to go further
than he himself wanted to.

Compared with Luther's later controversial writings, the polemical
tone of this book is still quite moderate. As far as the content is concerned, Luther expanded on statements that he had previously made,
particularly at the Leipzig Debate of 1519. These statements expressed
his thinking at that time about the church and the place of the pope in the
church. Up until this point, Luther had not dealt with these questions in
such an extensive way. Luther now expressed the idea that Christendom
is the congregation of all the believers in Christ on earth or a gathering in
the Spirit. He also asserted that it is necessary to distinguish between
Christendom as a spiritual and a physical entity. Only the spiritual Christendom is the true church. This true church has no head here on earth;
its only head is Christ, who is in heaven. We must be careful not to
interpret these statements of Luther as though he were thinking of an
invisible church. Even though many ideas might seem to point in this
direction, they must always be interpreted within the limits of the controversy. This controversy required Luther to express himself very
sharply. Therefore, if we wish to avoid a one-sided interpretation of
Luther's statements in this book, we must interpret them in terms of
Luther's many other writings about the church.

4.26 "To the Christian Nobility":
Luther as Advocate of Social Reform

In 1520 Luther also published *To the Christian Nobility of the German
Nation Concerning the Reform of the Christian Estate*.[146] This book
must be read against the background both of the longstanding official
protests against abuses in the life of the church *(gravamina)* presented
by the estates to the emperor at the imperial diets and the contemporary
discussion of the need for the reform of the church. This book is a part of
this discussion. Luther never again—neither before nor after this book—
made as many or as detailed proposals for reform. His proposals for
reform are, of course, primarily concerned with the life of the church.
They also deal, however, with the universities as well as with political and
social life. The most significant elements of this book, however, are not to
be found in these proposals for reform. Rather, the greatest significance of
this book lies in its theological basis. Specifically, Luther encouraged the

secular governments to take the initiative in reforming both the church and society because he no longer accepted the medieval idea that the spiritual estate is superior to the secular estate.

In place of the medieval assertion of the superiority of the spiritual over the secular estate, Luther asserted the thesis that all baptized are priests. Of course, it is not proper for everyone to exercise the office of a pastor or a bishop. In reading Luther, it is important to note that the distinction between all of the baptized as priests and as pastors can be expressed more exactly in Latin than in German: All of the baptized are priests *(sacerdotes)*, but only the pastors are the ministers *(ministri)*. This new theological approach led Luther to a significant transformation of the medieval view that the secular and spiritual authorities can each represent the other in an emergency. Luther still felt that the laity should help the church when this is necessary. In addition to this, Luther's sharp criticism of Rome also gave this book its far-reaching significance in world history. Luther summarized the various issues that arose in the controversy with the papacy with the picture of the three walls. Luther described the papacy as having established three walls as its three lines of defense against every attempt to reform it. The church built the first wall by asserting that the spiritual authorities are superior to the secular authorities. The second wall was the church's claim that only the pope may finally interpret the Scripture. And the third wall was the assertion that the pope is superior to the councils of the church. As a result, it had only recently become possible to assert the authority of the Scripture or of the councils over against the papacy. And the laity had been unable to do much at all. In this context, the doctrine of the universal priesthood of the baptized fulfilled the function of destroying these three walls built by the Roman Church. Thereby it freed the secular authorities to exercise their proper responsibility. In this book, as well as in his later book on government,[147] Luther supported the secular government in its assertion of independence over against the spiritual authority of the church. Of course, many of the people who supported Luther because of his opposition to Rome really disagreed with his theology on most other points.

4.27 "The Babylonian Captivity of the Church"

Luther's book addressed to the Christian nobility was concerned with external reforms. In the same year, 1520, Luther also discussed needed reforms in theology itself. Luther used *The Babylonian Captivity of the Church*[148] to discuss needed reforms in theology and particularly in the doctrine and administration of the sacraments. In this book—which Luther described as only a prelude to a far more basic and extensive discussion of this theme—Luther charged the Roman curia with having created and used the doctrine of the seven sacraments as the basis of its power. This charge was obviously historically inaccurate and could not be substantiated. The fact that Luther made this charge, however, was a sign of the fact that the papacy had become the central issue of the controversy.

Luther's criticism of the doctrine of the Lord's Supper was even more important. Whereas the letter to the nobility had described "walls," Luther now spoke of "captivities." The first captivity was the withholding of the wine from the laity in communion.[149] Luther incorrectly tried to describe this as the result of the tyranny of the Roman Church. The second captivity was the doctrine of transubstantiation, which Luther described as a human invention, but which actually was a responsible attempt to explain the mystery of Christ's presence in the sacrament. Luther defined the third captivity as the view that the celebration of the Mass is a good work and a sacrifice.

Luther labeled this third captivity of the doctrine of the sacrifice of the Mass as the worst of all. In order to understand Luther's own position as well as his attack on this doctrine, we must do more than compare his thinking with the scholastic doctrine of the Mass as it was taught, for example, by Thomas Aquinas. Rather, we can understand Luther's thinking at this point only by taking into account the almost magical piety that was then associated with the sacrifice of the Mass as well as the completely inadequate theology of the sacrifice of the Mass prevalent at that time.[150]

Luther's criticism of the other sacraments was basically less sharp than his critical analysis of the Mass. The reduction of the number of sacraments from seven to three or two—since Luther was not at all certain whether he thought of penance as a sacrament or not—cut deeply enough, however.

4.28 "The Freedom of a Christian"

Luther wrote his treatise *The Freedom a Christian*[151] in response to a suggestion made by Karl von Miltitz. In the autumn of 1520, Miltitz had, on his own initiative, attempted to reconcile Luther and Rome. *The Open Letter to Pope Leo X*[152]—which Luther printed as an introduction to this treatise on freedom—must be understood against the background of the situation in which it was written. Luther himself could not possibly have fully understood what was at that time actually happening in the relationship between himself and the papacy.

Luther described this book as containing the sum total of what he would have liked to teach about the Christian life. Luther began with the twofold thesis: "A Christian person is a free lord of everything and subject to no one. A Christian person is a ready servant of everything and subject to everyone."[153] This twofold thesis is the most successful and congenial statement of Paul's understanding of freedom ever achieved. On the basis of this understanding of freedom—and in full consistency with his own understanding of freedom—Luther would later criticize the demands for "fleshly" or physical freedom made by the peasants.[154] In this treatise, Luther established the connection between his doctrine of justification and the Reformation ethic. For our own study of Luther, it is useful to compare Luther's understanding of freedom in the years 1520 to 1521 with Melanchthon's understanding of freedom as developed in his *Loci communes*, published in 1521.[155] Similar comparisons could be made with Karlstadt's understanding of freedom[156] as well as with the Reformers' discussions of freedom during the Wittenberg Riots of 1521–22.[157]

4.29 "The Magnificat"

Luther's interpretation of the song of Mary, *The Magnificat*,[158] is a pearl among his interpretations of the Scriptures. Luther first worked on this manuscript from November 1520 through March 1521 in Wittenberg. His work was interrupted by his trip to Worms and he finished his work during the last part of May and the beginning of June 1521, while he was on the Wartburg. Neither the external confusion nor the inner tension of this period, however, is at all noticeable in the meditative style of this interpretation. Luther frequently demonstrated this ability to work simultaneously on completely different tasks. Indeed, it is sometimes hard to believe that two pieces of work written at the same time come from one and the same author. This reveals the extraordinary emotional and intellectual breadth of Luther. One way of observing Luther at work is to list what he did in a particular month and then to consider the variety of tasks and of topics as well as their possible interrelationships. In doing this, we should not ignore his extensive correspondence.

In terms of its content, *The Magnificat* is particularly important both for Luther's view of the virgin Mary as well as for his understanding of history.

4.30 Monastic Vows

The Judgment of Martin Luther on Monastic Vows[159] was written while Luther was on the Wartburg, within the brief space of some three weeks in November 1521. Before this, Luther had made occasional statements about monastic vows. Luther dedicated this book to his father who had earlier been so unhappy about his son's decision to enter the monastery. To this extent, this book can be understood as describing the way in which Luther came to terms with his own past. Obviously, the theological questions of monastic vows stand in the center of the discussion and the autobiographical problems only appear in the margins—just as Luther still continued to wear his monastic garb for several years. The careful outline of this book raises five basic questions about monastic vows. In so doing, it gives us unusually clear insights into the way in which Luther thought and argued. It should be noted that Luther continued to approve of monastic vows in a very limited sense.[160] This book on monastic vows was, as a matter of fact, Luther's last great controversy with Rome in those years. As such, it marks the end of his early period. Luther had already broken with the papacy and with the contemporary doctrine of the sacraments. In this book, he came to terms with the then commonly accepted principle that there were two sets of ethics: one for secular Christians and the other for monastics. Luther's argumentation cannot be adequately understood solely on the basis of a knowledge of the theology of monasticism. It is even more important to take into account the way in which these vows were actually understood by people at the time as well as the enormous social significance of the monasteries, particularly in the life of the cities.

4.31 "A Sincere Admonition Against Rebellion" (1522)

Following Luther's stay on the Wartburg and the disturbances that occurred in Wittenberg and elsewhere, the question of rebellion against as well as of obedience to the government became more significant. In the distance, the early warning signs of the approaching Peasants' War were clearly observable. Luther dealt with these problems in various publications. The booklet *A Sincere Admonition by Martin Luther to All Christians to Guard Against Insurrection and Rebellion* appeared in 1522.[161] This was Luther's response to his observations of the mood of the common people, observations that he made during his secret journey from the Wartburg to Wittenberg from December 4–9, 1521. Along the way, for example, he heard rumors of a coming mass murder of the clergy. Although Luther did not believe these rumors, he wanted to make his attitude concerning rebellion and insurrection clear.

4.32 The Limits of Obedience to Government

Luther wrote his book on the authority of the government toward the end of the year 1522: *Temporal Authority: To What Extent It Should Be Obeyed.*[162] This book was developed in response to specific situations at that time, especially to the decree issued by Duke George of Saxony demanding that all copies of Luther's translations of the New Testament be turned in and confiscated. Luther responded by developing his so-called doctrine of the two kingdoms, or of the two governments of God.

This doctrine is distorted when presented in an abstract systematized form that suggests we can understand Luther's position without first understanding the historical situation. On the contrary, this doctrine can be understood only in terms of the specific historical contexts in which it developed. It is particularly important to note that the basic theme of this book is the limits of the authority of the government and therefore also the limits of its claims to obedience.

4.33 The Reform of Worship

Luther first responded to the need for a new Protestant liturgy and discussed the problems connected with its development in 1523. He first published his very brief essay *Concerning the Order of Public Worship*[163] and followed it almost immediately with his more extensive *An Order of Mass and Communion for the Church at Wittenberg* (1523),[164] which also contains an order of worship. It is useful to compare Luther's position in this book with contemporary Protestant revisions of the liturgy— such as that of Thomas Müntzer. Such a comparison reveals that Luther was also conservative in the area of liturgical reform.

4.34 Educational Reform

To the Councilmen of All Cities in Germany That They Establish and Maintain Christian Schools[165] was published in 1524. This demonstrates the effects of the Reformation movement on education. Luther stated the basic presupposition of this book: "Let us be sure of this: we will not long preserve the gospel without the languages," that is, Hebrew and Greek.[166]

4.35 Capitalism and Lending Money for Interest[167]

This book demonstrates Luther's continuing interest in social and political questions. There is, however, no reason to describe Luther as an expert in economics—even if we take his other statements on these matters into account.[168] Luther's decisive presupposition is that since the gospel has once again been brought to the light of day, it condemns and denounces many works of darkness—in particular, greed. Luther's criticism of various abuses is worth our attention in this connection. His own proposals were not developed on the basis of detailed knowledge of the then-prevailing economic relationships, however, even though such relationships were very well understood by some of his contemporaries. By and large, Luther's attitude on questions of economics was very conservative.[169]

4.36 The Peasants' War (1525)

The uprising of the peasants in the spring of 1525 caused Luther to publish several items. Among these are: *Admonition to Peace, A Reply to the Twelve Articles of the Peasants in Swabia,*[170] *Against the Robbing and Murdering Hordes of Peasants,*[171] *Vertrag zwischen dem löblichen Bund zu Schwaben und den zwey Haufen der Bauern vom Bodensee und Allgäu. Luthers Vorrede und Vermahnung,*[172] and *An Open Letter on the Harsh Book Against the Peasants.*[173]

We can read Luther's writings about the Peasants' War from quite different perspectives. One approach is to examine the development of the peasant uprising and its basic characteristics—these are still difficult to determine accurately. Another approach is to examine Luther's influence on the specific demands made by the peasants and the interaction between the Reformation and the peasant movement. Still another approach is to investigate the establishment of the territorial state and the ways in which Luther supported this movement as well as the ways in which the peasants also contributed to it. We can also focus on Luther's political ethics or even on the ways in which his writings affected the outcome of the Peasants' War. Whatever approach we take to this question, we should avoid prematurely condemning one or the other of the movements or of the persons involved and, insofar as possible, attempt to maintain an unprejudiced attitude.

4.37 "The Bondage of the Will"

Luther's treatise *The Bondage of the Will*[174] is in many respects the most difficult of Luther's writings to interpret.[175] This is true not only because its internal structure, the point of departure, and the goal of Luther's argumentation are unusually disputed among scholars but also because this book must always be read in terms of Luther's controversy with Erasmus. Erasmus himself, however, in writing *On the Freedom of the Will: A Diatribe or Discourse*[176] did not achieve the high level of thoughtfulness and clarity that he ordinarily reached in his discussions of the ideas of God and the freedom of the will.

In studying Luther's book we should first carefully analyze what he said and clarify our own personal view of his presentation. In doing so, we may give particular attention to Luther's discussion of the relationship of necessity *(necessitas)* to compulsion *(coactio),* to our freedom to choose *(liberum arbitrium vs. servum arbitrium)* or to the contrast between the hidden God and the revealed God *(Deus absconditus vs. Deus revelatus).*

Beginners will find it somewhat more difficult but very rewarding to compare the positions of Luther and Erasmus with corresponding views in the earlier theological tradition, especially with the views of Augustine, Aquinas, Ockham, Gabriel Biel, or the views commonly accepted in the Renaissance. Comparing Luther's with Melanchthon's radically different positions in the first and the last editions of his *Loci*[177] or with that of other sixteenth-century theologians can make us aware of the great variations in thinking among the Reformers themselves. In any case, the Lutheran confessions did not adopt the more extreme assertions made by Luther in *The Bondage of the Will.*[178] And in his later writings even Luther himself usually discussed the question of predestination from the viewpoint of Christology.

4.38 The Lord's Supper

Luther's *Confession Concerning Christ's Supper* (1528)[179] is Luther's final extensive statement in the controversy with Zwingli on the Lord's Supper. We must read this book in the context both of our knowledge that the doctrine of the Lord's Supper played a different role in Luther's thinking than in Zwingli's and of the preceding controversy. It is also important to follow exactly the differences in the chain of argument, particularly the way in which Luther and Zwingli interpret "flesh" in John 6:63 ("the flesh is of no avail").

Such a comparison reveals the different approaches to interpretation of the Scripture as these are revealed in Luther's and Zwingli's divergent understandings not only of the word "is" but also of other scriptural assertions such as, "the Rock was Christ" (1 Cor. 10:4). Similarly, we should note the ways in which Luther and Zwingli both asserted that the unworthy reception of the Lord's Supper has physical effects on the recipient (1 Cor. 11:30). Luther's development of the doctrine of ubiquity, the relation of this doctrine to late scholastic thinking, and its significance in Luther's controversy with Zwingli may also be studied. It is also rewarding to compare the development of Luther's and Zwingli's thinking about the Lord's Supper with that of Calvin. It is particularly interesting to study the way in which the various doctrines influenced the ways in which the consecrated but undistributed bread and wine were dealt with. Similar studies may be made of the relationship of teachings about the Lord's Supper to penance and to the various regulations governing liturgical practice *(Kirchenordnungen)*. All of these studies will also help us to compare and contrast the various understandings of the gift communicated in the Lord's Supper.

Finally, Luther's personal confession of faith at the end of this book is of great significance.[180] This personal confession greatly influenced the development of Protestant confessions up to and including the Augsburg Confession. It clearly illustrates the way in which Luther combined his soteriological focus with his reception of the creeds of the early church.

4.39 The Large Catechism (1529)

The Large Catechism[181] developed out of Luther's involvement in the visitation of churches and schools carried out in Electoral Saxony. This catechism is the most comprehensive overview of the basic questions of dogmatics that Luther himself ever wrote. It may therefore—in a limited sense—be understood as a replacement for the dogmatics that he never wrote. For a closer study of the Large Catechism,[182] the following topics are particularly recommended: (1) a comparison with older catechisms; (2) a comparison of the Large Catechism with Luther's treatises on parts of the catechism from the first years of the Reformation; (3) a comparison of the statements about God in the Large Catechism with those in *The Bondage of the Will*. Similar comparisons could also be made of all the important theological questions in the Large Catechism and Luther's corresponding discussions of these questions in other writings. Any of these studies would be very rewarding. Such studies can make us aware of how much the current polemical situation influenced various formulations. The views expressed by Luther in the Large Catechism are, for the most part, not influenced by such polemical situations.

4.40 Luther and the Augsburg Confession

The *Exhortation to All Clergy Assembled at Augsburg*[183] was Luther's most significant contribution to the Diet of Augsburg in 1530. Luther addressed this to "all the clergy assembled at Augsburg" and thus not only to the Lutheran clergy. In comparison with Luther's other writings, his statements in this book are much less polemical. In place of polemicizing, Luther addressed the conscience of the clergy and pleaded with them to do everything possible "to do and accomplish much and great good through this diet."[184] Luther warned, however, that if the diet were to end without any significant results having been achieved, the people would become impatient and despair. Luther described himself as addressing this writing to the clergy only because he was so aware of the threatening dangers. This writing was therefore very important for Luther's political thinking at the time. In addition, Luther discussed a series of individual questions—including indulgences—that are not mentioned in the Augsburg Confession.

In order to gain a comprehensive picture of Luther's literary participation in the Diet of Augsburg, we should also consider the many letters that he wrote during this diet.[185]

4.41 Luther as Translator

On Translating: An Open Letter (1530)[186] gives us insight into the way in which Luther translated the Bible. He reported frequently using the help of other scholars such as Melanchthon or the Hebrew scholar Aurogallus. In addition, this brief writing is important for our understanding of Luther's hermeneutic—that is, his method of interpretation. It is rewarding to use this booklet as a guide and to explore the passages that it discusses in the Weimar Edition of Luther's Bible.[187] This edition provides the differing formulations used by Luther in the various revisions of the German Bible. By comparing these versions, we can each gain our own impression of how Luther constantly worked to improve his translation.[188]

4.42 A Word of Warning

Dr. Martin Luther's Warning to His Dear German People[189] was written by Luther in October 1530 as his response to the threatening situation that developed after the Diet of Augsburg. It was intended to strengthen the weak. Luther spoke far more sharply about the "papists" in this writing than he had in *Exhortation to All Clergy Assembled at Augsburg.*[190] As a result of the Diet of Augsburg, all hopes for improving relationships between the parties had disappeared. Luther was now worried that the emperor would begin to wage war against the Protestants. In Luther's opinion, such an action would be a battle against the gospel and therefore also a battle against God. This writing is particularly important for Luther's thinking about Germany as a nation. The student should compare it with another of Luther's writings, for example, *To the Christian Nobility of the German Nation Concerning the Reformation of the Christian Estate,*[191] in order to be able to trace the development of Luther's role in the movement to establish a German nation.

4.43 The Smalcald Articles

Luther wrote The Smalcald Articles in December 1536; they were published in 1537. Pope Paul III had summoned a council to convene in Mantua at Pentecost of 1537. The Protestant estates made intensive preparations for this council. Luther wrote these articles at the request of the Elector of Saxony—but also as his own personal position paper. In his outline, Luther took the elector's suggestions into consideration. In writing about each topic, however, he made his own judgment as to whether a particular article of doctrine was one on which there was common agreement, or whether it affected the basic understanding of the person and work of Jesus Christ. Luther also identified some "matters which we may discuss with learned and sensible men or even among ourselves."[192]

In spite of their generally polemical tone, The Smalcald Articles remain a significant contribution to the theological conversation—as long as Luther's threefold differentiation of the doctrines under discussion is taken into account. It will be particularly useful to compare Luther's statement on the Lord's Supper in The Smalcald Articles with the Wittenberg Concord of 1536.[193]

4.44 "On the Councils and the Church"

On the Councils and the Church,[194] published in 1539, is particularly important for our understanding of Luther's doctrine of the church as well as his view of the tradition of the early church and the significance of the decrees of the councils.

4.45 "Against Hanswurst"

Like On the Councils and the Church, Against Hanswurst[195] is a very important resource for our understanding of Luther's doctrine of the church. In addition, it is important for Luther's position in the conflict between Duke Henry of Braunschweig-Wolfenbüttel and Elector John Frederick of Saxony and Landgrave Philip of Hesse.

In both books, Luther came to terms with the Roman Church's claim to be the only true church. He discussed the marks of the church and identified these marks as they appear in the visible form of the church from the time of the early church to the sixteenth century. At the same time, Against Hanswurst particularly demonstrates how the polemics of the older Luther became increasing immoderate.[196]

4.46 Luther's Memories of the Beginning
of the Reformation

Luther used the Preface to the Complete Edition of Luther's Latin Writings (Wittenberg, 1545)[197] to reminisce about the beginnings of the Reformation and the path by which he arrived at the insights that led to the Reformation.

For a long time, these memories were the primary focus of discussions about when the Reformation actually began and when Luther gained the insights that resulted in the breakthrough.[198] Luther's description of the beginning stages of the Reformation has been interpreted in a variety of ways. In spite of this, however, this text remains one of the most important for our understanding of the "catastrophic event" and of the insights with which the Reformation began. Any interpretation of the breakthrough that contradicts Luther's own memories of it, in my opinion, is and remains unusually mischievous.

In any case, however, Luther's view of the whole early period of the Reformation is particularly interesting because the chief actor himself gives a retrospective description of events. This self-testimony is obviously not a "primary source" in the direct sense of the term, but can be regarded only as a secondary source.

It is not necessary at this point to do more than mention Luther's letters,[199] sermons,[200] and table talk.[201]

4.47 The Later Academic Disputations[202]

The text of these important disputations show us Luther, in the latter years of his life, at work as a theological scholar and give us a better perspective on his work than his later lectures do. In addition, Luther's concern for pure doctrine becomes particularly clear in these disputations. The subjects of some of these disputations were the doctrines of God, Christ, and the nature of the human being.

The other disputations dealing with antinomianism are particularly important. Luther used these disputations to express his sharp disagreement with Johann Agricola. In doing that, he presented his doctrine of law and gospel and defined its meaning over against various interpretations. Luther was, however, not able to prevent an outbreak of the dispute about the third use of the law soon after his death; nor was he able to prevent others from falsely attributing the doctrine of the third function of the law—that the law is the norm of the life of the Christian as a regenerate person—to him.[203] Luther's understanding of law and gospel can be studied more comprehensively on the basis of these disputations than anywhere else in his writings. It is, however, obviously necessary also to give attention to the way in which Luther practically applied the distinction between law and gospel in his sermons, expert opinions, and so forth.

The Disputation Concerning Man discusses the doctrine of the human being in a particularly broad and deep manner.[204]

5 | ASPECTS AND PROBLEMS OF LUTHER'S THEOLOGY

In this section, I shall not attempt to summarize the most important themes of Luther's theology. Rather, I shall analyze a series of important points that illustrate special problems that we need to consider in our study of Luther's theology. Some of these problems are not receiving adequate attention in current research. By focusing attention on these problems, I hope that this section will also contribute to the discussion of the most basic questions of contemporary Luther research.

5.1 THE METHODOLOGY OF DESCRIBING LUTHER'S THEOLOGY

The question as to whether and how it is possible to describe Luther's theology adequately has a number of differing but quite important dimensions.

5.1.1 Luther Made No Claim to Be an Innovative Theologian

First, we must ask ourselves whether Luther's self-understanding of his role as a theologian permits us to undertake the task of describing Luther's theology and whether such a description will serve any useful purpose. As already pointed out (see above, 3.43), Luther did not want people to call themselves Lutherans, because he did not want to be anyone's master or teacher.

Luther thus never claimed to have done anything new in theology. He never even claimed to have created a new point of departure for systematic theology that was superior to his predecessors. In declining to make such a claim, Luther agreed with almost all the theologians of the early and medieval church as well as Eastern Orthodox theologians down to the present day. The attempt to find a unique approach to the central questions of faith or to the relationship between theology and philosophy is a typically modern undertaking. The first theologian consciously to claim such a new and better approach was Gotthold Ephraim Lessing. He asserted the superiority of his method in contrast to the method of

139

Protestant Orthodoxy. Since Schleiermacher, such a claim has been made by many theologians.

Obviously, Luther's failure to claim that he had done something new does not mean that he actually did not do so. This same statement would be true for the theologians of the early church as well as of the medieval church. For example, theologians like Augustine, Anselm of Canterbury, or Peter Abelard represented new and decisive breakthroughs in theological method. Indeed, any critical confrontation of other theological or philosophical schools certainly indicates that the author is trying to develop his or her own new and unique perspective on theology. Since Luther more strongly and thoroughly criticized the traditional theology of his time than any of his predecessors had done, he certainly intended to develop his own independent approach to theology. Luther's goal, however, was not to develop further or transform theological thought but rather to return to the true doctrine that was present and—in spite of all later corruption—always available in Scripture.

Thus Luther was not concerned, as modern thinkers often are, with creating a new and easily defended position over against new questions and discoveries in natural science and philosophy. His theology is far removed from being such an apologetic theology. And in fact, there was no need for that kind of theology in the sixteenth century.

In terms of our evaluation of Luther's theology, the preceding conclusions mean that we cannot evaluate Luther—either as a custodian of the theological tradition, or as a critical restorer of central theological teachings on the basis of his study of Scripture—by comparing him with modern theologians. Rather, Luther must be understood in the context of the conditions of scholarship in the early sixteenth century. To say it very directly: Luther's theology demonstrates its incomparable power to generate new approaches, particularly in the way in which it maintains the central teachings of the traditions of the church. It was possible, however, for Luther to preserve this tradition only because he simultaneously engaged in critical examination of the falsifications of the tradition by scholastic theology—at least what Luther himself concluded were such falsifications.

5.1.2 How Should We Structure Our Presentation?

The attempt to present a comprehensive overview of Luther's theology reveals the need to provide some systematic structure. The question is, should we organize it in terms of the systematic relationship of the doctrines to one another or in terms of its historical development?

Any attempt to describe Luther's theology is confronted with particular difficulties in deciding how to divide the material and what to emphasize. Most presentations of Luther's theology proceed systematically. This is the case with Theodosius Harnack who wrote a two-volume study of Luther's theology.[1] Harnack gave his book the descriptive subtitle: "with particular reference to his doctrine of reconciliation and redemption." Both Reinhold Seeberg[2] and Erich Seeberg[3] organized their materials systematically. In addition, Paul Althaus,[4] Lennart Pinomaa,[5] Friedrich Gogarten,[6] Rudolf Hermann,[7] and Hans Joachim Iwand, whose final book on Luther was published posthumously,[8] all structure their materials systematically. Gerhard Ebeling also provides a systematic overview in *Luther: An Introduction to His Thought* (1964).[9]

On the other hand, however, Ebeling's extensive essay on Luther's theology[10] proceeded on a historical developmental basis. In such a treatment, Ebeling began by describing Luther's original position and then traced its further development in the course of the various controversies after 1517. Although many significant monographs on individual topics in Luther's theology that were published in the last decade have used this method, there is still no comprehensive treatment of Luther's theology that is structured in this way.

Without doubt, there are significant reasons for choosing either of these two forms of presentation. One of the strengths of the historical developmental form is that it enables us to observe the development of Luther's thought not only in the period of his early lectures but also during his controversies with Rome, the so-called enthusiasts, Müntzer, Zwingli, Erasmus, Agricola, and others. Ordinarily, the developmental picture does not affect our understanding of the core of Luther's thinking. Rather, it gives us significant insight into the way in which he more carefully defined, structured, extended, or even changed his positions on individual points. Our understanding of Luther's position on matters such as the church, the law, the Lord's Supper, the two kingdoms or the two governments, or the right of the congregation to evaluate teaching and to call and depose teachers will differ depending whether we use the earlier or later writings of Luther as normative.

The fact that Luther's thinking changed does not mean that he ever formulated a doctrine merely in terms of a particular discussion. Rather, his formulations always rest on deep systematic relationships to his whole pattern of thinking theologically—even though he often first verbalized his thinking in response to a particular question. The basic conception, however, which formed and shaped his writing about a particular doctrine as well as its specific formulation at a given time can only be identified on the basis of careful consideration of the various situations that led to the controversy. It is precisely for this reason that the historical developmental method is valuable. The problem with such a method is that it is in danger of losing sight of the total context of Luther's theology.

In contrast to such a historical developmental approach, a systematically comprehensive presentation of Luther's theology can make us aware of the interrelationship between the various themes of Luther's theology and the central position of the doctrine of justification. Such an approach, however, must beware of two dangers. One danger is not to give sufficient emphasis to the development of Luther's theology. The second danger results from the fact that Luther's statements are so closely related to the historical situation in which he found himself when he wrote. As a result, the attempt to reconstruct Luther's theology systematically may express more of the author's own pattern of thought than the inner development of Luther's thinking. The numerous systematic presentations of Luther's theology all too often only demonstrate the basic positions of their various authors. Frequently it is painfully obvious that a particular author could not have arrived at his or her conclusions through a study of Luther but rather that he or she developed them on the basis of other material.

In any case, the easily noticeable differences in the way in which various authors describe Luther's theology is remarkable. Thus Paul Althaus uses the concept of a "primal revelation" as an important part of his own dogmatics. His description of Luther's theology clearly reveals this emphasis in Althaus's own thinking. Similarly, the fact that Althaus first discussed the doctrine of the Trinity in the middle of his book on Luther's theology clearly corresponds to the fact that Althaus in his own dogmatics followed the example of Schleiermacher and discussed the doctrine of the Trinity only at the end of his dogmatics. Admittedly, Althaus's *The Theology of Martin Luther* discusses the doctrine of the Trinity in the middle of that book. Similar comments could be made about Friedrich Gogarten's presentation of Luther's theology. Not only his organization but also especially his line of argument reveal specific characteristics of Gogarten's own systematic position.

Rudolf Hermann's posthumously published lectures on Luther's theology are concerned with avoiding this danger by constantly taking the events of Luther's life and the contemporary situation into account. As a result, his lectures are very loosely organized from a systematic viewpoint. Although Hermann described some important dimensions of Luther's theology, he also excluded from his discussion some questions that are particularly important for understanding the systematic structure of Luther's thought. The structure of H. J. Iwand's posthumously published lectures on Luther's theology[11] is obviously similar to the structure of his own early study of the doctrine of justification and faith in Christ.[12]

He added, however, a section on "church, state, and society" in his study of Luther.

Having expressed these concerns, I wish to emphasize that someone can also structure their own systematic theology on the basis of an intensive study of Luther. As a result, it is true both that such an author's own systematic viewpoint has been developed under the influence of their study of Luther's theology and that Luther is read in terms of certain questions that are important to the author. This is, to a certain extent, especially true of Althaus; naturally it is also true of other authors.

5.1.3 The Significance of the Early Church's Doctrine of the Trinity for Luther

No matter which method we follow, we cannot avoid a one-sided reading of Luther. We do, however, have the right to expect all scholars to be very clear about their various points of departure and method of presentation. They should also compare and contrast their conclusions with the conclusions of other scholars.

We must also remember that Luther only infrequently explicitly discussed some very essential doctrines such as the Trinity and Christology. In spite of this, we must assume that, without any doubt, Luther considered such doctrines to be of basic significance for his whole theology. In *The Bondage of the Will* he says, "For what still sublimer thing can remain hidden in the Scriptures, now that the seals have been broken, the stone rolled from the door of the sepulcher [Matt. 27:66; 28:2], and the supreme mystery brought to light, namely, that Christ the Son of God has been made man, that God is three and one, that Christ has suffered for us and is to reign eternally?"[13]

What was the real significance of the doctrine of the Trinity for Luther? Does the fact that he said so little about it simply indicate that there was no disagreement between himself and Rome on this point? Should other specific elements of Luther's theology be more strongly emphasized in any systematic presentation than would seem to be justified on the basis of a cursory examination of his explicit references to these questions? In making a decision, we should also consider the fact that other sixteenth-century Reformers who did write their own dogmatics discussed the doctrine of God and the Trinity at the beginning of their work. This is true, for example, of the later editions of Melanchthon's *Loci*[14] or of Calvin's *Institutes of the Christian Religion*.[15] Would Luther have done the same?

5.1.4 The Basic Theme of Theology

Obviously, it is important to present a systematic summary of Luther's theology that is appropriate to his own theology. It is even more important, however, that our discussion of every point of Luther's doctrine be faithful to the way in which Luther himself practiced theology, especially on the basis of his understanding of the relationship of people to God. In his lectures on Psalm 51 Luther says, "The proper subject of theology is man guilty of sin and condemned, and God the Justifier and Savior of man the sinner. Whatever is asked or discussed in theology outside this subject is error and poison."[16] Whenever we look at individual theological problems from this viewpoint then the question of the way in which we systematize Luther's theology is of far less significance. Only on this basis can we succeed in avoiding both the danger of an orthodox systematization of Luther on the one hand and the danger of an attempt to reinterpret Luther in order to make him existentially relevant to a particular contemporary situation on the other.

5.2 IMPORTANT ASPECTS OF
THE THEOLOGICAL DEVELOPMENT OF THE YOUNG LUTHER

5.2.1 Who Are the "Young Luther" and the "Old Luther"?

When we speak of the "young Luther," we ordinarily think of Luther before 1517 or 1518. The end of the period of the "young Luther" is placed either in 1517, at the beginning of the controversy with Rome, or, if one dates the Reformation breakthrough in 1518 when Luther arrived at a mature formulation of the doctrine of justification, in 1518.[17]

The meaning of references to the "old Luther" is not nearly so clear. Sometimes people are referring to Luther's attitude during the Peasants' War in 1525, to the way in which he more firmly defined many of his positions, as well as to the way in which he began to work more closely with the government and began to fear the masses (*Herrn Omnes*). These characteristics first became apparent in 1525. Sometimes, however, people use the reference to the "old Luther" to describe the period in which Luther developed his doctrine of the sacraments in opposition to Zwingli. The emphasis in this reference is primarily on the process by which Luther consolidated his teaching. Sometimes, however, people use the phrase "old Luther" to refer to Luther's opposition to the enthusiasts in the spring of 1522. In any case, the undefined way in which scholars speak of the young and the old Luther should under no circumstances lead students to assume that there is a sharp boundary between the two periods. Rather, it is important for us to see both the continuity in Luther's development and a certain shift in emphasis in his thinking.

5.2.2 Theological Work of the Young Luther

Luther research in the twentieth century has particularly emphasized the study of the young Luther. These studies have been made possible through the rediscovery of the manuscripts of Luther's lectures from the years 1513 to 1518, or at least of the students' notes of these lectures. It was particularly Karl Holl (d. 1926) who began to break new ground with his study of the young Luther. In the decades since then, both the questions and the methods of research have been more carefully defined. There are still numerous problems to be worked through.

In very general terms, we still have much work to do on Luther's relationship to the late Middle Ages, as well as to the entire period of the Middle Ages. The following specific questions are, however, particularly the focus of current research: (1) Luther's relationship to the exegetical tradition—both in terms of the interpretation of Scripture as a whole and in terms of the interpretation of individual passages; (2) the significance of Augustine, of Ockhamism, as well as of mysticism for the theology of the young Luther—in examining this question, we are concerned not only with the extent of such influence but also with the independent way in which Luther received this influence, including the possibility of a "productive misunderstanding"; (3) the numerous theological topics ranging from the conception of God, the view of Christ, the understanding of the church, the understanding of word and faith, of repentance and judgment, of righteousness and justification, and including specific questions such as Luther's attitude toward the Roman Church or the view of the primacy of Peter. In studying these questions, careful attention must be given to Luther's own personal development as well as the development of his thinking about these doctrines.

The peaceful academic work of his years of teaching gave Luther the opportunity to lay the basis for his Reformation theology. The basic concepts, although not all the details, were already firmly established by 1517 or 1518. Luther obviously expanded on this basic position in the course of the many and various controversies of the following years, but he made no basic changes. It is very important for further research to be done on the continuity and development of Luther's world of thought from 1513 to the years of controversy. Frequently, we are able to establish that a particular idea was already developed in Luther's early years but that after the autumn of 1517, in the controversy with Rome, it took on a polemical form that it had not previously had. This is true, for example, for Luther's understanding of repentance. For example, Luther had already regained the broad New Testament understanding of repentance in his early years but it was only in the Ninety-five Theses on indulgences that his new understanding of repentance became the basis of his criticism of indulgences. It remains important for us to investigate the sources and development of Luther's theology in order to understand the nature of the Reformation and the depth of the conflict between Luther and Rome. We cannot, however, ignore the fact that we today already know more about Luther in this regard than most of his contemporaries did. Those who were able to read first became aware of Luther when he published *The Seven Penitential Psalms* in April 1517.[18]

It is also significant that the first material that Luther intentionally prepared for publication was written in German. In this, Luther, for the first time, revealed himself as the religious writer who would later become so popular. In reading this book, we must carefully distinguish between our present knowledge of the basis and content of Luther's new theology and what the general public could have understood about Luther—given the conditions in 1517–18. Of course, Luther had much earlier exercised significant influence through his work as a university teacher and preacher in Wittenberg as well as through other forms of oral communication. Luther was very influential long before he began to write for publication.

5.2.3 The Hermeneutical Method of the Young Luther

All of us must remain aware of the danger of systematizing Luther's thinking, especially the thinking of the young Luther, and of prematurely interpreting his thinking so that it agrees with the thinking of the later Reformer. Even observing this caution, however, there can be no doubt at all that Luther struggled with the traditional methods of interpreting Scripture and arrived at a new method of understanding the meaning of Scripture. He still had not yet overcome the ponderous method of interpreting Scripture in a fourfold sense (namely, the literal, allegorical, tropological, and anagogical senses). In this respect he was even less advanced than Nicholas of Lyra (who died c. 1350) and Faber Stapulensis (c. 1455–1536). Luther, however, used this scheme of a fourfold meaning of Scripture in order to arrive at a christological interpretation. Luther also placed the "spirit" and the "letter" in opposition to one another and at this point already began to distinguish our relationship to God *(coram Deo)* and to the world *(coram mundo)*. The category "spirit," however, also refers to the way in which God is hidden from us and unavailable to us, whereas the category of the "letter" refers both to human autonomy and to the wrath of God. Of course Luther does not separate "spirit" and "letter" from one another. Rather, the spirit is hidden in the letter. The same verse, the same word can at one and the same time be both letter and spirit. This means that each word can at one and the same time be a word of both divine judgment and divine grace. This approach to the interpretation of Scripture is particularly expressed in a statement such as this, "Note that the strength of Scripture is this, that it is not changed into him who studies it, but that it transforms its lover into itself and its strengths. . . . [Scripture says,] you will not change me into what you are [as the heretics do], but you will be changed into what I am."[19]

5.2.4 Judgment and Gospel in Luther's "First Lectures on the Psalms"

Luther's hermeneutical method automatically made the themes of judgment, self-accusation, humbling oneself, and confessing oneself to be a sinner as well as righteousness, justification, and grace the central focus of his theology. This was already clear in his first series of lectures on the Psalms.[20] Luther's discussion of these themes was partially determined by his own experience of the monastic life. At the same time, however, he presented basically new perspectives even on monasticism itself. Basically, then, this selection of themes as well as his discussion of them must be understood both in terms of his experience of spiritual temptation and of his intensive study of the Scriptures. It is essential that we understand what Luther meant when he said that God acts in a hidden way, doing "the opposite" *(sub contrario)* of what he seems to be doing. For Luther this meant that God's grace is always present as the hidden reality under his judgment. Thus, we can say that a new and deeper knowledge of the sinfulness of people was one of the first developments that led to the Reformation. Luther recognized that we are sinful not only because of specific acts but because we are self-centered and seek our own welfare. This is most true when we seek to become right with God by doing good works rather than trusting in God. Actually, the opposite is true: we are justified by God precisely when we accept God's judgment and acknowledge that we are sinners. Since we only then agree with the divine judgment, only then are we right with God.

Since judgment and gospel are such central themes in the *First Lectures on the Psalms,* other topics that Luther also discussed recede into the background. It is important to note these topics. The sacraments is one such topic. The detailed reasons for Luther's limited comments on the sacraments are disputed among scholars. Apparently Luther was concerned that the then-widespread teaching that the sacraments are automatically effective and convey grace even without faith could mislead people into a false security about salvation. Thus only the first traces of Luther's later teachings about the sacraments appear in these lectures. Beyond this, his sharp criticism of the corruption and abuses in the church is significant. This criticism appears very early in Luther's works. It is basically directed against weakness in faith and against a feigned desire to experience salvation.

5.2.5 The Lectures on Romans

The *First Lectures on the Psalms* document Luther's own struggle to gain clarity about central questions of faith. His lectures on Romans of

1515–16[21] present a more clearly defined account of the results of that struggle for his own theology. In his introductory statement to these lectures, Luther discussed the theme of judgment, "The chief purpose of this letter is to break down, to pluck up, and to destroy all wisdom and righteousness of the flesh. This includes all the works which in the eyes of people or even in our own eyes may be great works. No matter whether these works are done with a sincere heart and mind, this letter is to affirm and state and magnify sin, no matter how much someone insists that it does not exist, or that it was believed not to exist."[22] In these lectures on Romans, Luther also expressly criticized the scholastic doctrine of sin particularly because, in his opinion, it underestimated both the concupiscence and the *fomes,* or tinder, which Luther already understood as the selfishness of the will.[23] In a similar way, Luther also criticized other scholastic concepts, particularly in the context of the doctrine of grace.

Luther's lectures on Romans of 1515–16 reveal considerable progress in the doctrine of justification when compared with the *First Lectures on the Psalms.* At the very beginning of his lectures on Romans, Luther described the righteousness of God as coming to us from outside ourselves *(extranea, externa,* or *aliena iustitia);* he contrasted this with the righteousness that belongs to us and that comes from inside ourselves *(propria* or *domestica iustitia).*[24] Statements such as these clearly demonstrate that Luther was already thinking in terms of the Reformation's characteristic concept of grace as "outside of ourselves" *(extra nos).* Apparently Luther developed these ideas by himself. Perhaps the mystical concepts "rapture" or "ecstasy" stimulated his thinking.

Scholars are not agreed as to whether or not a so-called theology of humility is to be found in the lectures on Romans. Many scholars have attempted to prove that the Reformation view of the righteousness of God and the justification of people is already fully expressed in these lectures. Others, such as Ernst Bizer,[25] however, still understood humility as the necessary condition for the reception of salvation. It is true that many passages in the lectures on Romans do not yet express the Reformation position. At the same time, such important concepts as *imputare* and *reputare,* technical terms for God's declaring sinners righteous, are already encountered in the lectures on Romans. The important pair of concepts, promise and faith, which would later play such an important role in Luther's transforming reformation of the doctrine of the sacraments, appears in the lectures on Romans from the very beginning.[26] Even though we repeatedly find passages that cannot be interpreted in the sense of the Reformation, we can still hardly deny that these lectures not only express the theology of the Reformation with increasing clarity, but also specifically apply it in solving numerous individual questions. It is unusually stimulating and instructive to trace the ongoing process by which Luther became progressively aware of his insights in the years before the controversy on indulgences.

This process of transformation in Luther's theology had implications for very many problems. As far as the interpretation of Scripture is concerned, allegorizing already began to decrease. That, of course, was also related to the nature of the texts that Luther interpreted. The Psalms invite the application of the fourfold sense of Scripture to a greater extent than do the Pauline epistles. Together with this, however, Luther more and more tried to establish the literal meaning of Scripture. He no longer tried to find the spiritual meaning of a text alongside the literal meaning but rather within it. When we compare the lectures on Romans to the *First Lectures on the Psalms,* we also find more extensive discussions of the sacraments. Even though this change is primarily due to the content of the texts being interpreted, such as Romans 6, we still find the elements of an entirely new understanding of the sacraments. This appears most clearly in Luther's lectures on Hebrews.[27]

During these years, there are also new emphases in Luther's statements about the church as well as about monasticism. The Reformation's understanding of freedom first appears in his lectures on Romans. There is hardly a theological problem in which Luther did not demonstrate significant advances in his thinking. There is often a significant difference between what Luther began to say in 1515 and his later statements during the controversy on indulgences. The polemic against Rome and against certain abuses is also missing. Luther's criticism of scholasticism, however, for the sense of self-security and the weak kind of faith that it engendered was now much sharper than it had been in the *First Lectures on the Psalms.* Looking back, we can see that the conflict between Luther and Rome was inevitable. Theologically, Luther still had not completely moved away from the basis of the medieval church. His theology was so strongly influenced by the New Testament, however, that it was really only a question of time until the conflict would begin.

5.3 THE QUESTION OF LUTHER'S REFORMATION BREAKTHROUGH

5.3.1 Should It Be Dated Early or Late?

For many decades, Luther scholars have been arguing about when Luther broke through to consciousness about his Reformation insight into twofold meaning of the righteousness of God and of justification. How is the content of this insight to be defined in detail? This question could be intensively explored only after Luther's early lectures were once again

available. Since the beginning of the twentieth century, there have been
many comprehensive discussions of the significant questions. These discussions have usually ended after some time without any clear conclusion having been achieved. At the present, there is not very much
discussion of this question. This is probably due to the fact that scholars
are somewhat tired of the whole discussion. Obviously, however, the
question about the Reformation breakthrough is of considerable significance for our understanding of Luther himself as well as of the entire
Reformation.

So far as the dating of the Reformation breakthrough is concerned, the
two years most frequently proposed are 1514 or 1518. Some scholars,
however, still hold a view that was formerly very widespread. According
to this view, Luther had already gained his new insights before he began
his first lectures on Romans, that is, not later than 1513.[28] Some scholars,
on the other hand, still support a date of 1519 or even 1520. Together
with these different attempts to define the date, however, scholars in
recent years have also taken the view that the Reformation breakthrough
did not consist in a definite insight that was gained at some exact point of
time but rather that the Reformation breakthrough consisted in the
process by which Luther's new theological viewpoints gradually matured.
Only as Luther looked back on this long process did he become aware
that something had actually happened. According to this view, however,
the Reformation insight is basically to be understood as the presuppositions that had been implicitly present in Luther's theological work from
some point such as the beginning of the controversy on indulgences.[29]

5.3.2 What Was the Content of the
Reformation Insight?

The question about the content of the Reformation insight is no less
important than the question about the time at which it developed. Luther
himself frequently said that his new understanding of the righteousness
of God was the focus of this insight. According to Paul, Luther said, this
righteousness is not the distributive righteousness by which God judges
but rather the righteousness by which God gives. In 1545 Luther described this righteousness as "passive righteousness."[30] In faith, we receive this righteousness which sets us free. Luther said that, whereas he
had previously understood the righteousness of God as the righteousness
by which God demands something from us, he now understood it as
"causative" righteousness, that is, as God making people righteous.[31]
Thus, for Luther, the righteousness received in faith was not only the
forgiveness of sins but also the beginning of God's process of making us
righteous. In thinking about this, we must remember that Luther under-

stood that the righteousness of God as well as the justification of people would first be completely realized on the last day. Over against the background of this comprehensive arch that reaches from the present into the world beyond, however, the emphasis obviously lies on God's promise and on faith.

5.3.3 The Most Important Sources

Anyone who wishes to investigate the question of Luther's Reformation breakthrough must give special attention to the following problems:

Luther's Own Statements About His Discovery.[32] In analyzing Luther's statements, we must distinguish between the comments that he made in his table talk—statements which must be used very carefully because Luther not only made them without careful thought but also because of the uncertainty as to whether they were accurately recorded. Luther also made other statements in his letters or writings. Many scholars think that such a self-testimony is particularly significant. But other scholars disagree. The fact that Luther's own statements about his Reformation discovery sometimes disagree with one another gives added significance to the decision to emphasize some more than others. On what basis can we make such a decision?

The Early Lectures, Writings, and Letters Until 1518–19. We ought not expect to find something like a description of Luther's conversion in these texts. The fact is that even very intensive study and discussion of the significant material has still not produced any agreement about the timing and the first appearance of Luther's Reformation insight. We must carefully consider how we are going to use these texts. Precisely because the Reformation insight was so significant for Luther, existentially as well as theologically, we ought not assume that he one day discovered that he had suddenly solved all important problems. It would also be a mistake to expect that after a certain point in time Luther regularly and consistently expressed his new insights. Rather we need to think about the whole process of development in the young Luther's theological thinking, particularly as this appears in his lectures. His new insight can be identified in the context of this process of thought. It appears in connection with his focus on our understanding of Christ, on the position of people before God, and on the relationship between judgment and gospel. In describing this, we must also take into account that Luther gained his insight without becoming aware that he was now in opposition to the teaching of the church. Obviously anyone who asserts a late date for the Reformation breakthrough must at least see a connection between this breakthrough and Luther's incipient conflict with Rome.

The Relationship Between the Reformation and the Real Medieval

Church. We have, in the past decades, become increasingly clear about the complexity of this problem. This is particularly true since our study of the relationship between Luther and the Middle Ages has entered into a new stage. For example, we now have more objective studies of the relationship between Luther and Thomas Aquinas. The question as to whether and to what extent Luther's insight was something new in comparison with the traditional teachings can only be answered by carefully dividing the question. In thinking about this question, we need to distinguish between the traditional interpretation of Romans before Luther and the way in which systematic theologians described the righteousness of God and justification. Sometimes we find approaches that are remarkably similar to Luther's exegetical insight; however, we also find that no one drew theological conclusions similar to those of Luther. Special problems arise when we ask whether or not Luther's insight really does justice to Paul's intended meaning. And this question too cannot be answered only on the basis of asking whether Luther's interpretation was correct in a philological sense. Rather we must test whether or not Luther translated the Pauline theological concepts into the generally quite different thought structures of the early sixteenth century. Luther could have done so in a substantially correct manner even though certain emphases were different.

The Present Status of Research.[33] The discussion since then has not produced any basically new perspectives. Of course, it is amazing that certain viewpoints constantly reappear in spite of the radically changing and awkward situation that presently characterizes scholarly studies. It hardly seems possible that we will arrive at any resolution of these problems which will be generally satisfactory.

At the same time, however, it now seems clear that the view that Luther's Reformation insight is not to be understood as a definite event but rather as the pattern of presuppositions underlying Luther's theological work also brings very great difficulties with it. In his later life, Luther frequently said that the insight came to him as a specific describable event. If we adopt this view, these statements of Luther must be considered to be false, and we have no basis on which to ascribe such a significant lapse of memory to Luther. In other words, we simply have no adequate methodological basis on which to undertake such a far-reaching reinterpretation of Luther's own statements. The only basis on which such a reinterpretation would be acceptable would be that someone were able to prove that Luther suffered other lapses of memory as well. Since no one has yet done this, scholars cannot avoid dealing with this problem no matter how difficult the situation appears to be.

The dating of Luther's Reformation insight, as well as our definition of its contents, have considerable significance for our evaluation of the beginnings of Luther's conflict with Rome also. Those who support an early date thereby also assume that Luther taught a basically new theology before his controversy with the Roman Church and that this new theology of necessity eventually led to a conflict with Rome. Those who support a late date for the Reformation breakthrough thereby also share the view that Luther was first led to develop the really decisive stages of his Reformation theology through his conflict with Rome. For this reason, the decision for an early or late dating is probably more significant than our answer to the question of whether Luther actually posted the Ninety-five Theses or not.[34] Our answer to this latter question does, however, have important consequences for our evaluation of the way in which Luther became a public figure.

5.4 THE AUTHORITY OF SCRIPTURE

5.4.1 The Problem of Scripture and Tradition

The Reformation is commonly described as having asserted the authority of Scripture over against all human authority. This scriptural principle of the Reformation is then contrasted with the Roman Catholic assertion of the validity of tradition. This summary in slogans is certainly not inaccurate. The problems are, however, somewhat more complex when we look at individual issues.

If we wish to evaluate the Reformation's emphasis on the authority of the Scripture properly, we must be careful to keep a variety of questions in mind.

The theme of Scripture and tradition that we encounter in modern theological controversies is formulated in terms of the present discussion. As such, it is a result and not a presupposition of the Reformation. Neither the view of the Reformers nor of their Roman opponents is simply a continuation of the older view. In the early and medieval church, the question of the relationship between Scripture and tradition was not dealt with in any way which corresponds to its treatment in the sixteenth century. It was only in the course of the conflict between Luther and Rome that the idea of sharp opposition between Scripture and tradition developed. Its development in the sixteenth century determined the discussion for a long time afterward.

Both the early and the medieval church took the authority of Scripture for granted, although at certain points they did so in different ways. The principle of "Scripture alone" was never advocated before Luther, however. This fact is of major importance: Until Luther, the authority of Scripture as a totality was absolutely taken for granted in the church and the relationship between Scripture and tradition had not yet been identified as a problem. This reality made it possible for the Reformers to criticize the sixteenth-century church on the basis of the content and the authority of Scripture. It also enabled many people to accept their criticisms as valid.

The representatives of the old church were faced with a dilemma. They did not wish to wish to deny the watchword of the Reformation, "Scripture alone," because they also accepted the authority of Scripture. At the same time, they could not critically evaluate what the Reformers were doing because the Roman tradition had never thought through the relationship between Scripture and tradition. This is ultimately the reason why the Roman theologians at first simply asserted the authority of the pope against Luther and his supporters.

In spite of this assertion of the authority of the pope, however, theologians in the period before Luther generally understood the meaning of Scripture as compatible with the total context of the church's traditional teaching and interpreted it in harmony with the church's doctrinal decisions. Actually, this approach required the theologians of both the early and the medieval church to discuss the relationship of Scripture and tradition. These discussions, however, never resulted in the slightest suggestion that there might be a contradiction between Scripture and tradition. No one ever critically reexamined the tradition on the basis of Scripture. Rather there was a consistent movement toward the understanding of the relationship between tradition and Scripture that prevailed at the beginning of the Reformation. This is true for individual theologians such as Vincent of Lerins (who died before 450), who among all the theologians of the early church moved farthest in the development of a definition of tradition in the medieval sense in his *Commonitorium.*[35] This was also the basis on which the councils understood their work.

And yet, even theologians of the Middle Ages criticized the church on the basis of the Scripture. This happened most often particularly in the twelfth- and thirteenth-century movements that emphasized poverty as a Christian virtue, as well as in the movements under the leadership of John Wyclif and John Huss. These critics asserted the authority of the Scripture as the divine law over against mere human traditions. This did not lead to any closer consideration of the problem of the relationship between Scripture and tradition, however.

In addition to examining the problem of Scripture and tradition, we need to ask what level of significance was actually ascribed to the Scripture in theological work. With all of the radical certainty of a new movement that is just becoming aware of its strength, the Reformation accused scholasticism of having despised the Scripture and having based its theology on Aristotelian philosophy. This accusation appeared most frequently in the context of the discussion of the doctrines of sin and of grace, as well as in the discussion of the concept of God. There was some truth to this accusation—at least in the context of the Reformers' intensive attempts to establish the original text and the meaning of Scripture. In spite of this, however, the question as to whether a particular position is closer to or further from the substance of Scripture is more complex than those early Reformers could have known. This fact, taken together with the reality that Reformation theologians themselves, after the middle of the sixteenth century, began to make more and more use of Aristotelian philosophy, forces us to a somewhat more considered judgment. In any case, we must carefully consider the reasons that led to this change in the Reformation itself. We cannot allow ourselves to evade the issue by simply describing these realities as an abandoning of the basic Reformation position.

If we are willing to consider these problems carefully, we can better place the Reformation's scriptural principle into its proper historical context. In addition, we must also see the humanistic emphasis on returning "to the sources" *(ad fontes)* as a forerunner of the Reformation's scriptural principle, even though the differences between the two are still of significance.

5.4.2 The Authority of the Scripture and the Authority of Christ

As far as Luther's own understanding of the authority of Scripture is concerned, the following important factors must be considered.

Luther undoubtedly emphasized the authority of the biblical Word to an extent that was previously unknown. When he asserted the authority of Christ against the authority of the pope in the controversy on indulgences, he was thinking of the Christ who speaks to us through the Scripture. This was particularly true in his statements about repentance and faith. Similarly, in the controversy with Zwingli, Luther referred back to the exact wording of the words of institution when he argued against Zwingli's interpretation of "is" as though it meant "signifies." Specific statements of Scripture also occupy the central position in Luther's other controversies—for example, those with Karlstadt or Müntzer, although these controversies dealt more with questions of the understanding of the whole of Scripture and especially of the relationship between the Old and New Testaments.

Luther, however, in contrast to the early orthodox theologians of the later sixteenth century, did not develop any doctrine of verbal inspiration.[36] Quite the opposite is true. For example, Luther was openly critical of the substance of certain portions of Scripture, particularly of the Letter of James. His norm in making this criticism was the Pauline doctrine of justification.[37] The total breadth of Luther's understanding of the authority of Scripture can be represented by three quotations:

"Neither councils, fathers, nor we, in spite of the greatest and best success possible, will do as well as the Holy Scriptures, that is, as well as God himself has done."[38]

The cloths in which the infant Jesus was wrapped "are nothing but Holy Scripture, in which Christian faith lies wrapped up."[39]

"God and the Scripture of God are two things, no less than the Creator and the creature are two things."[40]

It is thus clear that Luther can describe the relationship between God and the Scripture in three ways: (1) he identifies the Bible and the Word of God; (2) he also describes the Word of God as the real content of the Bible without identifying this content with the external form in which we encounter it; (3) he also describes a dialectic relationship in which he differentiates the Bible and the Word of God by describing the one as the Creator and the other as the creature.

5.4.3 The Clarity of the Scripture

Luther's understanding of the clarity of Scripture also played an important role in his understanding of the authority of Scripture. Luther stated this very clearly in *The Bondage of the Will.* In this book Luther determined whether a passage was clear or obscure in terms of its witness to the central truths of the faith, the incarnation of Christ, the cross, and the resurrection. Luther did not assert, however, that Scripture gives a clear answer to all questions. At this point, there is a basic difference between Luther and the later orthodox doctrine of verbal inspiration. In the age of orthodoxy, theologians more and more understood the clarity of Scripture as meaning that doctrinal controversies could be decided by scriptural proofs.

5.4.4 Christ Is the Center of the Scripture

Luther can properly be described as one of the greatest interpreters of Scripture in the history of the church. This is true both in terms of the extent of his exegetical work and of its theological significance. In the course of his exegetical work, Luther succeeded in understanding Scripture from its center and was also able to rediscover this center in its various refractions through the individual witnesses and their unique testimonies. "Take Christ out of the Scriptures, and what will you find left in them?"[41] This led Luther directly to the conclusion that Scripture interprets itself. "The meaning of Scripture is, in and of Scripture itself, so certain, accessible, and clear that Scripture interprets itself and tests, judges, and illuminates everything else."[42]

5.4.5 Law and Gospel

Luther's important distinction between the law and the gospel is also closely related to his interpretation of the Scripture in terms of its center. The Word of God encounters people as law and as gospel, as a word of judgment and as a word of grace. This does not mean that we may simply equate the law with the Old Testament and the gospel with the New Testament. It is certainly true that there is more law than gospel in the Old Testament and more gospel than law in the New Testament. Luther's distinction between law and gospel, however, referred to something other than the division of biblical statements into the two parts of the biblical canon. This distinction rather describes the fact that *God* both judges and is merciful. And this twofold dimension of the Word of God must be taken into account in our interpretation of Scripture as well as in our preaching.

The unity of the two testaments is expressed in the fact that the Old Testament already contains the gospel in a hidden way as well as in the fact that the New Testament contains the law. As far as the hidden presence of the gospel in the Old Testament is concerned, Luther could say that he saw the whole content of the Scripture in the first chapter of the Bible.[43] Luther expressed this view very clearly in his explanation of the First Commandment. On the one hand, he saw the First Commandment as the summary of both the Decalogue and natural law. It summarizes all the demands that God makes of us, that is, that we should fear, love, and trust God more than anything or anyone else. To this extent, the First Commandment is a word of judgment. On the other hand, Luther also saw the First Commandment as God's promise. "Now this is the work of the first commandment, which enjoins, 'Thou shalt have no other gods.' This means, 'Since I alone am God, thou shalt place all thy confidence, trust, and faith in me alone and in no one else.' For you do not have a god if you [just] call him God outwardly with your lips, or worship him with the knees or bodily gestures; but [only] if you trust him with your heart and look to him for good, grace, and favor, whether in works or suffering, in life or death, in joy or sorrow."[44] The First Commandment thus also contains the promise that God wants to be our God. The First Commandment intends to teach people to despair of their own works and to trust in God's mercy alone.

Of course, the real meaning of this commandment was not yet revealed

in the Old Testament. During the time of the Old Testament, the First
Commandment primarily had the character of law. It was Christ who first
brought the hidden character of the divine commandment as promise to
the light of day. Through his message that God is a God of the living and
not of the dead (Matt. 22:32), Christ made the real meaning of the First
Commandment clear. There is still more: the New Testament finally has
no significance apart from the fact that it opens up the real meaning of
the Old Testament. The proclamation of the New Testament is, in a
certain sense, intended to express and proclaim only that which was
previously hidden in the letters and in the secret visions of the Old
Testament. "For the New Testament is nothing but an uncovering and a
revelation of the Old Testament. . . ."[45]

On the other hand, the New Testament not only contains the gospel
but also contains the law. In the New Testament, the law encounters us in
the Sermon on the Mount, for example. Only here is the actual, radical
meaning of the Old Testament commandments unveiled, that is, God's
original will for people. Even the cross of Christ is not just the fixed
symbol of divine love but is God's sharpest judgment on human sin. In
this respect too, it is true that the real meaning of the Old Testament is
first fully revealed through the New Testament.

The distinction between law and gospel is one of the most important
themes in Luther's theology. It is closely related not only to his understanding of Scripture but also to his Christology and doctrine of justification. If we look at the form in which this occurs, these themes are quite
different from the corresponding topics in the theology of the early and
medieval church. The distinction between law and gospel is not one
particular teaching or even a transformation of traditional viewpoints
within a single topic, as, for instance, the character of the theory of
satisfaction in the thinking of Anselm, or the doctrine of reconciliation in
Abelard, or the new epistemology and distinction between the absolute
and the mediated power of God that characterized Ockhamism. The
distinction between law and gospel is not one teaching that is added to
the other topics; rather, it is significant for the way in which we interpret
Scripture as well as for theological work in absolutely every doctrine.
Law and gospel must be distinguished in the doctrine of God, particularly
in our doctrine of the Holy Spirit as well as in the interpretation of the
commandments, in the doctrine of the sacraments, and in ethics. Dealing
with any doctrine in a formally correct manner is never enough unless
we also express the proper distinction between law and gospel in the
double nature of God's activity as well as our twofold relationship to God
as people who are both judged and who have experienced mercy. Precisely here we become most clearly aware of the powerful dynamic that

flows through Luther's theological work. At the same time, we can now begin to see that the simple theoretical assertion that Scripture alone is the authority in theology really says very little. The basic Reformation principle of "Scripture alone" will be correctly understood when we add the principles of "grace alone," "faith alone," and, particularly, "Christ alone." "Scripture should not be understood as meaning anything else than that people are nothing and Christ alone is everything."[46]

5.5 REASON AND FAITH

5.5.1 The Uniqueness of Luther's Understanding of Reason

The significance of reason in Luther's theological work is a theme that still needs much study. In particular there are still individual writings as well as specific theological themes that must be analyzed in order to describe more exactly the manner and way in which Luther uses reason.

Above all, it becomes evident again that Luther approached theological work in a different way than the scholastics did. He was very little concerned about an epistemological definition of reason, or with defining the boundaries between either reason and revelation or nature and grace. To this extent, Luther's view of reason can be compared neither with the Thomistic nor with the Ockhamistic position, although Luther began his theological work as an Ockhamist. In contrast to the scholastic treatment of reason, Luther clearly stood out as an especially sharp critic of reason. Of course when Luther described reason in matters related to faith as "blind" or as "the devil's whore," he was not simply scolding or asserting his own theological ideas without concern for understanding and insight. Rather, Luther at a very early point already understood that we are not able to engage in a neutral search for the truth in matters related to the knowledge of God. Sin also expresses itself in our attempt to know God. To put it very pointedly, we only know what we want to know about God. Reason and will are parallel to each other in this matter. In a certain sense, the act of knowing is also influenced by the will, for our knowledge of divine truth is every bit as much an existential act as our not knowing the divine truth. To this extent, we are at this point dealing with dynamics similar to those in Luther's doctrine of law and gospel.

5.5.2 The Question of the Natural Knowledge of God

Luther's answer to the question about the natural knowledge of God was ambivalent. Luther frequently seemed to agree with scholasticism that reason has some knowledge of God. Thus reason knows that there is a

God even though it is not able to speak correctly about the deity. Luther also said that reason knows something about God's goodness, wrath, or righteousness. "Reason can do this much: It can recognize God as a terrible, wrathful judge, who leaves us no place to hide, neither in this world nor in hell."[47] Reason also knows about God's commandment. And reason knows what is right and what is wrong. Reason even knows that we cannot enter into heaven until we have gotten rid of sin. Reason also knows that God works everything in everything and predetermines everything; such knowledge is written into the hearts of all of us.[48]

On the other hand, Luther also said that reason neither knows nor understands anything about God. It is particularly noteworthy that these negative statements about reason's understanding God frequently follow assertions that reason does know something about God. "The more you attempt to rely on reason, the farther you are removed from God."[49] Reason does not know the right way to God, although it knows that we ought to follow the right way. Luther put it even more sharply in *The Bondage of the Will* when he said that reason does not necessarily accept that there is a higher being and ascribe certain attributes to this being. Reason can equally well conclude that there is no God at all or at least that God is not righteous.[50] As far as human reason is concerned, God is simply incomprehensible and unreachable.

These two series of statements only appear to contradict each other. Rather they belong together. Luther always raised the question about whether there is a God together with the question about whether we have a God.[51] As Luther described it, reason always sees through a red or a blue lens and cannot remove it from its eyes. As a result, everything that reason looks at must be either red or blue.[52] Thus we make and create our own image of God which corresponds to our own wishes and hopes. Indeed, Luther even said that since reason sleeps, it also imagines a sleeping God.[53]

Alongside these statements about the knowledge of God, Luther made a number of very significant statements about reason's ability to know what God is not. Insofar as it can do this, reason is able to hold itself open for an encounter with transcendence. Luther's book *The Judgment of Martin Luther on Monastic Vows* (1521) gives important insights into this, because its systematic construction is a pattern for his style of theological thinking. "Reason does not comprehend what God is, but it most certainly comprehends what God is not."[54] Although reason cannot see that only faith is right and good in God's sight, it still knows that unbelief, murder, and disobedience are evil. Christ himself used these insights of reason when he pointed out that every kingdom that is divided against itself will be destroyed.[55]

Luther thereby clearly rejected every attempt to come to God with the aid of reason. The "affirmations" of reason are false. In spite of this, Luther still said that reason's "negations" can be true statements about what God is not. Luther was not thinking about some kind of negative theology *(via negationis)*, as though reason were able to make positive assertions about God by making a detour over negations. What Luther meant with this statement was that reason, when properly applied and aware of its limitations, preserves the possibility of revelation and thereby itself remains open in relationship to transcendence. He also probably intended to maintain the unity of truth and thus to avoid the theory of a twofold truth.

5.5.3 Luther's Relationship to Philosophy

Luther's attitude toward philosophy is similar to his answer to the question of the natural knowledge of God. Here, too, he made very many sharply critical judgments that must, however, be understood in terms of the context in which they were made. Luther rejected the dependence of theology on philosophy and particularly rejected the philosophical concept of God, because it does not pay attention to our relationship to God. Luther felt that the growing influence of philosophy on scholasticism's doctrine of grace and particularly in the doctrine of the sacraments, resulted in an alienation from the biblical statements. Luther was particularly critical of any philosophy that describes people without reference to the reality of sin and of our bondage to death and the devil as well as to our redemption through Jesus Christ.

5.5.4 Luther's Answer in Worms

Luther, of course, did not completely reject philosophy. Luther found philosophy to be completely acceptable as long as it respected its limitations. As far as reason is concerned, Luther ascribed the highest authority on earth to it within the above-named limitations. There are no limitations on the authority of reason in secular matters. In spiritual matters, Luther also made considerable use of reason. This is demonstrated particularly in the answer that he gave in Worms. "Unless I am convinced by the testimony of the Scriptures or by clear reason (for I do not trust either in the pope or in councils alone, since it is well known that they have often erred and contradicted themselves), I am bound by the Scriptures I have quoted and my conscience is captive to the Word of God. I cannot and I will not retract anything, since it is neither safe nor right to go against conscience."[56]

Luther here referred to three elements: the testimony of the Scriptures, the clear basis of reason, and a conscience that is bound by God's Word.

There is still much disagreement about the interpretation of individual details of Luther's statement. Obviously, reason can be understood as merely referring to conclusions drawn on the basis of the Scriptures. If we take into consideration Luther's statements in *The Judgment of Martin Luther on Monastic Vows,* however, a more comprehensive understanding is possible. In any case, Luther's statements about reason or about the conscience were never intended to assert the autonomy of either in the modern sense. When Luther said that his conscience was "captive to the Word of God," he asserted a similar captivity of reason. Luther was not speaking of an autonomous reason determined by his own ego, but rather spoke of reason set free to carry out its right and natural function through faith. Luther obviously meant, then, to deny that his teaching was absurd. As far as conscience is concerned, Luther was not talking about some independent entity, but he rather described the fact that nothing can take the place of our personal faith. For Luther, the conscience was not an organ of moral consciousness; rather it was the "bearer of our relationship to God."[57] The conscience is therefore also the personal function in which we experience the comfort and the healing power of the gospel. Once the conscience has been subjected to God's Word, it is no longer the controlling organ through which we evaluate our deeds and through which we seek to justify ourselves. "For conscience is not the power to do works, but to judge them."[58] Thus Luther's appeal to his conscience is based on the Reformation's understanding of Scripture.

5.5.5 The Significance of Reason for Theological Work

If reason is understood in terms of the above discussion, reason is also of considerable significance for Luther's theological work. Admittedly, Luther can say that faith kills reason, because reason is blind and unable to see God's Word. Luther, however, also described reason as being so enlightened by God that it becomes extremely meaningful for our renewal. In these cases, Luther said that faith is so high that it is beyond the grasp of reason itself, but that revelation illuminates reason in specific ways. Such illuminated reason must now "against its own will" confess that it is unable to comprehend God's work.[59] Thus even reason is at least partially renewed. The process by which people come to faith or experience justification can also be described in terms of understanding.

It would be a one-sided interpretation if we were to place either Luther's positive or negative statements about human reason in the foreground of the discussion. Rather, both kinds of statements must stand alongside each other and be understood in terms of their relationship to each other. At the same time, however, we ought not forget that Luther— in spite of his emphasis on the difference between theology and philosophy—never approved the theory of a twofold truth.

Similarly, Luther also described reason in the Christian in apparently paradoxical terms. On the one hand, he said that reason and faith are always in conflict, because even when we come to faith, reason is never freed of its independent and proud nature; even believers are still tempted to construct an image of God that corresponds to their own desires. On the other hand, Luther repeatedly emphasized that faith does not leave people unchanged. Rather, faith is the beginning of a process in which the whole person is transformed. Of course this process also includes the renewal of reason.

This new reason is not some habitual faculty that the Christian possesses and controls. Its existence cannot be proved; and it can be lost. It also cannot be clearly defined in contrast to the old reason. Luther did not distinguish—as later orthodox theologians did—between the reason of the natural person and the reason of the regenerate. Luther still asserted, however, that the first stages of this new reason, which no longer serves the purposes of people who are trying to justify themselves, are already present in the believer.

For these reasons, we cannot simply say that Luther described the Christian's reason and faith as being in total conflict, nor can we describe the functions of a totally enlightened reason. Luther simultaneously described faith and reason as in opposition to each another and as beginning to coexist in service to each other. The dialectic underlying this paradox corresponds to the dialectic of Luther's statements about believers being, at one and the same time, totally sinners and totally righteous, as well as to the dialectic underlying the tensions and the unity between law and gospel.

This dialectic also played a significant role in Luther's understanding of the function of reason in theology. First of all, there is no doubt that reason was of very great significance for theology as Luther understood it. Luther's own theological work, especially the critically and sharply reasoned method with which he himself conducted academic disputations, reveals Luther's own brilliant application of the human capacity for knowing and for understanding to the theological task.[60] Detailed investigation of some of Luther's other writings—especially those writings related to the controversies with the enthusiasts or with Zwingli on the doctrine of the Lord's Supper—would enrich this picture considerably. Similarly, the study of Luther's "rational" arguments in his political statements and opinions would be rewarding.

5.6 LUTHER'S ATTITUDE TOWARD THE CHURCH'S TRADITION

5.6.1 Faith and Doctrine

We can hardly overemphasize the significance of the traditional dogma for Luther. Scholars generally underestimate this, however. Luther's numerous and intense controversies, particularly with Rome, have permitted us to overlook what Luther shared in common with his opponents. And yet, Luther, in spite of occasional critical remarks, totally and completely accepted the doctrinal decisions of the early church. As far as the decisions of the medieval councils were concerned, Luther rejected the decree of the Fourth Lateran Council (1215), which defined the doctrine of transubstantiation. He also rejected the decree of the Council held in Florence in 1439 which required the Armenian church to accept the doctrine of the seven sacraments. In the sixteenth century, no decisions had yet been made about the position of the pope and the doctrine of Mary. It is only in more recent times that sharp disagreement about these doctrines has developed between the Roman Catholic and Protestant churches.

The basic significance of doctrine for Luther is illustrated by an occasional remark. Luther began *The Sacrament of the Body and Blood of Christ—Against the Fanatics* (1526) with the following introduction:

> In this sacrament there are two things that should be known and proclaimed. First, what one should believe. In Latin this is called the *objectum fidei*, that is, the work or thing in which one believes, or to which one is to adhere. Second, the faith itself, or the use which one should properly make of that in which he believes. The first lies outside the heart and is presented to our eyes externally, namely, the sacrament itself, concerning which we believe that Christ's body and blood are truly present in the bread and wine. The second is internal, within the heart, and cannot be externalized. It consists in the attitude which the heart should have toward the external sacrament. Up to now I have not preached very much about the first part, but have treated only the second, which is also the best part. But because the first part is now being assailed by many, and the preachers, even those who are considered the best, are splitting up into factions over the matter, ... the times demand that I say something on this subject also.[61]

Luther stated this principle in reference to the doctrine of the Lord's Supper. He always followed this pattern in other doctrines, however. Whenever Luther formulated confessions or articles of faith, he regularly began with the doctrine of God in its Trinitarian form. For this reason, it would seem appropriate to give the doctrine of God the central position in a presentation of Luther's theology.

5.6.2 The Evaluation of Luther's Attitude Toward the Doctrine of the Trinity in the Presentations of Luther's Theology

The authors of descriptions of Luther's theology differ remarkably in their evaluation of the importance of the doctrine of the Trinity for Luther. They also evaluate the didactic element in Luther's writings in very different ways. For example, Reinhold Seeberg in his history of doctrine[62] did not discuss Luther's understanding of God until section 77. This is followed by the discussion of sin in section 78. Section 7.9 discusses the doctrines of Christ, the Trinity, and the work of Christ.

Werner Elert followed a similar pattern. He began his study of Reformation theology by discussing basic questions that must be confronted in order to understand the existential context of Luther's theology. These include the so-called *Urerlebnis* (primal experience), sin, law, the wrath of God, anxiety, and natural theology. The doctrine of God is not discussed, however, until the second section under the heading "Dogma and the Church."[63]

Erich Seeberg went further in the same direction. In *Luthers Theologie in ihren Grundzügen*,[64] he described Luther's "view of God" in chapter 4. He discussed such topics as the hidden God, God and evil, God and sin, the "transcendent" God who reveals himself and becomes real for us in Christ. This is followed by a chapter on "Christ." This is primarily devoted to "spiritual elements of our theological commitment to Christ." Erich Seeberg never provided any longer section on the doctrine of the Trinity, however.

The same is true of Gerhard Ebeling's article on Luther's theology.[65] Ebeling did not mention the doctrine of the Trinity.

Paul Althaus began his book *The Theology of Martin Luther* with a discussion of "the general and the proper knowledge of God" and then of "God in himself and God as he reveals himself." Although there are earlier references to the doctrine of the Trinity, it is not explicitly discussed until the middle of his book. Then less than two pages are devoted to it.[66]

Such limited treatment of Luther's doctrine of the Trinity is unsatisfactory. At the very least, these presentations of Luther's theology fail to explain why this doctrine was so important to Luther. And the frequent distinction, even separation, between Luther's view of God and his doctrine of the Trinity needs to be further explained. Although it is certain that there are problems at this point, it is equally certain that Luther never thought of God without thinking of the Trinity.

5.6.3 Luther's Critical Remarks on
the Doctrine of the Trinity

Luther made many critical remarks about the dogma of the Trinity. He expressed reservations about the traditional concept of "threefoldness" *(Dreifaltigkeit)* because God is the highest unity *(summa concordia).* Luther felt that the term "threefoldness" was "risky," but that the term "threeness" *(Dreiheit)* was "blasphemous."[67] Luther also felt that comparisons of the three persons of the Trinity with three angels or with three persons would lead into error. The doctrine of the Trinity does not describe three gods but one God. "Call it some kind of threesome. I have no adequate term for it."[68] Luther saw all such terms only as attempts to describe the reality of God.[69]

5.6.4 The Real Importance of the Doctrine of
the Trinity for Luther's Theology

At the same time, Luther still completely and totally affirmed the substance represented by the doctrine of the Trinity. For example, he said that the doctrine of the Trinity was scriptural.[70] There are many passages in Scripture that "clearly" teach the doctrine of the Trinity.[71] Luther clearly considered the doctrine of the Trinity to be scriptural. He saw it as a summary of biblical statements about God and considered the teaching of this summary to be a binding obligation in the church. The following statement is very clear on this point. "Some councils, among them the Council of Nicaea, have clarified the articles of faith and formulated them on the basis of Scripture. Affirming these doctrines is the same as affirming God's Word."[72]

Luther, however, was also able to criticize the philosophical terms used in teaching the doctrine of the Trinity as inadequate. In so doing, he was following the example of St. Augustine. Augustine himself had expressed strong reservations about the usefulness of the concept of "person" and preferred the concept of "relationship." The substantive significance of the doctrine of the Trinity for Luther was, however, demonstrated by the fact that he began his personal confession of faith at the end of *Confession Concerning Christ's Supper* (1528) with the following affirmation of the doctrine of the Trinity: "First, I believe with my whole heart the sublime article of the majesty of God, that the Father, Son, and Holy Spirit, three distinct persons, are by nature one true and genuine God, the Maker of heaven and earth; in complete opposition to the Arians, Macedonians, Sabellians, and similar heretics. . . . All this has been maintained up to this time both in the Roman Church and among Christian churches throughout the whole world."[73] Luther here also affirmed the substance of Augustine's principle that the works of the Trinity in relationship to all that is outside the Trinity remain indivisible *(opera trinitatis ad extra sunt indivisa)*.

Luther makes a similar statement in the Smalcald Articles.

> The first part of the Articles treats the sublime articles of the divine majesty, namely:
> 1. That Father, Son, and Holy Spirit, three distinct persons in one divine essence and nature, are one God, who created heaven and earth, etc.
> 2. That the Father was begotten by no one, the Son was begotten by the Father, and the Holy Spirit proceeded from the Father and the Son.
> 3. That only the Son became man, and neither the Father nor the Holy Spirit.
> 4. That the Son became man in this manner: he was conceived by the Holy Spirit, without the cooperation of man, and was born of the pure, holy, and virgin Mary. Afterwards he suffered, died, was buried, descended to hell, rose from the dead, and ascended to heaven; and he is seated at the right hand of God, will come to judge the living and the dead, etc., as the Apostles' Creed, the Athanasian Creed, and the Catechism in common use for children teach.
> These articles are not matters of dispute or contention, for both parties [believe and] confess them. Therefore, it is not necessary to treat them at greater length.[74]

The two words in brackets in the above quotation, "[believe and]," are not included in the printed texts of the Smalcald Articles. They were part of Luther's original manuscript but were crossed out by Luther himself. As a result, the printed text at this point affirms only that Roman Catholics and Protestants agree in confessing the Trinitarian faith. Naturally, Luther did not intend to imply that the dogma of the Trinity was not firmly maintained in the Roman Church. For Luther, however, faith in the triune God simultaneously required a specific doctrine of the human person and a specific doctrine of salvation; that is, faith in the triune God required the Reformation doctrine of justification. For Luther, simply accepting the dogmas as true was not enough.

This makes it clear that Luther understood the dogmas of the early church in the light of the doctrine of salvation. To this extent, he was part of the line of theological development begun by Athanasius. Athanasius felt that the Arians' rejection of the doctrine that the Son was of one substance with the Father *(homoousios)* called the whole meaning of redemption into question. Luther felt, however, that this connection between the dogmas and soteriology is even closer. As far as Luther was concerned, it is important that the dogmas not only objectively express Christian truth but also that they clearly describe its existential significance. For this reason, Luther did not accept the dogmas because of the authority of the Roman Church—with which he was, of course, in great conflict—but rather because of what they actually said.

5.6.5 The Image of God and the Doctrine of God

Luther thus both interpreted the traditional dogma on the basis of his teaching about salvation and also defined it as an expression of the same doctrine of salvation. He thereby emphasized different aspects of the dogmas than the earlier church had. We might say that Luther gave the image of God equal rank with the doctrine of God. Luther did not intend to play the image of God off against the doctrine of God; rather he inseparably combined them with each other. What we experience in life is the presence and activity of the triune God and not of some anonymous power of fate.

In considering this, we must emphasize that Luther thought of God as always active. Luther described God as "an energetic power, a continuous activity, that works and operates without ceasing. For God does not rest, but works without ceasing."[75] That God has created the world does not mean only that God set it in motion and then abandoned it to itself; rather it means that God constantly works and acts in the world. Being God and being the Creator are basically one and the same thing. That is why God is the creator and preserver of all things. God is God. For that reason, it is God who is at work in history causing kingdoms to rise and to pass away—calling all people into life and also setting the end of their life. God, of course, acts in a hidden way. We can never experience God directly. In his interpretation of Jonah (1526), Luther said it in a very daring way: "All of this is a source of comfort and confidence for us. It teaches us to rely on God, with whom life and death are alike. They are both trivial to Him, playthings as it were, as He bestows the one and takes the other, or exchanges one for the other. But for us these are momentous and impossible things, which God employs to display His power and skill to us."[76]

Many of the terms that Luther used in such statements are related to the language of the mystics. Thus Luther wrote: "The almighty power of God ... cannot be at any one place, I say. For if it were at some specific place, it would have to be there in a circumscribed and determinate manner, as everything which is at one place must be at the place determinately and measurably, so that it cannot meanwhile be at any other place. But the power of God cannot be so determined and measured, for it is uncircumscribed and immeasurable, beyond and above all that is or may be."[77] Later he wrote, "His own divine nature can be wholly and entirely in all creatures and in every single individual being, more deeply, more inwardly, more present than the creature is to itself, and yet on the other hand may and can be circumscribed nowhere and in no being, so that he actually embraces all things and is in all, but no one being circumscribes him and is in him."[78] "Nothing is so small but God is still smaller, nothing so large but God is still larger, nothing is so short but God is still shorter, nothing is so long but God is still longer, nothing is so broad but God is still broader, nothing so narrow but God is still narrower, and so on. He is an inexpressible being, above and beyond all that can be described or imagined."[79]

Luther also used the traditional terms for speaking of God, such as the first cause.[80] But these ideas meant something different for Luther than they traditionally had. Luther did not think it possible to trace the chain of causality back to the first cause and thereby finally to encounter God as the first cause. Rather Luther used this term to express his conviction that God uses creatures to carry out divine activity. Creatures and objects are the means through which God carries out the divine plan. They are the masks God puts on, the forms behind which God hides. "All creatures are God's masks and disguises. He permits them to work with him and assist him in creating many things—although he could, and sometimes does, do all these things without their cooperation."[81]

5.6.6 The Distinction Between the Hidden God and the Revealed God

Luther's new formulation of the distinction between the hidden God (*Deus absconditus*) and the revealed God (*Deus revelatus*) is of considerable significance. Although it is principally found in *The Bondage of the Will*,[82] its content, and to some extent even its terminology, appears in Luther's other writings. This distinction was not intended to expand the traditional doctrine of the Trinity with an additional point of doctrine. It was certainly not intended as a practical replacement for that doctrine. Rather, Luther obviously saw it as the appropriate interpretation of the doctrine of the Trinity and as a necessary tool to deal with the questions at issue between himself and Erasmus. This distinction is therefore Luther's appropriate interpretation of the doctrine of the Trinity insofar as it warns us against attempting to speculate about God's unsearchable will and directs us to turn to God's self-revelation. It is also an appropriate interpretation of the doctrine of the Trinity insofar as Luther did not arrive at this distinction on the basis of a philosophical concept of God but rather developed it strictly on the basis of God's revelation.

Scholars have interpreted the details of Luther's distinction between the hidden God and the revealed God in quite different ways. According to Otto Ritschl[83] "Luther's dualistic structuring of the concept of God painfully reminds us of the Marcionite doctrine that there are two Gods."

Reinhold Seeberg[84] viewed this distinction as Luther's personal appropriation of the Scotist and Ockhamist doctrines of the absolute power of God *(potentia Dei absoluta)* and the mediated power of God *(potentia Dei ordinata)*.[85] According to Werner Elert,[86] the experience of the hidden God constitutes the "primal experience" of God's power, experienced as the power of fate without Christ.

Any proper understanding of Luther's distinction between the hidden God and the revealed God must first of all take into account the flow of thought in *The Bondage of the Will* and then must consider its exegetical context. As far as the first task is concerned, Luther's concluding section in *The Bondage of the Will* makes it clear that his formulation presupposes faith in Christ as the necessary basis for its understanding.[87] Furthermore, Luther makes this distinction in the course of his interpretation of Ezek. 18:23, "Have I any pleasure in the death of the wicked, says the Lord God, and not rather that he should turn from his way and live?"[88] Erasmus interpreted this passage as supporting his assertion of a limited freedom of the human will.

It is interesting to note that Luther later occasionally applied the distinction between the hidden and the revealed God directly to the individual persons of the Trinity.

> We distinguish therefore between the Holy Spirit in his nature and substance as God and the Holy Spirit as he is given to us. God, in his nature and majesty, is our enemy, because he demands that we fulfill the law. . . . This is also true of the Holy Spirit. When his finger writes the law on Moses' tablets of stone, he appears in his majesty, accuses us of sin, and terrifies our hearts. However, when he comes to us in tongues and other spiritual gifts, he himself is called "gift" because he makes us holy and gives us life. Without this "gift" of the Holy Spirit himself, the law condemns our sin, because the law is never "gift," but always is the word of the eternal and almighty God.[89]

By and large, however, such statements are isolated statements in Luther's writing. Luther did not discuss in any more detail the question of how the doctrine of the Trinity related to his distinction between the hidden God and the revealed God. Still, however, this clearly demonstrates that Luther's doctrine of God and his personal view of God are very closely connected with each other.

In addition, the distinction between the hidden God and the revealed God that we find in *The Bondage of the Will* must not be seen in isolation but rather must be placed into the total context of Luther's concept of God. This distinction, then, means that the holy, unapproachable majesty of God remains even in God's self-disclosure. No matter how much Luther thought through theological questions on the basis of his doctrine of salvation, no matter how emphatically he placed justification through faith alone on the basis of divine forgiveness in the center of his thinking, the reality and seriousness of the divine judgment never disappear. Rather, they are always constantly being overcome through trust in the gracious God revealed in Christ. The Christian is never "beyond law and gospel."[90]

The wrath of God is not a figment of our imagination but is rather the power of God at work in life as well as in history. We need to flee from this wrath to the love of God that has appeared in Christ. God's revelation in Jesus Christ breaks through the power of God's wrath, even though the latter continues to be active. Thus, according to Luther, even in self-disclosure God remains the unsearchable majesty in whose presence we would be destroyed if we did not take refuge in the God who is gracious in Christ. It is a paradoxical formulation—but in Luther's thinking it is valid and not at all an extreme formulation—to say that we must always flee from God to God. To this extent, Luther's distinction between the hidden God and the revealed God corresponds to his teaching of law and gospel. We must say this as clearly as we say that this teaching can only be understood on the basis of Luther's doctrine of God. On this basis, it becomes clear that faith, as Luther understood it, is absolutely necessary for salvation.

In reviewing the history of the interpretation of Luther's theology in the last century, we can now see that Albrecht Ritschl, who died in 1889, overlooked the reality of the wrath of God. Theodosius Harnack, who also died in 1889, properly drew attention to the wrath of God as a factor in Luther's theology.[91] More recently, Karl Barth and the Barthians once again have underestimated the significance of the wrath of God for Luther. Interpreters of Luther who are consciously "confessional," such as Werner Elert and others of the Erlangen school, have sometimes obviously overemphasized the double aspect of the wrath and love of God in Luther's theology.

It is this tension between wrath and love that constitutes the dynamic of Luther's concept of God. This dynamic is not simply a voluntaristic formulation of the doctrine of God. That was available long before Luther in the Scotist and Ockhamist traditions. Luther presented theology with a new approach. The presence of this tension between God's wrath and God's love also created an essential difference between Luther and the mystics, even though the mystics' concept of God influenced both the whole and specific parts of Luther's theology in significant ways. The student will find a detailed comparison of these differing ideas of God, with particular reference to those points which they share in common and those points at which they differ from one another, to be a stimulating project. In making such a comparison, it is useful to work not only with older concepts of God but also to take the ideas of God proposed by Luther's contemporaries, for example, Thomas Müntzer, into consideration.

As far as the dynamic of Luther's view of God is concerned, attention may here be drawn to a few points. First of all, it is important to note that Luther does not distinguish the various so-called attributes of God. It may be more helpful to say that Luther achieved the intention of the discussion of the attributes by recognizing that it is not really possible to differentiate between one attribute and the other attributes. Rather, each of God's so-called attributes constantly expresses the whole of God's activity. God's omnipotence or omniscience are never merely partial aspects of God; rather each always expresses the totality of God. As Luther put it, to say that God speaks is the same as saying that God creates.[92] Luther also emphasized that being God and being Creator are basically one and the same thing. In this way, God is always actively creating, and for Luther this meant that God never works without creating.

5.6.7 God as Creator

David Löfgren[93] interpreted Luther's statements about creation to mean that Luther did not see creation as a finished act but rather as an ongoing event. Luther understood creation as a present reality. For this reason, the very real goodness of the created world is not to be understood as part of its inherent nature or its own capacity but rather constantly rests on God's real and ongoing creative intervention. This interpretation might very well go too far. It is indeed correct that we cannot separate the different aspects of Luther's statements about God's activity. It is also true that Luther from time to time made no distinction between creation and preservation. In spite of this, however, this emphasis on creation as an ongoing process is carried too far if the independence of the created world from God—properly understood—is called into question.

Löfgren has asserted that God also constantly creates new natural laws; for this reason, he says, human reason always remains one step behind these laws.[94] Over against this, we need to remember that Luther clearly said that human reason evokes and formulates these natural laws, although "justice" is always a "creature of God."[95] Neither insight should be played off against the other. We should also distinguish between Luther's understanding of God's creation, the preservation of the created world, and God's activity. In so doing, it is very important to indicate clearly that each of these activities of God always describes the wholeness of God. Any restatement of Luther's doctrine of God, or any other doctrine, must avoid both the danger of an orthodox schematization and the danger of reducing everything to the same meaning.

An additional perspective that must also be taken into account in this context is the strong mystical tradition referred to above.[96] The following text from Luther's second lectures on the Psalms (1518–21) is very interesting at this point:

> When you hope in God, where do you have left to go except into your own nothingness? And where do you go when you enter into your own nothingness except into that from which you came? You, however, came out of this same nothingness, that is, you came from God. Therefore when you return into your own nothingness, you return to God. Even though you fall outside yourself and outside of all creation, you still fall into the hand of God. As Isaiah (40:12) says, he holds the whole world in the hollow of his hand. So run throughout the world, if you wish. Where will you run to? You will always run into the hand and bosom of God. Thus the souls of the righteous are in the hand of God, because they are outside the world.[97]

Luther was interpreting Ps. 5:12 on the basis of the Latin Vulgate. This translation provides hardly any basis for such a far-reaching interpretation. The text itself asserts that God will "dwell" in those who hope in God. This, however, points in quite a different direction than Luther's exegesis which focuses on our return to God. Luther's revision of the original intention of the text was significant. It was even more significant that Luther seemed almost to identify God and the nothingness of the human person, although Luther did not go quite so far as to assert that God is nothingness. On the contrary, he equated the nothingness of the human person with the being of God or with the hand of God. If the human person is destroyed in the literal sense of the word, she or he thereby comes to God—just as we all come from God and therewith from our own nonbeing.

It is, of course, not enough merely to assert that the mystical tradition underlies this statement. Rather, the fact is that there were decisive differences between Luther and mysticism. Unlike the mystics, Luther was not speaking about the mystical union or the exchange between the divine Thou and the human ego. Instead, in the process described by Luther, the human ego is destroyed when it comes to God. In such a statement, Luther gave an almost existential interpretation to the mystical tradition. Any kind of mythological thinking was excluded. And yet Luther preserved the duality between God and the human person which he took over from the mystics. This duality finds its highest expression precisely in the destruction of the human person. It is hard to imagine a statement more daring than this. Obviously, however, it would be one--

sided of us to try to derive the totality of Luther's idea of God from such texts or even only from his understanding of creation.

5.6.8 God Is God

The central focus of Luther's doctrine of God can, however, also be described from other viewpoints. Paul Althaus has said that "God is God" is the meaning of Luther's doctrine of justification.[98] Althaus has demonstrated that Luther rejected moralism or the legalistic fulfillment of the divine commandments not only because we are never really able to succeed in doing this, but rather also because moralism and legalism are finally idolatry and contrary to the nature of God. The human attitude that corresponds to the nature of God is much more that of a receiver who trusts only in divine mercy. Luther's criticism of works-righteousness is thus basically theocentric. "To have a God" and to want to be justified on the basis of the fulfillment of the law are thus two contradictory positions. Faith alone is the appropriate human attitude in relationship to God. Of course, it would also be wrong of us to carry the ideas that Althaus has so convincingly developed to an extreme—with the possible result that we would thereby overlook the reality of God's demands as well as the reality that it is God who both makes demands and judges us.

Wherever we begin when we seek to come to terms with Luther's understanding of God, we constantly come up against the unity of the doctrine of God and the image of God. This unity in Luther's thinking is obviously due to the fact that he always based his whole theology on the cross of Christ.

5.7 ECCLESIOLOGY,
THE OFFICE OF THE MINISTRY,
AND THE STRUCTURE OF THE CHURCH

5.7.1 The Absence of Any Ecclesiological Program in Luther's Thinking

In studying Luther's ecclesiology, or his doctrine of the church, we must again decide which of various methods we will follow. We must also decide how much weight we will give to certain teachings that Luther shared with his opponents and did not discuss because they were not a point of controversy. Here again the various possible interpretations of Luther's theology have diverged from one another in quite significant ways.

Any systematic treatment of Luther's doctrine of the church suffers from a serious disadvantage—particularly if it deals with his view of the structure of the church. It is all too easy to give to Luther's statements a

ASPECTS AND PROBLEMS OF LUTHER'S THEOLOGY

significance that they cannot possibly have. This is because all of them were developed in the context of Luther's numerous controversies. These statements tell us more about Luther's increasingly sharp criticism of the papacy and of the hierarchy of the church in general. In addition, it is far too easy to assume that Luther was proposing a definite structure for the church. The fact is that Luther had no such vision. Particularly in the early period of the Reformation, both his criticism of certain abuses in the medieval church and his own thinking about the church were meaningful only in the context of the situations that were the subject of controversy. It is almost impossible to separate Luther's statements about the church from those controversies.

Neither side in these sixteenth-century controversies—most certainly not Luther—was working out of a coherent set of ideas that were in conflict from the beginning of the controversy. Rather, the various views of the church were first sharply defined in the course of the conflict. Of course, certain ideas were present from the beginning on both sides which various parties considered to be absolutely essential. We must be very clear about these decisive elements of the various understandings of the church. We have no reason to assume, however, that it was absolutely necessary for the following controversies to develop as they actually did. These same presuppositions might have led to quite different results.

It is also important to note that the doctrine of the church was considerably less well developed than the doctrines of the Trinity or of the person and work of Christ. The great works of scholastics do not contain any doctrine of the church. Naturally there were individual writings—such as Cyprian's "On the Unity of the Church" or Augustine's anti-Donatist writings. These were quite significant and much was said about the church indirectly. Not least of all, church law was in many ways significant for the understanding of the church. As far as the papacy was concerned, its authority and leadership role in the church were generally accepted. This was the truth even though the conciliar movement of the fifteenth century for some time raised the question whether the pope or an ecumenical council was the highest authority. In the sixteenth century, however, the conciliar movement was no longer very significant. In spite of this, when we study the controversies of the early sixteenth century, we must take into account the fact that there were very many open questions. At that point in time, no established norms were available for the doctrine of the church as there were for the doctrine of the Trinity and for the person and work of Christ.

As far as the unity of the church is concerned, we must remember that people in the sixteenth century were aware of two significant schisms. The one was the schism between Eastern and Western Christianity, which had been a reality ever since 1054. Even though Eastern Orthodox Christians were far away, the constant threat of attack by the Turks kept the memory of the fall of Constantinople in 1453, and therewith also the Eastern church, constantly alive in the sixteenth century. The question about the necessity of papal authority in the church that arose from this schism was very significant for the early history of the Reformation. It may therefore be taken for granted that the existence of the Eastern Orthodox church soon became significant for the controversy centered around Luther, particularly in the year 1519.

The second schism that was important for the early Reformation was that of the Hussite movement. John Huss had been condemned and executed by the Council of Constance in 1415. In 1433, however, the Council of Constance agreed to the so-called *Compactata* of Prague, which made certain concessions to the Hussites. This agreement was, however, never approved by the pope. Thus, although Huss himself continued to be considered a heretic, and although the Hussite Wars with their widespread destruction, particularly in the area of Saxony, were still a living memory among the people, the Hussites continued to represent an open wound on the body of the one Christendom.

It was also important for the question of the unity of the church that the terrible schisms in the papacy itself (1378–1415) were still well remembered by people at the time of Luther. All this meant that obedience to the pope could no longer be taken for granted in the way in which it had been in other times.

In addition, one must consider: First, no one intended to bring about a split in the church. What Luther intended was the reformation of the church according to the Word of God. He was not concerned about a list of definite reforms, but rather desired to bring an end to the obvious abuses as well as to restore the proclamation of the pure Word of God. Even when the Reformation was introduced in many other territories as well as in cities, almost no one at all thought about the possibility of founding a new church. On the contrary, an appeal was made to the example of late medieval reforms that had been introduced in many territories by the secular authorities. The situation was undoubtedly more difficult in the sixteenth century, because many assumed that there were contradictions between the authority of the Scripture and the authority of the church. It is at this point that the line of separation between "Roman Catholic" and "Protestant" can be most easily traced. There was, however, almost no subjective consciousness of a split in the church at all.

Second, this description of the situation is confirmed by the fact that the church was still dealt with as a unity by the legal authorities of the empire even at the time of the Religious Peace of Augsburg of 1555. It was only in the Peace of Westphalia of 1648 that the actually existing split in the church was sanctioned and accepted as a reality by the law of the empire. Until then, people worked on the basis of a fiction that assumed the ongoing unity of the church and spoke of "religious parties." The emperor was, however, not able to function as the protector of the Roman Catholic Church in Protestant territories.

Third, the discussion at the time of the Reformation dealt neither with the split in the church nor with ways to overcome it; the significant issue was where to find the true church. People thus worked on behalf of the unity of the church, but they did so by establishing criteria for the presence of the true or the false church. This explains not only the severity of the mutual polemic but also the far-reaching agreement that continued to exist in spite of everything. Just as was the case in the doctrines of the Trinity and of the person and work of Christ, the common basis that both sides accepted without question was of considerable significance. This was true even though they hardly ever thought about the importance of this common agreement. The fact is, however, that there was probably considerably more agreement in the doctrine of the church than is ordinarily recognized.

5.7.2 Traditional and New Elements in Luther's Doctrine of the Church

We might risk saying that we find all the traditional elements of the doctrine of the church in Luther; the difference lies in the emphasis that Luther placed on these various elements. It is also true, however, that Luther also made a radically new beginning in that he established the gospel and faith as the norm for determining whether the true and therefore the one church is present. Both these assertions must be seen in close relationship with one another. It is not valid to play one side of Luther's doctrine of the church off against the other.

5.7.3 Luther's Early Attitude Toward the Pope

At the beginning of the controversy on indulgences, Luther had absolutely no intention of calling the authority of the church, the pope, or the bishops into question.[99] Luther's opponents of course drew attention to certain consequences that his teachings had for the authority of the pope and the councils. They were not entirely wrong in doing so. Luther himself, however, sincerely regarded the pope as the shepherd and teacher of Christendom. Luther's mixed feelings about the pope were clearly expressed in his letter of May 30, 1518, dedicating his *Explanations of the Ninety-five Theses* to Pope Leo X. In this letter, Luther on the one hand said, "Holy Father, I throw myself before your feet and offer myself together with all that I am and have. Make me alive or kill me, accept or recant, agree to or reject [what I have written]. Whatever you decide is acceptable to me. I shall recognize your voice as the voice of Christ, who leads [the church] through you and speaks through you. If I have deserved death, I shall not refuse to die."[100] On the other hand, Luther had just a few lines earlier declared, "I am unable to recant."[101] Anyone reading both of these statements at a later time would see them as contradicting each other. Luther, however, did not see them as being in opposition to each other. His words of submission to the pope were not written as a matter of tactics. Luther could not imagine anything else than that Christ himself actually led the church through the pope. At the same time, Luther had reached insights into the questions under controversy through his study of the Bible. These insights were firmly established in his thinking and he was not ready to abandon them.

In the following years, Luther, of course, could not maintain this attitude. The process of his excommunication under church law, the simple challenge to recant without discussion of the issues, the increasingly sharper polemics, as well as the refusal of the ecclesiastical authorities to abolish obvious abuses, finally brought Luther in 1518–19 to the certainty that the pope is the antichrist. Therefore, as a result of this conclusion, subjection to the authority of the pope was no longer possible for Luther. Luther now denied that it was necessary for the church to have an earthly head.

This happened most pointedly in his first writing explicitly dealing with the church, *On the Papacy in Rome* (1520).[102] Luther here distinguished between Christendom as a gathering of all those on earth who believe in Christ in the sense of the creeds and Christendom as a gathering in one house, in one parish, in one diocese, in one archbishopric, or in the papacy—in each case his attention is focused on the external appearance. When Scripture speaks of the church, however, it exclusively refers to the gathering together of those who believe in Christ. Since only this gathering in the Spirit can be the true Christendom, it can have no head here on earth. Rather, this Christendom is ruled only by Christ as its heavenly head.[103]

5.7.4 'The Two Churches'

In this context, Luther even spoke of "two churches." "Therefore, for the sake of better understanding and brevity, we shall call the two churches by two distinct names. The first, which is natural, basic, essential, and true, we shall call 'spiritual, internal Christendom.' The second, which is man-made and external, we shall call 'physical, external Christendom.'

Not that we want to separate them from each other; rather, it is just as if I were talking about a man and called him 'spiritual' according to his soul, and 'physical' according to his body."[104] This distinction between "spiritual" and "physical" Christendom has various meanings. "Physical," and also "external," refer (1) to the contrast between the external church and the true, spiritual nature of the church. This distinction is particularly applied to the papacy.[105] (2) This terminology describes the twofold nature of the church in comparison to the human person, which has both a body and a soul. Although body and soul are distinct from each other, they are always present in the human person. The soul is the essential element, but we cannot think of the soul apart from its relationship to the body.[106]

Scholars who have attempted summary descriptions of Luther's ecclesiology, his doctrine of the church, have not always adequately taken this varying use of the term "physical" *(leiblich)* into account in their reading of this book as well as of Luther's other writings in which this term occurs. As a result, an absolutely inaccurate and unacceptable description of Luther's doctrine of the church was, and even today frequently still is, taken for granted. This erroneous interpretation presents Luther as having described the real church only in terms of its internal characteristics, sometimes described as the "invisible" church. In Luther's polemics against the pope as the representative of "physical" Christendom, he was protesting against the way in which the papacy of his time had, for all practical purposes, set aside the gospel in the church. Luther, however, was not protesting against the external nature of the church itself, nor did he understand Christendom as "invisible." To this extent, Luther is only being consistent when, in this same writing, he calls baptism, the Lord's Supper, and the gospel the signs "by which the existence of the church can be noticed externally."[107]

5.7.5 Luther's Attitude Toward the Office of the Bishop

Although Luther clearly rejected the authority of the papacy, he never polemicized against the office of the bishops in the same way. Quite the contrary, scholars generally agree that Luther himself thought it important to preserve the episcopal structure of the church. Luther was not thinking about the question of apostolic succession in any way—neither side of the controversy raised that question at all. Luther also was simply not thinking about the traditional office of the bishop as it had developed in the history of the church. Rather Luther understood the office of the bishop as responsible for the ministry of the gospel. At that time, it was customary for the bishops to exercise both spiritual and secular authority. Similarly, the bishops also had judicial powers, for example, in matters related to marriage. Luther rejected this integration of spiritual and secular authority. He, however, often expressed his opinion that there should be bishops in the church, for example, in his preface to the *Instructions for the Visitors of Parish Pastors in Electoral Saxony* (1528).[108]

The Lutheran churches in Germany developed the office of the superintendent, also called the "superattendent." As it was described in the regulations governing the life of the church *(Kirchenordnungen)*, this office is basically that of the bishop. The duties of the bishop include proclaiming the gospel, administering the sacraments, and visiting the pastors. Later, Luther made several attempts to introduce Lutheran bishops.[109] Of course, here too the gospel was Luther's critical norm. In terms of the traditional question, the office of the bishop does not belong to the essence *(esse)*, but it certainly belongs to the well-being *(bene esse)* of the church. The Smalcald Articles illustrate how Luther simply took the office of the bishop for granted: "The church cannot be better governed and maintained than by having all of us live under one head, Christ, and by having all the bishops equal in office (however they may differ in gifts) and diligently joined together in unity of doctrine, faith, sacraments, prayer, works of love, etc." It should be noted that Luther follows this statement immediately with a reference to a statement of St. Jerome, which the Reformers generally interpreted to mean there originally was no distinction between the office of pastor and the office of bishop.[110] This interpretation of the historical development of the office of the bishop is substantially correct. Luther's ideal structure of the church can best be described of bishops working together with synods.[111]

5.7.6 The Necessity of the Church to Salvation

Furthermore, Luther did not disagree with the tradition that the church is necessary for salvation. "Therefore he who wants to find Christ, must first find the church. . . . The church is not wood and stone but the assembly of people who believe in Christ. With this church one should be connected and see how the people believe, live, and teach. They certainly have Christ in their midst, for outside the Christian church there is no truth, no Christ, no salvation."[112] Of course, Luther did not understand the statement that there is no salvation outside the church in exactly the same sense as medieval theologians had. Although Luther also considered the sacraments to be necessary, the decisive factor is faith in that salvation which is offered and given to us through the Word and sacrament.

5.7.7 The Marks of the Church

Luther's understanding of the relationship between the spiritual and the physical nature of the church has just been discussed. This same relationship underlies his understanding of the "marks of the church" *(notae ecclesiae)*. Traditionally, theologians described four marks of the church: unity, holiness, catholicity, and apostolicity. Over against this, Luther stated his own opinion very sharply. "The one, eternal, and unmistakeable mark of the church is, and always has been the Word."[113]

In other places, however, Luther himself listed a whole series of marks. In *On the Councils and the Church* (1539), he listed (1) the Word, (2) baptism, (3) the Lord's Supper, (4) the Office of the Keys, (5) the calling and ordination of pastors and bishops, (6) prayer and giving praise and thanks to God, and (7) the bearing of the cross as well as of spiritual temptation.[114]

In *Against Hanswurst* (1541), he listed (1) baptism, (2) the Lord's Supper, (3) the Office of the Keys, (4) the office of preaching the Word of God, (5) the Apostles' Creed, (6) the Lord's Prayer, (7) the respect that is owed to secular government, (8) the praise of marriage as an order created by and acceptable to God, (9) the suffering of the true church, and (10) the willingness to endure persecution without seeking revenge. In addition, Luther rejected the accusation that the Lutherans do not fast and emphasized that instead of fasting in their own self-chosen way, they endure the sufferings that God lays upon them.[115] It is, however, significant that Luther closed this list with the assertion, "Thus we have proved that we are the true, ancient church" in contrast to the papists who "are the new false church."[116] Nevertheless, it is important that Luther traced the marks of the church into the physical existence of the church. This indicates again that Luther did not simply think of the church as spiritual in the sense of being invisible.

Although Luther denied that the papists are the church, he willingly conceded that there was much that was Christian under the papacy. "We on our part confess that there is much that is Christian and good under the papacy; indeed everything that is Christian and good is to be found there and has come to us from this source. For instance we confess that in the papal church there are the true holy Scriptures, true baptism, the true sacrament of the altar, the true keys to the forgiveness of sins, the true office of the ministry, the true catechism in the form of the Lord's Prayer, the Ten Commandments, and the articles of the creed."[117] Thus, in spite of his radical criticism of the papal church, Luther conceded that the Roman Church also bore the marks of the church. "The church was always present, even though it could not always be identified. However, where were the true marks of the church preserved? In God's marvelous plan, the true Scripture was kept and preserved in the papal church. Baptism, the sacrament of the altar, and absolution were also miraculously preserved by God. Thus many died in true faith."[118]

On the other hand, we must recognize that Luther's sharp condemnation of the Roman Church stood in contrast to this positive view. Luther did not only respond to the papal bull threatening excommunication by burning it, but also, by exercising the authority given to him in his baptism, he excommunicated the pope and the cardinals, or at least declared them to be excommunicated.[119] Luther later repeated this condemnation in a variety of ways. Apparently, Luther did not see these two aspects of his attitude against Rome as being in contradiction to one another.

5.7.8 The Office of the Ministry and Ordination

There were tensions not only in Luther's attitude toward the organization of the church of the time but also in his understanding of the office of the ministry and of ordination. In any case, scholars have described and evaluated Luther's understanding of the office of ministry and of ordination in quite different ways. Generally, we can say that Luther in his early period—especially from 1520 until about 1523—emphasized the universal priesthood of the baptized. He sometimes did this in such a way that he seemed to derive the special office of the ministry from the universal priesthood. In contrast to this, Luther in his later years generally gave more emphasis to the special and independent mission of the office of the ministry.

Luther scholars have, as a result, based their description of Luther's understanding of the office of the ministry either on the position of the old Luther or of the young. Wilhelm Brunotte, for example, asserted the independence of the office of the ministry from a "congregational" understanding of the basis for this office. He was correct—insofar as Luther during his early period actually did not derive the office of the ministry from the universal priesthood of the baptized.[120] In contrast, Hellmut Lieberg speaks of Luther's "bipolar" doctrine of the ministry.[121]

At one point in his life, Luther derived the office of the ministry from the universal priesthood of the baptized—a view that emphasized the importance of the pastor's call by the congregation. At another time Luther derived the office of the ministry from the institution of this office by Christ—a view that emphasized the importance of ordination.

It is also important to note Peter Manns's proof of his thesis that Luther never—not even in the stormiest early days of the Reformation—approved the celebration of communion in a private residence.[122] Quite the contrary is true. Luther repeatedly resisted every attempt to separate the celebration of the communion from its relationship to the office of the ministry and to the congregation. This clearly demonstrates that we cannot adequately develop Luther's doctrine of the ministry simply on the basis of his explicit statements. Rather, we must also take his practice into account.

As in the case for Luther's ecclesiology as a whole, so we must always take the specific situation and controversy in which Luther made a particular statement into account in interpreting its meanings. For this reason, we must avoid reading too much into his early statements.

For example, Luther formulated the concept of the universal priesthood of the baptized in 1520—after several preliminary attempts. It is not to be understood as a constitutive principle for the organization of the church. The "universal priesthood" obviously corresponds to Luther's Reformation view of justification and faith as well as of every Christian's direct relationship to God. At the same time, we ought not overlook the polemical context in which this doctrine was formulated. Luther particularly emphasized this thesis of the universal priesthood of the baptized in *To the Christian Nobility of the German Nation Concerning the Reform of the Christian Estate*. In this context he uses it to break down the "three walls of Rome."[123] Elsewhere, however, Luther always maintained that the bishops are responsible for the care of the pastors who preach the gospel. Congregations may take the initiative only when and if the bishops do not fulfill their responsibility. At a later time, however, Luther felt that the secular government should intervene.

5.7.9 Differing Emphases in Luther's Doctrine of the Ministry

The following controversies were the contexts of Luther's various statements about the ministry and ordination. Each resulted in a particular pattern of emphasis.

From 1517 to 1520 Luther was in conflict with the authorities of the church and developed his concept of the universal priesthood of the baptized.

The period 1520 to 1523 began with the breaking off of relationships between Luther and Rome and is characterized by Luther's polemic against the priesthood and the sacrifice of the Mass.

Beginning in 1524 Luther was constantly in opposition to the enthusiasts.

After 1530 the Reformation developed under less-conflicted conditions. In this context, Luther developed a comprehensive structure of the

Protestant church and was increasingly able to realize it in practice. He now emphasized the coordination of the office of the ministry, ordination, and the church.

5.7.10 The Ministry and the Universal Priesthood

In addition, it is important to remember that Luther's terminology ordinarily distinguished between the ordained ministry and the universal priesthood of the baptized. He used the term "sacerdotium" in discussing the universal priesthood, but reserved the term "ministerium" for the ordained ministry. As far as ordination is concerned, Luther, after 1520, consistently denied that it is a sacrament. Luther, however, also consistently maintained that the office of the preaching of the Word and of the administration of the sacraments was instituted in the church by Christ himself.

Luther's list of the marks of the church[124] also clearly indicates that he thought of the ordained ministry as essential to the church. His rejection of the sacramental character of ordination came from his strict definition of a sacrament, which he first stated in 1520. There is no external sign in ordination, such as the water of baptism or the bread and wine of communion. Luther, however, continued to emphasize the divine mission of the ministry as well as the promise that God speaks and acts when the pastor acts in accordance with pastoral duty. Luther basically also agreed with the traditional understanding that ordination confers the gift of the Holy Spirit on the pastor as a resource for carrying out the ministry.

In discussing Luther's view of the ministry and ordination, we must consider the orders of service that the Reformers prepared for the ordination of pastors—as well as Luther's statements in his publications and letters. Additional important matters must also be considered, including the communion of the sick, the exorcism in baptism, and the so-called conditional baptism that was administered when there was doubt as to whether a child had already been baptized.

As far as the organization of the church as a whole is concerned, the fact is that no one really expected that the sixteenth-century schism in the church would be permanent. This means that we cannot assume that the Reformers were raising or answering questions related to basic issues. As long as there was still hope that the whole church would be reformed or that, at the very least, the Protestants would be given freedom to preach the gospel, there was no reason to think about a basic reorganization of the church. Luther's early statements were, almost without exception, aimed at removing the limitations on or even the suppression of the Reformation's preaching of the gospel. Had these efforts been successful, significant changes in the organization of the church would almost certainly have followed—most likely in a more Lutheran understanding of the office of the bishop. In spite of such changes, however, it is quite likely that the German Reformation, like the English Reformation, would have preserved the episcopal structure of the church.

Since no bishop, at that time, supported the German Reformation, and since the congregations suffered under widespread uncertainty about and disorder in their relationship to the church, it became absolutely necessary for the Reformers to create some kind of order. The monasteries and nunneries had been dissolved almost everywhere. And there was as yet no brief summary of the teachings of the Reformation—so that completely contradictory ideas were often presented as the teaching of the Reformation. In the early years of the Reformation as well, there had been no need for new orders of the service of worship.

The Peasants' War had clearly demonstrated that many viewpoints being proclaimed in various places in the name of the Reformation were quite dangerous to individuals and to society. It was clearly the duty of the Reformers to restore clarity and order for the sake of the church; it was also a political necessity of the highest order. No one can dispute this. Given the conditions of those times, there was only one single authority who could do what was necessary in the situation. That was the secular government. Whoever, by virtue of hindsight, thinks that Luther and the other Reformers might have been able to avoid calling on the help of the secular government simply does not understand the limited possibilities with which they were working.

At the beginning of the Reformation, Luther had told the congregations that they were free to appoint pastors for themselves without the cooperation of their bishops or even in opposition to their bishops. He said this very clearly in *That a Christian Assembly or Congregation Has the Right and Power to Judge All Teaching and to Call, Appoint, and Dismiss Teachers, Established and Proven by Scripture* (1523).[125] In the same year, Luther had already asserted that secular governments had previously sometimes installed pastors without the approval of the bishops and the popes. Luther saw this fact as establishing a precedent that the Reformers were free to follow. In addition, Luther had, in 1520, suggested that secular government should take the lead in calling an ecumenical council—which the Reformers hoped would bring about a genuine reformation of the church.[126] In 1526 and in the following years, however, Luther and the other Reformers took steps that went considerably beyond the position they had taken in 1523.

It is important for us to keep in mind the very problematical legal situation under which they worked. Among both the theologians and the secular officials—who were actually legally responsible for instituting the

Reformation—such actions were justified by reference to the agreements made at the Diet of Speyer in 1526. At that diet all the estates of the empire had agreed to act in such a way that they could answer both to God and the emperor. This agreement obviously applied only to the enforcement of the edict of the earlier Diet of Worms and was not intended to give the Protestant estates the right to reform the church. Thus, although the Reformers cited the decree of the Diet of Speyer in 1526 as the basic authorization for the secular government to intervene in the life of the church, they did so in a way that was absolutely contrary to its original intention and wording.[127]

5.8 CHURCH AND STATE: LUTHER'S DOCTRINE OF THE TWO KINGDOMS

5.8.1 The Doctrine of the Two Kingdoms: Historical Significance

Luther's doctrine of the two kingdoms is without doubt the single theme of Luther's theology that has been most discussed in recent decades. In this process, it has long been the custom of many to assume that Luther had already been tried and convicted of uncritically accepting the power of the secular government. Together with this, he is accused of having taught the subjects of those governments to respond with absolute obedience and he is therefore described as being largely responsible for the authoritarian form of government that existed in Germany for centuries. At the very least, Luther is condemned for having prevented the development of a democracy in Germany because of his attitude during the Peasants' War. Such accusations are particularly based on what is described as his one-sided interpretation of the thirteenth chapter of Romans.

Modern secular literature also frequently expresses a condemnation of Luther. Dieter Forte's play *Martin Luther und Thomas Münzer oder die Einfürung der Buchhaltung* (Martin Luther and Thomas Müntzer or the Introduction of Double-Entry Bookkeeping) was very popular when first produced in 1971 and for some time afterward, and is symptomatic of this interpretation. The Marxist critique of Luther is considerably older, although it has obviously undergone many changes since the days of Marx and Engels. Current Marxist attitudes toward Luther are much more discriminating than earlier critiques.

Modern church people and theologians have sharply attacked Luther's attitude from two perspectives. On the one hand, Luther is accused of having indirectly contributed to the glorification of the orders of creation and to that extent at least making it difficult for Lutherans to take a

critical attitude toward the Third Reich, the National-Socialist government from 1933 to 1945. On the other hand, Luther is also held responsible for the "conservative" attitude of many Lutheran churches toward the
political situations and the revolutionary movements for freedom in
countries of the Third World.

There can be no argument with the assertion that Luther's doctrine of
the two kingdoms has had far-reaching effects on history and remains
influential today. No matter whether any of the various twentieth-century
attitudes toward Luther is right or wrong, however, there is absolutely no
reason for Luther scholars to describe Luther's viewpoint in terms of
slogans and prejudices. Such inadmissible generalizations and simplistic
evaluations of Luther are occasionally even found among scholars who
have otherwise made significant contributions to our understanding of
Luther.

5.8.2 The History of the Background of
the Doctrine of the Two Kingdoms
in the Tradition of the Church

If we propose to investigate the complex group of doctrines that can be
summarized under the heading of the doctrine of the two kingdoms, we
must begin by recognizing that the problem identified with this doctrine
has had a long prehistory in the tradition. It even now seems that the
question of the opposition or the coordination of the secular and the
spiritual areas of life is a unique element of the Jewish-Christian tradition.
In any case, it is obvious that other cultures do not set these two in
opposition to one another in the same way that the Jewish-Christian
tradition does. Rather they are, in one way or another, much more closely
bound together with one another or even fused into some kind of unity.
Thus there was no corresponding distinction between these two areas in
classical antiquity.

This was particularly obvious in the Roman worship of the emperor.
The heathen Romans viewed such worship as basically nothing more than
an act of political loyalty—even though it occurred in the context of a
religious ceremony. Christians were, to be sure, prepared to live as loyal
citizens but not to prove this by offering the prescribed ritual sacrifice to
the emperor. The basic distinction between the spiritual and the secular
areas of life reappeared as a totality in the age of the state church, even
though from time to time the pre-Christian unity of these two areas also
reappeared.

The basic theme of the relationship of the spiritual to the secular or of
the relationship between the empire and the church has therefore been
dealt with in every age of theology. Ulrich Duchrow has given us the most

extensive study of this history of the tradition—even though his study is
by no means exhaustive.[128]

Augustine's understanding of two cities, one of God, the other of Satan,
was particularly influential on the future development of these concepts
and their manifold effects on the historical development in the Middle
Ages. The controversy over investiture in the eleventh and twelfth centuries is also part of the history of this topic, as are the fourteenth-
century controversies between Ludwig of Bavaria and the papacy. There
is hardly any other topic of ethics and of ecclesiology that has such a rich
and varied history as the distinction and the relationship between the
secular and the spiritual realms. The so-called doctrine of the two kingdoms is therefore to be understood, first of all, as an attempt to understand an important theme of Christian tradition in terms of the teaching
of Scripture and to present them in a way that would be relevant to the
issues at the time of the Reformation. This required a new formulation of
the doctrine.

5.8.3 The Term 'Doctrine of the Two Kingdoms'

Luther himself never used the concept of the "doctrine of the two
kingdoms." This has only become apparent as a result of the discussion of
this doctrine in recent years. This term seems to have been used for the
first time in 1922; however, it then very quickly passed into common
usage. This concept represents a brief formula that may possibly be useful
in describing a much more comprehensive complex of doctrines. Obviously any such brief formula is easily in danger of being systematized in
an impermissible way. As far as Luther is concerned, we can see the
reality of such a danger when we remember that he did not understand
the secular realm, or the kingdom of this world, as being limited to the
state or to government. Rather, he included under this term the whole
secular realm including nature, the family, the arts, and all the sciences.
Thus the relationship between the church and secular government is
only one small section of this doctrine, even though a very important
section. Contemporary discussions of the doctrine of the two kingdoms,
however, seem ordinarily to presuppose that the issue is exclusively the
relationship between the church and the secular state.

5.8.4 Is the Secular Realm Autonomous?

For a long time, Luther's view was misrepresented under the presupposition that it attributes "autonomy" to the secular realm. This was the
position even of a scholar such as Reinhold Seeberg. Seeberg emphasized
that Luther's view of the secular realm played a very significant role in the
spiritual and political development of Germany. As a result, the autonomy

of secular life and the state's control of culture were well established.[129] Seeberg's conclusion is right insofar as we encounter much less "legalism" in Lutheranism than in Calvinism. And, properly understood, the concept of autonomy may describe this. As the intense discussions of these issues after 1945 have shown, however, it is better to describe this factor in terms of "independence" rather than "autonomy." In the period after 1933, the description of Luther's view in terms of autonomy could easily lead to an uncritical approval of the actions of the secular government.

5.8.5 Survey of the Newer Studies of Luther's Doctrine of the Two Kingdoms

A radical change in the evaluation of Luther's view manifested itself when scholars began to focus on the terminology of the two "governments" as well as the two "kingdoms." The first effort to do so was that of Ernst Kinder.[130] The work of Gustav Törnvall[131] was considerably more extensive and significant. Over against the common assertion that Luther radically distinguished between the two kingdoms or realms, Törnvall demonstrated that Luther also spoke of two governments. God rules in a twofold way, that is, in a secular and spiritual manner: on the one hand, through the sword of the secular government and, on the other hand, through the word of the church's proclamation. The frame of reference within which these two governments are described leaves no room for either to assert its autonomy. Törnvall overemphasized the basic thesis of his book—in spite of the very valuable critical contributions that he made to the discussion of many questions that arose in the period of the struggle of the church in the Third Reich (1933–45). The fact is, however, that Luther thought in terms of both the two kingdoms and the two governments. These concepts are not simply interchangeable; rather each expresses a very definite perspective.

Johannes Heckel presented a very sharply defined position in his various studies.[132] Heckel's basic thesis was that Luther's doctrine of the two kingdoms is the equivalent of the old contrast between the kingdom of God and the kingdom of the devil. Heckel therefore did not understand Luther as putting God's twofold way of ruling in the center but rather saw him as attempting a further development of Augustine's understanding of the two cities. Heckel thereby emphasized a viewpoint that was not previously adequately taken into account in the scholarly discussion. At the same time, however, it has been properly pointed out that the citations that Heckel presents in proof of his thesis are primarily derived from the writings of the young Luther (1520–23). The statements of the old Luther which carry a different emphasis were not adequately taken

into account in his studies, however.[133] This means that any study of
Luther's doctrine must take into account the development of his
viewpoints.

Paul Althaus once again directed our attention to the need of placing
God's twofold way of ruling in the center of his doctrine of the two
kingdoms as well as of his other statements.[134] It is simply not adequate
to define Luther's statements only in terms of the New Testament opposition between the kingdom of God and the kingdom of Satan. Rather it is
necessary for us to take into account that Luther addressed himself to
different situations and that the changes in the situation led to a definite
change in the viewpoints themselves. It is only in this way that the actual
intention of the New Testament concepts can be preserved. Admittedly
Althaus does agree—in spite of his defense of Luther's doctrine of the two
kingdoms—that Luther's viewpoint left no room for the Christian congregation to engage in social criticism as part of its activity and therefore
also did not permit it to engage in activities that would help to shape and
form society.[135]

Both Franz Lau[136] and Heinrich Bornkamm[137] presented well-balanced
studies of this doctrine of the two kingdoms. Bornkamm examined both
the parallels and the differences between Augustine and Luther.

> In speaking of two "kingdoms" Luther is describing not only the two realms
> of church and state, proclamation and lawmaking, but also at the same time
> the two sets of relationships within which the Christian lives. On the one
> hand, there is his own existence, his personal attitude to his fellow men, his
> witness for the gospel—in this realm the unconditional commandment of
> forgiveness, endurance, and sacrifice prevails. On the other hand, there is
> the common "life together" of mankind in general, in which law must of
> necessity set firm limits against evil; here the Christian must help to see that
> no one suffers injustice or becomes the victim of another.[138]

Gerhard Ebeling demonstrated that the doctrine of the two kingdoms
is a necessity if we are to proclaim the message of salvation in a way that
is really in agreement with the gospel. "The Gospel engages with
(eingehen auf) the lex [law] and does not appear as some sort of
supplementary factor accidentally competing with the lex. The regnum
Christi [kingdom of Christ] does not appear beside the regnum mundi
[kingdom of this world] without a motive. For the necessity of the
regnum Christi is its engaging with the godlessness of the regnum
mundi."[139] Thus Ebeling understood Luther's doctrine of the two kingdoms as being in close relationship to his distinction between "in the
judgment of God" (coram Deo) and "in the judgment of the world"
(coram mundo). Ebeling was thereby able to emphasize the close rela-

tionship between Luther's doctrine of the two kingdoms and his doctrine of justification.

Since 1970, scholars have been engaged in a new series of discussions that are less concerned with Luther himself and more concerned with the ways in which the doctrine of the two kingdoms has affected the course of history. These discussions have indirectly been of considerable significance for the study of Luther.[140] Even though it seldom becomes explicit, these publications generally contain an implicit critical and negative reevaluation of Luther.

5.8.6 The Meaning and the Problematical Nature of the Concept of the Doctrine of the Two Kingdoms

Luther of course is not a historical monument protected against criticism for all time. There is much that is problematical, however, in recent critical evaluations of Luther's position.

Duchrow investigated the history of the tradition preceding Luther's doctrine and also took the young Luther into account.[141] Still, he permitted an adequate investigation of Luther's position after the mid–1520s as well as of the theology of the nineteenth and twentieth centuries to retreat into the background in favor of Duchrow's own almost ideological usage of the doctrine of the two kingdoms. Luther himself never used the concept of the doctrine of the two kingdoms. In spite of this now well known fact, it has become a facile slogan for expressing contemporary criticisms of Luther. This is not the place to investigate further whether these criticisms are correct or not. Whatever our evaluation of the attitudes of Lutheran theologians and churches in the nineteenth and twentieth centuries may be, it is simply impossible to describe their position with the concept of the doctrine of the two kingdoms. In terms of methodology, it is important to distinguish between the history of traditional understandings of Luther's concept of the two kingdoms and the actual political position of Lutheranism. Lutheranism's political position has only partially been determined by Luther's concept. The doctrine of the two kingdoms is a slogan that can no longer be used to describe a much more comprehensive and complex set of facts.

The brief slogan of the doctrine of the two kingdoms is also misleading insofar as it conceals the fact that Luther did not restrict his understanding of the secular kingdom to government and the state but rather included all secular functions. Anyone who is going to criticize Luther's understanding of the "autonomy" of the state can do so honestly only if they are willing to reject Luther's position that reason is unquestionably the highest authority for the way in which we respond to and handle questions about life in this world. Scholars who simply select a limited although important aspect of the kingdom of this world do justice neither to Luther nor to the Lutheran churches.

This brief slogan also is not appropriate insofar as it is not able to express the complex and varied pattern of practical action of both Luther and Lutherans. Since there are naturally significant differences between the sixteenth and the nineteenth and twentieth centuries, our criticism at this point is restricted to the use of the slogan of the doctrine of the two kingdoms in reference to Luther. Attention is drawn to recent discussions about Luther's practical proposals.[142]

Apart from any of the above, however, many critics have with good reason criticized Duchrow's selection of texts as subjective and not really representative of the viewpoints under discussion.

5.8.7 Open Questions and Further Tasks

In terms of methodology it is particularly important for the student to give attention to the following problems so as to lead the consideration of the two-kingdoms doctrine beyond the limited focus of the discussion up until now.

It is necessary to continue and to deepen previous studies in the development of the doctrine before Luther. Such studies must analyze the particular situation that led medieval theologians to deal with the topic of the two kingdoms, especially the political context within the secular world and the church.

The relationship of the so-called doctrine of the two kingdoms to other themes in Luther's theology must also be explored. In the future, more attention must be given to its relationship to Luther's eschatology. Careful consideration must also be given to the doctrines of God and creation, as well as to Luther's view of history.[143]

The relationship between Luther's statements and the specific contemporary situation he was addressing needs to be explored more carefully than it has been until now. It is undoubtedly true that Luther always worked with some basic structures whenever he spoke of the two kingdoms or governments. At the same time, however, it is very important to understand what he actually said in the context of the then-current situation. It makes quite a difference for our understanding of a specific statement to know whether it was addressed to the Wittenberg Riots of 1521–22, or was a contribution to the discussion of the nature of authority in the Duchy of Saxony in 1522 and 1523, or was a response to the Peasants' War, to the various phases of the Turkish invasions of southeastern Europe, to the Smalcald League, or to the constantly changing questions about the right of the Protestant estates to resist the emperor in armed conflict.

The question as to whether the Protestants had the right or even the duty to resist the emperor, should he attempt to force them to conform to his own religious position by using military force, is a good place to begin our analysis of Luther. In these discussions, all of the problems that are associated with the doctrine of the two kingdoms appear in a very basic form. In analyzing the discussion, we must carefully distinguish between questions about the right of persons who are governmental authorities in their own right to resist the emperor and/or other authorities, and questions about the right of such resistance to authority on the part of those who are subjects. It is important to note that Luther asserted it is not only a right but a duty to resist. He thought differently, however, about resistance in the secular world and in the church. The exploration of the basis for this difference will prove very interesting. It also will be necessary to study Luther's understanding of resistance in contrast to contemporary opinions.

Luther's view of the rights and duties of rulers deserves special attention. It is true that Luther's view did not yet adequately take into account the growing power of the territorial states. In spite of this, it is still significant that Luther defined the primary tasks of the rulers in terms of protecting the people, preserving the peace, and administering justice, that is, solely in terms of preserving life. For this reason, Luther considered a "revolution" to be possible only if the ruler were insane. He never explicitly discussed the possibility that governmental authority might be perverted and evil.

We should also pay attention to the specific persons who were Luther's secular authorities. To put it bluntly: Luther's view of secular authority was clearly determined by his experience with Frederick the Wise and the government of Electoral Saxony. In this context, Luther experienced that it is possible for government to function to maintain the peace in a way that cares for people and takes their actual situations into account. We can certainly say that Luther would have responded differently to questions regarding the doctrine of the two kingdoms had his experiences been different. We may also assert that the quite different experiences of people such as Thomas Müntzer determined, in turn, quite different responses to the significant questions.

5.9 LUTHER'S VIEW OF HISTORY

5.9.1 The Theological Dimensions of History

Luther's style and method of thinking can best be studied on the basis of his understanding of history. His interpretation of history, like all his thinking, was closely related to numerous theological themes. We name only a few: history and revelation, God's activity in history, the question of the meaning of history, suffering and the cross in history, the necessity of events beyond our control and the limitations of human planning and acting, the goal of history, and the place of the individual person in history.

Luther's view of history was thoroughly determined by his theology. In spite of the fact that it was Luther who first asserted the rightful role of human reason in life, Luther can still without the slightest concern say that either God or the devil is working in all of history. Today we find this lack of concern about such an assertion to be strange. There was nothing unusual about it, however, given the context of that time. Many others spoke of the activity of God or the devil in history. In so doing, they used the concepts and terms used in the Bible.

5.9.2 The Hidden Meaning of God's Activity: 'sub contrario'

Luther, however, was unique in his understanding of God and the devil as directly intervening in historical events. The principle is the same one Luther followed in understanding the meaning of the cross. God is revealed through self-veiling. God is never totally at our disposal, and is never under our control. God's working cannot be predicted. To this extent, the meaning of God's work is never clear and simple. Rather, we need faith to recognize God's revelation as it is concealed in the events of history.

At this point, Luther's view is quite different from that of people such as Müntzer and the so-called enthusiasts. They thought that they could absolutely identify specific events as the work of God. They saw themselves as representatives of the coming kingdom of God, having prophetic authority to speak on God's behalf. Luther thought that this approach bypassed the whole question of spiritual temptation and faith and resulted from their own inadequate self-awareness. For this reason, Luther saw the outcome of the Peasants' War, and particularly the tragic end of Müntzer, as a judgment of God. In other cases, however, in which those involved had not made the same kinds of claims as the enthusiasts, Luther was much more reluctant to express an opinion.

In spite of all this, however, the categories Luther used to describe the events and epochs of history are totally different from those in modern usage. As an interpreter of history, Luther was solely and exclusively an interpreter of Scripture. At the same time, he observed events with a sharp and discriminating eye. Even though he collected his data in a natural and rational manner, his value judgments were shaped by the Bible. This is particularly clear in his statements about international relationships, justice, the duties of rulers, and the great people of history. The historical accounts of the Old Testament provided the primary model for Luther's view of historical events. He gave little thought to the completely different situations in which he and his contemporaries lived.

5.9.3 History as the Battle Between God and Satan

Luther's central presupposition was that history is ultimately the arena in which God and Satan struggle. This presupposition is in the great tradition of historical interpretation that was primarily explicated in Augustine's *City of God.* The severity of Luther's criticism of the pope, as well as his understanding of himself, can be understood only in terms of this view of history. We must be very intentional about remembering this because Luther himself never developed these connections in any clear way. Against this background we can understand what he means when he describes the conflict between the papal church and the church of the Reformation as the battle between God and Satan. Adherents of the Reformation who endured persecution and martyrdom for the sake of the faith were understood as martyrs to Christ just as the early Christian martyrs were. Luther was convinced that the Lutherans presented a new confession to Christ at the Diet of Augsburg in 1530. Similarly, the attacks of those supporting the pope against the Protestants were understood to be assaults of the devil.

5.9.4 Luther's Self-Understanding in the Context of His View of History

This view of history also determined Luther's self-understanding.[144] Luther thought of himself as having been stationed in the middle of this battle between God and Satan. After the Diet of Worms in 1521, Elector Frederick the Wise ordered him to go into hiding on the Wartburg for his own safety. In a letter written on March 5, 1522, Luther asked permission to return to Wittenberg. He argued, "The devil knows very well that I did not hide from cowardice, for he saw my heart when I entered Worms. Had I then known that as many devils were lying in wait for me as there were tiles on the roofs, I should nevertheless have leaped into their midst with joy."[145] Both God and the devil not only know what is going on in our hearts but also take a part in the struggles of our spirits. We might suppose that this consciousness that God is, finally, active in everything could have led to Luther's restricting his own activity. Quite the contrary is true. Luther's knowledge that God is not ultimately dependent on him alone to get things done gave him the freedom and the confidence to work energetically. Whatever the work in which he was involved, Luther saw it as God's own work.

This consciousness is more important for our interpretation of Luther's self-understanding than the fact that he could occasionally refer to himself as a "reformer" or "a prophet of the German people." In using such terms, Luther was of course aware of his own role in the church and in history. This awareness did not mean, however, that he intended to give himself specific titles. And there is enough evidence to make it very questionable whether he ever actually referred to himself as a "reformer." In this respect, Luther was quite different from Müntzer. Müntzer signed his last letters, "Thomas Müntzer, a servant of God," or, more characteristically, "Thomas Müntzer, with the sword of Gideon." Such references clearly expressed Müntzer's claim to lead the eschatological battle that would result in the extermination of the godless. Unlike Luther, Müntzer could not see himself as only a tool in the hand of God who could easily be replaced by someone else. Rather, Müntzer felt that his personal active participation was necessary to the coming of the kingdom of God. Luther, on the other hand, saw himself as an interpreter of the Word. The Word was there prior to him and independently of him and would be equally effective without him.

Luther was so consistent in maintaining that God's power alone does everything that he saw every occurrence as the result of God's working. Admittedly, most of what God does is hidden under its opposite. As a result, history is never clearly recognizable as God's work. The category of "hiddenness" is thus extraordinarily important, both in Luther's theology of the cross and in his view of history. God creates life by putting us to death. When judging us, God is being gracious to us. This obviously does not mean that we can be certain to find God by simply reversing the apparent meaning of our experiences. There is no *via negationis*, no negative theology. Revelation and hiddenness are available only as a dialectical unity. Only in Jesus Christ do we encounter God as our savior.

The assertion that God's activity is hidden is associated with Luther's conviction that people are co-workers with God in the life of this world. We can even speak of a limited independence in what we do. God's activity and human activity cannot be balanced against each other; they are not in competition. This is the same principle that underlay Luther's description of the presence of Christ's body and blood in the Lord's Supper as a presence "in, with, and under" the bread and wine.

Luther's view of history as the battle between God and the devil and his view of God's work as hidden determined his focus on individuals and their situations rather than on the larger epochs of history. Luther did wish to look at all of history; however, his viewpoint was solely derived from the old original apocalyptic view of history. This history is seen as a drama beginning with the creation of the world and ending with the last judgment. Luther never tried to subdivide it into various epochs, however. At the very most, we only say that Luther was aware of definite phases in history. For example, in the controversy with Rome he pointed out that papal primacy and mandatory clerical celibacy were relatively late developments. He had no interest in trying to understand the process of that history itself, however.

5.9.5 History as a Summons to Believe

What was really important for Luther was that history ultimately summons everyone to believe. We are repeatedly tested as to whether we really want to hear God's Word or not. For only faith can bear the dark periods of history, only faith sees them in light of the cross of Christ. Each person, therefore, is summoned to meet the spiritual temptations that come to us through our experience of history with firm trust in God.

5.9.6 Luther Has No Theory of the Inevitable Decline of Civilization

Luther's point of departure in his understanding of history did not result in any theory of the inevitable decline of civilization. In this, he was quite different from many of his contemporaries, not only Humanists but also people in the "left wing" of the Reformation, like Müntzer. The development of such a theory would have been useful for Luther. With its help he could have developed additional arguments for his battle with Rome. He at most hinted at such an idea, however. For the most part, however, Luther did not only not develop such an idea for himself; rather, he explicitly rejected it. He did so because he was convinced that God is the one who really works in history and that God's Word is always present and effective. Even in the worst of times under the papal church, this Word was always present. Luther never asserted that the Word of God could not be heard in the papal church.[146] His rejection of the authority of the pope did not lead him to deny that the means of grace continued to be present and effective in the Roman Church. Luther never broke with the tradition of the church, as though the Word of God were no longer present in it.

5.9.7 Luther's Thought About Specific Issues

A good way to become involved with Luther's view of history is to read *The Magnificat* (1521)[147] or *Against the Antinomians* (1539).[148] Neither of these is primarily devoted to the topic of history. Both, however, contain much relevant material. *Against the Antinomians* is particularly useful, because its polemical statements contain frequent references to contemporary situations. These readings provide a vital awareness of the way in which Luther thought specifically and concretely about history. Luther described God acting here, the devil there. He also reported his own self-understanding. One of Luther's remarks about church history is particularly useful. First, the Word of God began to shine on the world. A group gathered together in its light. The devil, however, soon noticed the light and blew against it from all directions in his attempt to blow it out. This is the way it will be until the last judgment. Until the very end, the devil will never give up struggling against the light.[149] Luther said this about the church, "For after all, we are not the ones who can preserve the church, nor were our forefathers able to do so. Nor will our successors have this power. No, it was, is, and will be he who says, 'I am with you always, to the close of the age.' "[150]

6 | THE HISTORY OF THE INTERPRETATION OF LUTHER

6.1 TASKS, PERSPECTIVES, PROBLEMS

This chapter does not intend to present a comprehensive treatment of the themes described in its title and subtitles. The limited space available in this introductory study would require me so to compress the material that it would be distorted. Rather, I shall now attempt to introduce you, the reader, to the much larger topic of the history of Luther interpretation by drawing your attention to the most basic issues and suggesting possibilities for your independent study.

6.1.1 The History of the Interpretation of Luther as Questions Addressed to Luther by Later Generations

There are a variety of reasons why it is important to study the history of the interpretation of Luther. First, this can help us see the Reformer's many levels of activity and their unusually broad significance. There have, of course, been many one-sided interpretations of Luther and many that are of very questionable validity. There is also no doubt, however, that each of the various epochs of Luther interpretation have focused our attention on different aspects of his person and work. As a result, it is entirely possible that different interpretations do not always exclude, but rather complement one another.

It is indeed true that Luther was primarily a theologian and an interpreter of the Holy Scripture. He was at the same time, however, a reformer and prophet of the German people—even though he understood himself in different categories. Luther also had far-reaching significance for the development of the German national state. We cannot deny his influence on the development of politics and government, just as we must recognize his influence on the development of society. Luther also greatly influenced the further development of cultural and intellectual history—understood in the broadest possible terms. For example, he deeply influenced the history of the German language, its vocabulary, and its style of expressing thoughts. He thereby shaped the concepts and forms of expression that were available to later thinkers who used the German language. His translation of the Bible into German transmitted his new version of the concept of God as well as of Paul's doctrine of justification to many generations.

Our study of the history of Luther's influence today leads us far beyond the borders of Germany and the areas where German is spoken. Countries that officially introduced the Lutheran Reformation, such as Scandinavia, are especially important. He was quite influential in southeastern Europe. The image of Luther in France, England, Italy, Spain, and—in more recent times—in North America, is also important. It does not matter whether Luther has been represented in positive or in negative terms or what prejudices, hero worship, or negative criticisms have determined or distorted his image. Whatever its form, the image of Luther is a significant part of the history of his influence and we cannot simply ignore any of this in our studies. We must be willing, at least, to consider the possibility that even the most negative distortions make us aware of problematic elements in his person and work. No one should ever rush to the conclusion that the one true image of Luther has been found. It is basically true that, in studying anyone, we will encounter problematic sides to their character and factors that we are not able to understand. We ought not simply ignore these because we see ourselves as defending the individual.

An engagement with the history of the image of Luther will provide all who are concerned about issues growing out of scholarly research an opportunity to test the validity of various interpretations of Luther. To name only a few examples: Studies of his theology must stand the test of being congruent with what he actually did. Luther's view that it is the primary task of government to preserve order and peace rather than to control peoples' souls must be seen in terms of his relationship to Karlstadt or Müntzer. It is as important for us to know how Karlstadt and Müntzer perceived Luther as it is to know how he perceived them. The same is true of his representation of the papacy. As important as it is for us to discover Luther's own motives and intentions, in order to understand him correctly, it is equally important for us to give a fair hearing to his opponents. In so doing, we must concede that people sometimes had other and better motives and intentions than they were able to express, given the limitations of the situation. Especially at this point, Protestant Luther research needs to learn something from the openness that Roman Catholic theologians have brought to the study of Luther in the last decades. We need to be equally open in our understanding of his Roman Catholic opponents in the sixteenth century.

Every image of Luther, from every period, must be critically evaluated in terms of all that we know about Luther himself. Contemporary scholars who have studied Luther more intensively generally conclude that the history of Luther interpretation presents us with a series of fundamental misunderstandings. Thus even though our study of the image of Luther will reflect various aspects of the "genuine" Luther, it is still for the most part a history of misunderstandings.

6.1.2 Luther as the Protestant Church Father

We ought, for methodological reasons alone, to be skeptical of the fact that, until recently, almost every theological and ecclesiastical movement as well as a variety of political orientations have asserted that they were the heirs of Luther. In theology, for example, this has been true of such diverse schools as seventeenth-century Orthodoxy, Pietism, the Enlightenment, many Romanticists, conservative nineteenth-century theology, liberal theology, dialectical theology, and the German Christians. The same is true of various political movements. In the twentieth century, appeals to the authority of Luther have been made by the National Socialists as well as by the Communists—although the latter appealed to him only reluctantly and with some limitations.

This universal appeal of being, in one way or another, disciples of Luther reveals his far-reaching significance. Even movements that have quite different and contradictory purposes from his own, have not been able to evade his influence entirely. His significance was so great that even revolutionary movements have not been able to escape it in the long run. Even when he has been misrepresented and the data misinterpreted, the "genuine" Luther has gradually always asserted himself. In any case, we frequently observe a struggle between efforts to capture Luther in order to exploit him and efforts to become acquainted with the "real" Luther. It would be wrong for us to conclude that the history of the interpretation of Luther is only the history of the tendentious misreading of him.

6.1.3 Studies of the Image of Luther

There is a whole series of good descriptions of the history of the interpretation of Luther. The works of Horst Stephan,[1] Ernst Walter Zeeden,[2] and Heinrich Bornkamm[3] have been especially important. In addition, there are many studies of his relationships to individual problems and topics. Walther von Loewenich[4] analyzed the significance of a study of the history of the development of theology since the Enlightenment in terms of both our understanding of Luther and modern theology. Similar studies have not yet been made of other epochs of the interpretation of Luther. In summary, we can say that many detailed studies of the history of the image of Luther are still needed; it is therefore not possible at present to provide a very satisfactory overview. Many themes are available for research in this area.

6.1.4 Early Prototypes of the Image of Luther

The following sketch of the history of the interpretation of Luther can do little more than draw attention to some important developments and views. I shall discuss the basic characteristics of each epoch, but shall not attempt to note all of the significant differences within the epoch itself. As a preliminary observation, it should be noted that the prototypes of many later images of Luther appeared in the early years of the Reformation. We do not yet have a summary overview of the images of Luther during these years; however, such a study could show us the early Luther as he was reflected in others' opinions of him. It would probably show us the whole range of possible opinions about him.

On the one extreme of this range of opinion, we would find enthusiastic support of Luther on the part of people whose own positions were quite different from one another's and sometimes from Luther's. These people had a wide variety of expectations of Luther. On the other extreme, we would find his Roman Catholic opponents expressing passionate opposition to him. These opponents, too, would as individuals have held a wide variety of personal positions about Luther. Between these two extremes, we would find the Humanists, some of whom expressed cautious admiration, others disappointed rejection of Luther. Others who were working out of entirely different presuppositions from Luther's would at first respond positively but would then slowly begin to express their opposition. Some first became aware of this opposition at the time of the Wittenberg Riots when they found themselves unable to approve of his cooperation with the Electoral Saxon government. A little later, the controversy with Johann Agricola would produce the first differentiation between the young Luther (whom Agricola supported) and the old Luther (who seemed to Agricola to be in opposition to the young Luther).[5]

This factor in the image of Luther is quite significant today, even though it appears in different forms. This distinction between the young Luther and the old Luther is used in discussing the way in which his theology constantly grew more and more explicit in opposing the enthusiasts. It is also used to describe the development from an almost revolutionary movement to closer cooperation with the authorities. In addition, it can be used as a very generalized contrast between the early dynamic stages of the Reformation and the later period of consolidation or even petrification.

The development of the Protestant state churches and their confessional consolidation, and the development of the Roman Catholic Reformation, produced a polarization in the image of Luther that would determine the future development for a long time. Roman Catholics saw him as the arch-heretic and a rebel. Among the Protestants, the criticisms of Luther that had been expressed ever since 1520 were now silenced. It would be a long time before this image of Luther was overcome.

6.2 THE IMAGE OF LUTHER IN SEVENTEENTH-CENTURY ORTHODOXY

6.2.1 Luther as an Infallible Teacher

During his lifetime, Luther had unusual authority among the Protestants as a teacher of the church. This authority became still greater in the course of the intra-Protestant controversies of the 1550s and 1560s and up through the adoption of the Formula of Concord in 1577. For example, the Formula of Concord decided controversies about the Lord's Supper and the person and work of Christ by interpreting the earlier confessions in terms of Luther's theology, rather than interpreting Luther so that he agreed with these confessions. In this process, a rather limited number of his thoughts were adopted—the first stages of the development of Lutheran Orthodoxy.

As a result of this process, the characteristic image of Luther in seventeenth-century Lutheran Orthodoxy developed. Lutheran theologians were almost totally interested in Luther's theology and showed very little interest in his person. He was given a role as church father that was shared by no one else. This corresponds to the fact that the literature about him was almost all written by theologians. Theologians, however, ascribed to him the exercise of an almost infallible teaching office— comparable to the office that they denied to the pope.

These Lutherans were also absolutely convinced that God had personally called Luther to lead the reformation of the church. They were uncertain only as to whether the call had come to him directly or through means. If they said it came directly, they could ascribe the greatest possible authority to him. If they said it came through means, they could use him as their best illustration in rejecting the position of the enthusiasts—who believed that they received direct revelations from the Holy Spirit, an assertion that he had rejected.

This position of Lutheran Orthodoxy resulted in an almost total interest in Luther's theology and very little interest in his person. Revelation 14:6 was interpreted as a biblical prophecy of the sending of Luther: "Then I saw another angel flying in midheaven, with an eternal gospel to proclaim to those who dwell on earth, to every nation and tribe and tongue and people." This also expresses the eschatological element, the supposition that the Reformation was a significant event in the coming of the end of the world. Such biblical proof texts basically placed Luther on a level with the authors of the Holy Scripture. The legitimacy of this ascription of authority to Luther was demonstrated by very detailed exegesis. Such an attitude completely excluded the possibility of any critical examination of him.

In spite of this highest possible evaluation of Luther, there were differences in the details of the image of Luther. These differences resulted primarily from the diverse structures of the various orthodox systems. Each orthodox theologian claimed the full authority of Luther for himself. Since their views and methods of presentation sometimes differed, however, they eventually developed different methods and this soon produced diversity in the interpretation of Luther. After the end of the sixteenth century, the question as to whether Luther's Reformation still needed to be completed by a "second Reformation" was no longer significant. Even though there were many questions whether there would be such a "second Reformation," the adoption of the Book of Concord in 1580 was the "official" declaration that another reformation was not needed.

6.2.2 The Introduction of Reformation Jubilees

It is characteristic that the age of Orthodoxy also introduced the custom of celebrating Reformation jubilees. From early on, of course, there had been days on which the Reformation was especially remembered. The regulations for the life of the church in northern Germany, beginning with the regulations introduced in Braunschweig in 1528, prescribed an annual commemoration of the introduction of the Reformation or of the adoption of the new ecclesiastical regulations. Such directives are also found in the later sixteenth century. Here and there, the custom of celebrating specific dates in Luther's life developed. Thus in Pomerania, St. Martin's day (November 11), the anniversary of Luther's baptism, was a day for remembering the Reformer. Luther died on February 18 in Eisleben, where that day was celebrated in memory of Luther. In some places, special days were set aside for remembering the introduction of the distribution of the wine to the laity in the Lord's Supper. These were, however, individual holidays with quite different content. As yet there was still no day generally observed as a day on which to remember the Reformation.

This all changed in the early seventeenth century. Congregations were instructed to celebrate the hundredth anniversary of the publication of Luther's Ninety-five Theses as a jubilee festival. It is significant that the initiative for this action came from the Reformed. At the beginning of 1617, some well-known Reformed theologians, particularly Abraham

Scultetus, the senior preacher to the court of the elector of the Palatinate in Heidelberg, observed the centennial of Luther's beginning the cleansing of the church. The idea was taken up by Elector Friedrich V of the Electoral Palatinate. He was the director of the Protestant Union and apparently wanted to document his leadership. In any case, he used the occasion of a conference of the Union in Heilbronn in April, 1617, to remind the Protestant estates of the approaching centennial anniversary. He pointed out that a joint celebration of the festival by Lutherans and Reformed would emphasize the fact that the Reformed subscribed to the Augsburg Confession. This would demonstrate their right to toleration under the terms of the Religious Peace of Augsburg of 1555. In addition, a common celebration would create the impression that Protestants stood together in a common front over against Roman Catholicism. The Heilbronn conference responded on April 23, 1617, by resolving that all members of the Union should observe November 2, 1617, as a festival. In their worship they were to remember that God had brought about the Reformation through Luther and "other godly people" and pray God to continue protection of and blessing on the Protestant churches. This day of remembrance was also observed by some nonmembers of the Protestant Union.

Electoral Saxony went its own way. At approximately the same time that the Heilbronn conference was passing its resolution, that is, on April 22, 1617, the theological faculty of the University of Wittenberg asked the Saxon elector, Johann Georg II, to hold a jubilee celebration in Wittenberg. The elector, however, ordered that a jubilee should be celebrated throughout all of Electoral Saxony from October 31 through November 2, 1617. Some neighboring territories joined in this jubilee celebration. Some other territories, however, chose other dates. Braunschweig-Wolfenbüttel celebrated November 9, 1617; Hesse celebrated January 4, 1618. Electoral Brandenburg, like some other territories, did not celebrate at all.

The tone of the sermons preached at these jubilees corresponded completely to the image of Luther common at that time. These jubilee celebrations constituted a kind of canonization of Luther.

6.2.3 The Beginnings of a New Image of Luther

The orthodox Lutheran image of Luther did not begin to change until the end of the epoch—at a time when Pietism had already affected extensive areas of German Protestantism. These changes were primarily brought about by the learned legal scholar and political scientist, Veit Ludwig von Seckendorf (1626–92), when he published the first edition of his *Historical and Apologetic Commentary on Lutheranism or the Reformation*

(Commentarius historicus et apologeticus de Lutheranismo seu de Reformatione) (1688–92). It is already interesting that Seckendorf did not follow the custom of Lutheran Orthodoxy and designate the teaching activity of the old Luther as the most important part of the Reformation but rather saw the first seven years of the Reformation as the "real history of Luther." Once again, the person of Luther and the beginnings of the Reformation movement had been placed in the center of attention. Having thus shifted the point of emphasis, Seckendorf could also place a different value on the fact that Luther was an ordinary human person. Without in any way moving away from the heart and center of the teaching of the Reformation, he did not hesitate to express moderate criticism of Luther. Seckendorf also differed from most of the Lutheran orthodox theologians by emphasizing the common elements in the churches. He concluded his book with a prayer for the unity of Christianity.[6]

6.3 THE IMAGE OF LUTHER IN PIETISM

6.3.1 Variations in the Image of Luther

Pietism was significant for the history of the interpretation of Luther in several ways. First, it changed the rigid image of Luther common to the Lutheran orthodox theologians. Without questioning Luther's rank as the chief teacher of the church, it gave even more emphasis to his spirituality. Everything that he had said was no longer accepted without discrimination and without thinking; rather the Pietists recognized that some statements were more valuable than others. Such an independent attitude toward his authority was unknown until then. Even though there had been differences among the Lutheran orthodox images, we can still speak of a typical Lutheran orthodox image. We cannot make such an assertion about Pietism. Of course, Spener, Francke, Zinzendorf, and especially the radical Pietists like Gottfried Arnold, were all agreed in their positive evaluation of Luther's work in opposition to the Roman Church. They differ significantly from one another, however, in their evaluation of Luther's rejection of the enthusiasts. Since then, there has been no common image of Luther—even among Protestants. Quite the opposite is the case. Since 1700 the differences in various images and interpretations of Luther have rapidly become broader and deeper.

6.3.2 Philip Jacob Spener

Philip Jacob Spener was the first significant representative of German Pietism. He had no intention of making a radical break with the then-dominant style of Lutheran orthodox theology. He was therefore not critical of Luther in any way. Even when his Pietist approach to the Christian life came under attack, Spener tried to find a way of establishing common ground with his opponents. Accordingly, Spener's image of Luther is not totally opposed to that of Lutheran Orthodoxy. Still there are undeniable shifts in emphasis.

In his *Pia Desideria* (1675)[7] and in other writings Spener repeatedly appealed to Luther in support of his position on being born again and spirituality. The frequency of these references to Luther, however, should not cause us to overlook the fact that Spener was always referring to the same passages in Luther. These are primarily found in Luther's *Preface to the New Testament* (1522),[8] *The German Mass and Order of Service* (1526),[9] and Luther's edifying writings. The significance of this limited selection becomes apparent when we compare it with the great variety of other thoughts from Luther's works. Spener simply did not refer to passages in Luther that did not seem to support his position. Spener also revealed the difference between his and the Lutheran orthodox image of Luther by criticizing some aspects of Luther's person. Spener said that there was much about Luther that was "human" and "natural" and that still needed to be overcome. It is especially important that when Spener used concepts like faith and justification, he did not give them new content, yet they had a different tone than they had when discussed by Lutheran orthodox theologians. He was always discussing personal characteristics, experience, being raised to new life, sanctification, and even rebirth. As a result he no longer emphasized pure doctrine, but rather the realization of faith in prayer, in love of God and the neighbor, and in discipleship. From this perspective, Spener and many other Pietists were convinced that Luther's Reformation still needed to be completed. In the process of arriving at this conclusion, Spener cautiously adopted ideas that had originally been held by the "left wing" of the Reformation.

6.3.3 Nikolaus Ludwig Zinzendorf

Other leaders of Pietism, in a way basically similar to that of Spener, emphasized specific aspects of Luther's person and work. Each made this selection on a different basis, however. Nikolaus Ludwig Zinzendorf is particularly interesting in this regard. On the one hand, Zinzendorf understood the basic character of the Reformation doctrine of justification, as well as its relationship to the person and work of Christ, much better than Spener had. On the other hand, however, Zinzendorf used concepts and fantasies from the realm of emotion to express his understanding of Christianity. In this process, he often far exceeded the limits of good taste. In comparison with Spener's Pietism, therefore, Zinzendorf understood the totality of Reformation Christianity better but also sub-

jected it to greater distortions. There is a kind of ambivalence in this that
corresponds to the basic dialectic that Erich Beyreuther has identified in
Zinzendorf's method of theological thinking.[10] Zinzendorf had learned
his dialectic from Pierre Bayle, the best dialectician of the time. The
unique manner in which he assimilated and came to terms with Luther,
however, demonstrated a new and independent approach.

6.3.4 Gottfried Arnold

What we have just said about Zinzendorf's approach to Luther is even
more true of Gottfried Arnold. His great work, *Unparteiische Kirchen-
und Ketzerhistorie* (1699–1700),[11] for the first time placed the heretic
in the center of attention. Arnold concluded that the right position in
every controversy had been represented not by the victorious Orthodox
but by the heretics whom the church condemned. Arnold postulated that
the official church had betrayed the true nature of the faith by entering
into an alliance with the secular powers. In this situation, the heretics
preserved the true faith. Arnold defined this truth in terms of the Spirit
and the fruits of the Spirit; he never found it in the letter, or in the
external forms of the church's orthodox doctrine and life.

This approach was of decisive significance for the image of Luther.
Arnold put a much sharper edge on the distinction between the young
and the old Luther that had been used so frequently by his predecessors.
Arnold thus more carefully evaluated Luther's and the Reformation's
significance for the cleansing of the church. He was, however, also now
much sharper in his criticism of Luther. Arnold not only regretted that
there was much too much that was still human about Luther but also
rejected any claim that Luther possessed infallible authority in the realm
of doctrine. He was especially critical of the Reformation for having
externalized Christianity by entering into an alliance with the secular
government. As a result, the congregations have not achieved maturity
and the church has been violated by the state. On this basis, Arnold now
took the sharp criticism that Luther had directed against Rome and
applied it to the Lutheran state church: human doctrines and human
works have corrupted the nature of Christianity.

Arnold, however, exempted Luther's person from such accusations. He
distinguished between Luther's intentions and the actual results of his
work. In addition, Arnold based his own understanding of Christianity
primarily on Luther. He considered the confessions not as some kind of
paper pope, but rather described them in Luther's terms as "a witness and
confession of our faith." They must, therefore, be understood as instruction in the faith. In interpreting Christianity in such internalized categories, however, Arnold also forcibly separated from one another elements

that Luther had considered to be inseparably joined together. Luther had affirmed their unity particularly in his controversy with the enthusiasts.

The quite different, even contradictory, ways in which Orthodoxy and Arnold approached Luther for the first time revealed the tremendous breadth that must be described in any history of Luther's influence. Thinkers and movements that were passionately opposed to one another could with equal right appeal to Luther. It was impossible to harmonize these various approaches—even though contemporary Luther scholars are now certain that both sides represented genuine ideas of Luther. Something had been divided in the course of the historical development, and the original unity could never again be found. This situation calls us to attempt to find a new basis for establishing this unity. Such an attempt was not made in the eighteenth century, however. Rather, we can only say that Arnold's interpretation of Luther gave new expression to many questions that had remained unresolved in the controversy between Luther and people like Karlstadt and Schwenckfeld. Arnold's interpretation of Luther raised significant questions that must still be asked of Luther.

6.4 THE IMAGE OF LUTHER IN THE ENLIGHTENMENT

The Enlightenment generally shared the feeling of great respect for Luther that had been the dominant attitude. Once again, however, new aspects of Luther's person and work were discovered and made the focus of attention, while others were allowed to recede into the background.

As far as Luther's person was concerned, the Enlightenment introduced a differentiated view. The simplistic contrast between the young and the old Luther was replaced by a more considered evaluation. As a result, Luther's opponents could also be treated in a fairer way. Although progress in this respect was very great, however, the representatives of the Enlightenment had almost no understanding at all for Luther's theology, neither for that of the young nor for that of the old Luther.

6.4.1 Luther as Leader in the Struggle for Reason and the Freedom of the Conscience

In the Enlightenment, certain aspects of Luther's struggle with the Roman Church became the center of attention in a new way. Luther's refusal to submit to the pope was seen as a struggle for reason and the freedom of the conscience. Luther had set us free from the dark superstitions of the Middle Ages. This liberation was given its own new religious interpretation when it was seen as a work of divine providence. Therewith the earlier interpretation of the Reformation in the context of the history of theology that saw Lutheran Orthodoxy as the container in which the Reformation had been both contained and preserved was now replaced by an interpretation in the context of the Enlightenment's faith in progress. This also gives new meaning to the old idea that the Reformation still needed to be continued or completed. It was no longer the remnants of the papal church that needed to be overcome, but rather now it was everything that was not in agreement with reason. In accordance with this view, each chose for themselves what they felt they could take from Luther and the Reformation and use in their own time.

6.4.2 The Beginning of the Historical-Critical Method: Johann Salomo Semler

The Enlightenment's approach to the Reformation was applied on a broad front. As part of that, some thinkers began to work on the development of a historical-critical method and thereby laid the ground for a scholarly approach to Luther and the Reformation. Among all the Enlightenment theologians, Johann Salomo Semler (1725–91) was the most significant in this respect.

Semler is generally considered to be the founder of the historical-critical method of studying the biblical books. In this connection, he was also of considerable significance for the image of Luther and the Reformation. When Semler laid the foundation for critical study of the Bible, he also destroyed the claim that the confessions were infallible and without error. Such a claim could simply not be made, Semler concluded, because the situation in which Luther spoke and worked was unique and will never occur again in the same form. Semler asserted that the same was true of early Christianity, which therefore also cannot be made into the norm for later times.

From this perspective, the task was seen to be that of first understanding the unique nature of the present day and then to ask very soberly and responsibly how we can make the biblical message meaningful in our situation. Semler himself set an example by giving a new interpretation to central biblical thoughts in relation to the significant questions that were being asked in the theology and church of his time. This work was of considerable significance both for the interpretation of the Bible and for the application of this material to the then-current situation. In this process, Semler recognized that the various other movements in the church all had some limited validity. In contrast to more radical representatives of the Enlightenment, Semler was careful to preserve his independent position in this respect. He revealed this in discussing other questions as well, for example, questions about the relationship between the state and the church or the freedom of conscience. As a scholar who avoided all one-sided, radical solutions, Semler was the first scholar who on many points represented the Reformation in a balanced, differentiated, and scholarly manner. Semler thereby significantly stimulated the development of a new image of Luther.

6.4.3 Gotthold Ephraim Lessing

Gotthold Ephraim Lessing (1729–81) also developed a differentiated view of Luther, although he approached Luther in another way.[12] Lessing fully approved of Luther as a person and a Reformer—even though he, more clearly than earlier students of Luther—saw that Luther had many weaknesses and was limited by the time in which he lived. At all decisive points, however, Lessing's image of Luther was determined by his view of reason and revelation. It is very difficult to give a brief description of this. On the one hand, Lessing sharply attacked the coordination of reason and revelation that the Lutheran orthodox theologians of that time asserted. He frequently said that revelation will sometime become obsolete and pass away. On the other hand, Lessing sometimes spoke as though the outcome of the struggle between reason and revelation is still undecided. Luther was unusually significant for each of these viewpoints. Naturally, when Lessing rejected the Lutheran orthodox position, he also rejected the Pietist view that Luther had reformed the church once and for all and that nothing more was necessary than to achieve a higher degree of spirituality than Luther had. Lessing found Luther's struggle against the papacy to be especially significant: it set the pattern for the continuation of his work in the future.

Lessing was absolutely certain that the right to appeal to Luther's authority belonged only to those who continued the struggle of the Reformation in the present—not to those who were unwilling to go beyond Luther. Lessing praised Luther for having set us free from the yoke of tradition. At the same time, he asked who it is that will bring us freedom from the unbearable yoke of the letter. The place of the papacy in the sixteenth century was occupied by the "letter" in the eighteenth century. Lessing thought primarily of the "letter" of the Bible and of the Lutheran confessions. As a result, he concluded that the real way to continue Luther's work was to join the fight for tolerance and freedom and against Lutheran Orthodoxy. Lessing agreed that the Lutheran orthodox theologians could appeal to the letter of Luther's work—but they could not appeal to his spirit. Lessing understood this spirit to be the spirit of freedom. Thus Lessing made the claim to be the administrator of the legacy of the Reformation. He was not prepared to abandon Luther to his Lutheran orthodox opponents.

Lessing's position changed the context in which the image of Luther was developed. This context was now the question of truth in its widest sense. At the same time, it is also quite clear that no one, including Lessing, is able to take a neutral position over against Luther. Anyone who speaks about Luther cannot avoid taking a personal position on both the questions related to the religion and world view of the sixteenth century and to contemporary problems.

Other representatives of the Enlightenment administered the legacy of the Reformation in much sharper ways and with less differentiation of various elements of its substance than Lessing had. Frederick the Great, for example, compared Luther with his own enlightened age and called him a poor devil. He praised the Reformers for having brought freedom from the yoke of the clergy and in addition for having increased the income of the state by confiscating church property. Such a utilitarian view obviously completely misses the point of the Reformation. Still, the great majority of the leading spirits of the time thought of themselves much more as disciples of Luther than of the Roman Catholic Church. At this time, the concept "Protestant" took on connotations of enlightenment and of subjectivism that still determine its use today.

6.5 THE IMAGE OF LUTHER IN THE GERMAN CLASSICAL PERIOD

6.5.1 Klopstock, Kant, Hamann, Herder

The increasing variations in the interpretation of Luther in the late eighteenth century can be described with reference to such contrasting figures as Klopstock, Kant, Hamann, and Herder.

Compared to his contemporaries, Friedrich Gottlieb Klopstock understood the central questions of Luther's theology quite well. In any case, he had access to the problems of sin and redemption, although he too had paid his tribute to the spirit of the age.

Immanuel Kant probably did not read anything written by Luther except for the Small Catechism. If it is really true, as has sometimes been asserted, that there is a deep relationship between the theology of the Reformation and Kantian philosophy, Kant himself never gave any indication of this fact.

Johann Georg Hamann, the so-called Magus of the North, had considerably more understanding for the central themes of Lutheran theology, particularly for the concept of the "Word."[13] Hamann's interpretation of Luther was generally not determined by the spirit of the age. At the same time, he clearly recognized the one-sided interpretations of the Rationalists and other groups of the Enlightenment.

In contrast to Hamann, Johann Gottfried von Herder presented an interpretation of Luther that was equally far removed from both Hamann and the Enlightenment.[14] To put it briefly, Herder applied the then new concept of the genius to Luther and saw Luther as a religious hero who could only be understood in the context of the new discipline of ethnic history. On this basis, Herder could present Luther as a "personality" and relate him more closely to the new intellectual age that was developing in Weimar. Because Herder served this intermediary function, his interpretation of Luther was disproportionately more influential than that of Hamann—although Hamann's interpretation was far superior to that of all his contemporaries.

6.5.2 Johann Wolfgang von Goethe

Herder's suggested new directions for the interpretation of Luther never achieved their deserved effectiveness in the German classical period. Johann Wolfgang von Goethe, for example, never became well acquainted with Luther. Like the Enlightenment, he valued Luther's liberating activity and placed an extraordinary value on Luther's translation of the Bible into German.[15] In addition, some of Goethe's literary characters incorporate characteristics of Luther, as Goethe knew him, and there are some indirect references. Luther never had any significance for Goethe that is worth discussing, however, not even for his understanding of the Christian faith. Even at those times of life when Goethe stood quite close to Christianity, he responded to Pietistic groups rather than to the Reformer. Goethe's understanding of church history was basically determined by Arnold.[16] Goethe frequently made judgments based on Arnold's view of the role of the heretic in the church. The fact that Goethe never really became involved with Luther is due, however, not so much to Arnold's influence as to his totally different approach to life. Admittedly, we can find "Protestant" tones in Goethe in every period of his life and particularly during his Italian journeys. Goethe wanted nothing to do with the Roman Catholic sympathies of many other Romanticists. And on the occasion of the Reformation jubilees of 1817 and 1830, Goethe expressed his respect for and gratitude to Luther. In spite of this, there are significant points of difference between Luther's radical theology of sin and grace and Goethe's ideal of the human person. No amount of respect for Luther, no acknowledgment of his great work can hide this reality. And the fact that the greatest German poet never achieved a very close relationship to Luther undoubtedly contributes to the fact that the leaders of the German cultural and intellectual world after Goethe have also kept their distance from Luther.

6.5.3 Friedrich Schiller

Friedrich Schiller also did not achieve any significant understanding of
Luther and his work. He repeated the then already common and widespread statements about Luther's liberating activity or about the en-
thronement of reason.[17] Schiller's own deep awareness of the tragic
realities of life and our inevitable involvement in guilt really provided a
basis on which he would have been able to rediscover many of Luther's
long-forgotten ideas. Obviously that did not happen. Still, Schiller's historical works reveal a concise and insightful appreciation of the revolutionary events that came about as a result of the Lutheran Reformation. In so
doing, Schiller clearly recognized the multiplicity of motives and interests that led to new alliances of states and peoples in Europe as well as to
sharp divisions between Roman Catholic and Protestant territories. Of
course Schiller, like Goethe, never spoke of faith in the midst of spiritual
temptations or of the way in which God carries out his work in such a
way that he seems to be doing the opposite. Although close together
geographically, Wittenberg and Weimar were quite distant from one
another.

6.5.4 Johann Gottlieb Fichte

What we have said about the great poets is also true of the philosophers
of the German classical period. Kant did not really study Luther. Johann
Gottlieb Fichte knew somewhat more about Luther and also understood
Luther's struggle to save his soul. Basically, however, Fichte remained
within the limits of the ordinary Enlightenment view of Luther: Luther
set Christianity free from its bondage to external forms and shifted the
focus of attention to the inner life. Apparently Fichte himself was well
aware of the distance between his position and that of Luther and the
Reformation. In any case, he never appealed to the authority of Luther in
developing his philosophy of religion.[18]

6.5.5 Georg Wilhelm Friedrich Hegel

No other significant philosopher of the early nineteenth century gave
such deliberate and careful attention to the Reformation as did Georg
Wilhelm Friedrich Hegel.[19] In that process, Hegel to a large extent
overcame the misinterpretations of the Reformation that had been so
taken for granted since the time of the Enlightenment. Certainly Hegel
could also get quite emotional about the idea of freedom, and this
tendency was strengthened by his concept of subjectivity. Hegel, however, strongly emphasized that the Lutheran Reformation understood
freedom in a very specific sense; it spoke of freedom in relationship to
God. Hegel was also aware that this understanding of freedom was based

on faith. Hegel, however, also reinterpreted this by equating the God of Christianity with the "absolute spirit" of Hegelian philosophy. Luther's understanding of faith thus became the process by which the spirit gains the consciousness of its freedom.[20] The subjective spirit that receives the divine spirit was understood to be the divine spirit itself. Faith and the reception of the divine spirit were accordingly seen as the spirit relating to itself. Faith was therefore understood as involving participation in the divine spirit.

These thoughts enabled Hegel to gain a much better orientation to the Lutheran style of Christianity. Specifically, faith was obtained in the church. The Reformation's overcoming of the difference between the clergy and the laity was also of significance here, as was the Lord's Supper. All of these were understood in terms of the divine spirit and of the way in which the spirit becomes a present reality. Admittedly this was a new distortion of the theology of the Reformation, different from that of the Enlightenment or of Goethe. In contrast, Luther himself had been primarily concerned about properly distinguishing between the Creator and the creature, a distinction that was important both for the understanding of the creation of people as well as for the understanding of sin.

6.6 THE IMAGE OF LUTHER IN ROMANTICISM

6.6.1 Novalis

The German classical period and the Age of Romanticism were generally simultaneous and also influenced each other. The two writings that were most typical of Romanticism were published in the eighteenth century: Novalis's *Die Christenheit oder Europa* (Christianity or Europe) and Schleiermacher's *On Religion: Speeches to Its Cultured Despisers (Über die Religion. Reden an die Gebildeten unter ihren Verächtern)*[21] were both published in 1799. Novalis had no special acquaintance with Luther. And he understood neither Luther nor the Reformation. It is true that he says in his book that the Reformation was provoked by the corruption of the church in the late Middle Ages. His real ideal, however, was the restoration of an idealized medieval unity with the pope at the head. He thought that religion could be rediscovered only by a revival of medieval Christianity. For Novalis, however, this did not mean that the Middle Ages should simply be replicated. Rather he thought of a new, more comprehensive Reformation that would restore the unity of Christianity—and so on a higher level of Christianity than had been the case in the Middle Ages.

Novalis conceded that the early period of the Reformation was like the light of a meteor streaking across the sky. Soon, however, Christianity was finished. "From then on, no more was left."[22] Novalis thought that the Reformation was the cause of the modern age of unbelief. In so doing, he adopted basic views that originally came from Roman Catholic polemical literature that was directed against the Reformation. And yet, Novalis was not in favor of any kind of restoration of the medieval church. At the same time, it is understandable that a whole series of leading representatives of Romanticism converted to the Roman Catholic Church and Romanticism gave the general impression of being a return to Rome.

6.6.2 Friedrich Schleiermacher

Naturally the image of Luther created by the Protestant theologian Friedrich Schleiermacher was quite different. Any negative evaluation of the Reformation is understandably completely absent. At the same time, Schleiermacher did not achieve a closer relationship to Luther. Luther played no significant role in Schleiermacher's reflections on religion in his famous lectures on religion. Schleiermacher neither made use of anything that Luther had said nor did he define his position in contrast to Luther. In his lectures on religion, Luther was simply listed as a "hero of the Reformation."[23] And even in terms of basic content, Luther had not said much that interested Schleiermacher, the Romanticist. Schleiermacher's later writings also give no special significance to Luther. Of course, Schleiermacher was very clear that he was Protestant and proud of it. And Luther had made decisive contributions by protesting against the Roman Church and by refusing to go against his better knowledge and submit to the authority of Rome. To this extent, the Reformation was important for Schleiermacher. At the same time, Schleiermacher did not even define his position over against the theology of the Reformation which was so very different from the theology that he himself presented in *The Christian Faith.*[24]

On most of the important theological themes, Schleiermacher and Luther disagreed. This is true for the basic understanding of the relationship between philosophy and theology. Whereas Luther had seen these two in sharp contrast—although he carefully defined the nature of this relationship—Schleiermacher saw them as being harmoniously united. There is a similarly great difference in their basic approach to sin and grace. There are also deep and basic differences in their understanding of the church. Finally each saw the place and the importance of the dogmatic teaching differently.

There was one similarity between Luther and Schleiermacher. Both lived and worked in a radically new situation and sought to respond to the demands of their times. For this reason, we cannot limit our comparison of them to an analysis of the details of their doctrines. Rather we must compare their theological approaches in their totality. A comparison like this, which also considers the basic possibilities of understanding life according to their respective epochs, has not yet been published. Paul Seifert has written a brief but important sketch of this comparison.[25] Nothing, however, can diminish the importance of the fact that Schleiermacher felt that nothing much was to be gained from studying the theology of the Reformation.

This fact is even more important in view of Schleiermacher's extraordinarily great influence on theology in the nineteenth and early twentieth centuries. The very least we can say is that Schleiermacher did not stimulate anyone to a new study of Luther. This was true not only of Schleiermacher but also of all of Romanticism. As radically different as the religious and confessional positions of various theologians of the Romantic movement were, they made as little contribution to the new study of Luther as the theologians of the German classical period had made.

6.7 THE BEGINNING OF THE SCHOLARLY STUDY OF LUTHER

6.7.1 The Erlangen Edition

The publication of the Erlangen Edition *(EA)* of Luther's works[26] created a new basis for the study of Luther. Although we can, in retrospect, recognize many inadequacies in this edition, for example, in terms of not having used the best available manuscripts, in the work of editing, and in the scholarly apparatus, this edition was far superior to anything else then available. It was the first attempt at a complete edition of Luther's works and the first edition to apply critical methods in editing the text. In the course of time, the method of reconstructing the original text was significantly improved on—but it must be noted that this was done on the basis of the experience of the editors of this edition. As a result, some volumes are better than others. Those volumes that E. L. Enders helped to edit are particularly solid. It is also noteworthy that the Erlangen Edition for the first time made it possible for wider circles of people to engage in their own intensive personal study of Luther.

6.7.2 Leopold Ranke

Leopold Ranke provided dynamic stimulus to scholarly Luther research even before the publication of the Erlangen Edition. Ranke apparently began to study Luther in a new and different way while he was still a student at the University of Leipzig. A fragment of his studies at that time was published in 1926:[27] the first example of this new kind of Luther research that has since come to be taken for granted. This fragment shows how Ranke collected excerpts from Luther and other sixteenth-century sources. He then added his own reflections, the most important being the note that he made on October 31, 1817. It expressed very high praise of Luther. At the same time, it expressed dissatisfaction with the basically inadequate literature that was published in preparation of the three hundredth anniversary of Luther's Ninety-five Theses. This dissatisfaction led Ranke to begin his own intensive study of Luther and the other sources. Having a sharp sense for identifying the most important sources, Ranke read them from his own independent perspective and reached his personal conclusions.

This fragment of Ranke's early Luther research is important because it is the first example of an analysis of Luther and the Reformation that did not base its assumptions and concerns on particular philosophical presuppositions or on some other set of preconceived assumptions. Rather, Ranke sought to develop his image of Luther directly out of the sources. Ranke also represented a significant advance over the confessional interpretations of Luther. He saw Luther against the background and in the context of the history of the Reformation. Thus he was the first to recognize the religious significance of the Reformer on the scale of world history. In reading Luther, Ranke gave special attention to Luther's interpretation of Psalm 101 (1534/35).[28] In this interpretation of the psalm, Luther developed his own theological view of history. These views were obviously quite influential in the development of Ranke's own thinking, although Ranke translated Luther's statements into the categories of Fichte's philosophy.

In 1817, Ranke was a twenty-one-year-old student. The discoveries and insights that developed out of his study of Luther at that time were incorporated into his *Deutsche Geschichte im Zeitalter der Reformation.* This work was first published over twenty years later in 1839–47. It marks the beginning of a new era of historical study. It establishes a radically new basis for the study of the history of the Reformation as well as for the interpretation of Luther. Although Ranke was still somewhat influenced by the interpretation of Luther in Romanticism, no one else came close to his comprehension of Luther's motives in the controversy with Rome nor in his theology in general. Theologians needed quite a bit of time before they were able to assimilate Ranke's deep insights into Luther and to incorporate them into the basis of their own study of Luther.

Space does not permit us to trace the broad variety of interpretations of Luther provided by German historians in the nineteenth century. Nor are we able to explore the specific ways in which the political and

cultural currents influenced the constant revision of the various images of
Luther. We can merely observe that historical research—usually under
the influence of Ranke, but sometimes in explicit disagreement with
him—constantly sought to develop its own image of Luther. In so doing,
scholars were significantly influenced by the manifold political tensions
and conflicts of their time. One of the most important of these influences
was the conflict between the conservative politicians and the progressive
revolutionary forces. This conflict reached a climax in 1848. It is important for us here because it produced a variety of contradictory Luther
interpretations. The "reactionaries" could appeal to Luther's demand for
obedience to authority. The "leftists," such as Marx and Engels, saw
Luther as a lackey of the princes. The latter party had no understanding of
Luther's theology, but rather interpreted it as a phenomenon of social
conditions in the early sixteenth century. They could not possibly see
religion as anything more than a production of the prevailing situation in
society. The party that claimed Luther's authority in support of their own
privileged position in government and society were, however, equally
one-sided in their interpretation. For example, they presented Luther as
the "greatest German of all" and were convinced that his work had finally
been completed by Bismarck. No one at that time recognized that all
these different interpretations of Luther were greatly distorted by their
subjection to alien ideologies.

6.7.3 Albrecht Ritschl

Ranke's effort to develop an image of Luther that was based on scholarly
research and as free as possible of extraneous presuppositions was not
the only such attempt. Two theologians also undertook this task and each
produced an interpretation of Luther that we need to take very seriously—even though they differed significantly from each other on
important issues. Both of these works were very influential in later Luther
research.

One of these pace-setting interpretations of Luther was developed by
Albrecht Ritschl (1822–89). Both in his systematic presentation of doctrine[29] and in his historical study of Pietism,[30] Ritschl developed an
important image of Luther. This was superior to previous interpretations
of Luther in another way than Ranke's interpretation had been. Ritschl
went beyond Ranke in his efforts to see Luther and the whole Reformation in the context of the history of theology from the late Middle Ages
through the modern age. Ritschl felt that Luther's greatest achievement
was his overcoming of the influence of speculative metaphysics as well as
of mysticism. Ritschl freely admitted that Luther occasionally demonstrated that he had been influenced by Nominalism. He thought that was

the case in *The Bondage of the Will*.[31] In that book Luther had worked
with the nominalist distinction between God's various powers. Basically,
however, Ritschl saw Luther as the one who announced and brought
freedom and independence. The Enlightenment had understood the
freedom that Luther brought as the first stage of tolerance. Ritschl emphasized its meaning as freedom over against the laws of nature and of
history as well as the basis of an inner process by which we can master
the world. One of Ritschl's favorite Luther quotes was "where there is
forgiveness of sins, there are also life and salvation."[32] Ritschl made
important contributions by interpreting the Christian faith in contrast to
modern natural science as well as to philosophy and by his intensive
discussion of questions of political ethics. He always thought of Luther as
his most important teacher.

In contrast to his understanding of Luther, Ritschl described Pietism as
a movement that was derived from mysticism and that was basically more
in the medieval Catholic than in the Protestant tradition. Ritschl thereby
also expressed his opposition to the various forms of the nineteenth-
century Awakening movement.

The most important result of Ritschl's interpretation of Luther was that
theologians began to become aware of the significance of Luther's theology. Luther, before Ritschl, was a church father whose writings were
reverently quoted but hardly ever read. After Ritschl, Luther was a theologian who had decisive contributions to make to the situation of the
later nineteenth century—even though this was quite different from the
situation of the sixteenth. At the same time, Ritschl's image of Luther
suffered from serious weaknesses. No one drew attention to those more
clearly than did Theodosius Harnack. Ritschl had abridged or completely
overlooked basic elements of Luther's theology. Among these were the
ideas of the wrath of God, judgment, the dialectical distinction between
the law and the gospel, as well as Luther's more radical statements about
sin and grace. Ritschl took concepts that were really theological concepts
for Luther and redefined them in terms of inner freedom and of ethics.
Thus Ritschl's highest achievements and his greatest limitations in the
interpretation of Luther were closely related: he was able to make the
theology of the Reformation relevant to the current situation, but he
could do so only at the cost of misinterpreting it.[33]

6.7.4 Theodosius Harnack

The other pace-setting interpretation of Luther in the nineteenth century
was the result of Theodosius Harnack's fresh approach to Luther.
He wrote the first comprehensive study of Luther's theology, *Luthers
Theologie mit besonderer Beziehung auf seine Versöhnungs- und*

Erlösungslehre.[34] The fact that it was reprinted in 1927 indicates the great value of this study. And this overview of Luther still occupies a unique place among the efforts to interpret Luther.

Harnack's work is characterized by his opposition to Ritschl. He was especially energetic in his rejection of Ritschl in the second volume. Harnack criticized Ritschl for having overlooked the distinction between the law and the gospel and the fact that judgment and grace appear side by side. As a result Harnack said that Ritschl had failed to understand the central meaning of the Lutheran doctrine of justification which requires an understanding of Christ's death on the cross. The subtitle of Harnack's book is significant. It puts the doctrines of reconciliation and redemption in the center. These doctrines are the absolutely necessary basis for understanding the relationship between law and gospel, which was a decisive factor in Luther's whole theological work.

Because of this, Harnack gave special prominence to themes that Ritschl had quite improperly ignored. One of these is the question of the hiddenness of God. Harnack was the first to demonstrate the meaning of this concept, which was so central to *The Bondage of the Will.*[35] Harnack clearly showed that we cannot understand Luther's thinking simply on the basis of God's love. Alongside this love stands the reality of God's wrath. Luther as presented by Harnack is basically the orthodox Luther— but the image has been enriched by a number of genuine characteristics of Luther's thought that Orthodoxy itself had forgotten and that were not discussed until Harnack did so.

Of course, Harnack's image also suffered from significant weaknesses. Unlike Ritschl, Harnack made almost no attempt to understand Luther's place in the history of theology of the late Middle Ages and of the early modern age. As a result, his interpretation was not anchored in history and Harnack had no sense of the limitations of Luther's achievements. Furthermore, Harnack read Luther's works thoroughly but paid very little attention to the historical situations in which they had been written. Instead he collected a great many quotations from Luther's works and organized them on the basis of a set of systematic themes. With this material before him, he wrote his description of Luther's theology. Finally, Harnack never placed Luther's theology in any relationship to the cultural and theological movements of the nineteenth century. This gives the reader the impression that Luther's theology developed outside the context of time. This may be the reason why Harnack's work, which was very significant in and of itself, attracted no significant attention outside the circles of conservative confessional Lutheran theologians. Only much later did Luther scholars discover that Harnack's book contains significant treasures that ought not be ignored.

Of course, the significant tension between these two methods, the one presenting Luther in a basically uncritical way, and the other relating Luther to whatever happened to be the controversies of the the contemporary situation, was not limited to the two so contrary works of Ritschl and Harnack. Rather this tension is also present today. In a certain sense, both choices are one-sided. The one choice runs the danger of abstracting Luther from history and failing to make any contribution to the current controversies. The other at best leads to an ingenious attempt to make Luther relevant but is also very likely to distort seriously Luther's position in the process.

6.7.5 Feuerbach, Burckhardt, Nietzsche, Kierkegaard

Ludwig Feuerbach attempted to interpret Luther in a very peculiar manner.[36] He claimed that Luther was the spiritual father of Feuerbach's own atheistic philosophy, which described faith in God as the projection of the human spirit on to the eternal.[37] Jacob Burckhardt never dealt with the Reformation in his published work. His personal notes as well as various lectures, however, reveal a deep dislike for Luther's non-Humanist, radical style.[38] Friedrich Nietzsche had condemned Luther's "insolence" much more sharply.[39] Søren Kierkegaard attacked the comfortable middleclass form of Christianity that Luther had supposedly introduced.[40]

6.7.6 Ernst Troeltsch

Wilhelm Dilthey, Graf York von Wartenburg, and others contributed to a completely new emphasis on the image of Luther. The most significant member of this group was Ernst Troeltsch.[41] Troeltsch made significant contributions to the study of universal history and developed a sociological approach to the study of history. In the course of this work and at a time when German scholars were extravagantly praising Luther as a national hero, Troeltsch drew attention to the importance of the Anglo-Saxon Free churches and their traditions of freedom and democracy as important factors in our approach to Luther. Viewed in this context, Luther still appeared to think about life as though he lived in the Middle Ages. For example, he had introduced the confessional age and thereby extended the era in which the ancient dogmas were dominant.

Troeltsch especially criticized Luther for his political ethic as well as for his personal political actions. Troeltsch felt that these had strengthened the power of government to function in a one-sided way. Luther was therefore guilty of having caused the absolute power of governments that developed later. In addition, Luther's distinction between the Christian and the secular person supported the concept of a twofold morality that has also had very detrimental effects on Germany's political development.

At the same time, Troeltsch remained very aware of Luther's unusually great contributions to religion. Although Luther remained part of the Middle Ages, his deep understanding of the Christian faith resulted in the liberation whose full implications had only gradually and in unexpected ways been fully realized in Protestantism.

Troeltsch's magnificent work was influential far beyond the boundaries of theology; it was especially important for the history of ideas and for sociology. I would agree most heartily with many of Troeltsch's criticisms of Luther. We cannot ignore the fact, however, that Troeltsch's theses are also subject to very serious questions, both from the perspective of history in general and from the perspective of the history of theology. Many of Troeltsch's judgments were simply wrong—and they still influence the thinking of many scholars today.[42]

6.8 THE SIGNIFICANCE OF KARL HOLL FOR LUTHER RESEARCH

We can only speak of Luther research in the true sense of the term since the beginning of the twentieth century. The significant breakthroughs were made by Karl Holl (1866–1926). Every variety of modern Lutheran research owes Holl a debt of gratitude for his basic contributions.[43]

6.8.1 The Weimar Edition

The great advances which have been made in Luther research would not have been possible without the great Weimar Edition *(WA)*.[44] When the first volume was published in 1883, the Erlangen Edition was not yet complete.[45] From the very beginning, however, it was clear that the Weimar Edition would be far superior to the Erlangen Edition. Unlike the Erlangen Edition, the Weimar Edition did not separate Luther's German from his Latin writings but rather tried to group Luther's publications and manuscripts in chronological order. Luther's letters, table talk, and Bible translations were published in separate sections of the edition. It soon became clear that the great care devoted to developing the best edition of a text was worth the effort. Very soon, never before published manuscripts written by Luther in the early years of the Reformation were discovered. Among these were the lectures on the Psalms (1513–15) and on Romans (1515–16).[46]

The publication of these lectures created a totally new basis for the study of the young Luther, that is, Luther before 1517. Now scholars could trace the paths followed by Luther from the time he entered the monastery through the beginning of his teaching activity until he became a public figure. It was now possible to liberate the study of Luther's

motives and original intentions from the tug of war of ideological prejudices that for centuries had dominated the study of Luther. Once set free
from this bondage, Luther research was free to give far more adequate
answers to questions about Luther.

6.8.2 Holl's Contributions to Luther Research

Among all the Luther scholars at the beginning of the twentieth century,
Karl Holl's studies are on a higher level than those of anyone else. The
reason was that Holl was very learned in all facets of church history and
was better able than anyone else to place Luther in the context of the
history of theology. In addition, he understood the Christian faith in a
scholarly, precise manner and knew how to present his material in a very
interesting manner. Finally, he so presented his version of Reformation
theology that it became the center of the contemporary theological
discussions. This was a new way of making Luther heard.

Holl never wrote a comprehensive summary of Luther's theology;
rather he presented his research in a series of monographs. Since these
essays reflect a unified view of Luther which Holl always presented in a
perspective appropriate to the particular topic, however, these essays
present us with an impressively comprehensive view of Luther. Holl was
the first to combine historical and systematic perspectives in his study of
Luther. He also investigated the historical genesis of the problem and
then traced the historical development of certain aspects of Luther's
thought. Holl was, however, simultaneously interested in questions of
systematic theology. He thoroughly understood how to present these in
such a way that he made their relevance for contemporary theological
discussions quite clear.

Holl began to publish his essays in a variety of ways. The most important were "Die Rechtfertigungslehre in Luthers Vorlesung über den
Römerbrief mit besonderer Rücksicht auf die Frage der Heilsgewissheit"
(appeared in 1910);[47] "Luther und das landesherrliche Kirchenregiment"
(in 1911);[48] "Die Enstehung von Luthers Kirchenbegriff" (in 1915);[49]
What Did Luther Understand by Religion? (a festival lecture delivered at
the University of Berlin on October 31, 1917);[50] *The Reconstruction of
Morality* (published in 1919);[51] "Luther und die Schwärmer" (in
1922).[52] The reader who is familiar with German history during these
years will understand that Holl always chose subjects that were relevant
to the then contemporary discussion.

6.8.3 Luther's Religion as the Religion
of the Conscience

Holl focused his interpretation of Luther around the question of our
position in relationship to God. As human beings, we know that we are

confronted by an absolute demand that we cannot meet. We experience both this absolute demand and our own inadequacy in our conscience. This is the place where we meet God. This experience of God's ethical demand and our own failure to meet that demand is the basis on which we experience the judging and the gracious God.[53] It is this experience which is the specifically religious experience. It was characteristic of Holl's interpretation that he understood Luther's religion as "a religion of conscience."[54] Unlike those religions, such as those of Augustine and most of the Middle Ages, which Holl characterized as religions of salvation or of blessedness, Luther's religion included the element of "duty" *(Pflicht)*.[55] Holl felt that Luther's religion was also incomparably deeper than the religion of mysticism and the Renaissance. Luther was the first to present a really personal religion. At all basic points, Luther had taken his material directly from Paul. At the same time, however, Luther laid the necessary basis for a personal as well as a political ethic.

Holl's detailed analysis of specific texts, his careful historical interpretation, as well as his clear understanding of the consequences of his research for systematic theology all combined to make his essays on Luther so influential. In addition, Holl was also a very talented academic teacher. In any case, a large number of prominent Luther scholars received their training from him, scholars such as Emanuel Hirsch, Heinrich Bornkamm, and Hanns Rückert. The years following the First World War were a time of theological renewal; Holl made substantial contributions to that process.

6.8.4 Limitations of Holl's Interpretation of Luther

Holl's interpretation of Luther also had its limitations, however. First, neither his assertion that Luther had taught "a religion of conscience" nor his thesis that the breakthrough of the Reformation led to a restructuring of ethics can be maintained as he presented them. Holl's focus on ethics really did not do justice to Luther. Furthermore, his criticism of earlier religion, especially of Augustine's religion as a eudemonistic religion, was not valid. It is much more difficult than Holl thought to define the differences between Luther and the traditional teaching of the church. Holl's reconstruction of the late medieval position was not accurate. As far as Luther himself was concerned, the road to Reformation did not begin with a new ethos nearly as much as with a new understanding of faith centered around questions of judgment and repentance. Holl committed an even more serious error when he asserted that "Luther's piety was not Christ-centered in the sense that his whole faith was based totally and solely in Christ."[56] This thesis about "the forgetting of Christ"[57] has since been properly abandoned by Luther scholars of all persuasions. At this point, it is necessary to disagree explicitly with Holl and to assert that Luther's theology is focused on Jesus Christ as the crucified and risen Lord.

This leads to the final question: Did Holl too quickly present a modernized version of Luther without adequately reflecting that Luther's times and the situations in which he spoke were quite different from Holl's? Holl's famous lecture *What Did Luther Understand by Religion?* has many overtones that are easily understood by someone who reads them in the context of the very dangerous situation at the end of the First World War. Although these statements were meaningful in the context of Holl's situation, however, they did not fairly represent Luther's position.

The same is true of Holl's lecture in Wittenberg, "Luther und die Schwärmer." Holl was responding to the inadequate study of Thomas Müntzer that Ernst Bloch had recently published.[58] Holl developed very deep insights into Müntzer and other Spiritualists as theologians. He did so in a very one-sided way, however, because he studied them from Luther's point of view. Holl's thesis that the enthusiasts were orginally adherents of the Reformation who then fell away is still popular today. This thesis is historically untenable, however. Some of Holl's assertions are even more problematical: he also presented Luther as the prototype of German history whereas Müntzer was seen as the prototype of Anglo-Saxon history. Holl very unfairly described the enthusiasts as mere agitators in contrast to Luther who was described as having "represented creative religious truth."[59]

In the situations in which these essays were written, such statements could only mean that Holl was using the authority of Luther in public support of the nationalistic conservative political movement. That was also clearly Holl's intention. In that, however, Holl's interpretation of Luther went far beyond the limits of any permissible modernization of Luther's thought. As a result, Holl's view of Luther was not adequately defended against its misuse by nationalistic politicians, who attempted to claim Luther's authority in support of their position. This produced evil fruit after 1933. We should, therefore, not be surprised that some of the leading members of the group who called themselves "German Christians"—a group that supported the messianic claims of the National Socialist Party—had been trained by Holl, particularly Emanuel Hirsch.

Holl was unfortunately not able to see that some of Troeltsch's suggestions about the significance of Luther could have been very useful. Holl expressed his opposition to Troeltsch on a broad range of topics. Holl was far superior to Troeltsch as a Luther scholar and in Luther research. And yet something more was needed than Holl's merely defensive response to Troeltsch's assertions. Troeltsch's theses and his critical questions addressed to the Lutheran Reformation were far too significant to be dealt with so simply. It was therefore inevitable that Troeltsch's contribution would take on new meaning in a later period.

6.9 RECENT CURRENTS IN THE INTERPRETATION OF LUTHER

Holl died in 1926 at the age of sixty. Thus he could not play an active role in the theological and political controversies that began to develop at the time. Even before 1933, and even more strongly after Hitler's rise to power, theologians and church people were sharply divided into three groups, the "German Christians," a broad middle-of-the-road party, and the "Confessing Church." Many members of the Confessing Church were influenced by Karl Barth.[60] Holl was not able personally to apply his interpretation of Luther to these controversies. If he had, the theological discussion might have followed quite a different path. Holl's image of Luther was so broadly formulated and meaningful that it might very well have played as significant a role as Barth's theology did.

6.9.1 Emanuel Hirsch

The most significant representative of Holl's school was Emanuel Hirsch (1888–1972).[61] Unfortunately Hirsch's political and theological positions after 1933 discredited Holl's legacy. As a result conversations about Luther in the church and in theology were dominated by other persons and viewpoints than those associated with Holl's interpretation of Luther. This fact also concealed the reality that even Hirsch was working with specific traditions of the Reformation—although he developed these in his own arbitrary fashion.

6.9.2 Karl Barth

Karl Barth (1886–1968) was a Reformed theologian and the author of a multivolume *Church Dogmatics*.[62] It was of considerable significance that he, in all his theological work and particularly in writing his dogmatics, engaged in a more intensive study of the broad theological tradition than previous modern theologians had. For Barth, Luther was the most important theologian of the past. In contrast to Holl's method of interpreting Luther, Barth did not focus as much on the young Luther as on the older Luther, who had in a certain sense become a teacher of the church after 1530. Unlike the Lutheran orthodox theologians, Barth was not concerned with disproving other theological approaches and establishing his own, but rather sought a responsible and comprehensive interpretation of the teaching of the church. No other theologian since

the days of Lutheran Orthodoxy had ascribed the same significance to the
old Luther as Barth did. In so doing, Barth repeatedly drew attention to
what he saw as Luther's limitations. Barth thought that Luther's distinction between the hidden God and the revealed God threatened to destroy
the unity of God. Barth also shared the old Reformed concern that
Luther's assertion of the ubiquity of Christ according to his human nature
improperly restricted the reality of his human nature. Barth also criticized the Lutheran understanding of law and gospel. It must be admitted
that many Lutherans have understood the distinction between the law
and the gospel as a separation in which one is spoken at one time, the
other at another time, rather than as a dialectical relationship of mutu-
ality. Over against this distortion, Barth emphasized the primacy of the
gospel over the law. The law is simultaneously the necessary form in
which the gospel expresses itself. Barth defined the relationship between
Christianity and the secular community in the same way; Christianity is
the inner kernel of the secular community.[63]

Barth expressed many concerns and criticisms about Lutheranism, as
well as about Luther himself. These are most sharply expressed in the
assertion that the Lutheran tradition ascribes autonomy to the orders of
creation as well as to the state. Barth felt that the almost inevitable result
of this was the separation of the law from the gospel, of nature from
grace, and of the secular government from the spiritual government.
Barth was well aware of the danger of that "legalism" that Lutheranism
was trying to avoid, but he always tried to guard against this danger in a
different way, by emphasizing the sovereignty of Christ. He thought that
Lutheranism had not sufficiently emphasized the importance of this
sovereignty of Christ.

6.9.3 Friedrich Gogarten

Friedrich Gogarten interpreted Luther in quite a different way than Barth
did.[64] He was one of the early representatives of dialectical theology but
later disagreed with Barth and more carefully defined his own position.
Gogarten also corrected Holl's interpretation of Luther. He emphasized
that the doctrine of the person and work of Christ was at the center of
Luther's theology. Gogarten asserted this correction in connection with
the debate between Holl and Troeltsch.

This debate between Troeltsch and Holl was very significant for the
development of Gogarten's own approach to ethics. Whereas Troeltsch
had accused Lutheran theology of promulgating a double ethic, Gogarten
tried to show that Luther had freed people who had been deceived into
depending on external authorities and granted them a very appropriate
kind of autonomy. This gave a new meaning to the old thesis that Luther

had set people free: Luther set us free to take mature responsibility for the control of our own lives. Stated in other terms: The Reformation first gave the world freedom to be really worldly or secular.

Gogarten, however, did not intend to say that the Reformation became superfluous once this freedom had been achieved. Reason can fulfill its task in the world without falling back into false dependence on various authorities or ideologies only as long as faith remains alive. Faith empowers reason to enjoy the freedom that it deserves. The assertion that it was faith that gave freedom to reason is more than a description of historical reality. The fact is that reason will lose this freedom as soon as it is not preserved through faith. It is not accidental that true worldliness became a historical possibility in the history of the Western world and that this happened only at a time when faith and reason mutually respected the differences in their areas of competence and tasks. To this extent, secularization was the legitimate result of the Reformation's understanding of the Christian faith. On the other hand, secularism results when human reason becomes the sole and absolute authority.

Gogarten thought that faith does not directly determine the answers that either reason or political ethics give to the questions of life. Gogarten, therefore, rejected the possibility of developing a special Christian ethics. Rather, ethics are based on the work of reason. The role of faith is to establish reason's freedom to be truly rational.

Gogarten's interpretation of Luther provoked discussions in which the scholars intensively explored the relationship between the Reformation and the development of the modern world. These studies demonstrated that this relationship is far more complex than Gogarten thought it was. It became quite clear that the modern world was produced by a broad stream of developments that began in the late Middle Ages. The Reformation helped to shape and made some contribution to this process but the modern world would have developed without the Reformation.

With regard to specific questions of the interpretation of Luther, Gogarten obviously did not always do justice to Luther's ethics. Gogarten's distinction between Christianity and rationality does not correspond to Luther's own thinking. Even when he was speaking about political matters, Luther argued on the basis of "Christian" principles. He saw the motivating power of private as well as of public actions as love.

In the German-speaking world, the interpretations of Luther offered by Gogarten and Barth were—alongside those of Holl—the sharpest and most influential. This was the case even though neither Barth nor Gogarten were primarily Luther scholars whose main work was devoted to the study of Luther and the Reformation.

6.9.4 The Swedish Interpretation of Luther

Among the interpretations of Luther that developed outside of Germany, the Swedish approach was particularly important. In any case, it developed its own particular characteristics in the last decades. The uniqueness of the Swedish image of Luther consists primarily in the way in which it focused on the "motif of conflict" in analyzing various theological questions.

Beginning in the 1920s, the leading images of the Swedish school[65] of interpreting Luther included scholars such as Gustaf Aulén,[66] Anders Nygren,[67] Ragnar Bring,[68] and Gustaf Wingren.[69] In this connection, the Finnish school of Luther research should also be mentioned, particularly Lennart Pinomaa.[70] As has been mentioned, the "motif of conflict" played a more important role in Scandinavia than questions about the orders of creation. Thus, special attention was given to the conflict between God and Satan and the corresponding struggle of the spirit against the flesh in people. Nygren developed a history of Christian doctrine around the basic themes of "eros" and "agape." He presented Luther as the most pronounced advocate of agape religion. Swedish theologians were especially interested in discussing the question of law and gospel. In addition, the Swedes gave particular emphasis to the terminology of the two governments of God in order to avoid a one-sided view of the two kingdoms.[71] They thereby made it clear that, in spite of the conflict between these two governments, God ultimately works in each of them and rules the world in two ways. Pinomaa devoted special attention to Luther's concept of the wrath of God and showed that this concept, which had been developed by St. Paul, was also of considerable significance for Luther.

The Scandinavian emphasis on the theme of conflict was a necessary counterbalance to a one-sided emphasis on justification and certainty of salvation. The Swedish interpretation of Luther did not lead to the kind of conclusions that Barth had criticized. It was therefore better equipped than the German interpretation of Luther to counter Barth's critical attacks with its own critical questions about Barth's own theology.[72]

6.9.5 The End of the Old Schools of Luther Interpretation

Certain differences in the interpretation of Luther can be explained by differing perspectives of various scholars. The starting points and the focus of interest are not the same for a church historian as they are for a systematician. Generally, Luther research in Germany was more dominated by church historians, in Sweden by systematic theologians. This was one of the reasons why the Swedes were comparatively less interested in the question of the young Luther than the Germans were. The Swedes, however, paid more attention to questions related to the historical development of specific motifs or themes.

Luther research in other countries cannot be so broadly characterized in terms of specific approach and method as—recognizing a variety of individual differences—was possible in Sweden and Finland. This is increasingly becoming the case in all Luther research. As time goes on, the early clustering of theologians around a few approaches to the interpretation of Luther have made way for a great variety of methods. For this reason, it is no longer possible to speak of the development of "schools" in the old sense and such schools play an increasingly less important role.

This is not to say, however, that the great attempts to present a summary statement of Luther's theology, which were made after the time of Karl Holl, are no longer influential. The most significant comprehensive statements of Luther's theology are those of Reinhold Seeberg, Erich Seeberg, and Paul Althaus.

Reinhold Seeberg[73] was a product of the Lutheran tradition represented by the Erlangen School and accordingly presents a solid but "conservative" evaluation of Luther.

Erich Seeberg's projected three-volume overview of Luther's theology[74]—only two volumes of which were published—focuses in a unique way on the meaning of mysticism and Luther's understanding of the Spirit. This led to his concept of Christ as the "primal image of God *(Urbild)* as well as to his special understanding of the nature of faith. His unpublished third volume was intended to develop the significance of Luther's understanding of the Holy Spirit for the development of his theology. That volume would probably have consistently developed the implications of this approach to the interpretation of Luther.

Paul Althaus's description of Luther's theology[75] and of Luther's ethics[76] drew on the rich variety of Luther's statements more fully than anyone else had. The great variety of quotations and insights of Luther that are reported by Althaus repeatedly demonstrates that no systematic approach is ever going to be adequate to contain Luther within a single system. Luther constantly breaks out of rigidly schematized conceptions.

Rudolf Hermann did not attempt to systematize Luther's theology.[77] Rather, he focused on the dynamic contrasts underlying pairs of concepts such as faith and repentance, flesh and spirit, law and faith.

6.9.6 Gerhard Ebeling

In recent years, Gerhard Ebeling has made especially important contributions to Luther research.[78] He has intensively investigated Luther's relationship to the medieval tradition, with special reference to the interpretation of Scripture. Ebeling and some of the scholars whom he trained have researched the many interrelationships between the doctrine of the person and work of Christ and hermeneutics and have thereby more clearly traced Luther's theological development. In addition, Ebeling has in his own unique way raised questions about Luther's relationship to modern thought. Ebeling concluded that there is no simple answer to this question. On the one hand, the development of modern thought is an unusually complex process, on the other hand there are dimensions of Luther's thought that the modern world has completely forgotten—and forgotten to its own disadvantage. Ebeling has thereby raised the discussion of the important but extraordinarily complex question of Luther's relationship to the modern world to a new level of scholarly insight.

6.10 THE NEW ROMAN CATHOLIC IMAGE OF LUTHER

The changes in the Roman Catholic understanding of Luther in this century can only be called revolutionary. From the early sixteenth century on, the Roman Church described Luther as the arch-heretic, who had destroyed the unity both of the church and of the West. The Lutherans thought the papacy was the antichrist; Roman Catholics responded in kind. Occasionally there were genuine encounters. And there were praiseworthy exceptions to the general rule that people on both sides simply condemned one another. For the most part, however, relationships between Lutherans and Roman Catholics were, until well into the twentieth century, dominated by massive prejudices and suspicions. This situation was reinforced by the conflicts of the German "Kulturkampf."[79] During the time of the Second German Empire (1871–1919), Roman Catholics were slandered as being "Ultramontanists," that is, as having political interests determined by those of Rome, anti-German, and against the emperor, who was Protestant.

6.10.1 Heinrich Denifle and Hartmann Grisar

At the beginning of the twentieth century, the Dominican Heinrich Denifle[80] and the Jesuit Hartmann Grisar[81] wrote very comprehensive descriptions of Luther. Both still exemplified the traditional Roman Catholic prejudices against Luther. In his book, however, Denifle also stimulated Luther research in unusually important ways. He was the first scholar who gave a scholarly explanation of what was new in the Reformation in comparison to the Middle Ages.

Denifle, however, also asserted that Luther's doctrine of justification, by grace alone and through faith alone, was devised to enable him to lead his dissolute life in security, without having to worry about the results. This thesis is so without foundation that it cannot be taken seriously. Denifle's polemic against Luther was so bitter and emotional that it has obscured the very real contribution that Denifle made. Among Protestants, Holl took the lead in responding to Denifle and Grisar. He failed to distinguish between their polemic excesses and the very real contributions that they had made to Luther research, however.

6.10.2 Franz Xaver Kiefl and Sebastian Merkle

About 1910, however, various Roman Catholic theologians began to think about Luther in a different way. Franz Xaver Kiefl[82] and Sebastian Merkle[83] made important contributions to this process of change. They made the very meaningful step of simply trying to understand Luther in terms of his intentions for the practice of religion and for the life of the church. They were more concerned with understanding Luther than with passing judgment on him. This presupposed that they were also ready to examine realistically the life of the church at the end of the Middle Ages without needing to pretend that it was better than it really was. The achievement of this group is especially significant because the Roman Catholic Church generally did not approve of this approach. Indeed their work was carefully examined, often misunderstood, and sometimes given minor condemnation by the Holy Office of the Roman Curia, which was at the time responsible for defining the official teaching of the Roman Church and identifying real or even possible error.

6.10.3 Joseph Lortz

A new epoch of Roman Catholic Luther studies began in 1939 when Joseph Lortz (1887–1975) published *Die Reformation in Deutschland*.[84] Lortz had previously published a number of smaller monographs. This, however, was a completely new, well-researched image of Luther. If Protestants and Catholics had not had so many positive experiences with one another in their common opposition to the National Socialist regime, this book might never have been written. For whatever reasons, however, Lortz was able to try to see both the greatness of Luther and his one-sidedness and limitations.

Lortz was merciless in his criticism of the late medieval church, its practice of indulgences, its abuses in religious practice, the hardly satisfying nature of its theological work, and finally the unspiritual nature of the Roman curia. Lortz asserted that Luther had turned against a kind of medieval Catholicism that was no longer completely Catholic. To this extent, Lortz could properly approve of Luther's attacks on the Roman Church. He also did something similar in evaluating Luther's theology. Lortz thought that Luther had had extraordinarily deep insights into Paul and that his seriousness about repentance and his emphasis on the certainty of faith were simply exemplary.

Lortz, however, still concluded that Luther's interpretation of the faith was one-sided. Luther did not hear all of Scripture. He had not only isolated Paul from the other biblical writings but also understood Paul only in a very limited way. Lortz found the cause of this in Luther's "subjectivism." Luther did not think out of the full experience of the church but rather had absolutized his own, very deep but still limited, understanding of faith. As a result, the Lutheran Reformation inseparably combined a genuine experience of faith, deeper and richer than had been known before, with heretical error. Therefore, even though the Reformation had renewed and enriched the church, it had also caused the great schism. Lortz thereby replaced the older Roman Catholic criticism of Luther's morals with a critical analysis of his theology.

In later works, Lortz somewhat modified his views. In 1939, he had, for example, concluded that Luther's lectures on Romans (1515–16)[85] were, at the decisive points, no longer in the Catholic tradition. He later said that there was nothing in these lectures that was not essentially Catholic. This, however, raised a new kind of question as to what is really Catholic and what the Reformation really was. Lortz's position also remained caught in the disturbing tension created by his readiness to recognize the corruption of the later medieval church, while he at the same time rushed to defend the Roman Church and its exercise of its teaching office to condemn Luther from any kind of criticism.[86]

6.10.4 Erwin Iserloh

A number of Roman Catholic theologians were either trained as scholars by Lortz or significantly influenced by him. They not only extended his work but also revised both his basic questions and his conclusions. Iserloh published a number of studies in which he both carefully documented the decline of theology in the late Middle Ages and also convincingly described differences among the Reformers themselves.[87] For example, Melanchthon had tried to preserve the office of the bishop but had not succeeded. Iserloh made these and similar observations in order to facilitate the reunification of the churches: If the Reformation church would have adopted the office of the bishop together with apostolic succession, one of the main barriers to church union would have been overcome.

6.10.5 Stephan Pfürtner and Otto Hermann Pesch

Other Roman Catholic theologians have advanced the conversation in the area of theology. Stephan Pfürtner[88] and Otto Hermann Pesch[89] have demonstrated that when we take their intention and the errors that they were trying to correct into consideration, we find no absolute disagreement between Thomas of Aquinas and Luther. These scholars have convincingly demonstrated this in studies of justification and of the certainty of faith. These were the basic questions, however, the point at which the break occurred in the sixteenth century. We are, therefore, now in a position to reopen the discussions about the meaning of the Reformation and to approach them in a completely new way.

It must be noted, however, that only some individual theologians have been able to achieve this level of insight. The Roman Church has not explicitly approved their work. We, therefore, still do not know what the practical consequences of this work will be. We can at this point say, however, that this change in the Roman Catholic image of Luther is an example of the way in which scholarly research can overcome even strong prejudices. And in any case, the relationships between the Roman Catholic and the Protestant churches have been so affected that we will hardly ever again be able to be in conflict with each other without having really understood each other.

6.11 PROBLEMS AND PERSPECTIVES OF LUTHER RESEARCH

6.11.1 A New Approach to the Reformer

As far as the image of Luther in general is concerned, we are again today faced with the task of finding a fresh approach to the Reformer. Germans have a special problem in this regard, because their relationship to their historical past is, for many reasons, so emotionally loaded. The difficulty in creating a realistic image of Luther is connected to this crisis in our historical consciousness. Earlier images of Luther are for the most part obsolete. The long misuse of the idea that Luther was the hero of the German people has forever discredited the image of Luther as a German nationalist. Even when we describe Luther's work as a work that has liberated people from a variety of bondages and has introduced the period of cultural tolerance that resulted from the Reformation, people are far too ready to focus on its limits and to make the Reformation responsible for the development of authoritarian government. And although Luther was primarily a reformer and an author, people who have an agnostic pessimism about the possibility of ever knowing the truth cannot get to know him on that basis.

6.11.2 New Tasks

The task of developing a contemporary image of Luther becomes all the more difficult when we think of all the new tasks that we must fulfill in order to be able to present a well-founded image of someone like Luther.

One of those tasks is to come to terms with the Marxist view of the Reformation. Friedrich Engels and Karl Marx set a pattern of sharply condemning Luther. Several decades of noteworthy historical research have now resulted in a more differentiated reaction to Luther, even though this reaction is still often determined by ideological considerations. For example, until now Marxists have been unwilling to recognize religion as an independent area of human life; rather, they have always identified it as the byproduct of other economic and social realities, like all questions dealing with the meaning and potential wholeness of human life. As long as Marxists took this position, they could never arrive at any appropriate understanding of Luther. At the same time it is also true that the difficult questions that the Marxists ask of theology must be taken very seriously. This is not the time or the place to become defensive.

Another cluster of tasks is related to those just discussed. We need to take the results of research into the history of society into consideration. This new branch of research basically leads to a more holistic view of historical events and personalities. Attention is given to economic, financial, and social factors in the broadest sense of those terms. This field is just beginning to be developed. We shall for a long time therefore be engaged in important studies that will certainly change our present picture of the sixteenth century. Those engaging in scholarly research about Luther must take this method and its results into consideration if we intend to create a respectable image of Luther.

The difficult task will be to establish the relationship between theology and social history. It is never possible to isolate and study the "religious" or the "theological" elements of a situation in a pure culture; rather, they are always intertwined with other human factors and activities. Still we must ask whether religious and theological motives play a decisive role at any specific point or not. And even when other factors seem to be dominant, we still cannot deny the presence of religious and theological dimensions and must carefully assess their significance.

As far as Luther is concerned, this means that we have to research a whole variety of issues before we can develop a new image of this Reformer and man of God that will be believable and convincing to our contemporaries.

In addition, we shall need to answer two other questions that were discussed earlier and for which solution after solution has already been offered: What was Luther's relationship to the Middle Ages? What was Luther's relationship to the modern world? We may confidently expect that much of what we presently take for granted will be called into question. New understandings of the relationships between the confessional churches will also affect our image of Luther. And we also need to integrate insights into the variety of the early Reformation movements—insights which have long been available but have remained largely unused—into our image of Luther.

Alongside the especially important work on these larger questions, we will also need to carry on research about the smallest details. Although there is some reason for concern about too great a preponderance of technical theological studies, there is hardly an area in which we do not need more such research. These studies will make a valuable contribution to a new and more complex image of Luther.

We also need a comprehensive biography of Luther. Such a biography should put Luther into the context of the political and cultural history of his time and show how he functioned in his multiple roles of theologian, churchman, counselor, and advocate, as well as give us information about his personal life. The fact that no one has for so long attempted such a comprehensive biography is the result not only of the difficulty and scope of the work but also of our being so uncertain about our own image of Luther.

7 | EDITIONS, SCHOLARLY JOURNALS, AIDS TO THE STUDY OF LUTHER

A detailed overview of all the important complete editions of Luther's works that have been published since the sixteenth century has been published by Kurt Aland.[1] Aland also provides a chronological list of Luther's writings. The most extensive list is the alphabetical list of Luther's works with their locations in the various editions. By coordinating these various lists, it is relatively easy to find where a citation from one edition can be found in another.

[Aland's references can be coordinated to the American Edition of Luther's Works (*LW*) by using Heinrich J. Vogel, *Vogel's Cross Reference and Index to the Contents of Luther's Works.*—Trans.][2]

In the following, I will describe only the most important editions.

7.1 The Weimar Edition (*WA*)

This is the largest and usually the best edition of Luther's works. The *WA* consists of four parts: Writings (*WA*); Letters (*WA* Br); Table Talk (*WA* TR); and the German Bible (*WA* DB). Only the first part containing the "writings" is not yet finished. It is to be hoped that it will be completed in the foreseeable future.

The original plan was to publish Luther's writings in chronological order. After the first volumes had been published, however, new manuscripts from Luther's early years or students' lecture notes were discovered. For this reason, the chronological sequence is not strictly followed for the years through 1518. Thus anyone who wishes to read all of Luther's writings from a particular period should not simply depend on their order in the *WA*. Rather, one must follow the chronological list provided by Aland. Often, later volumes of the Writings and the Letters correct or supplement the texts in earlier volumes. Aland's alphabetical listing gives the necessary references to this supplementary material.

It is also important to note that the *First Lectures on the Psalms* that were originally published in *WA* 3 and 4 are being reedited in *WA* 55. The new edition proved to be necessary because Luther's difficult handwriting was not always correctly deciphered and the references to direct and indirect quotations were inadequate. Apart from this, no new editions of any volumes of the *WA* are presently planned.

Items that might appear in such a new edition appear in the supplementary series *Archiv zur Weimarer Ausgabe (AWA)*. This occasional publication provides new editions, supplementary publications, and newly published texts that are directly related to the texts in the *WA*. The first volumes provided a new edition of the *Operations in Psalmos*, Luther's second series of lectures on the Psalms, 1518–21. Since the editorial work in the earlier volumes of the *WA* is sometimes inadequate, additional new editions will certainly appear. There are, however, many reasons why there will not be a new edition of the *WA* for a long time.

7.2 The Erlangen Edition *(EA)*

After the *WA,* the Erlangen Edition (*EA*) is the most easily available and the best. In this edition, the German and the Latin writings are published in two separate series. The German writings were published from 1826 to 1857. The first twenty-six volumes were reissued in a revised second edition from 1862 to 1885. The Latin writings related to biblical interpretation *(Exegetica opera latina)* appeared from 1829 to 1886. The remaining Latin writings *(Opera latina varii argumenti)* were published from 1865 to 1873.

The Erlangen Edition was a great advance at the time it was published. Admittedly, its edition of the texts is often inferior to that of *WA.* The later volumes were more adequately edited, however. The distinction between the Latin and the German writings is unfortunate, because it ignores the common context of these writings. The *EA* should not now be used as the primary basis of scholarly research. Volumes 66 and 67 contain an index of key words that can provide a useful although very general orientation to Luther's works.

The eighteen volumes of Luther's Letters originally intended as part of the *EA* were edited by E. L. Enders. After 1909, Enders's edition of the Letters was published independently. Enders's edition was very good and is still useful alongside *WA* Br.

7.3 The Walch Edition (Walch)

The first edition of the Johann Georg Walch's edition of Luther's works was published from 1740–53. Seen in the context of that time, it was a significant achievement. Luther's Latin works were translated into German, translations that are still valuable for comparison today.

A second revised edition of the Walch Edition was published in St. Louis from 1880 to 1910. In some instances, the revisions were based on

better manuscripts and improved on Walch significantly. Many copies of
this edition circulated in Germany after the Second World War. German
scholars, for example, Aland,[3] refer to it more frequently as the second
edition of Walch than as the St. Louis Edition. It is still a significant
resource today—although it, too, has translated all the Latin texts into
German.

In both editions of Walch, volumes 15–17 are an especially significant
resource. These volumes contain the texts of many documents from the
history of the Reformation, documents that are hard to find at all or so
scattered that it is hard to know even where to look. All of the Latin
documents, however, have been translated into German. In order to do
scholarly work, other, critical editions must be used. Volume 23 contains
an index of key words that is more extensive than the similar index in *EA.*

7.4 The Braunschweig Edition *(Br)*

This edition was prepared by specialists in the study of Luther and was
published from 1889 to 1905. It was intended for "Christians to read at
home." The basic eight volumes as well as the two supplementary volumes offer a good selection of Luther's works in translation. Many of the
editors' comments are still a useful resource for scholars today.

7.5 The Clemen *(Cl)* or the Bonn *(BoA)* Edition

This edition was edited by Otto Clemen with the assistance of Albert
Leitzmann. The first edition was published from 1912 to 1933. The first
four volumes contain a selection of Luther's writings presented in their
entirety. Volumes five to eight contain selections from Luther's early
lectures, letters, sermons, and table talk. The text of Clemen's edition is
sometimes superior to the text of the Weimar Edition. Any text that
appears in both should be compared. The notes are excellent although
brief and contain a number of editorial comments as well as references to
sources, etc. At this point too, Clemen is sometimes superior to the
Weimar Edition.

7.6 The Munich Edition *(Mü)*

The first edition appeared in 1914 and later; the second in 1934 and
following; a third edition appeared from 1948 to 1965, and there have
been some reprintings. It contains six basic volumes *(Mü)* and seven
supplementary volumes *(Mü Erg).*[4] It is clearly the most popular German
edition of Luther. The Latin writings have been translated; the text of the
German writings is slightly modernized. The brief commentary is sometimes very good. The translations of *The Bondage of the Will,*[5] the

lectures on Romans,[6] and of Luther's writing *Against Latomus*[7] are especially noteworthy.

7.7 Luther Deutsch *(LD)*

Kurt Aland edited an eleven-volume set (ten volumes plus an index volume) of Luther called *Luther deutsch.*[8] Three volumes of commentary were planned. The third, called *Lutherlexikon* [Dictionary of Luther's German], has already been published. The other two, which were to present a study of Luther in the judgment of history and a biography of Luther, have not appeared. In addition to differences in the selection of texts that are included, this edition is different from others because it modernized Luther's text more than other editions. The index volume and the "Dictionary of Luther's German" are useful to scholars. They do, of course, limit their concerns to the material contained in Aland's edition, but they are more useful than the index of the Erlangen Edition.

7.8 The New Calwer Edition[9]

The first ten volumes contain a selection of Luther's writings in modernized German. The selection is intended for the general reader. As a result the scholarly notes are brief and very general. Volumes 11 and 12 contain Heinrich Fausel's biography of Luther. This is a very good piece of work. It contains many selections from Luther's works which are joined together by a brief sketch of Luther's life. This combination of biography and theological evaluation was successful, even though it cannot take the place of a larger biography.

7.9 Martin Luther Studienausgabe

This edition of Luther's works was edited by Hans Ulrich Delius.[10] This volume contains texts from Luther's early lectures, the best reconstruction of the text of the *Heidelberg Disputation* of 1518 presently available, sermons from 1519 and 1520, and selections from the prefaces to the biblical books. Volume 2 contains writings from the history of the Reformation, including *Against Latomus.* The third volume presents writings about secular authority and the Peasants' War, the fourth, Luther's major writing on the Lord's Supper, the fifth, the Smalcald Articles and the *First Disputation Against the Antinomians.* The sixth volume is to translate some of the Latin writings and also contain a glossary of early High German terms. The planned selection of Luther's writings contains some selections not usually reprinted but quite important. The decision to translate the Latin writings into German is a realistic response to the level of the contemporary knowledge of Latin. It seems that this edition will be as important as that of Clemen. In any case, its text of the *Heidelberg Disputation* is the only text to be currently used in scholarly work.

7.10 The American Edition of Luther's Works *(LW)*[11]

Many editions of Luther's works have appeared outside of Germany. The fifty-four volume American edition of *Luther's Works (LW)* is far and away the best.[12] It also offers the most extensive selection of Luther's works. The German reader will sometimes find the notes useful. This is especially true of the notes to Luther's correspondence.[13]

7.11 The Index Volume to the Weimar Edition

The lack of a comprehensive index to Luther's works has been often and painfully felt. Alongside the brief index volumes of the Erlangen Edition and Walch, a few volumes of the *Weimar Edition* contain indexes, especially the volumes containing the table talk.[14]

An index of subjects and theological concepts for the volumes containing Luther's correspondence in the Weimar Edition is in preparation. An index of scriptural references is also being planned. *WA Br* 15 already contains indexes of persons and places.[15]

The complete index to Luther's writings in the Weimar Edition is being prepared by the "Institut für Spätmittelalter und Reformation" at the University of Tübingen. The plan is not merely to present a concordance but rather an index of concepts, with some classification of the various meanings of each concept. The printed index will often contain only a representative selection of these references. The complete list will be available from the institute, however. A ten-volume index is projected for publication, five volumes for the German writings and five volumes for the Latin writings.[16]

7.12 Dictionaries of Luther's German and Latin

There are no comprehensive dictionaries of the words appearing in Luther's Latin or German writings. In reading the Latin writings, we are dependent on the standard Latin dictionaries—and they are not always helpful. The German dictionaries are a little better, although not much. There is no comprehensive dictionary of Early Modern High German and there is no dictionary of Luther's German. A few aids are available.[17]

7.13 International Congress for Luther Research 1956–

Beginning in 1956, the International Congress for Luther Research has been convened at various intervals. This congress has increasingly become the meeting place for Luther scholars from many countries, with many interests. Here scholars discuss basic and general questions of Luther research as well as special research projects, for example, the indexes to the Weimar Edition.

As of this writing, six meetings have been held and reports of their proceedings have been published.[18]

7.14 Scholarly Journals

The following scholarly journals are entirely or largely devoted to Luther and Reformation research as well as to the interpretation of Luther: *Luther-Jahrbuch; Luther. Zeitschrift der Luther-Gesellschaft; Archiv für Reformationsgeschichte; The Sixteenth Century Journal.* Many important articles also appear in a variety of theological and historical journals as well as in journals for Germanic studies.

An excellent overview of current publications dealing with Luther is provided by the yearly bibliography published in the *Luther-Jahrbuch.*

ABBREVIATIONS

AKG	Arbeiten zur Kirchengeschichte
ARG	*Archiv für Reformationsgeschichte*
AWA	*Archiv zur Weimarer Ausgabe*
BC	*The Book of Concord: The Confessions of the Evangelical Lutheran Church.* Translated and edited by Theodore G. Tappert. Philadelphia: Fortress Press, 1959.
BoA	Bonn Edition of Luther's Works
Br	Braunschweig Edition of Luther's Works
Cl	Clemen Edition of Luther's Works. Edited by Otto Clemen. 8 vols. 1st ed., 1912–33.
CR	*Corpus reformatorum*
EA	Erlangen Edition of Luther's Works
FKDG	Forschungen zur Kirchen- und Dogmengeschichte
HTR	*Harvard Theological Review*
JES	*Journal of Ecumenical Studies*
KLK	Katholisches Leben und Kämpfen. Münster, 1927–.
KlT	Kleine Texte für (theologische und philologische) Vorlesungen und Übungen. 1902–.
LCC	Library of Christian Classics. 26 vols.
LD	*Luther deutsch.* Edited by Kurt Aland.
LM	*Lutherische Monatshefte.* Hamburg, 1962–.
LuJ	*Luther-Jahrbuch*
LW	*Luther's Works.* Edited by Jaroslav Pelikan, Hilton C. Oswald, and Helmut T. Lehmann. Vols. 1–30, St. Louis: Concordia Publishing House, 1955–. Vols. 31–55, Philadelphia: Fortress Press, 1957–.
Mü	Munich Edition of Luther's Works
Mü Erg	Supplementary volumes of Munich Edition (7 vols.)
NF	Neue Folge
NS	New Series
QFRG	*Quellen und Forschungen zur Reformationsgeschichte*
RGG³	*Religion in Geschichte und Gegenwart.* 3d ed., 5 vols. Tübingen: J. C. B. Mohr (Paul Siebeck). 1957–65.

SBAW.PPH	Sitzungberichte der bayerischen Akademie der Wissen- schaften in München—philosophisch-philologisch-historische Klasse. Munich, 1871–.
SF	Studia Friburgensia. NS 1: 1947–.
SVRG	Schriften des Vereins für Reformationsgeschichte
ThA	Theologische Arbeiten. 1954–.
ThLZ	*Theologische Literaturzeitung*
TThZ	*Trierer theologische Zeitschrift*
WA	*D. Martin Luthers Werke.* Kritische Gesamtausgabe. Weimar, 1883–.
WA Br	*D. Martin Luthers Werke.* Briefwechsel. Weimar, 1930–.
WA DB	*D. Martin Luthers Werke.* Deutsche Bibel. Weimar, 1906–61.
WA TR	*D. Martin Luthers Werke.* Tischreden. Weimar, 1912–21.
ZEE	*Zeitschrift für evangelische Ethik*
ZKG	*Zeitschrift für Kirchengeschichte*

NOTES

Preface

1. Heinrich Böhmer, *Luther in the Light of Modern Research*, trans. E. S. G. Potter (New York: Dial Press, 1930).
2. *Luther's Works*, ed. Jaroslav Pelikan, Hilton C. Oswald, and Helmut T. Lehmann (vols. 1–30, St. Louis: Concordia Publishing House, 1955–; vols. 31–55, Philadelphia: Fortress Press, 1957–).
3. Herbert Wolf, *Martin Luther. Eine Einführung in germanistische Luther-Studien* (Stuttgart: Metzler, 1980).

Chapter 1: Luther's World

1. Karlheinz Blaschke, *Sachsen im Zeitalter der Reformation*, SVRG no. 185, vols. 75/76 (Gütersloh: Gütersloher Verlagshaus, Gerd Mohn, 1970), 39.
2. See, for example, Francis Griffin Stokes, trans., *Epistolae Obscurorum Virorum; The Latin Text with an English Rendering, Notes, and an Historical Introduction* (London: Yale University Press, 1925). A selection has been reprinted by Lewis W. Spitz, ed., *The Northern Renaissance* (Englewood Cliffs, N.J.: Prentice-Hall, 1972), 29–39.

Chapter 2: Questions Related to Luther's Life

1. Heinrich Bornkamm, *Luther in Mid-Career 1521–1530*, ed. Karen Bornkamm, trans. E. Theodore Bachmann (Philadelphia: Fortress Press, 1983).
2. *Explanations of the Ninety-five Theses*, Cl 1:57; WA 1:557–58; LW 31:129–30.
3. See the brief references in Heinrich Böhmer, *Luther and the Reformation in the Light of Modern Research*, trans. E. S. G. Potter (New York: Dial Press, 1930), 183–205, and in Bornkamm, *Luther in Mid-Career*, 553–64.
4. Preserved Smith, "Luther's Early Development in the Light of Psycho-analysis," *American Journal of Psychology* 24 (1913): 360–77.
5. Paul J. Reiter, *Martin Luthers Umwelt, Charakter und Psychose*, 2 vols. (Copenhagen: Leven & Munksgaard, 1937–41).
6. Ibid., 2:574.
7. Ibid., 1:383.
8. Ibid., 2:295.
9. Ibid., 21.

10. [For example, Erik H. Erikson, *Young Man Luther: A Study in Psycho-analysis and History* (New York: W. W. Norton, 1958), 206ff.—Trans.]

11. Ulrich Becke, "Eine hinterlassene psychiatrische Studie Paul Johann Reiters über Luther," *ZKG* 90 (1979): 85–95.

12. *LW* 10 and 11.

13. *LW* 25.

14. *LW* 27:151–410.

15. *LW* 29:107–241.

16. *Cl* 5:320–26; *WA* 1:224–28; *LW* 31:9–16.

17. *Cl* 1:3–9; *WA* 1:233–38; *LW* 31:25–33.

18. *Cl* 3:94–293; *WA* 18:600–787; *LW* 33:15–295.

19. *Cl* 4:292–320; *WA* 50:192–254; *BC*, 287–318.

20. Erasmus, *On the Freedom of the Will: A Diatribe or Discourse*, LCC 17:35–97.

21. See above, n. 18.

22. *CR* 1:753–56, no. 344; and *ZKG* 21 (1901): 596–98; Preserved Smith and Charles M. Jacobs, *Luther's Correspondence and Other Contemporary Letters*, 2 vols. (Philadelphia: Lutheran Publication Society, 1918), 2:324–27. [Note that there are two versions of this letter; both are translated by Smith and Jacobs.—Trans.] Cf. Bornkamm, *Luther in Mid-Career*, 409.

23. *WA Br* 3:541; *LW* 49:117.

24. "Accordingly, we (the imperial commissioners), also Electors, Princes, and Cities of the empire and embassies of the same, have here and now at this imperial diet reconciled and united ourselves with one accord until such time of the council or national assembly . . . that together with our subjects in such matters as may pertain to the edict—promulgated by imperial majesty at the diet of the empire held in Worms—each of us will so live, govern, and deport ourselves as we severally hope and trust will be answerable before God and the Imperial Majesty." W. Friedensburg, quoted in Bornkamm, *Luther in Mid-Career*, 616. Bornkamm contains an extensive discussion of the events related to the Diet of Speyer.

25. At this time, a technical term for those who protested against the declarations of the Diet of Speyer in 1529.

26. *Cl* 4:104–43; *WA* 30²:268–356; *LW* 34:9–61.

27. *WA* 31¹:65–182, 588; *LW* 14:43–106.

28. *WA* 30²:435–507; 30³:584–88; *LW* 40:325–77.

29. *WA* 30²:517–88; *LW* 46:213–58.

30. *Cl* 4:179–93; *WA* 30²:632–46, 694; *LW* 35:181–202.

31. *WA* 26:545–54.

32. *BC*, 571. Another English translation is provided by Henry E. Jacobs, ed., *The Book of Concord; or The Symbolical Books of the Evangelical Lutheran Church, with Historical Introduction, Notes, Appendices, and Indexes*, 2 vols. (Philadelphia: G. W. Frederick, 1883), 2:253–57. Bucer's interpretation of the Wittenberg Concord also appears in Jacobs's edition.

33. These are found in *WA* 39¹,²; some have been translated in *LW* 34:109–96.

34. *WA Br* 9:457, 460–63.

35. *Cl* 4:194–228; *WA* 30³:276–320; *LW* 47:11–55.

Chapter 3: Luther's Role in the Complicated Controversies of His Time

1. *Cl* 1:3–9; *WA* 1:233–38; *LW* 31:25–33.

2. *Cl* 5: 320–26; *WA* 1:224–28; *LW* 31:9–16.

3. *Cl* 1:7, 17–18; *WA* 1:236, 22–24; *LW* 31:31.

4. *Disputation Against Scholastic Theology, Cl* 1:6, 3–31; *WA* 1:235, 20–38; *LW* 31:12.

5. *Cl* 5:377–404; *WA* 1:353–74; *LW* 31:39–70. Recently the text of the Heidelberg disputation has been more accurately edited by Helmar Junghans, *Martin Luther: Studienausgabe,* ed. Hans Ulrich Delius, 6 vols. (Berlin: Evangelische Verlagsanstalt, 1979), 1:186–218.

6. *Cl* 5:379, 5–6; *WA* 1:354, 21–22; *LW* 31:40 (thesis 21). *Cl* 5:388, 33—389, 10; *WA* 1:362, 21–34; *LW* 31:68–69. Cf. *Cl* 1:128, 29–38; *WA* 1:613, 21–28; *LW* 1:225.

7. *WA* 2:36, 26–30.

8. Cf. his letter to Wenzel Link of December 18, 1518, *WA* Br 1:121, no. 1.

9. *WA* 2:279, 11–17.

10. Ibid., 24–32.

11. [See Carl Mirbt, *Quellen zur Geschichte des Papsttums und das römische Katholizismus,* 2d ed. (Tübingen: J. C. B. Mohr [Paul Siebeck], 1901), 183–85. Also B. J. Kidd, ed., *Documents Illustrative of the Continental Reformation* (Oxford: Clarendon Press, 1911), 75–79.—Trans.]

12. *Why the Books of the Pope and His Disciples Were Burned by Doctor Martin Luther, Cl* 2:28–37; *WA* 7:161–82; *LW* 31:383–95.

13. [E. G. Schwiebert, *Luther and His Times: The Reformation from a New Perspective* (St. Louis: Concordia Publishing House, 1950), 825 n. 266, says that the original text has been lost but that a later revision is available.—Trans.]

14. *Cl* 1:363–421; *WA* 6:404–69; *LW* 44:123–217.

15. *Cl* 1:426–512; *WA* 6:497–573; *LW* 36:11–126.

16. *Cl* 2:2–27; *WA* 7:49–73; *LW* 31:333–77.

17. *Cl* 2:188–298; *WA* 8:573–669; *LW* 44:251–400.

18. *Eight Sermons at Wittenberg 1522, Cl* 7:366, 3–6; *WA* 10³:9, 10–13; *LW* 51:73.

19. *WA* Br 2:15–16, no. 312.

20. *Cl* 2:300–310; *WA* 8:676–87; *LW* 45:57–74.

21. *Cl* 2:302, 35–36; *WA* 8:679, 26–27; *LW* 45:61.

22. *Cl* 2:360–94; *WA* 11:245–81; *LW* 45:81–129.

23. *Cl* 2:379, 36; *WA* 11:265, 5–7; *LW* 45:109.

24. *Cl* 2:365, 27–30; *WA* 11:250, 18–20; *LW* 45:89.

25. *Cl* 2:366, 8–16; *WA* 11:251, 1–10; *LW* 45:90.

26. *Cl* 2:366, 21–23; *WA* 11:251, 15–18; *LW* 45:91.

27. *LW* 46:8–16.

28. *Cl* 3:47–68; *WA* 18:291–334; *LW* 46:17–43.

29. *Cl* 3:69–74; *WA* 18:357–61; *LW* 46:49–55.

30. Cf. Johannes Wallmann, "Ein Friedensappell—Luthers letztes Wort im Bauernkrieg," in *Der Wirklichkeitanspruch von Theologie und Religion: Ernst*

Steinbach zum 70. Geburtstag, ed. Dieter Henke, Günter Kehrer, and Gunda Schneider-Flume (Tübingen: J. C. B. Mohr [Paul Siebeck], 1976), 57–75.

31. "Tumultus rusticorum: Vom 'Klosterkrieg' zum Fürstensieg," in *Deutscher Bauernkrieg 1525,* ed. Heiko A. Oberman, *ZKG* 85, no. 2 (1975): 172.

32. *Cl* 2:133–87; *WA* 7:544–604; *LW* 21:297–358.

33. Siegfried Bräuer, "Thomas Müntzers Weg in den Bauernkrieg," in *Thomas Müntzer: Anfragen an Theologie und Kirche,* ed. Christoph Demke (Berlin: Evangelische Verlagsanstalt, 1977), 65–85, esp. 71.

34. *Cl* 3:317–51; *WA* 19:623–62; *LW* 46:93–137.

35. *Cl* 3:317, 18—318, 2; *WA* 19:623, 20–22; *LW* 46:93.

36. *Cl* 3:318, 4–6; *WA* 19:623, 24–26; *LW* 46:93.

37. *Cl* 3:319, 17–24; *WA* 19:625, 3–9; *LW* 46:95.

38. *Cl* 3:319, 17–24; *WA* 19:625, 21–24; *LW* 46:95.

39. *Cl* 3:325; *WA* 19:632; *LW* 46:103.

40. *Cl* 3:331, 34–35; *WA* 19:639, 24–26; *LW* 46:112.

41. *Cl* 3:336, 15–16; *WA* 19:645, 9–10; *LW* 46:118.

42. *Cl* 6:2, no. 2; *WA* Br 1:70, no. 27; *LW* 48:24.

43. LCC 17:35–97.

44. Ibid., 47.

45. Ibid., 37.

46. [Erasmus of Rotterdam, *De libero arbitrio diatribe sive collatio (Gespräch oder Unterredung über den freien Willen). Hyperaspistes diatribae adversus servum arbitrium Martini Lutheri liber primus (Erstes Buch der Unterredung 'Hyperaspistes' gegen den 'Unfreien Willen' Martin Luthers),* trans. Winfried Lesowsky, vol. 4 of *Erasmus-Studienausgabe. Lateinisch und deutsch,* ed. Werner Welzig (Darmstadt: Wissenschaftliche Buchgesellschaft, 1969), 272.—Trans.]

47. *Cl* 3:101, 20–29; *WA* 18:606, 22–29; *LW* 33:26.

48. *Cl* 3:210, 41—211, 5; *WA* 18:715, 17—716, 1; *LW* 33:185.

49. *Cl* 3:177, 34–39; *WA* 18:685, 19–24; *LW* 33:140.

50. *Cl* 3:178, 2–4; *WA* 18:685, 27–28; *LW* 33:140.

51. *Cl* 3:291, 23—292, 4; *WA* 18:786, 3–20; *LW* 33:293.

52. *The Adoration of the Sacrament, WA* 11:431–56; *LW* 36:275–305.

53. See, for example, *The Holy and Blessed Sacrament of Baptism, Cl* 1:196–212; *WA* 2:727–37; *LW* 35:49–73.

54. *Cl* 1:299–322; *WA* 6:353–78; *LW* 35:79–111.

55. *Cl* 1:426–512; *WA* 6:497–593, 632; 9:801; *LW* 36:11–126.

56. *WA* 18:62–125, 134–214; *LW* 40:79–223.

57. *CR* 90:807, 11–14.

58. [For a detailed survey of this controversy and references to the publications of Luther's opponents, see Robert H. Fischer's historical introductions to *LW* 37 (xi–xxi) and to the individual documents in the same volume as well as Martin E. Lehmann's introductions to *LW* 38 and to individual documents. For a detailed running account of the controversy, see Heinrich Bornkamm, *Luther in Mid-Career 1521–1530,* ed. Karen Bornkamm, trans. E. Theodore Bachmann (Philadelphia: Fortress Press, 1983), 501–51.—Trans.]

59. [Luther's most important writings are *The Sacrament of the Body and Blood of Christ—Against the Fanatics (WA* 19:482–523; *LW* 36:335–61); *That*

These Words of Christ, "This Is My Body," etc., Still Stand Firm Against the Fanatics (*WA* 23:64–283; *LW* 37:13–150); *Confession Concerning Christ's Supper* (*Cl* 3:352–516; *WA* 26:261–509; *LW* 37:161–372); *Commentary on St. John's Gospel* (Chapters 6—8) (*WA* 33:1–675; *LW* 23).—Trans.]

60. See *The Marburg Colloquy and The Marburg Articles, LW* 38:15–89.

61. [For the text of the Augsburg Interim of 1548, see Kidd, *Documents,* 359–62. It was called an "Interim" because it was in effect until the final resolution of the controversy. The Protestants agreed to significant limitations on their teaching and practice. Many of them repudiated this agreement through the Leipzig Interim. For the text of this latter document, see *CR* 7:259ff.; for an English translation of the Leipzig Interim, see Henry E. Jacobs, ed., *The Book of Concord; or The Symbolical Books of the Evangelical Lutheran Church, with Historical Introduction, Notes, Appendices, and Indexes,* 2 vols. (Philadelphia: G. W. Frederick, 1883), 2:260–72. The matter was more finally resolved by the Peace of Augsburg of 1555, Kidd, *Documents,* 363–64.—Trans.]

62. *The Babylonian Captivity of the Church, Cl* 1:496, 18–19; *WA* 6:559, 20ff.; *LW* 36:104.

63. Rudolf Sohm, *Outlines of Church History,* trans. May Sinclair (Boston: Beacon Press, 1958), 169–75.

64. *Cl* 5:288, 31–37; *WA* 56:478, 26–32; *LW* 25:471.

65. *Cl* 1:363–421; *WA* 6:404–69; *LW* 44:123–217.

66. *WA* 26:195–240; *LW* 40:269–320.

67. The relevant texts have been reprinted by E. Sehling (ed.) in *Die Evangelischen Kirchenordnungen des 16. Jahrhunderts* (Leipzig: O. R. Reisland, 1902), 1:142–74.

68. *WA* 26:197, 15–29; *LW* 40:271.

69. *WA* 26:200, 29–34; *LW* 40:273.

70. Hans-Walter Krumwiede, *Zur Entstehung des landesherrlichen Kirchenregiments in Kursachsen und Braunschweig-Wolfenbüttel* (Göttingen: Vandenhoeck & Ruprecht, 1967), 52.

71. *Cl* 5:242, 11; *WA* 56:274, 14; *LW* 25:61.

72. *Cl* 4:322–78; *WA* 51:469–572; *LW* 41:185–256.

73. See the editors' introductions in *Cl* 4:321; *WA* 51:462; *LW* 41:182.

74. *Cl* 4:322, 1–13; *WA* 51:469, 3–16; *LW* 41:185.

75. *Cl* 4:322, 16–21; *WA* 51:469, 19–24; *LW* 41:185.

76. *WA* 7:835, 1–5; *LW* 32:111.

77. *Cl* 4:325, 19–20; *WA* 51:472, 16–17; *LW* 41:188.

78. For example, *Cl* 4:325, 27; *WA* 51:472, 24; *LW* 41:188.

79. *Cl* 4:344, 6–7; *WA* 51:510, 23–24; *LW* 41:212.

80. *Cl* 4:338, 35—339, 11; *WA* 51:498, 23—499, 20; *LW* 41: 204–5.

81. *Cl* 4:339, 8–9; *WA* 51:498, 33—499, 17; *LW* 41:206.

82. *Cl* 4:339, 26; *WA* 51:500, 18–19; *LW* 41:206.

83. *Cl* 4:346, 20; *WA* 51:515, 27; *LW* 41:219.

84. *Cl* 4:343, 12; *WA* 51:508, 23; *LW* 41:211.

85. *Cl* 4:340, 29; *WA* 51:502, 23–24; *LW* 41:207–8.

86. *Cl* 4:345, 11; *WA* 51:512, 28–29; *LW* 41:213.

87. *WA* 50:367, 25ff.; *LW* 34:284. See also *LW* 41:205 n. 29.

88. *Cl* 4:361, 21–35; *WA* 51:542, 28—543, 28; *LW* 41:235.

89. *WA* 54:206–99; *LW* 41:263–376.

90. *Cl* 1:422, 1—425, 17; *WA* 6:462, 12—465, 21; *LW* 44:207–12.

91. *WA* 54 contains these pictures in an illustrated supplement. For additional sources, see *LW* 41:260–61.

92. For the titles of Luther's writings about the Jews, see below, 4.7 under "Writings on the Jews."

93. *WA* 11:314–36; *LW* 45:199–229.

94. *WA Br* 1, no. 202, p. 35; Preserved Smith and Charles M. Jacobs, eds. and trans., *Luther's Correspondence and Other Contemporary Letters*, 2 vols. (Philadelphia: Lutheran Publication Society, 1918), 1:220.

95. *A Sincere Admonition by Martin Luther to All Christians to Guard Against Insurrection and Rebellion*, *Cl* 2:308, 5–17; *WA* 8:685, 4–15; *LW* 45:70–71.

96. *Receiving Both Kinds in the Sacrament*, *Cl* 2:333, 27–32; *WA* 10²:40, 7–12; *LW* 36:265.

97. *Cl* 1:20, 26–32; *WA* 1:528, 27–31.

98. *Commentary on the Alleged Imperial Edict*, *WA* 30³:386, 14—387, 4; *LW* 34:103–4.

99. *Eight Sermons at Wittenberg 1522*, *Cl* 7:369, 31—370, 1; *WA* 10³:18, 14–19; *LW* 51:77–78.

100. *Cl* 6, no. 255, 6–12; *WA Br* 5, no. 1635, 6–12; *LW* 49, no. 223, 367–68. This is Luther's letter to Justus Jonas of July 9, 1530.

Chapter 4: Luther's Writings

1. *WA* 50:657, 2–3; *LW* 34:283.

2. *WA* 50:660, 31—661, 3; *LW* 34:287–88.

3. Heinrich Bornkamm, *Luther als Schriftsteller*, reprinted in *Luther: Gestalt und Wirkungen*, SVRG no. 188 (Gütersloh: Bertelsmann, 1975), 39–64.

4. Ibid., 55.

5. Ibid., 59.

6. *Cl* 1:426–512; *WA* 6:497–573; *LW* 36:11–126.

7. *Cl* 2:188–298; *WA* 8:573–669; *LW* 44:251–400.

8. *Cl* 1:16–147; *WA* 1:525–628; *LW* 31:77–252.

9. *BC*, 291–92.

10. *WA* 50:509–653; *LW* 41:9–178.

11. See above, n. 7.

12. *WA* 5:19–673. Luther lectured on Psalms 1—22 in this series of lectures. *LW* 14:279–349 provides a translation of the lectures on Psalms 1 and 2.

13. Ulrich Nembach, *Predigt des Evangeliums. Luther als Prediger, Pädagoge und Rhetor* (Neukirchen-Vluyn: Neukirchener Verlag, 1972). Gerhard Krause's review of Nembach's book raises significant questions and disagrees (*ThLZ* 99 [1974]: 271–75).

14. Klaus Dockhorn, "Luthers Glaubensbegriff und die Rhetorik. Zu Gerhard Ebelings Buch 'Einführung in theologische Sprachlehre,'" in *Linguistica Biblica. Interdisziplinäre Zeitschrift für Theologie und Linguistik* 21/22 (February 1973): 19–39.

15. *WA* 31¹:552–615; *LW* 14:41–106.

16. For example, see *WA* 39¹,²; some have been translated, *LW* 34:105–96, and 38:235–77.

17. At this point, we should refer to the recent rediscovery of the text of an early disputation in which Luther participated and which illuminates a number of problems in the early controversies: Gerhard Hammer, "Militia Franciscena seu militia Christi. Das neugefundene Protokoll einer Disputation der sächsischen Franziskaner mit Vertretern der Wittenberger theologischen Fakultäat am 3. und 4. Oktober 1519," *ARG* 69 (1978): 51–81, and 70 (1979): 59–105.

18. *WA* 1:158–220.

19. *CI* 2:133–87; *WA* 7:544–604; *LW* 21:295–355.

20. *CI* 1:11–14; *WA* 1:243–46.

21. *CI* 1:196–212; *WA* 2:742–58; *LW* 35:45–73.

22. *CI* 1:299–322; *WA* 6:353–78; *LW* 35:75–111.

23. See above, n. 8.

24. *WA* 2:183–240.

25. See above, n. 7.

26. *WA* 11:431–56; *LW* 36:275–305.

27. *CI* 4:180–93; *WA* 30²:632–46; *LW* 35:181–202. The full title is *Ein Send-brief D. M. Luthers. Von Dolmetschen und Fürbitte der Heiligen,* that is, *An Open Letter: On Translating and on Intercessory Prayer Addressed to the Saints.*

28. *WA* 1:281–314.

29. *WA* 1:647–86.

30. See above, n. 6.

31. *WA* 6:579–94, 632.

32. *WA* 7:94–151. Cf. *Defense and Explanation of All the Articles of Dr. Martin Luther Which Were Unjustly Condemned by the Roman Bull, LW* 32:7–99.

33. *WA* 7:705–78.

34. *WA* 8:43–128; *LW* 32:137–260.

35. *WA* 18:62–125, 134–214; *LW* 40:79–223.

36. Cf. above, 3.29–35.

37. *WA* 54:206–99; *LW* 41:263–376.

38. *CI* 2:427–41; *WA* 12:205–20; *LW* 53:19–40.

39. *CI* 3:294–309; *WA* 19:72–113; *LW* 53:61–90.

40. *WA* 53:231–60. This is Luther's *Order for the Consecration of a Truly Christian Bishop.*

41. See below, 4.17.

42. *CI* 1:362–425; *WA* 6:404–69; *LW* 44:123–217.

43. *CI* 2:1–27; *WA* 7:42–73; *LW* 31:333–77.

44. *CI* 2:395–403; *WA* 11:408–16; *LW* 39:305–14.

45. *WA* 15:238–40.

46. *WA* 15:391–97; *LW* 40:65–71. See also *LW* 49:94–96.

47. *CI* 2:442–64; *WA* 15:27–53; *LW* 45:347–78.

48. *CI* 3:47–68; *WA* 18:291–334; *LW* 46:17–43.

49. *CI* 3:69–74; *WA* 18:357–61; *LW* 46:49–55.

50. *CI* 3:75–93; *WA* 18:384–401; *LW* 46:63–85.

51. *Cl* 3:317–51; *WA* 19:623–62; *LW* 46:93–137.
52. *BC,* 358–61.
53. *BC,* 338–56.
54. *BC,* 288–318.
55. *WA* 7:784–91; *LW* 42:183–86.
56. *Cl* 1:161–73; *WA* 2:685–97; *LW* 42:99–115.
57. *WA* 23:402–31; *LW* 43:145–65.
58. *WA* 53:205–8; *LW* 43:247–50.
59. *WA* Br 10:489–94.
60. *WA* 11:314–36; *LW* 45:199–229.
61. *WA* 15:741–58.
62. *WA* 53:417–552; *LW* 47:137–306.
63. *WA* 53:579–648.
64. *WA* 30^2:107–48; *LW* 46:161–205.
65. *WA* 30^2:160–97.
66. *WA* 51:585–625; *LW* 43:219–41.
67. Not in *WA*. For text, see *EA* 64:277–78.
68. *WA* Br 6:20–21, no. 1773; *LW* 50:5–6.
69. *WA* 15:146–54.
70. *WA* 30^3:496–509. Luther added a preface, marginal notes, and commentary.
71. For a selection of these sermons, see *LW* 51 and 52.
72. *Cl* 3:317–51; *WA* 19:658, 21–34; *LW* 46:135–36.
73. *WA* 35:632.
74. *WA* 51:608–10; *LW* 43:232–33.
75. *WA* Br 11:112, 16–25.
76. *WA* 35:569–70.
77. *WA* 35:577.
78. *WA* 35:601.
79. *WA* 35:589–90.
80. *WA* 35:590–91.
81. See *LW* 48, 49, and 50.
82. *Cl* 7:20–38 and 8:1–354; *WA* Tr 1–6; *LW* 54.
83. *WA* Br 9:443–45.
84. *WA* 1:153. The author of this book was an unknown mystic, see *LW* 31:73–74.
85. *WA* 1:378–89; *LW* 31:75–76.
86. *WA* 53:22–184.
87. *CR* 12:712–1094.
88. *WA* 35:411–15, 487–88; *LW* 53:214–16.
89. *WA* 35:422–25, 493–95; *LW* 53:219–20.
90. *WA* 19, after 72; *LW* 53:82–83, cf. 60, 282.
91. *WA* 2:386–87.
92. *WA* 49:278–79.
93. Ricarda Huch, *Luthers Glaube, Briefe an einem Freund,* 1st ed. (1917), 160.
94. *Cl* 1:213, 227; *WA* 6:63, 3, and 202, 2; *LW* 39:7 and 44:21.
95. *Cl* 2:300, 2–8; *WA* 8:676, 4–10; *LW* 45:57.

96. *Cl* 2:310, 20–25; *WA* 8:687, 21–26; *LW* 45:74.

97. *Cl* 2:360, 5; *WA* 11:245, 6; *LW* 45:81.

98. *Cl* 2:404, 1–19; *WA* 12:11, 3–20; *LW* 45:169.

99. *Cl* 5:222–304; *WA* 56:3–528; *LW* 25:3–524.

100. *Cl* 1:161–73; *WA* 2:685–97; *LW* 42:99–115.

101. See Luise Klein, "Die Bereitung zum Sterben: Studien zu den frühen reformatorischen Sterbebüchern" (dissertation, University of Göttingen, theological faculty, 1959).

102. *Cl* 1:165, 13–22; *WA* 2:689, 3–11; *LW* 42:104.

103. *Cl* 1:173, 18–24; *WA* 2:697, 14–21; *LW* 42:114.

104. *Cl* 1:166, 27–28; *WA* 2:690, 16–17; *LW* 42:105.

105. *Cl* 6:103, 21—105, 11; *WA* Br 2, no. 455, pp. 455, 39—456, 85; *LW* 48:390–91.

106. Wilhelm Walther, *Die deutsche Bibel Übersetzung des Mittelalters,* 3 vols. (Braunschweig: H. Wollermann, 1889–92), as well as his *Luthers deutsche Bibel* (Berlin: Ernst Siegfried Mittler und Sohn, 1917).

107. Gustav Roethe, "Luthers Septemberbibel" *LuJ* 5 (1923): 1–21.

108. Hans Vollmer, "Die deutsche Bibel," *LuJ* 16 (1934): 27–50.

109. Heinrich Bornkamm, "Die Vorlagen zu Luthers Übersetzung des Neuen Testaments," in *Luther: Gestalt und Wirkungen,* SVRG, no. 188, (Gütersloh: Bertelsmann, 1975), 73.

110. Heinz Bluhm, *Martin Luther: Creative Translator* (St. Louis: Concordia Publishing House, 1965).

111. [Heinz Bluhm, *Luther: Translator of Paul* (New York: Peter Lang, 1984).— Trans.]

112. Siegfried Raeder, "Voraussetzungen und Methode von Luthers Bibelübersetzung," in *Geist und Geschichte der Reformation. Festgabe Hanns Rückert zum 65. Geburtstag,* AKG 38 (1966): 152–78.

113. *Cl* 4:180–93; *WA* 30²:632–46, 694; *LW* 35:181–202.

114. See below, 7.11.

115. See above, 4.7 under "The Translation of the Bible."

116. *WA* DB 10¹:400–401. In the 1524 edition the text reads: "Herr du bist unser zuflucht worden, Fur und fur." The text in 1531 and 1545: "Herr Gott du bist unser zuflucht, Fur und fur."

117. *WA* 40³:502, 4–5; *LW* 13:84, 87.

118. *WA* 40³:497–508; *LW* 13:83–91.

119. See below, 7.1.

120. See below, 7.5.

121. See below, 7.11.

122. See below, 7.6 and 7.8.

123. See below, 7.10.

124. See below, 7.2.

125. See below, 7.3.

126. Kurt Aland, Ernst Otto Reichert, and Gerhard Jordan, *Hilfsbuch zum Lutherstudium,* 3d ed. (Witten/Ruhr: Luther–Verlag, 1970).

127. Heinrich J. Vogel, *Vogel's Cross Reference and Index to the Contents of Luther's Works* (Milwaukee: Northwestern Publishing House, 1983).

128. *Cl* 2:188–298; *WA* 7:544–604; *LW* 21:297–358.

129. Since the documents referred to in the following paragraphs will be discussed in more detail in the following sections of this chapter, references to sources are usually not given here.

130. Theodore G. Tappert, ed., *Selected Writings of Martin Luther,* 4 vols. (Philadelphia: Fortress Press, 1967).

131. Translations of parts, and sometimes all, of these lectures are provided in exegetical sections of *LW.* A selection of the original texts is available in *Cl* 5.

132. Selections of these are found in *Cl* 5.

133. See also *LW* 10 and 11 (Psalms), 25 (Romans), 29 (Hebrews).

134. *Cl* 5:344–77; *WA* 57:3–238; *LW* 31:39–70. The text in volume 1 of Hans Ulrich Delius's *Studienausgabe Martin Luther* (vols. 1–3, Berlin: Evangelische Verlagsanstalt, 1979–83; vol. 4, forthcoming), 1:186–218, incorporates new findings and is the best text. See below, 7.9.

135. The necessary texts are available in Walter Koehler, ed., *Dokumente zum Ablass Streit von 1517,* 2d ed. (Tübingen: J. C. B. Mohr [Paul Siebeck], 1924).

136. *Sermon on Grace and Indulgences* (1518), *Cl* 1:11–14; *WA* 1:243–46.

137. *Cl* 1:3–9; *WA* 1:233–238; *LW* 31:25–33.

138. *Cl* 1:16–147; *WA* 1:525–628; *LW* 31:83–252.

139. Simply "15" in *LW. Cl* 1:53–58; *WA* 1:554–58; *LW* 31:125–30.

140. *Cl* 1:7, 31—8, 3; *WA* 1:236, 35—237, 6; *LW* 31:234–40. This is the discussion of theses 69–74. See Johannes Heckel, *Initia juris ecclesiastici Protestantium,* in SBAW.PPH. 1949, 5 (1950).

141. They are characterized by the fact that the title begins with *Sermo* or *Sermon*—which does not describe a preached sermon, but rather a written treatise. This term is not always preserved in the English translations of *LW.*

142. Published in 1519: *The Sacrament of Penance* (*Cl* 1:174–84; *WA* 2:713–23; *LW* 35:9–22); *A Sermon on Preparing to Die* (*Cl* 1:161–73; *WA* 2:685–97; *LW* 42:99–115); *A Sermon on the Estate of Marriage* (*WA* 2:166–71; *LW* 44:7–14); *Two Kinds of Righteousness* (*WA* 2:145–52; *LW* 31:297–306); *On Rogationtide Prayer and Procession* (*WA* 2:175–79 + ; *LW* 42:87–93); *A Meditation on Christ's Passion* (*Cl* 1:154–60; *WA* 2:136–42; *LW* 42:7–14); *The Blessed Sacrament of the Holy and True Body of Christ, and the Brotherhoods* (*Cl* 1:196–212; *WA* 2:742–58; *LW* 35:49–73); *The Holy and Blessed Sacrament of Baptism* (*Cl* 1:185–95; *WA* 2:727–37; *LW* 35:29–43); *[Kleiner] Sermon von dem Wucher (Usury)* (*WA* 6:3–8 and 9:798).

Published in 1520: *Sermon on the Ban* (*Cl* 1:213–26; *WA* 6:63–75; *LW* 39:7–22); *A Treatise on the New Testament, That Is, the Holy Mass* (*Cl* 1:299–322; *WA* 6:353–78; *LW* 35:79–111 [See also *WA* 6:78–83, 630, and 9:799 and 21:161.]); *Treatise on Good Works* (*Cl* 1:227–98; *WA* 6:202–76; *LW* 44:21–114); *[Grosser] Sermon von dem Wucher* (*WA* 6:36–60, 630, and 15:314–20).

143. *Cl* 1:299–322; *WA* 6:353–78; *LW* 35:79–111.

144. *Cl* 1:324–61; *WA* 6:285–324, 631; *LW* 39:55–104.

145. See *LW* 39:51–54.

146. *Cl* 1:363–421; *WA* 6:404–69; *LW* 44:123–217.

147. *Temporal Authority: To What Extent It Should Be Obeyed* (1523), *Cl* 2:360–94; *WA* 11:245–80; *LW* 45:81–129.

148. *Cl* 1:426–512; *WA* 6:497–573; *LW* 36:11–126.

149. [For a thorough discussion of the process leading to giving only the bread to the laity, see James J. Megivern, *Concomitance and Communion: A Study in Eucharistic Doctrine and Practice,* SF NS 33 (Fribourg: The University Press, 1963).—Trans.]

150. Erwin Iserloh, *Der Kampf um die Messe im den ersten Jahren der Auseinandersetzung mit Luther,* KLK 10 (1952): esp. 56–60. [See also James F. McCue, "Luther and Roman Catholicism on the Mass as Sacrifice," *JES* 2.2 (Spring 1965): 205–33.—Trans.]

151. [Luther published this book both in Latin and German at the explicit request of his order. He first wrote and published it in Latin (*WA* 7:49–73; *LW* 31:343–77), and then made his own free translation of it into German (*Cl* 2:10–27; *WA* 7:20–38). A translation appears in Bertram Lee Woolf, *Reformation Writings of Martin Luther,* 2 vols. (London: Lutterworth Press, 1952–56), 1:356–79. Although the differences do not always come through clearly in the translations, a comparison of these two versions can be helpful in showing the difference between Luther's style of thinking in each of these languages. See above, 4.23.—Trans.]

152. *WA* 7:42–49; *LW* 31:333–43; the German version: *Cl* 2:2–10; *WA* 7:3–11; Woolf, *Reformation Writings of Luther,* 1:336–47, 888.

153. *Cl* 2:11, 6–9; *WA* 7:21, 1–4; *LW* 31:344.

154. *Admonition to Peace: A Reply to the Twelve Articles of the Peasants in Swabia, Cl* 3:64, 34—65, 14; *WA* 18:327; *LW* 46:39.

155. See below, 4.37 n. 176.

156. See Andreas Karlstadt, *Von Abtuhung der Bilder und das keyn Bedtler vnther den Christen seyn sollen, 1522,* ed. Hans Lietzmann, KlT 74 (Bonn: A. Marcus und E. Weber's Verlag, 1911). For a detailed study of the problems see Ronald J. Sider, *Andreas Bodenstein von Karlstadt: The Development of His Thought 1517–1525* (Leiden: E. J. Brill, 1974), 148–73; Bernhard Lohse, "Luther und der Radikalismus," *LuJ* 44 (1977): 7–27.

157. See particularly Luther's "Invocavit Sermons (March 9–16, 1522)," *Cl* 7:363–87; *WA* 10³:1–64; *LW* 51:70–100. A good survey over these discussions has been given by Helmar Junghans, "Freiheit und Ordnung bei Luther während der Wittenberger Bewegung und der Visitationen," *ThLZ* 97 (1972): 95–104; Mark U. Edwards, Jr., *Luther and the False Brethren* (Stanford, Calif.: Stanford University Press, 1975), 6–33.

158. *Cl* 2:133–87; *WA* 7:544–604; *LW* 21:297–358.

159. See above, n. 7.

160. *Cl* 2:257, 31–35; *WA* 8:632, 39—633, 4; *LW* 44:315–16.

161. *Cl* 2:300–310; *WA* 8:676–87; *LW* 45:57–74.

162. *Cl* 2:360–94; *WA* 11:245–81; *LW* 45:81–129.

163. *Cl* 2:424–26; *WA* 12:35–37; *LW* 53:11–14.

164. See above, n. 38.

165. See above, n. 47.

166. *Cl* 2:451, 25–26; *WA* 15:38, 7–8; *LW* 45:360.

167. *Cl* 3:1–46; *WA* 15:293–313. The second half of the book is a reprint of an earlier work on usury, published in 1520: this text is found in *WA* 6:36–60; *LW*

45:245–310. A brief addition was made in the 1524 reprinting, *WA* 15:15, 321–22; *LW* 45:308–10.

168. Günter Fabiunke has attempted to do this. (*Martin Luther als Nationalökonom* [Berlin: Akademie-Verlag, 1963]).

169. See, for example, Max Weber, *The Protestant Ethic and the Spirit of Capitalism,* trans. Talcott Parsons (New York: Charles Scribner's Sons, 1958), 84, 60, 126, 240.

170. See above, n. 48.

171. See above, n. 49.

172. *WA* 18:336–43.

173. *Cl* 3:75–93; *WA* 18:384–401; *LW* 46:63–85.

174. *Cl* 3:94–293; *WA* 18:600–787; *LW* 33:15–295. The most useful English translation is in *LW* 33. The best German translation is in the Munich Edition of Luther's Works, Supplementary Volume I—Hans Joachim Iwand's commentary is especially helpful. Klaus Schwarzwäller has presented a very useful analysis of the structure of Luther's book in *Theologia crucis; Luthers Lehre von der Prädestination nach De servo arbitrio, 1525* (Munich: Chr. Kaiser, 1970). For a description of the history of the doctrine of the freedom of the will, see Henry J. McSorley, *Luther: Right or Wrong? An Ecumenical–Theological Study of Luther's Major Work, The Bondage of Will* (Minneapolis: Augsburg Publishing House, 1969).

175. See above, 3.27.

176. LCC 17:35–97.

177. [*Loci communes* might be translated "common points" or "commonplaces"—although the latter has some negative connotations in English not intended by Melanchthon. Melanchthon's *Loci* appeared in various editions, beginning with the *Loci communes* of 1521. Two modern translations of this edition are available: *The Loci Communes of Philip Melanchthon,* trans. Charles Leander Hill (Boston: Meador Publishing Co., 1944), and *Loci Communes Theologici,* trans. Lowell J. Satre, ed. Wilhelm Pauck, LCC 19:18–152. The 1555 edition has also been translated: *Melanchthon on Christian Doctrine: Loci Communes, 1555,* trans. and ed. Clyde L. Manschreck (New York: Oxford University Press, 1965). The last edition of the *Loci* was that of 1559 and is somewhat more explicit in revising earlier thinking than even the 1555 edition. See Hans Engeland, "Introduction," in LCC 19:xxv–xlii.—Trans.]

178. See, for example, Articles II and IV of the *Apology of the Augsburg Confession*—a confessional document written by Melanchthon—or Article II of *The Formula of Concord, BC,* 102–13, 519–39.

179. *Cl* 3:352–516; *WA* 26:261–509; *LW* 37:161–372.

180. *Cl* 3:507–15; *WA* 26:499–509; *LW* 37:360–72.

181. *BC,* 358–461.

182. See Johann Michael Reu, *Dr. Martin Luther's Small Catechism* (Chicago: Wartburg Press, 1929) and *Quellen zur Geschichte des kirchlichen Unterrichts in der evangelischen Kirche Deutschland zwischen 1530 und 1600,* 9 vols. (Gütersloh: Bertelsmann, 1904–35). See also Carl Volz, ed., *Teaching the Faith* (River Forest, Ill.: Lutheran Education Association, 1967); Johannes Meyer, *Historischer Kommentar zu Luthers kleinem Katechismus* (Gütersloh: Bertelsmann, 1929).

183. *Cl* 4:104–43; *WA* 30²:268–356; *LW* 34:9–61.

184. *Cl* 4:104; *WA* 30²:268; *LW* 34:9.

185. See *LW* 49:280–437.

186. *Cl* 4:179–93; *WA* 30²:632–46; *LW* 35:181–202.

187. *WA* DB, 9 vols.

188. See above, 4.11–15.

189. *Cl* 4:194–228; *WA* 30³:276–320; *LW* 47:11–55.

190. See above, 4.40.

191. See above, 4.26.

192. *BC,* 302.

193. See above, 2.20.

194. *WA* 50:509–653; *LW* 41:9–178.

195. *Cl* 4:322–78; *WA* 51:469–572; *LW* 41:185–256. See above, 3.40.

196. See above, 3.40.

197. *Cl* 4:421–28; *WA* 54:179–87; *LW* 34:327–38.

198. See below, 5.2.

199. *Cl* 6; *WA* Br 1—11; *LW* 48—50.

200. It is almost impossible to draw a clear boundary around Luther's sermons in the *WA.* See, however, the selected sermons in *LW* 51 and 52 and *Cl* 7.

201. *Cl* 7:20–38 and 8:1–354; *WA* Tr 1—6; *LW* 54.

202. *WA* 39¹,²; *LW* 34:104–96 (a selection); unfortunately, *Cl* omits these entirely.

203. *WA* 39¹:485, 16–24. See Gerhard Ebeling, "On the Doctrine of the *Triplex Usus Legis* in the Theology of the Reformation," in *Word and Faith*, trans. James W. Leitch (Philadelphia: Fortress Press, 1963), 62–78.

204. *WA* 39¹:175–80; *LW* 34:137–44. See Gerhard Ebeling, *Lutherstudien,* 2 vols. (Tübingen: J. C. B. Mohr [Paul Siebeck], 1971, 1982), see particularly 2:1–22.

Chapter 5: Aspects and Problems of Luther's Theology

1. Theodosius Harnack, *Luthers Theologie mit besonderer Beziehung auf seine Versöhnungs- und Erlösungslehre,* 2 vols., 1st ed. (vol. 1, Erlangen: Theodor Bläsing, 1862–66; vol. 2, Erlangen: Andreas Deichert, 1886; reprinted Munich: Chr. Kaiser, 1927); in one volume (Amsterdam: Rodopi, 1969).

2. Reinhold Seeberg, *Lehrbuch der Dogmengeschichte,* 4th ed., 5 vols. (Leipzig: A. Deichert, 1933), vol. 4/1. The English translation, *The History of Doctrines,* trans. Charles E. Hay (Grand Rapids: Baker Book House, 1952), was based on a special revision of the first edition; later German editions were substantially revised.

3. Erich Seeberg, *Luthers Theologie, Motive und Ideen,* vol. 1, *Die Gottesanschauung* (Göttingen: Vandenhoeck & Ruprecht, 1929); vol. 2, *Christus, Wirklichkeit und Urbild* (Stuttgart: Kohlhammer, 1937). This work was never finished. A summary volume was published, however, *Luthers Theologie in ihren Grundzügen* (Stuttgart: Kohlhammer, 1940; rep. 1950).

4. Paul Althaus, *The Theology of Martin Luther,* trans. Robert C. Schultz (Philadelphia: Fortress Press, 1966).

5. Lennart Pinomaa, *Faith Victorious: An Introduction to Luther's Theology*, trans. Walter J. Kukkonen (Philadelphia: Fortress Press, 1963).

6. Friedrich Gogarten, *Luthers Theologie* (Tübingen: J. C. B. Mohr [Paul Siebeck], 1967).

7. Rudolph Hermann, *Gesammelte Studien zur Theologie Luthers und der Reformation* (Göttingen: Vandenhoeck & Ruprecht, 1960), and idem, *Luthers Theologie*, ed. Horst Beintker (Göttingen: Vandenhoeck & Ruprecht, 1967).

8. Hans Joachim Iwand, *Luthers Theologie*, ed. Johann Haar (Munich: Chr. Kaiser, 1974).

9. Gerhard Ebeling, *Luther: An Introduction to His Thought*, trans. R. A. Wilson (Philadelphia: Fortress Press, 1970).

10. In *RGG*³, 4:495–520.

11. Iwand, *Luthers Theologie.*

12. Hans Joachim Iwand, *Rechtfertigungslehre und Christusglaube* (Leipzig: J. C. Hinrichs, 1930).

13. *Cl* 3:101, 23–28; *WA* 18:606, 24–28; *LW* 33:25–26.

14. Philip Melanchthon, *Melanchthon on Christian Doctrine: Loci Communes, 1555*, trans. and ed. Clyde L. Manschreck (New York: Oxford University Press, 1965).

15. John Calvin, *Institutes of the Christian Religion*, LCC 20 and 21.

16. *WA* 40²:328, 1ff.; *LW* 12:310.

17. See below, 5.3.1–3.

18. *WA* 1:158–220. A second edition appeared in 1525, *WA* 18:479–530. This second edition has been translated into English, *LW* 14:140–205.

19. *First Lectures on the Psalms*, *WA* 3:397, 9–11; *LW* 10:332–33.

20. *Cl* 5:38–221; *WA* 3, 4, and 55; *LW* 10 and 11. For the revised edition and additional notes, see *WA* 55. *Cl* contains a selection; *LW* translates only the scholia, with occasional translations of the glosses in the notes. *LW* incorporates some of the material in *WA* 55.

21. *Cl* 5:222–304 (selections); *WA* 56:3–528. (See also 57:127, 131–232; *LW* 25:3–524. In using *WA* 57, remember that there are three sets of page numbers in the volume.)

22. *Cl* 5:222, 1–6; *WA* 56:157, 2–6; *LW* 25:135.

23. *Cl* 5:239, 11—246, 20; *WA* 56:269, 21—291, 14; *LW* 25:258–78.

24. *Cl* 5:222, 7–11; *WA* 56:158, 10–14; *LW* 25:136–37.

25. Ernst Bizer, *Fides ex auditu. Eine Untersuchung über die Entdeckung der Gerechtigkeit Gottes durch Martin Luther* (Neukirchen: Neukirchener Verlag, 1958; 3d ed., 1966), 45–52.

26. For example, *Cl* 5:240–41; *WA* 56:272–73; *LW* 25:260–61. See also *WA* 56:46, 13–19; *LW* 25:39–40.

27. *Cl* 5:344–74 (selections); *WA* 57³:5–238; *LW* 29:107–241.

28. For example, Regin Prenter, *Der barmherzige Richter. Iustitia dei passiva in Luthers Dictata super Psalterium 1513–1515*, Acta Jutlandica 33, no. 2 (Copenhagen, 1961), 20.

29. For example, Heiko Oberman, "'Justitia Christi' and 'Justitia Dei.' Luther and the Scholastic Doctrines of Justification," *HTR* 59 (1966): 1–26.

30. *Preface to the Complete Edition of Luther's Latin Writings, Cl* 4:427, 40; *WA* 54:186, 7; *LW* 34:336–37.

31. Luther does not himself use the term "causative," but he has often described the Hebrew way of thinking in such a way that the term "causative" does adequately render Luther's interpretation of the terms such as "justice or righteousness of God" and "love of God."

32. Large numbers of these statements have been collected by Otto Scheel, *Dokumente zu Luthers Entwicklung,* 2d rev. ed. (Tübingen: J. C. B. Mohr [Paul Siebeck], 1929). Since then, researchers have sometimes considered even more statements of Luther to be relevant to the discussion.

33. Many important studies of scholars have been gathered and reprinted in B. Lohse, ed., *Der Durchbruch der reformatorischen Erkenntnis bei Luther* (Darmstadt: Wissenschaftliche Buchgemeinschaft, 1968).

34. See above, 3.4.

35. *The Commentary of Vincent of Lerins,* trans. T. Herbert Bindley (London: S.P.C.K., 1914).

36. The doctrine of verbal inspiration was developed after the middle of the sixteenth century, mainly over against the Tridentine definition of the relation between Scripture and tradition.

37. *WA* DB 7:384–87; *LW* 35:395–98. *WA* prints the editions of 1522 and 1545 side by side so that it is possible to see the changes. The notes to *LW* quote Luther's statements in earlier editions that were much sharper in tone.

38. *Preface to the Wittenberg Edition of Luther's German Writings, WA* 50:657, 25ff.; *LW* 34:284.

39. *The Gospel for Christmas Eve, Luke 2[:1–14], WA* $10^{1.1}$:75, 6–7; *LW* 52:21.

40. *The Bondage of the Will, Cl* 3:101, 6–8; *WA* 18:606, 11ff.; *LW* 33:25.

41. Ibid., *Cl* 3:101, 29; *WA* 18:606, 29; *LW* 33:26.

42. *Assertio omnium articularum M. Lutheri per bullam Leonis X. novissimam damnatorum* (1520), *WA* 7:97, 23–24.

43. *WA* Tr 3, no. 3043a.

44. *Treatise on Good Works, Cl* 1:234, 21–27; *WA* 6:209, 24–30; *LW* 44:30.

45. *The Gospel for the Festival of the Epiphany, Matthew 2[:1–12], WA* $10^{1.1}$:625–26, 3; *LW* 52:205.

46. *WA* 15:527, 35–37; a sermon preached in 1524.

47. *WA* 17^{1}:431, 2–4; a sermon preached in 1525.

48. *Cl* 3:214–15; *WA* 18:719; *LW* 33:191.

49. *WA* 9:448, 37—449, 1; a sermon preached in 1520.

50. *Cl* 3:290, 7–10; *WA* 18:784, 36–39; *LW* 33:290.

51. Ebeling, *Luther: Introduction to His Thought,* 249ff.

52. *WA* 16:143, 17–19.

53. *Cl* 3:200, 38–41; *WA* 18:706, 22–24; *LW* 33:171.

54. *Cl* 2:253, 32–33; *WA* 8:629, 26–27; *LW* 44:336.

55. *Cl* 2:253, 33–37; *WA* 8:629, 27–30; *LW* 44:336.

56. *WA* 7:838, 4–8; *LW* 32:112.

57. Emanuel Hirsch, *Lutherstudien,* 2 vols. (Gütersloh: Bertelsmann, 1954), 1:127–28.

58. *Cl* 2:226, 26–32; *WA* 8:606, 30–35; *LW* 44:298.

59. *WA* 28:608, 21–29.

60. See Gerhard Ebeling's extensive analysis of Luther's disputation on the human person *(de homine)* in *Lutherstudien*, 2 vols. (Tübingen: J. C. B. Mohr [Paul Siebeck], 1971–77), 2/1.

61. *WA* 19:482, 25—483, 19; *LW* 36:335.

62. Reinhold Seeberg, *Lehrbuch der Dogmengeschichte*, 4/1.

63. Werner Elert, *The Structure of Lutheranism*, trans. W. A. Hansen (St. Louis: Concordia Publishing House, 1962).

64. See above, n. 3.

65. See above, n. 10.

66. Althaus, *Theology of Martin Luther*, 199–200.

67. *WA* 46:436, 7–13.

68. *WA* 46:436, 71–72, a sermon preached in 1538; see *WA* 49:237, a sermon preached in 1541.

69. *WA* 41:270, 2–23; 272, 1–19; *WA* 52:338, 1–10.

70. *WA* 39²:304, 16. The statement was actually made by Georg Major in the course of theological disputation at which Luther presided.

71. *WA* 39²:382, 6–7; 323, 20–21. The second reference is to another statement by Major.

72. *Von der Beichte, ob der Papst Macht habe zu gebieten. Der 118. Psalm* (1521), *WA* 8:149, 34—150, 4.

73. *Cl* 3:508, 11–17; *WA* 26:500, 27–32; *LW* 37:361.

74. *BC*, 291–92.

75. *The Magnificat*, *Cl* 2:161, 21–23; *WA* 7:574, 29–31; *LW* 21:328.

76. *WA* 19:232, 21–25; *LW* 19:82.

77. *This Is My Body*, *WA* 23:133, 26–28; *LW* 37:57.

78. Ibid., *WA* 23:137, 31–36; *LW* 37:60.

79. Ibid., *Cl* 3:404, 33–38; *WA* 26:339, 39—340, 2; *LW* 37:228.

80. *WA* 40³:209–15.

81. A postil: on Matt. 4:1–11, *WA* 17²:192, 28–30. See also John Nicolas Lenker, ed., *Sermons of Martin Luther: On the New Testament*, 8 vols. (Grand Rapids: Baker Book House, 1983; reprint of 1904 edition—paging and volume number differ from earlier edition), 2:141.

82. See above, 3.23–27.

83. Otto Ritschl, *Dogmengeschichte des Protestantismus; Grundlagen und Grundzügen der theologischen Gedanken und Lehrbildung in der protestantischen Kirche*, 4 vols. (vols. 1–2, Leipzig: J. C. Hinrichs, 1908–12; vols. 3–4, Göttingen: Vandenhoeck & Ruprecht, 1926–27), 3:16.

84. Reinhold Seeberg, *Lehrbuch der Dogmengeschichte*, 4/1:182. For an English translation of an earlier version, see *The History of Doctrines*, 2:151, 243–45, 265.

85. See above, 1.18 and 3.27. *Potentia Dei ordinata* is frequently translated "the ordained power of God." It refers to God working through and limiting himself by the structures and processes of the created world.

86. Elert, *Structure of Lutheranism*, 24, see also 19.

87. *Cl* 3:291–93; *WA* 18:786–87; *LW* 33:293–95. See above, 3.26–27.

88. *Cl* 3:174–77; *WA* 18:682–84; *LW* 33:135–38.

89. *WA* 39¹:370, 12—371, 1.

90. Hans Joachim Iwand, "Um den rechten Glauben," in *Gesammelte Aufsätze* (Munich: Chr. Kaiser, 1959), 87–109.

91. See below, 6.7.3–4.

92. *WA* 31¹:445, 3–24; *LW* 14:124.

93. David Löfgren, *Die Theologie der Schöpfung bei Luther* (Göttingen: Vandenhoeck & Ruprecht, 1960).

94. Ibid., 83.

95. *WA* 40³:221, 6ff.

96. See above, 5.6.5.

97. *WA* 5:168, 1–8.

98. Althaus, *Theology of Luther,* 105ff., and "Gottes Gottheit als Sinn der Rechtfertigungslehre," *LuJ* 13 (1931): 1–28.

99. See above, 3.5.

100. *CI* 1:21, 31–35; *WA* 1:529, 23–26.

101. *CI* 1:21, 7; *WA* 1:529, 3.

102. *CI* 1:324–61; *WA* 6:285–324; *LW* 39:49–104.

103. *CI* 1:333, 28—337, 20; *WA* 6:295, 12—298, 36; *LW* 39:68–72.

104. *CI* 1:335, 28ff.; *WA* 6:286, 35ff.; *LW* 39:70.

105. *CI* 1:325, 28ff.; *WA* 6:286, 35ff.; *LW* 39:59.

106. *CI* 1:333, 28ff.; *WA* 6:295, 12ff.; *LW* 39:68.

107. *CI* 1:339, 16–17; *WA* 6:301, 3–4; *LW* 39:75.

108. *WA* 26:19, 195, 1—200, 21; *LW* 40:269–72.

109. Peter Brunner, *Nikolaus von Amsdorf als Bischof von Naumburg. Eine Untersuchung zur Gestalt des evangelischen Bischofamtes in der Reformationszeit,* SVRG, no. 161 (Gütersloh: Gerd Mohn, 1961).

110. *BC,* 300. [see Philip Melanchthon's *Treatise on the Power and Primacy of the Pope, BC,* 331.—Trans.]

111. Peter Brunner uses the term "Synodaler Episkopalismus." See "Von Amt des Bischofs," in *Pro Ecclesia Gesammelte Aufsätze zur dogmatischen Theologie* (Hamburg: Lutherisches Verlagshaus, 1962), 1:264.

112. *The Gospel for the Early Christmas Service, Luke 2[:15–20], WA* 10¹·¹:140, 8–17; *LW* 52:39–40.

113. *WA* 25:97, 32–33. The quotation is from Luther's scholia on Isaiah. *LW* 16:32 translates student notes of this lecture (*WA* 31²:22, 34–35): "By the Word alone, therefore, the church is recognized, and in the glory of the Word the reign of Christ is described."

114. *WA* 50:628ff.; *LW* 41:150–66.

115. *CI* 4:330ff.; *WA* 51:479ff.; *LW* 41:194–99.

116. *CI* 4:333–34; *WA* 51:487; *LW* 41:199.

117. *Concerning Rebaptism, WA* 26:147, 13ff.; *LW* 40:231–32. The statement was made in 1528 in a book condemning the practice of rebaptism.

118. *Luthers Bedenken über die Sequestration* (August 1532), *WA* 39²:167, 8—168, 1.

119. *WA* 6:604, 19–38.

120. Wilhelm Brunotte, *Das geistliche Amt bei Luther* (Berlin: Lutherisches Verlagshaus, 1959).

121. Hellmut Lieberg, *Amt und Ordination bei Luther und Melanchthon*, FKDG (Göttingen: Vandenhoeck & Ruprecht, 1962).

122. Peter Manns, "Amt und Eucharistie in der Theologie Martin Luthers," in *Amt und Eucharistie*, ed. Peter Bläser (Paderborn: Bonifacius–Druckerei, 1973), 68–173, esp. 72–76.

123. See above, 4.26.

124. See above, 5.7.7.

125. *Cl* 2:395–403; *WA* 11:408–16; *LW* 39:305–14.

126. *Cl* 1:372, 15—373, 20; *WA* 6:413, 1—414, 4; *LW* 44:136–37.

127. For a fuller discussion of the development of the state church and Luther's participation in this process, see above, 3.38.

128. Ulrich Duchrow, *Christenheit und Weltverantwortung. Traditiongeschichte und systematische Struktur der Zweireichelehre* (Stuttgart: Ernst Klett, 1970). A parallel work in English is Karl H. Hertz, ed., *Two Kingdoms and One World: A Sourcebook in Christian Social Ethics* (Minneapolis: Augsburg Publishing House, 1976).

129. Reinhold Seeberg, *Lehrbuch der Dogmengeschichte*, 4/1:340–41. Compare *The History of Doctrines*, 2:273.

130. Ernst Kinder, *Geistliches und weltliches Regiment Gottes nach Luther* (Weimar: H. Böhlau, 1940).

131. Gustav Törnvall, *Geistliches und weltliches Regiment bei Luther. Studien zu Luthers Weltbind und Gesellschaftsverständnis* (Munich: Chr. Kaiser, 1947).

132. See especially Johannes Heckel, *Lex charitatis. Eine juristische Untersuchung über das Recht in der Theologie Martin Luthers*, SBAW.PPH, NF 36 (1953), and idem, *Im Irrgarten der Zwei–Reiche–Lehre. Zwei Abhandlungen zum Reichs– und Kirchenbegriff Martin Luthers* (Munich: Chr. Kaiser, 1957).

133. Paul Althaus, "Die beiden Regimente bei Luther. Bermerkungen zu Johannes Heckels 'Lex charitatis'," *ThLZ* 81 (1956): 129–36, and idem, "Luthers Lehre von den beiden Reichen im Feuer der Kritik," *LuJ* 24 (1957): 40–68.

134. Althaus wrote a number of very significant essays on this subject, particularly "Luthers Lehre von den beiden Reichen im Feuer der Kritik."

135. Ibid., 67.

136. Franz Lau, *Luthers Lehre von den beiden Reichen*, 2d ed. (Berlin: Lutherisches Verlagshaus, 1953).

137. Heinrich Bornkamm, *Luther's Doctrine of the Two Kingdoms in the Context of His Theology*, trans. Karl H. Hertz, Facet Books (Philadelphia: Fortress Press, 1966).

138. Ibid., 8.

139. Gerhard Ebeling, "The Necessity of the Doctrine of the Two Kingdoms," in *Word and Faith*, trans. James W. Leitch (Philadelphia: Fortress Press, 1963), 386–406; the quotation is on 390.

140. The discussion began with a series of, publications—in which Ulrich Duchrow was most prominently represented. First, he published his extensive description of the history of the tradition of the doctrine of the two kingdoms (Duchrow, *Christenheit und Weltantwortung*). Then, he and Heiner Hoffmann jointly edited a collection of sources, *Die Vorstellung von Zwei Reichen und Regimenten bis Luther* (Gütersloh: Gütersloher Verlagshaus Gerd Mohn, 1972).

Then Duchrow, in collaboration with others, edited other volumes of sources—
(with Wolfgang Huber) *Umdeutungen der Zweireichelehre Luthers im 19. Jahrhundert* (Gütersloh: Gütersloher Verlagshaus Gerd Mohn, 1975); *Die Am-
bivalenz der Zweireichelehre in lutherischen Kirchen des 20. Jahrhunderts*
(1976). See also Duchrow's essay: "Zweireichelehre als Ideologie. Folgenreiche
Umdeutungen Luthers im 19. Jahrhundert" *LM* 14 (1975): 296–300. Then Duchrow edited the volume *Lutheran Churches—Salt or Mirror of Society? Case
Studies on the Theory and Practice of the Two Kingdoms Doctrine* (Geneva:
Lutheran World Federation, Department of Studies, 1977). This volume begins
with a brief historical and systematic summary written by Duchrow himself; then
various contributors give critical evaluations of the effect of the doctrine of the
two kingdoms on the attitude of the Lutheran churches in various countries.

141. Duchrow, *Christenheit und Weltverantwortung.*

142. For example, Hermann Kunst, *Evangelischer Glaube und politische
Verantwortung. Martin Luther als politischer Berater seiner Landesherrn und
seine Teilnahme an den Fragen des öffentlichen Lebens* (Stuttgart: Evangelisches
Verlagswerk, 1976); Eike Wolgast, "Die Wittenberger Theologie und die Politik
der evangelischen Stände," *QFRG* 47 (1977). Important contributions to the
discussion of Duchrow's work were made by Trutz Rendtorff, Review of Ulrich
Duchrow and Wolfgang Huber, eds., *Umdeutungen der Zweireichelehre Luthers
im 19. Jahrhundert,* in *ZEE* 20 (1976): 64–70. Duchrow and Huber response,
ibid., 144–53. See also Martin Honecker, "Zur gegenwärtigen Interpretation der
Zweireichelehre," *ZKG* 89 (1978): 150–62.

143. For Luther's view of history, see below, 5.9.1–7.

144. See above, 3.43–45.

145. *Cl* 6, no. 54, 104, 7–11; *WA Br* 2, no. 455, 50–54; *LW* 48:390.

146. See above, 5.6.7.

147. *Cl* 2:133–87; *WA* 7:538–604; *LW* 21:295–358.

148. *WA* 50:468–77; *LW* 47:107–19.

149. *WA* 50:475–76; *LW* 47:15–118.

150. *WA* 50:476; *LW* 47:118.

Chapter 6: The History of the Interpretation of Luther

1. Horst Stephan, *Luther in den Wandlungen seiner Kirche* (1st ed., Geissen:
Töpelmann, 1907; 2d ed., Berlin: Töpelmann, 1951).

2. Ernst Walter Zeeden, *Martin Luther und die Reformation im Urteil des
deutschen Luthertums. Studien zum Selbstverständnis des lutherischen Protestantismus von Luthers Tode bis zum Beginn der Goethezeit,* 2 vols. (Freiburg:
Herder, 1950–52).

3. Heinrich Bornkamm, *Luther im Spiegel der deutschen Geistesgeschichte. Mit
ausgewählten Texten von Lessing bis zur Gegenwart* (1st ed., Heidelberg: Quelle
& Meyer, 1955; 2d rev. ed., Göttingen: Vandenhoeck & Ruprecht, 1970).

4. Walther von Loewenich, *Luther und der Neuprotestantismus* (Witten/Ruhr:
Luther-Verlag, 1963).

5. See above, 5.2.1. Agricola did not yet use the terms "young Luther" and "old
Luther." But he referred to earlier writings of Luther's in the years 1517 through
1519. For further details see Joachim Rogge, *Johann Agricolas Lutherverständnis*

unter besonderer Berücksichtigung des Antinomismus, ThA 14 (Berlin: Evangelische Verlagsanstalt, 1960), 104–10.

6. Zeeden, *Martin Luther und die Reformation,* 2:167ff.

7. Philip Jacob Spener, *Pia Desideria,* trans. Theodore G. Tappert (Philadelphia: Fortress Press, 1964).

8. *WA* DB 6:2–11; *LW* 35:357–62.

9. *Cl* 3:294–309; *WA* 19:72–113; *LW* 53:51–90.

10. Erich Beyreuther, "Theologia crucis. Zinzendorf und Luther," in *Studien zur Theologie Zinzendorfs. Gesammelte Aufsätze* (Neukirchen-Vluyn: Neukirchener Verlag, 1962), 235–47.

11. Published in many editions. For example, Gottfried Arnold, *Unparteyische Kirchen- und Ketzer-Historien, vom anfang des Neuen Testaments biss auff das Jahr Christi 1688,* 3 vols. (Schaffhausen: Emanuel und Benedict Hurter, 1740–42).

12. [See Bornkamm, *Luther im Spiegel der deutschen Geistesgeschichte,* 199–202.—Trans.]

13. [See ibid., 202–5.—Trans.]

14. [See ibid., 205–15.—Trans.]

15. [See ibid., 215–19.—Trans.]

16. See above, 6.3.4.

17. [See Bornkamm, *Luther im Spiegel der deutschen Geistesgeschichte,* 219–20.—Trans.]

18. [See ibid., 220–25.—Trans.]

19. [See ibid., 225–37.—Trans.]

20. [See ibid., 199–202. The specific reference is to Georg Friedrich Wilhelm Hegel, *The Philosophy of History,* trans. J. Sibree, vol. 46 of Great Books of the Western World, ed. Robert Maynard Hutchins (Chicago: Encyclopaedia Britannica, 1952), 353.—Trans.]

21. Friedrich Schleiermacher, *On Religion: Speeches to Its Cultured Despisers,* trans. John Oman (New York: Harper Torchbooks, 1958).

22. Novalis is a pseudonym for Friedrich von Hardenberg. Novalis, *Die Christenheit oder Europa* (1799), in Novalis, *Werke,* in einem Band, ed. Uwe Lassen (Hamburg: Hoffman & Campe, n.d.), 294. [Quoted by Bornkamm, *Luther im Spiegel der deutschen Geistesgeschichte,* 240.—Trans.]

23. Schleiermacher, *On Religion,* 269. [See also Bornkamm, *Luther im Spiegel der deutschen Geistesgeschichte,* 274–77.—Trans.]

24. Friedrich Schleiermacher, *The Christian Faith,* ed. H. R. Mackintosh and J. S. Stewart (Philadelphia: Fortress Press, 1977).

25. Paul Seifert, "Luther und Schleiermacher," *Luther* 40 (1969): 51–68.

26. See below, 7.2.

27. Leopold von Ranke, *Deutsche Geschichte im Zeitalter der Reformation,* ed. Paul Joachimsen (Meersburg and Leipzig: F. W. Hendel, 1926), 6:313–99. [For further information, see Bornkamm, *Luther im Spiegel der deutschen Geistesgeschichte,* 42 n. 2.—Trans.]

28. [For selections from Ranke, see Bornkamm, *Luther im Spiegel der deutschen Geistesgeschichte,* 249–58; Luther's explanation of Psalm 101 is in *WA* 51:200–264; *LW* 13:145–224.—Trans.]

29. Albrecht Ritschl, *Die christliche Lehre von der Rechtfertigung und Versöhnung*, 3 vols. (1st ed., Bonn: Marcus, 1870–74; 2d rev. ed., 1882–83). Two of the volumes have been translated into English. The first edition of vol. 1, in which Ritschl analyzed the history of the doctrine, was translated as *A Critical History of the Christian Doctrine of Justification and Reconciliation*, trans. John S. Black (Edinburgh: Edmonston, 1872). The second edition of vol. 3 was translated as *The Christian Doctrine of Justification and Reconciliation: The Positive Development of the Doctrine*, ed. H. R. Mackintosh and A. B. Macaulay (Edinburgh: T. & T. Clark, 1902).

30. Albrecht Ritschl, *Geschichte des Pietismus*, 3 vols. (Bonn: Marcus, 1880–86).

31. See above, 3.26–27 and 4.37.

32. *BC*, 352, 6 (explanation of the Lord's Supper).

33. [David W. Lotz, *Ritschl and Luther: A Fresh Perspective on Albrecht Ritschl's Theology in the Light of His Luther Study* (Nashville: Abingdon Press, 1974). Lotz has translated Ritschl's "Festival Address" celebrating the four hundredth anniversary of Luther's birth, 187–202.—Trans.]

34. Theodosius Harnack, *Luthers Theologie mit besonderer Beziehung auf seine Versöhnungs- und Erlösungslehre*, 2 vols. (vol. 1, Erlangen: Theodor Bläsing, 1862–66; vol. 2, Erlangen: Andreas Deichert, 1886; reprinted, Munich: Chr. Kaiser, 1927; and in one volume, Amsterdam: Rodopi, 1969).

35. See above, 3.26–27 and 4.37.

36. Ludwig Feuerbach, *The Essence of Faith According to Luther*, trans. Martin Cherno (New York: Harper & Row, 1967).

37. [See Bornkamm, *Luther im Spiegel der deutschen Geistesgeschichte*, 299–305.—Trans.]

38. [See ibid., 266–74.—Trans.]

39. [See ibid., 305–14.—Trans.]

40. [See ibid., 95–100.—Trans.]

41. [See ibid., 373–83.—Trans.]

42. [Three of Ernst Troeltsch's works on the Reformation have been translated into English: *The Social Teachings of the Christian Churches*, trans. Olive Wyon, 2 vols. (New York: Macmillan Co., 1931), esp. 2:459–576; "Renaissance and Reformation," in *The Reformation: Material or Spiritual?* ed. Lewis W. Spitz (Lexington, Mass.: D. C. Heath, 1962), 17–27; *Protestantism and Progress: A Historical Study of the Relation of Protestantism to the Modern World*, trans. W. Montgomery (Boston: Beacon Press, 1958).—Trans.]

43. [See Bornkamm, *Luther im Spiegel der deutschen Geistesgeschichte*, 389–97.—Trans.]

44. See below, 7.1.

45. See below, 7.2.

46. See above, 2.12, 4.22, and 5.2.4–5.

47. Karl Holl's essays on Luther were collected and published in his *Gesammelte Aufsätze zur Kirchengeschichte*, vol. 1: *Luther*, 7th ed. (Tübingen: J. C. B. Mohr [Paul Siebeck], 1948). [In the following notes, this volume is referred to as "*GA* 1."—Trans.] "Die Rechtfertigungslehre in Luthers Vorlesung über den

Römerbrief mit besonderer Rücksicht auf die Frage der Heilsgewissheit," in *GA* 1:111–54.

48. Karl Holl, "Luther und das landesherrliche Kirchenregiment," in *GA* 1:326–80. [Another essay dealing with some of the same subject matter and written at the same time has been translated: *The Cultural Significance of the Reformation*, trans. Karl Hertz and Barbara Hertz (New York: Living Age, 1919).—Trans.]

49. Karl Holl, "Die Enstehung von Luthers Kirchenbegriff," in *GA* 1:288–325.

50. Karl Holl, *What Did Luther Understand by Religion?* ed. James L. Adams and Walter F. Bense, trans. Fred W. Meuser and Walter E. Wietzke (Philadelphia: Fortress Press, 1977).

51. Karl Holl, *The Reconstruction of Morality*, ed. James L. Adams and Walter F. Bense, trans. Fred W. Meuser and Walter E. Wietzke (Minneapolis: Augsburg Publishing House, 1979).

52. Karl Holl, "Luther und die Schwärmer," in *GA* 1:420–67.

53. Holl, *What Did Luther Understand by Religion?* 32–48.

54. Ibid., 48–62.

55. Ibid., 36 and often.

56. Ibid., 79.

57. Ibid.

58. Ernst Bloch, *Thomas Münzer als Theologe der Revolution* (Munich: Kurt Wolff, 1921).

59. Holl, "Luther und die Schwärmer," in *GA* 1:467.

60. [See Bornkamm, *Luther im Spiegel der deutschen Geistesgeschichte*, 409–12.—Trans.]

61. Emanuel Hirsch, *Lutherstudien*, 2 vols. (Gütersloh: Bertelsmann, 1954).

62. Karl Barth, *Church Dogmatics*, trans. G. T. Thomsen, 4 vols. in 13 parts (Edinburgh: T. & T. Clark, 1936–69; index volume, 1977).

63. [Karl Barth, *Community, State, and Church: Three Essays*, trans. and ed. Will Herberg (Garden City, N.Y.: Doubleday Anchor Books, 1960). Herberg's introduction is an extended essay dealing with the disagreement between Barth and Gogarten on this issue.—Trans.]

64. Friedrich Gogarten, *Luthers Theologie* (Tübingen: J. C. B. Mohr [Paul Siebeck], 1967). [See Bornkamm, *Luther im Spiegel der deutschen Geistesgeschichte*, 400–408.—Trans.]

65. Philip Watson, *Let God Be God* (Philadelphia: Muhlenberg Press, 1947), introduced the accents of this school to the English–speaking reader.

66. Gustaf Aulén, *Christus Victor*, trans. A. G. Hebert (London: S.P.C.K., 1931); idem, *The Faith of the Christian Church*, trans. Eric H. Wahlstrom and G. Everett Arden (Philadelphia: Muhlenberg Press, 1948); idem, *Eucharist and Sacrifice*, trans. Eric H. Wahlstrom (Philadelphia: Muhlenberg Press, 1956).

67. Anders Nygren, *Agape and Eros: A Study of the Christian Idea of Love*, trans. A. G. Hebert (London: S.P.C.K., 1941).

68. Ragnar Bring, "The Subjective and the Objective in the Concept of the Church," in *This Is the Church*, ed. Anders Nygren, trans. Carl C. Rasmussen (Philadelphia: Muhlenberg Press, 1952), 205–25; idem, *Das Verhältnis von Glauben und Werken in der lutherischen Theologie*, trans. Karl–Heinz Becker (Munich: Chr. Kaiser, 1955); idem, *Commentary on Galatians*, trans. Eric H.

Wahlstrom (Philadelphia: Muhlenberg Press, 1961); idem, *How God Speaks to Us: The Dynamics of the Living Word* (Philadelphia: Muhlenberg Press, 1962).

69. Gustaf Wingren, *Luther on Vocation,* trans. Carl C. Rasmussen (Philadelphia: Muhlenberg Press, 1957).

70. Lennart Pinomaa, *Faith Victorious: An Introduction to Luther's Theology,* trans. Walter J. Kukkonen (Philadelphia: Fortress Press, 1963).

71. See above, 5.8.5.

72. [Gustaf Wingren, *Theology in Conflict: Nygren—Barth—Bultmann,* trans. Eric H. Wahlstrom (Philadelphia: Muhlenberg Press, 1958); Anders Nygren, *Commentary on Romans,* trans. Carl C. Rasmussen (Philadelphia: Muhlenberg Press, 1949).—Trans.]

73. Reinhold Seeberg (1859–1935) was professor of systematic theology at Erlangen University from 1889 through 1898 when he was called to the University of Berlin. See his *Lehrbuch der Dogmengeschichte,* 4th ed., 5 vols. (Leipzig: A. Deichert, 1933); *The History of Doctrines* (Grand Rapids: Baker Book House, 1952); see chap. 5 n. 2.

74. Erich Seeberg, *Luthers Theologie in ihren Grundzügen,* (Stuttgart: Kohlhammer, 1st ed. 1940, reprinted 1950). See also above, chap. 5 n. 3.

75. Paul Althaus, *The Theology of Martin Luther,* trans. Robert C. Schultz (Philadelphia: Fortress Press, 1966).

76. Paul Althaus, *The Ethics of Martin Luther,* trans. Robert C. Schultz (Philadelphia: Fortress Press, 1972).

77. Rudolf Hermann, *Luthers Theologie,* ed. Horst Beintker (Göttingen: Vandenhoeck & Ruprecht, 1967).

78. For example, Gerhard Ebeling, *Lutherstudien,* 2 vols. (Tübingen: J. C. B. Mohr [Paul Siebeck], 1971–82); idem, *Luther: An Introduction to His Thought,* trans. R. A. Wilson (Philadelphia: Fortress Press, 1970).

79. In the German "Kulturkampf" (1871–86) Bismarck tried to push back the political influence of the Roman Catholic Church.

80. Heinrich Denifle, *Luther and Lutherdom from Original Sources,* trans. Raymond Volz (Somerset, Ohio: Torch Press, 1917).

81. Hartmann Grisar, *Martin Luther: His Life and Work,* adapted from the 2d German edition by Frank J. Eble, ed. Arthur Preuss (Westminster, Md.: Newman Press, 1950).

82. Franz Xaver Kiefl, "Martin Luthers religiöse Psyche," *Hochland* 15 (1917/18): 7–28.

83. Sebastian Merkle, *Gutes an Luther und Übles an seinen Tadlern, Luther in ökumenischer Sicht,* ed. Alfred von Martin (Stuttgart: Frommann, 1929), 9–19.

84. Joseph Lortz, *The Reformation in Germany,* trans. Ronald Walls, 2 vols. (New York: Herder & Herder, 1968).

85. See above 2.12, 4.22, and 5.2.5. As to Lortz's evaluation of Luther's lectures on Romans see, on the one hand, his *Reformation in Germany,* 1:210–13, and on the other hand, "Luthers Römerbriefvorlesung. Grundanliegen," *TThZ* 71 (1962): 129–53, 216–47.

86. Erwin Iserloh, "The Basic Elements of Luther's Intellectual Style," in *Catholic Scholars Dialogue with Luther,* ed. Jared Wicks (Chicago: Loyola University

Press, 1970), 3–33. This collection of essays gives the reader who knows only English a good sample of Roman Catholic scholarship at the time.

87. See particularly Erwin Iserloh, *Geschichte und Theologie der Reformation im Grundriss* (Paderborn: Bonifacius–Druckerei, 1980); idem, *The Theses Were Not Posted: Luther Between Reform and Reformation,* trans. Jared Wicks (Boston: Beacon Press, 1968); idem, "Luther's Christ–Mysticism," in *Catholic Scholars Dialogue with Luther,* 37–58. Isersloh also wrote large sections of the *Handbook of Church History,* ed. Herbert Jedin and John Dolan—chaps. 41–44, 47, and 58–61 of Vol. 4: *From the High Middle Ages to the Eve of the Reformation,* trans. Anselm Biggs (New York: Herder & Herder, 1970); "Part One: The Protestant Reformation," (except for chap. 27), in Vol. 5: *The Protestant Reformation,* trans. Anselm Biggs and Peter W. Becker (New York: Herder & Herder, 1980).

88. Stephan Pfürtner, *Luther and Aquinas—A Conversation: Our Salvation, Its Certainty and Peril,* trans. Edward Quinn (New York: Sheed & Ward, 1964).

89. Otto Hermann Pesch, "Existential and Sapiential Theology: The Theological Confrontation Between Luther and Thomas Aquinas," in *Catholic Scholars Dialogue with Luther,* 61–81; idem, *The God Question in Thomas Aquinas and Martin Luther,* trans. Gottfried G. Krodel (Philadelphia: Fortress Press, 1972). See further Otto Hermann Pesch, "Luther and the Catholic Tradition," *Lutheran Theological Seminary Bulletin, Gettysburg, Pa.,* 64 (Winter 1984): 3–21.

Chapter 7: Editions, Scholarly Journals, Aids to the Study of Luther

1. Kurt Aland, Ernst Otto Reichert, and Gerhard Jordan, *Hilfsbuch zum Lutherstudium,* 3d ed. (Witten/Ruhr: Luther–Verlag, 1970).

2. Heinrich J. Vogel, *Vogel's Cross Reference and Index to the Contents of Luther's Works* (Milwaukee: Northwestern Publishing House, 1983). [Vogel gives the Aland reference numbers. In addition to the American Edition, he coordinates references to the Weimar Edition, to the St. Louis Edition (Aland's "2. Walchschen Ausgabe"), and the Erlangen Edition.—Trans.]

3. Aland, Reichert, and Jordan, *Hilfsbuch zum Lutherstudium.*

4. *Martin Luther: Ausgewählte Werke,* ed. H. H. Borcherdt and Georg Merz, 3d ed. (Munich: Chr. Kaiser, 1951–65).

5. *Mü Erg,* vol. 1.

6. Ibid., vol. 2.

7. Ibid., vol. 6.

8. Kurt Aland, ed. *Die Werke Martin Luthers in neuer Auswahl für die Gegenwart,* 11 vols. (Göttingen: Vandenhoeck & Ruprecht, 1959–83); and idem, *Lutherlexikon* (Göttingen: Vandenhoeck & Ruprecht, 1960–75).

9. *Calwer Luther–Ausgabe,* ed. Wolfgang Metzger, 12 vols. (Gütersloh: Gütersloher Verlagshaus, 1964–68). This edition also appears in the popular series of German paperbacks called Siebenstern–Taschenbücher.

10. *Martin Luther Studienausgabe,* ed. Hans Ulrich Delius (vols. 1–3, Berlin: Evangelische Verlagsanstalt, 1979–83; vol. 4, forthcoming).

11. [German writers sometimes refer to this edition as *Am.*—Trans.]

12. *Luther's Works,* ed. Jaroslav Pelikan, Hilton C. Oswald, and Helmut T. Lehmann. The first thirty volumes were published in St. Louis by Concordia

Publishing House. Volumes 31 through 54 were published in Philadelphia by Fortress Press. The index volume, vol. 55, published by Fortress Press, will be available in the fall of 1986.

13. *LW* 49, 50, 51, ed. and trans. Gottfried G. Krodel.

14. Other indexes have been referred to above. [The user of *LW* will find the indexes to each volume a very helpful guide, pending the appearance of an index to the whole edition in the fall of 1986.—Trans.]

15. For a brief overview of the plan of the indexes to the Weimar Edition, see Karl–Heinz zur Mühlen and Klaus Lämmel, "Das Register der Weimarer Lutherausgabe," *Luther* 50 (1979): 138–47.

16. [An additional resource is Heinz Bluhm's index of Luther's German writings. This work can be consulted through the Department of German, Boston College, Chestnut Hill, Massachusetts. Heinz Bluhm, "Die Indices zu Werken Martin Luthers in Boston College, Chestnut Hill, Massachusetts," *LuJ* 51 (1984).—Trans.]

17. Alfred Götze, *Frühneuhochdeutsches Glossar,* 7th ed. (Berlin: Walter de Gruyter, 1971).

Wilhelm Müller and Friedrich Zarnke, *Mittelhochdeutsches Wörterbuch,* 3 vols. (Leipzig: Hirzel, 1854–66; reprinted Hildesheim: Georg Olms, 1963).

Philipp Dietz, *Wörterbuch zu Dr. Martin Luthers deutschen Schriften,* vols. 1 and 2 only (Leipzig: Vogel, 1870–72; reprinted Hildesheim: Georg Olms, 1973). Apart from never having been completed, the user cannot be certain that the words listed by Dietz actually were used by Luther. The *WA* indexes will clarify this problem. In case of doubt, check the listings of the *Institut für Spaätmittelalter und Reformation* in Tübingen.

Johannes Erben, *Grundzüge einer Syntax der Sprache Luthers* (Berlin: Akademie–Verlag, 1954). Presupposes specialized knowledge of German grammar.

For a brief overview of these and other important aids, see Birgit Stolt, "Germanistische Hilfsmittel zum Lutherstudium," *LuJ* 46 (1979): 120–35.

18. *Lutherforschung Heute. Referate und Berichte des 1. Internationalen Lutherforschungskongresses Aarhus. 18.–23.8.1956,* ed. Vilmos Vajta (Berlin: Lutherisches Verlagshaus, 1958).

Luther and Melanchthon in the History and Theology of the Reformation, Second International Congress for Luther Research, August 8–13, 1960, ed. Vilmos Vajta (Philadelphia: Muhlenberg Press; Göttingen: Vandenhoeck & Ruprecht, 1961).

Kirche, Mystik, Heiligung und das Natüriche bei Luther. Vorträge des Dritten Internationalen Kongresses für Lutherforschung Järvenpää, Finnland, 11.–16.8.1966, ed. Ivar Asheim (Göttingen: Vandenhoeck & Ruprecht, 1967).

Luther and the Dawn of the Modern Era: Papers for the Fourth International Congress for Luther Research (Saint Louis, Mo., 22.–27.8.1971), in Studies in the History of Christian Thought, vol. 8, ed. Heiko Oberman (Leiden: E. J. Brill, 1974).

Luther und die Theologie der Gegenwart. Referate und Berichte des 5. Internationalen Kongresses für Lutherforschung Lund 14.–20.8.1977, ed. Leif Grane and Bernhard Lohse (Göttingen: Vandenhoeck & Ruprecht, 1980).

The papers of the Sixth International Congress for Luther Research, which had been held at Erfurt, German Democratic Republic, 14.–20.8.1983, have been published in *LuJ* 52 (1985).

SELECT BIBLIOGRAPHY OF
WORKS IN ENGLISH

Aland, Kurt. *Martin Luther's 95 Theses: With the Pertinent Documents from the History of the Reformation.* Translated by P. J. Schroeder. St. Louis: Concordia Pub. House, 1967.

Althaus, Paul. *The Theology of Martin Luther.* Translated by Robert C. Schultz. Philadelphia: Fortress Press, 1966.

———. *The Ethics of Martin Luther.* Translated by Robert C. Schultz, Philadelphia: Fortress Press, 1972.

Asheim, Ivar, ed. *The Church, Mysticism, Sanctification and the Natural in Luther's Thought: Lectures Presented to the Third International Congress on Luther Research, Järvenpää, Finland, August 11–16, 1966.* Philadelphia: Fortress Press, 1967.

Atkinson, James. *The Trial of Luther.* New York: Stein & Day, 1971.

Bainton, Roland, H. *Here I Stand: A Life of Martin Luther.* New York: Abingdon & Cokesbury, 1950.

———. *Women of the Reformation in Germany and Italy.* Minneapolis: Augsburg Pub. House, 1971.

Baylor, Michael G. *Action and Person: Conscience in Late Scholasticism and the Young Luther.* Leiden: Brill, 1977.

Bluhm, Heinz. *Martin Luther: Creative Translator.* St. Louis: Concordia, 1965.

———. *Luther: Translator of Paul.* New York: Peter Lang, 1984.

Boehmer, Heinrich. *Martin Luther: Road to Reformation.* Translated by John W. Doberstein and Theodore G. Tappert. Philadelphia: Muhlenberg Press, 1957.

Bornkamm, Heinrich. *Luther's World of Thought.* Translated by Martin H. Bertram. Philadelphia: Fortress Press, 1958.

———. *Luther's Doctrine of the Two Kingdoms.* Translated by Karl H. Hertz. Philadelphia: Fortress Press, 1966.

———. *Luther and the Old Testament.* Translated by Eric W. and Ruth C. Gritsch, and edited by Victor I. Gruhn. Philadelphia: Fortress Press, 1969.

———. *Luther in Mid-Career 1521–1530.* Translated by E. Theodore Bachmann, and edited by Karin Bornkamm, Philadelphia: Fortress Press, 1983.

Brecht, Martin. *Martin Luther: His Road to Reformation, 1483–1521.* Translated by James L. Schaaf. Philadelphia: Fortress Press, 1985.

Carlson, Edgar M. *The Reinterpretation of Luther.* Philadelphia: Muhlenberg Press, 1948.

Cranz, Ferdinand E. *An Essay on the Development of Luther's Thought on Justice, Law and Society.* Cambridge, Mass.: Harvard Univ. Press, 1959.

Davies, Rupert E. *The Problem of Authority in the Continental Reformers. Luther, Zwingli, and Calvin.* London: Epworth Press, 1946.
Dickens, A. G. *The German Nation and Martin Luther.* New York: Harper & Row, 1974.
Duchrow, Ulrich. *Two Kingdoms: The Use and Misuse of a Lutheran Theological Concept.* Geneva: Lutheran World Federation, 1977.

Ebeling, Gerhard. *Luther, An Introduction to His Thought.* Translated by R. A. Wilson. Philadelphia: Fortress Press, 1970.
Ebon, Martin, trans. *The Last Days of Luther by Justus Jonas, Michael Coelius and Others.* Garden City, N.Y.: Doubleday & Co., 1970.
Edwards, Mark U. *Luther and the False Brethren.* Stanford, Calif.: Stanford Univ. Press, 1975.
————. *Luther's Last Battles: Politics and Polemics, 1531–1546.* Ithaca, N.Y.: Cornell Univ. Press, 1983.
Edwards, Mark and George H. Tavard, editors. *Luther—Reformer for the Churches: An Ecumenical Study Guide.* Philadelphia: Fortress Press, 1983.
Elton, G. R. *Reformation Europe 1517–1559.* New York: Harper & Row, 1966.
Erikson, Erik H. *Young Man Luther: A Study in Psychoanalysis and History.* New York: W. W. Norton, 1958.

Friesen, Abraham. *Reformation and Utopia: The Marxist Interpretation of the Reformation and Its Antecedents.* Wiesbaden: Franz Steiner, 1974.

Gerrish, Brian A. *Grace and Reason: A Study in Luther's Theology.* Oxford: At the Clarendon Press, 1962.
Grisar, Hartmann. *Luther: His Life and Work.* 3 vols. in 1. Translated by E. M. Lammond, and edited by Luigi Cappadelta. St. Louis: Herder, 1930.
Gritsch, Eric W. *Martin—God's Court Jester: Luther in Retrospect.* Philadelphia: Fortress Press, 1983.
Gritsch, Eric W. and Robert W. Jenson. *Lutheranism: The Theological Movement and Its Confessional Writings.* Philadelphia: Fortress Press, 1976.

Haendler, Gert. *Luther on Ministerial Office and Congregational Function.* Translated by Ruth C. L. Gritsch, and edited by Eric W. Gritsch. Philadelphia: Fortress Press, 1981.
Haile, Harry G. *Luther: An Experiment in Biography.* New York: Doubleday & Co., 1980.
Headley, John M. *Luther's View of Church History.* New Haven, Conn.: Yale Univ. Press, 1963.
Hendrix, Scott H. *Luther and the Papacy: Stages in a Reformation Conflict.* Philadelphia: Fortress Press, 1981.
Hertz, Karl H., ed. *Two Kingdoms and One World.* A Sourcebook in Christian Social Ethics. Minneapolis: Augsburg Pub. House, 1976.

Holl, Karl. *The Cultural Significance of the Reformation*. Translated by Karl and Barbara Hertz and John H. Lichtblau. New York: Meridian Press, 1959.
————. "Luther on Luther." Translated by H. C. Erik Middlefort. *Interpreters of Luther: Essays in Honor of Wilhelm Pauck*, 9–34. Philadelphia: Fortress Press, 1968.
————. *What Did Luther Understand by Religion?* Translated by Fred W. Meuser and Walter R. Wietzke, and edited by James L. Adams and Walter F. Bense. Philadelphia: Fortress Press, 1977.
————. *The Reconstruction of Morality*. Translated by Fred W. Meuser and Walter R. Wietzke, and edited by James L. Adams and Walter F. Bense. Minneapolis, Augsburg Pub. House, 1979.
Holmio, Armas, K. E. *The Lutheran Reformation and the Jews: The Birth of the Protestant Jewish Mission*. Hancock, Mich.: Finnish Lutheran Book Concern, 1949.

Iserloh, Erwin. *The Theses Were Not Posted: Luther Between Reform and Reformation*. Translated by Jared Wicks. Boston: Beacon Press, 1968.

Jensen, De Lamar, ed. *Confrontation at Worms: Martin Luther and the Diet of Worms*. Provo, Utah: Brigham Young Univ. Press, 1973.
Johnson, Roger A., ed. *Psychohistory and Religion: The Case of Young Martin Luther*. Philadelphia: Fortress Press, 1977.
Justification Today. Studies and Reports. Lutheran World Supplement no. 1. Geneva: Lutheran World Federation, 1965.

Karant-Nunn, Susan. *Luther's Pastors: The Reformation in the Ernestine Countryside*. Philadelphia: American Philosophical Society, 1979.
Kirchner, Hubert, *Luther and the Peasants' War.* Translated by Darrell Jodock. Philadelphia: Fortress Press, 1972.

Lazareth, William H. *Luther on the Christian Home: An Application of the Social Ethics of the Reformation*. Philadelphia: Muhlenberg Press, 1960.
Lienhard, Marc. *Luther's Witness to Jesus Christ*. Translated by Edwin H. Robertson. Minneapolis: Augsburg Pub. House, 1982.
Lohse, Bernhard. "The Development of the Offices of Leadership in the German Lutheran Churches: 1517–1918." *Episcopacy in the Lutheran Church? Studies in the Development and Definition of the Office of Leadership*, edited by Ivar Asheim and Victor R. Gold, 51–71. Philadelphia: Fortress Press, 1970.
Lortz, Joseph. *The Reformation in Germany.* 2 vols. Translated by Ronald Walls. New York: Herder & Herder, 1968.

Mackinnon, James. *Luther and the Reformation*. 4 vols. New York and London: Longmans, Green & Co., 1928–30.
Manns, Peter and Harding Meyer, editors. *Luther's Ecumenical Significance: An Interconfessional Consultation*. Philadelphia: Fortress Press, 1983.

Oberman, Heiko A. *Masters of the Reformation: The Emergence of a New Intel-*

lectual Climate in Europe. Translated by Dennis Martin. New York: Cambridge
Univ. Press, 1981.

_____. *Luther and the Dawn of the Modern Era: Papers for the Fourth Interna-
tional Congress for Luther Research* [in St. Louis, Missouri, 22–27 August
1971]. Leiden: Brill, 1974.

Olivier, Daniel. *The Trial of Luther*. Translated by John Tonkin. St. Louis: Concordia Pub. House, 1978.

Oyer, John S. *Lutheran Reformers Against Anabaptists: Luther, Melanchthon and
Menius and the Anabaptists of Central Germany*. The Hague: Nijhoff, 1964.

Pelikan, Jaroslav. *Obedient Rebels: Catholic Substance and Protestant Principle
in Luther's Reformation*. New York: Harper & Row, 1964.

Pesch, Otto H. *The God Question in Thomas Aquinas and Martin Luther*.
Translated by Gottfried G. Krodel. Philadelphia: Fortress Press, 1972.

Preus, James. H. *From Shadow to Promise: Old Testament Interpretation from
Augustine to Luther*. Cambridge, Mass.: Harvard Univ. Press, 1969.

_____. *Carlstadt's Ordinances and Luther's Liberty: A Study of the Wittenberg
Movement, 1521–1522*. Cambridge, Mass.: Harvard Univ. Press, 1974.

Reu, Michael J. *Luther's German Bible: An Historical Presentation Together With
a Collection of Sources*. Columbus, Oh.: Lutheran Book Concern, 1934.

Rupp, Gordon E. *The Righteousness of God: Luther Studies*, 3d ed. London:
Hodder & Stoughton, 1968.

_____. *Patterns of Reformation*. Philadelphia, Fortress Press, 1969.

Rupp, Gordon E. and Philip S. Watson, eds. *Luther and Erasmus: Free Will and
Salvation. Library of Christian Classics*, vol. 17. Philadelphia: Westminster
Press, 1969.

Schwiebert, Ernest G. *Luther and His Times*. St. Louis: Concordia, 1950.

Siggins, Ian D. *Martin Luther's Doctrine of Christ*. New Haven, Conn. and London:
Yale Univ. Press, 1970.

_____. *Luther and His Mother*, Philadelphia: Fortress Press, 1981.

Spitz, Lewis W. *The Renaissance and Reformation Movements*. 2 vols. St. Louis:
Concordia Pub. House, 1980.

_____. "Luther's Impact on Modern Man." *Concordia Theological Monthly*
41(1977)1:26–43.

Steinmetz, David M. *Luther and Staupitz: An Essay in the Intellectual Origins of
the Reformation*. Durham, N.C.: Duke Univ. Press, 1980.

Strauss, Gerhard. *Luther's House of Learning: Indoctrination of the Young in the
German Reformation*. Baltimore: Johns Hopkins Univ. Press, 1978.

Tentler, Thomas N. *Sin and Confession on the Eve of the Reformation*. Princeton:
Princeton Univ. Press, 1977.

*Theses Concerning Martin Luther 1483–1983. The Luther Quincentenary in the
German Democratic Republic*. Berlin and Dresden: Verlag Zeit im Bild, 1983.

Todd, John M. *Martin Luther: A Biographical Study*. London: Burns & Oates,
1964.

————. *Luther: A Life.* New York: Crossroad, 1982.

Watson, Philip J. *Let God Be God. An Interpretation of the Theology of Martin Luther.* 1947. Reprint. Philadelphia: Fortress Press, 1966.

Wicks, Jared. *Catholic Scholars Dialogue with Luther.* Chicago: Loyola Univ. Press, 1970.

Wingren, Gustav. *Luther on Vocation.* Translated by Carl Rasmussen. Philadelphia: Muhlenberg Press, 1959.

Yule, George. *Luther: Theologian for Catholics and Protestants.* Edinburgh: T. & T. Clark, 1985.

INDEX OF NAMES

INDEX OF SUBJECTS

Lightning Source UK Ltd.
Milton Keynes UK
UKOW05f1826031116

286826UK00027B/688/P